D0860892

HANDBOOKS
TREES

TREES

ALLEN J. COOMBES

Photography by
MATTHEW WARD

NEW EDITION

DK LONDON

US Editor Jenny Wilson
Managing Editor Angeles Gavira Guerrero
Managing Art Editor Michael Duffy
Senior Production Editor Andy Hilliard
Production Controller Meskerem Berhane
Jacket Design Development Manager Sophia M.T.T.
Associate Publishing Director Liz Wheeler
Art Director Karen Self
Publishing Director Jonathan Metcalf

DK DELHI

Senior Editor Nidhilekha Mathur
Consultant Editor Alka Thakur Hazarika
Project Art Editor Shipra Jain
Managing Editor Soma B. Chowdhury
Senior Managing Art Editor Arunesh Talapatra
Jacket Designer Juhi Sheth
Senior Jackets Coordinator Priyanka Sharma Saddi
DTP Designers Satish Chandra Gaur, Rakesh Kumar
Assistant Picture Researcher Shubhdeep Kaur
Production Manager Pankaj Sharma
Pre-production Manager Balwant Singh
Creative Head Malavika Talukder

Author Allen J. Coombes

This American Edition, 2023
First American Edition, 1992
Published in the United States by DK Publishing
1745 Broadway, 20th Floor, New York, NY 10019

23 24 25 26 27 10 9 8 7 6 5 4 3 2 1
001-333989-Aug/23

Published in Great Britain by Dorling Kindersley Limited.

A catalog record for this book
is available from the Library of Congress.
ISBN 978-0-7440-7420-8

Printed and bound in China

For the curious
www.dk.com

This book was made with Forest Stewardship Council™ certified paper - one small step in DK's commitment to a sustainable future.
For more information go to www.dk.com/our-green-pledge

Contents

INTRODUCTION 6

CONIFERS AND THEIR ALLIES 34

BROADLEAVES 84

LOOKING AT TREES

WHETHER STANDING IN isolation on a windy hillside, crowded together in dense forest, or lining a city street, trees form an important element of nearly every landscape. The almost infinite variation of trees through the seasons not only in shape, size, color, and texture, but also in the finer details of leaves, flowers, fruit, and bark makes the study of these familiar plants an ever-changing, yet enduring, source of delight.

The fact that trees survive almost everywhere means that you can appreciate and study them wherever you happen to be. In the countryside, they grow, hopefully but not always, as nature intends; in urban environments, planted along streets, and in parks and public gardens, they give comfort and solace among man-made structures. Of course, while there is nothing to compare with seeing trees growing wild in their natural habitat, towns and cities are still excellent places for observing and learning more about them.

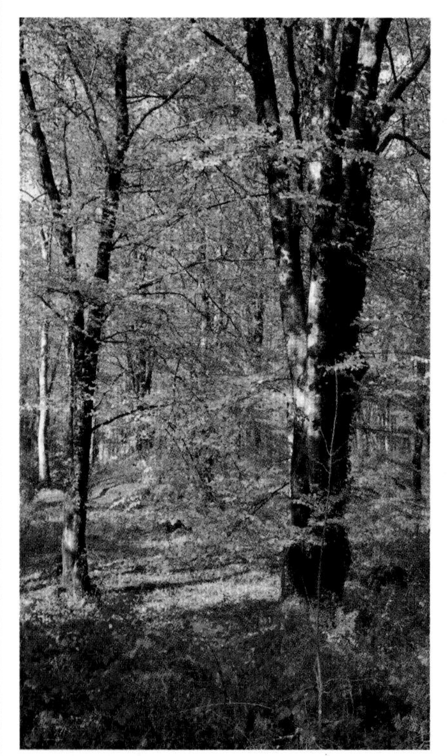

Beech wood in fall
An English beech wood is one of the glories of fall. Its densely leafy canopy allows little light to penetrate, with the result that little else can grow beneath it.

THE TREE SELECTION

This book includes only those species of tree that grow wild in the temperate regions of the world. In the northern hemisphere, this covers most of Asia, North America, Europe south to the Mediterranean, the Himalayas, and most of China; in the southern hemisphere, it includes South America, the cooler regions of Australia, and New Zealand. From within this extensive area, I have made a selection of plants that illustrates the amazing diversity of trees that can be found throughout the world. At the same time, I have tried to include most of the species that you are likely to find planted in gardens, backyards, and along streets, as well as a few that are unusual or more rare.

CONSERVATION ISSUES

In recent years, the destruction of the tropical forests has excited a good deal of attention, and rightly so: these last great areas of natural diversity are home to numerous plants and animals, whose continuing existence may be of vital importance to humankind. Faced with so large a debate, it is easy to forget that most forests in temperate zones have already suffered the fate that is threatening those in tropical regions. In the developed world, extensive areas of natural woodland have been lost through human demand for paper, building materials, and other wood-based products, as well as through the need for agricultural land, creating the relatively unnatural countryside we see today.

Oriental Beech (*Fagus orientalis*)

In developing parts of the world, temperate woods are still under threat in places like the Himalayas and South America. Particularly in areas of heavy rainfall, the felling of trees—with scant regard to the far-reaching consequences of this action—causes problems such as flooding and mud landslides, when the vegetation that once stabilized entire hillsides is gone.

It has been estimated that about 30 percent of the world's trees are threatened. These are mostly tropical species, with about 25 percent from temperate regions. One example is the Spanish fir (*Abies pinsapo*, see p.61), which grows wild on very few mountainsides in a small area of southern Spain. Years ago, its timber was a valuable local resource. Now, any further cutting might extinguish these glorious forests for ever. We must make special efforts to protect this and other such endangered species.

Chinese Chestnut (*Castanea mollissima*)

Threatened species
Diseases can nearly destroy a species. Chestnut blight from East Asia has killed all but a few wild American chestnuts (*Castanea dentata*, see p.143). The Chinese chestnut (*Castanea mollissima*, see p.143) is being used to help breed resistant trees.

Survivor from China ▷
The bark of *Magnolia officinalis* var. *biloba* (see p.182) was once harvested to produce medicines, causing the species to become rare in the wild. Cultivation has ensured that it still grows in gardens and yards.

HABITAT AND ENVIRONMENT

By adapting to an extensive range of environmental conditions, trees are able to grow in many different habitats. Generally speaking, it is the conifers that inhabit the most hostile situations. Their slender shape minimizes damage by snow; evergreen leaves make the best use of a growing season that may be short, and mean that the plant can survive extended periods of drought when the ground is frozen; and wind pollination eliminates the need for insect visitors, which may be sparse or nonexistent in unfavorable habitats.

Friendlier habitats produce a longer growing season, and encourage deciduous species. Here, there is time for the plant to produce new leaves, and shed old ones, every year in a continuous cycle of regeneration. In shady places, large leaves are needed to intercept as much sunlight as can filter through; in wet areas, tapered tips allow for the rapid shedding of water; in dry areas, grey or silvery leaves reduce water loss; and fragrant or showy flowers ensure a good chance of pollination by insects.

◁ **Adaptation for survival**
The larches (*Larix*, see pp.64–5) grow wild in the harshest conditions. They produce their foliage on numerous short side shoots—an adaptation that allows them to take advantage of favorable conditions as they come into leaf.

Hybrid plants
A hybrid is produced when two different species cross together. The plant that results usually shows characteristics that are intermediate between the two parents. Some hybrids occur only through cultivation in gardens and backyards, because the parent plants do not grow together in the wild.

◁ **Parent one**
Tarajo holly (*Ilex latifolia*, see p.93) has rather large leaves, which are toothed at the margin but not spiny.

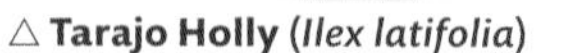

△ **Tarajo Holly (*Ilex latifolia*)**

Parent two ▷
The familiar common holly (*Ilex aquifolium*, see p.90) has leaves that are typically edged with spiny teeth.

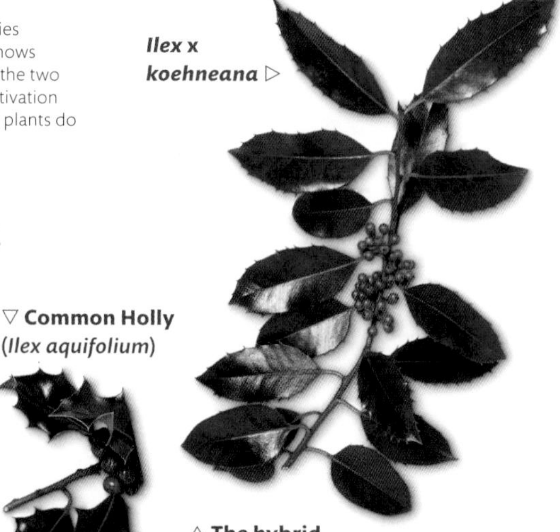

▽ **Common Holly (*Ilex aquifolium*)**

Ilex* x *koehneana ▷

△ **The hybrid**
Ilex x *koehneana* (see p.93) has the large leaves of *I. latifolia*. The spiny margin of the leaves is inherited from *I. aquifolium*.

A FAMILY TREE

FAMILY

A family contains a single genus or several related genera. The family name is always written in roman type, eg Rosaceae.

Rosaceae

GENUS, GENERA

A genus contains a single species or several related species. The genus element is always written in italic type, eg *Prunus*, *Cormus*.

Prunus

Cormus

This genus has only one species.

SPECIES

Species are the basic units into which genera are divided. For example, *Prunus padus* (Bird Cherry) and *Prunus lusitanica* (Portugal Laurel) are different species in the genus *Prunus*.

padus

lusitanica

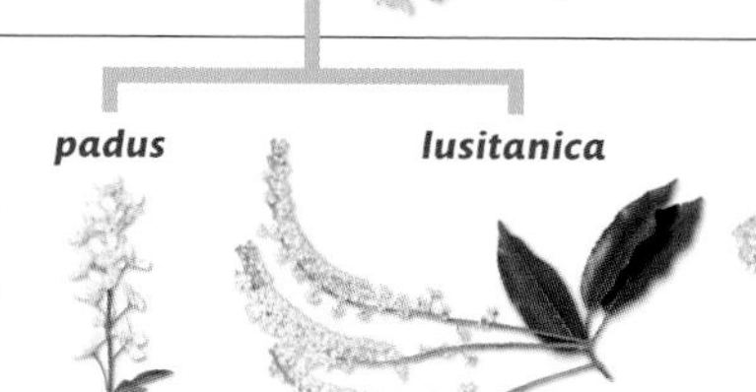

domestica

SUBSPECIES

A subspecies is a major division of a species: the two elements are always written in roman and italic type, eg subsp. *azorica*. Variety (var.) and forma (f.) are minor divisions of a species.

subsp. *azorica*

GROUPS

Groups include variants of a species not recognized botanically but regarded as distinct in gardens and yards. They are written in roman type, eg Pomifera Group.

Pomifera Group

Pyrifera Group

CULTIVAR

A cultivar is a form selected and named for its garden and yard merit. The cultivar name is written in roman type, with quotation marks, eg 'Watereri.'

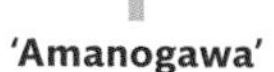

'Watereri'

OBSERVING AND RECORDING TREES

Keeping written notes about the trees you see is not only an enjoyable activity at the time: it also makes interesting reading at a later date. Choose half a dozen favourite trees close to where you live or work. Visit each one several times during the four seasons and build up a fact file that records their special features at different times of the year.

MEASURING A TREE'S HEIGHT

Cut a straight piece of stick that is the same length as the distance between your eye and your fist. Hold it vertically at arm's length and walk toward or away from the tree to align the top of the stick with the top of the tree and the base the stick with the base of the tree. Mark the point at which you are now standing and measure the distance on the ground to the base of the trunk. This distance equals the height of the tree.

Keeping a photographic record

Photographing trees can help you to keep a record of what you have seen and is preferable to cutting a piece that in some places may be illegal. Photograph the whole tree and take close-ups to show its features. If you cannot identify the tree from these, try sharing with your friends.

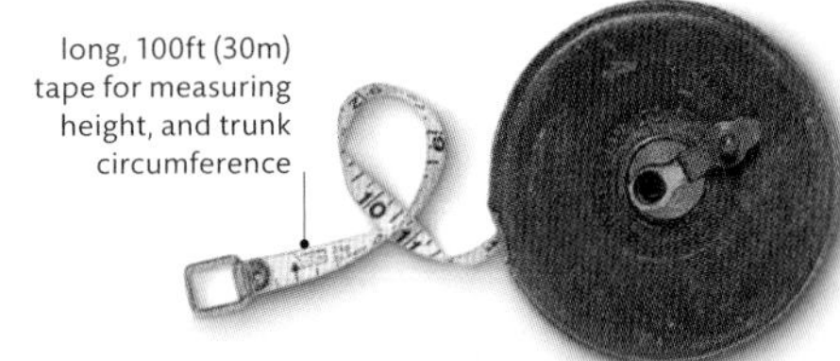

long, 100ft (30m) tape for measuring height, and trunk circumference

Taking field notes

Jot down the tree's height, the circumference of its trunk, and the color and texture of the bark. Note details of its leaves, flowers, and fruit (depending on the time of year), its location, and the date. Expand your notes at home.

colored pencils for making sketches

small sketch book for visual note-taking

reference photographs

wax crayon and paper for making bark impressions

cut specimen to take home for more detailed examination, but be sure to ask if permission is needed for you to do this

label with string tie for cut specimens

magnifying glass

HOW THIS BOOK WORKS

THE BOOK IS ARRANGED according to the major groups of tree: Conifers and their Allies, and Broadleaves. The groups are divided, alphabetically, into families. A short introduction to each family tells you how many genera and species it contains, and describes the general characteristics and features of the plants that belong to it. The entries that follow are arranged, alphabetically, by genus and by species within each genus. They give detailed information, in words and pictures, about selected species that are found in that family.

Each entry begins with the common name, or the scientific name if there is no single, accepted common name for that plant. Many plants do not have a common name: indeed, they are well enough known under their scientific name not to need one. This example shows how a typical entry is organized.

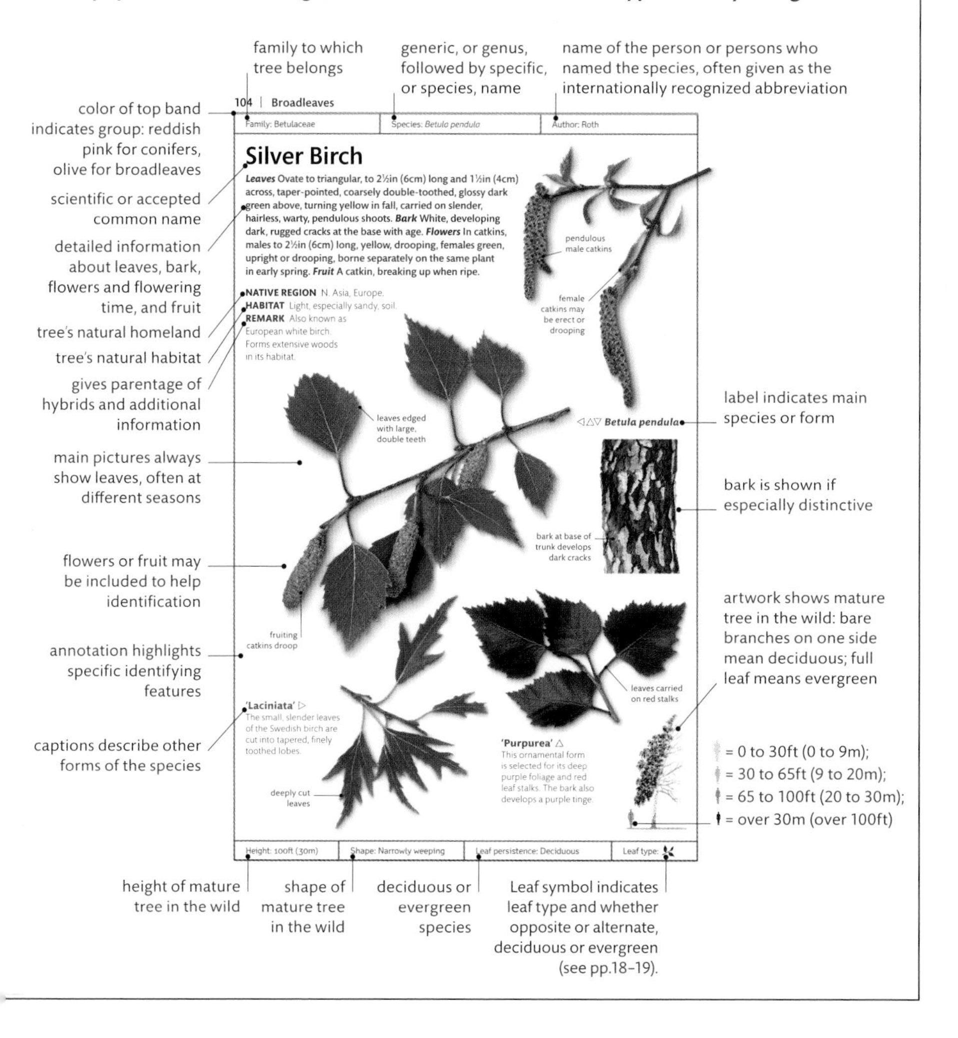

WHAT IS A TREE?

A TREE IS a living thing. It has a woody stem, the trunk, a root system, and branches clothed in season with leaves. It may have flowers and, later, fruit.

Size and habit distinguish a tree from a shrub. A tree usually attains 17ft (5m) or more and has a single stem that may divide; a shrub is usually smaller and has many stems growing from the base. Habit is related to habitat. A species that is a tallish tree in a fertile valley may be only a low shrub on an exposed hillside. Open sites allow the plant to develop a spreading crown; in dense forest, where the trees are crowded, it may form an altogether narrower shape.

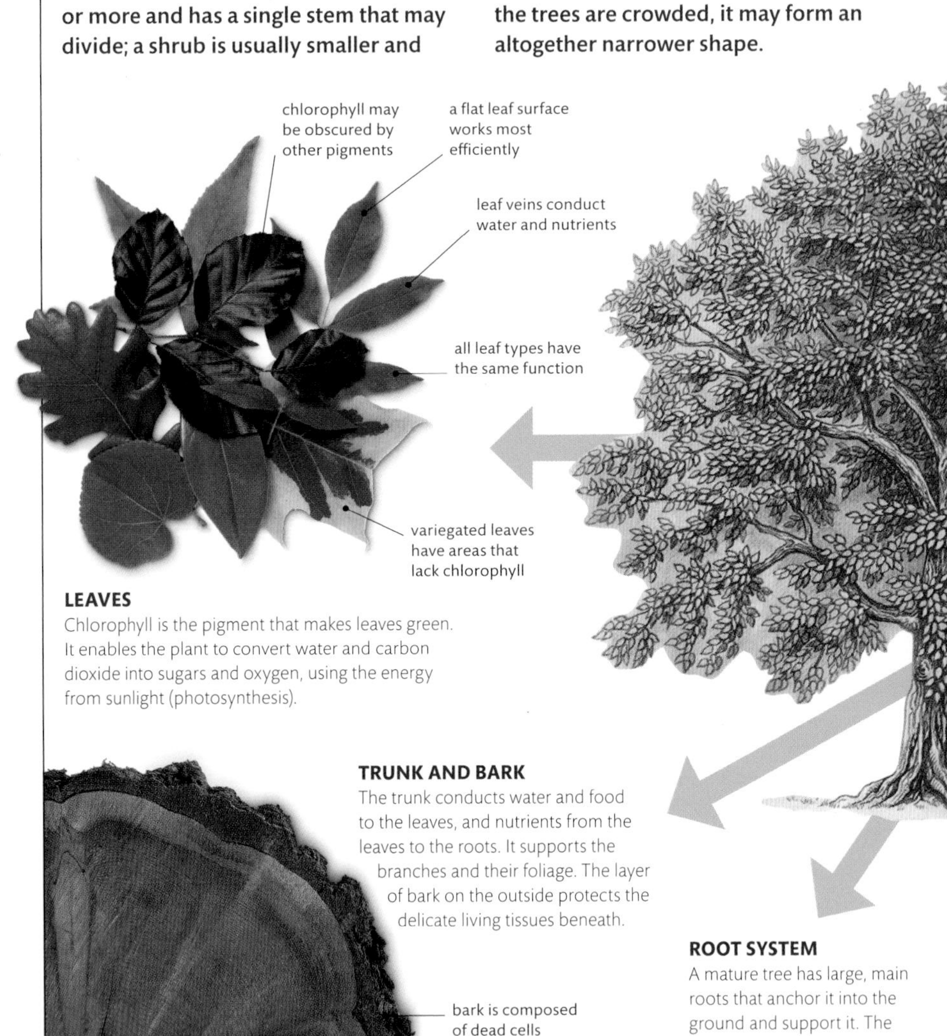
chlorophyll may be obscured by other pigments
a flat leaf surface works most efficiently
leaf veins conduct water and nutrients
all leaf types have the same function
variegated leaves have areas that lack chlorophyll
bark is composed of dead cells
growth rings in the trunk show annual increase in size

LEAVES
Chlorophyll is the pigment that makes leaves green. It enables the plant to convert water and carbon dioxide into sugars and oxygen, using the energy from sunlight (photosynthesis).

TRUNK AND BARK
The trunk conducts water and food to the leaves, and nutrients from the leaves to the roots. It supports the branches and their foliage. The layer of bark on the outside protects the delicate living tissues beneath.

ROOT SYSTEM
A mature tree has large, main roots that anchor it into the ground and support it. The surrounding network of very fine roots takes up water and minerals for transporting to its actively growing parts.

BUDS AND SHOOTS

Young leaf growths inside a layer of scales form buds on the shoots during winter. The scales protect the young leaves until they are ready to expand in spring. The shoots carry water and nutrients, and support the leaves.

FLOWERS

The flowers produce pollen and receive it from other plants. It is usually transferred by wind or insect activity. Successful pollination results in the formation of seed-containing fruit.

FRUIT

The fruit protects the seeds as they ripen, and helps to disperse them when they are mature. Fleshy fruit is usually eaten by animals, which travel and spread the seeds; dry, winged fruit is carried away by wind.

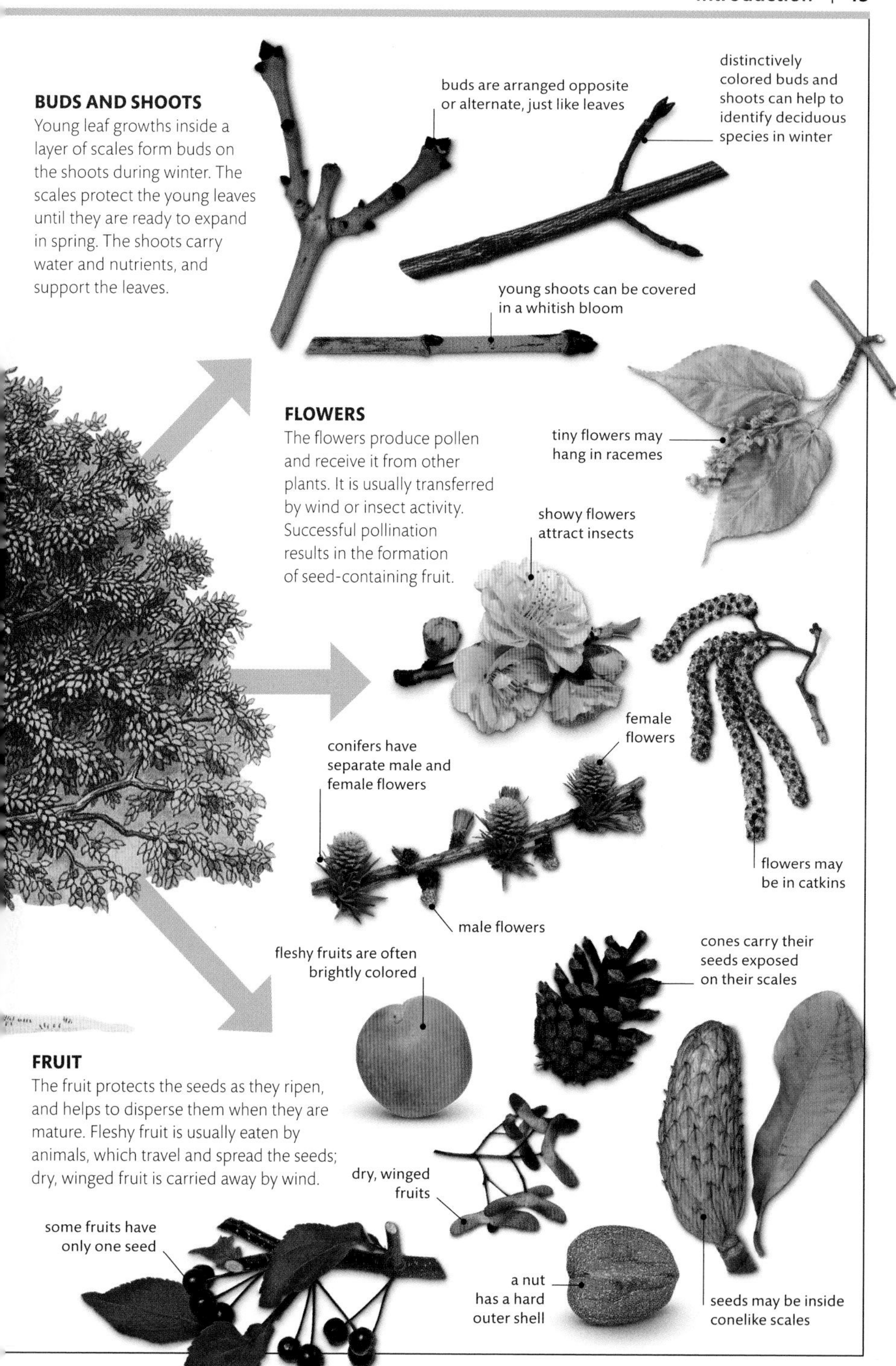
buds are arranged opposite or alternate, just like leaves
distinctively colored buds and shoots can help to identify deciduous species in winter
young shoots can be covered in a whitish bloom
tiny flowers may hang in racemes
showy flowers attract insects
female flowers
conifers have separate male and female flowers
flowers may be in catkins
male flowers
fleshy fruits are often brightly colored
cones carry their seeds exposed on their scales
dry, winged fruits
some fruits have only one seed
a nut has a hard outer shell
seeds may be inside conelike scales

THE PARTS OF A TREE

BECOMING FAMILIAR WITH the principal parts of a tree, and their variety, can help you to identify trees at any season of the year; and it is useful to recognize the special words that describe them. These pages illustrate typical leaves, flowers, fruit, and bark. If you can relate the words to the pictures, you can see in your mind what the parts of the tree look like as you read the entries.

TEN BASIC LEAF SHAPES

Leaves occur in a great variety of shapes; each also has variations within its basic shape. Every leaf may not fit exactly into one of the shapes shown below: it may be between two different ones. These shapes apply not only to simple leaves, but also to the individual leaflets of compound leaves. A simple leaf is one that is not divided into separate parts. A compound leaf is divided into two or more parts: each separate division is known as a leaflet.

Needlelike leaves are parallel-sided and taper-pointed.

Linear leaves are parallel-sided and have a blunt tip.

Rounded leaves are more or less circular in outline.

Oblong leaves are parallel-sided or nearly so.

Elliptic leaves are broad, narrowing at each end.

Heart-shaped leaves have a deep indent at the base.

Ovate leaves are widest below the middle.

Obovate leaves are widest above the middle.

Lanceolate leaves are slender and widest below the middle.

Oblanceolate leaves are slender and widest below the middle.

THE PARTS OF A FLOWER

Whereas leaves may vary greatly within any one genus, the flowers of related species and genera are usually similar, at least in structure. Those found on trees are often small, sometimes insignificant and without petals, or even inconspicuous; alternatively, they can be large and showy. Some tree flowers are fragrant; some smell unpleasant; some have no scent at all. How they are borne—singly or together in clusters—is also a notable identifying feature.

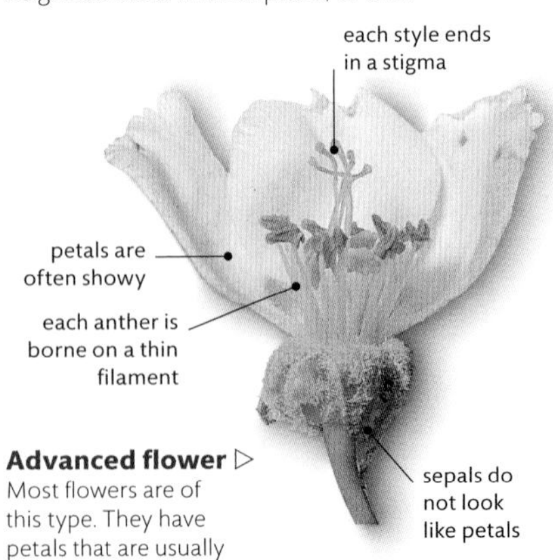

Advanced flower ▷
Most flowers are of this type. They have petals that are usually distinct from the sepals.

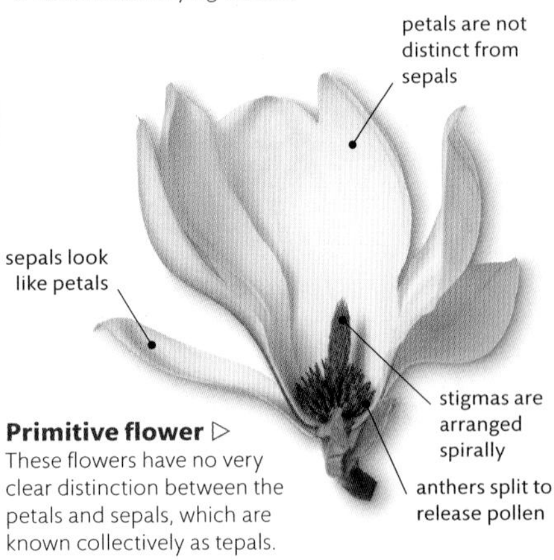

Primitive flower ▷
These flowers have no very clear distinction between the petals and sepals, which are known collectively as tepals.

TYPES OF FRUIT

Fruits develop from flowers, and so it follows that—as with flowers—the type of fruit a tree bears is characteristic of the genus or even the family to which it belongs. Most fruits originate from a single flower. Others, such as the fig (*Ficus carica*, see p.195), are derived from several flowers, which fuse together to form multiple fruits.

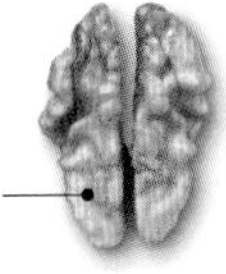
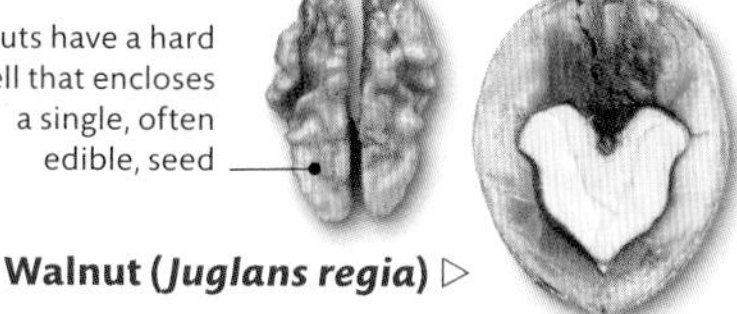

nuts have a hard shell that encloses a single, often edible, seed

Walnut (*Juglans regia*) ▷

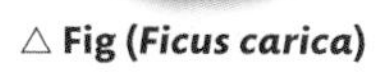

a fleshy receptacle contains many tiny seeds that develop from flowers borne inside it

△ **Fig (*Ficus carica*)**

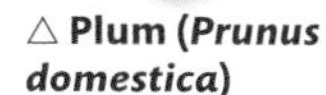

stone fruits are fleshy, with a single seed

△ **Plum (*Prunus domestica*)**

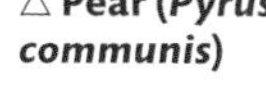

fleshy fruits may have several seeds and are often edible

△ **Pear (*Pyrus communis*)**

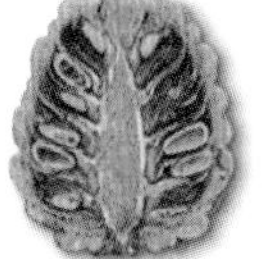
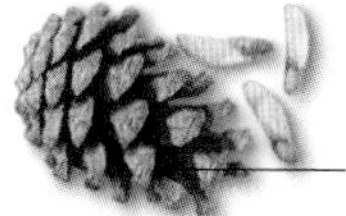

cone seeds are borne naked on the inner surface of the scales, which stay tightly closed until the seeds are ripe

△ **Winged cone seeds**

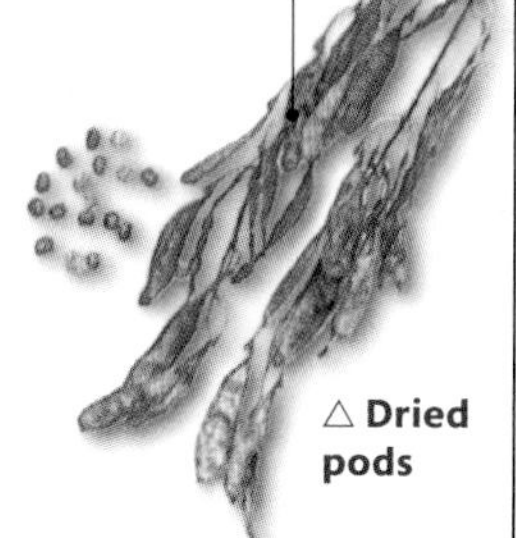

pods dry and split open to release one or more seeds

Pod seeds ▷

△ **Dried pods**

TYPES OF BARK

Trees develop their characteristic bark patterns and textures as a means of dealing with the increasing circumference of the trunk as they grow. Because the outer bark is composed of dead cells, it cannot grow and so, as the trunk expands, the bark cracks or peels in various ways. Bark is a useful feature in identification, since it can be used at any time of the year.

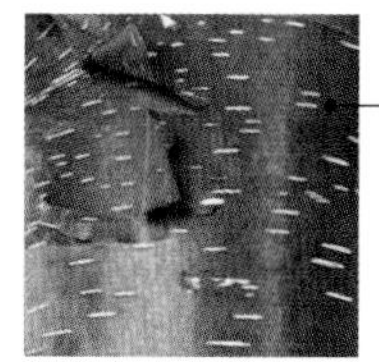

smooth bark is dotted with lenticels

Smooth bark is a feature of many young trees. It may crack or peel as they age.

bark of young tree was all white

Plates are irregular areas of bark, often flaking, with fissures or cracks in between.

younger bark can be seen at base of ridges and fissures

Ridges and fissures may develop as thick bark cracks. They can be raised and prominent or deep.

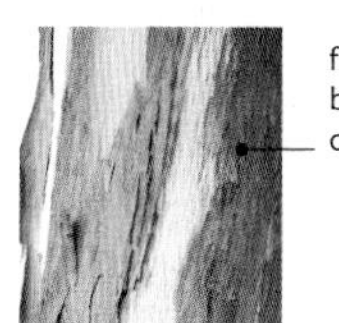

freshly exposed bark is distinctively colored

Vertically peeling bark often hangs and falls from the tree in long strips and ribbons.

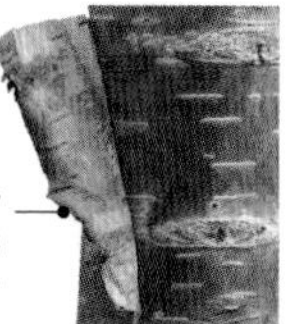

peeling bark by hand harms the tree

Horizontally peeling bark may unwind from the tree in paper-thin strips and wide sheets.

flaking bark shows many ages and colors

Irregularly flaking bark reveals different age layers, and gives the trunk a shaggy appearance.

CONIFER OR BROADLEAF?

CHARACTERS VISIBLE ONLY with a microscope can provide hidden clues that help with identification. But for most people, careful, detailed observation of what is immediately visible must do. If you can recognize the distinctive features that categorize the two major groups, it is easy to distinguish conifers and their allies from broadleaves, and vice versa. The main characteristics are described and illustrated on these two pages. The reproductive structures of conifers (strobili) are very different from those of the broadleaves, but for simplicity are referred to here as flowers and fruits.

CONIFERS AND THEIR ALLIES

Leaves

Most conifers are evergreen: they retain their leaves in winter. A few are deciduous: they renew their leaves annually. The leaves are usually narrow and sharp-pointed or small and scalelike. The foliage is often sweet and aromatic.

Flowers

Conifer flowers are male or female. They are borne on the same or different plants. They do not have petals, yet some can be quite ornamental. Female flowers often have brightly colored scales; males release powdery pollen.

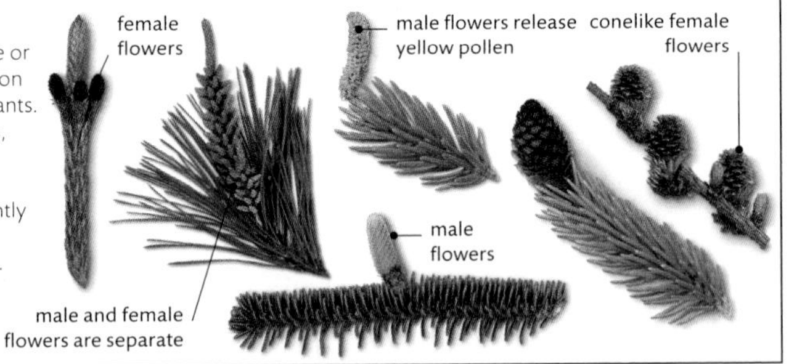

Fruit

The fruit of most conifers is a cone, composed of often woody scales, and colored brown when ripe. Juniper species have fleshy scales, so the fruit resembles a berry. Some of the trees listed here have been regarded as distinct from the conifers. Examples of this are the yews, of which the fruit is a seed covered with a fleshy coat.

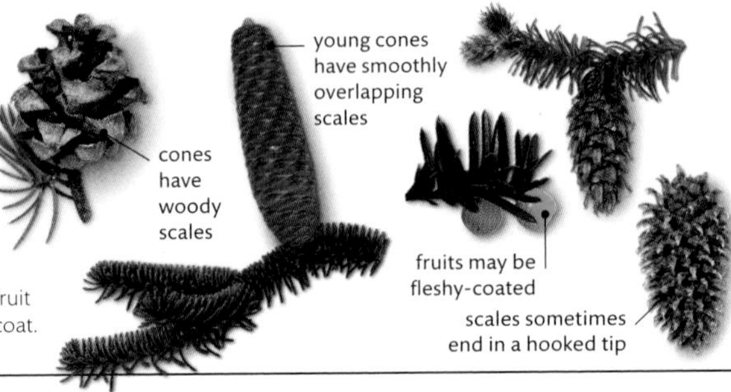

THE BOTANICAL DIFFERENCE

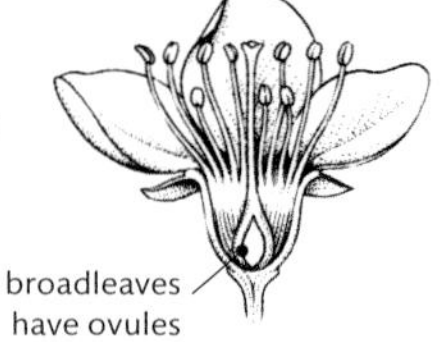

conifers bear naked seeds

Conifers

Conifers and their allies are classed as gymnosperms: plants with naked seeds not enclosed in an ovary. They are considered to be more primitive than broadleaves.

Broadleaves

Broadleaves are classed as angiosperms: plants with ovules enclosed for protection in an ovary. Following successful fertilization, the ovules develop into seeds.

BROADLEAVES

Leaves

Broadleaves are evergreen or deciduous. The leaves are simple or compound, usually flattened, and have a distinct network of fine veins. They vary greatly in shape. The foliage may have an aromatic scent, but lacks the resinous quality of conifers.

Flowers

Broadleaf flowers are usually bisexual: male and female parts are in the same flower. Separate males and females are borne either on the same or different plants. Both types usually have petals, and are often fragrant. They can be small or large.

Fruit

The fruit of broadleaves has much more diversity than that of most conifers, and comes in many forms. It may be a berry, acorn, capsule, nut, or pod; woody, fleshy-coated, or dry; spiny, rough, or smooth; inedible or edible; and any color when ripe.

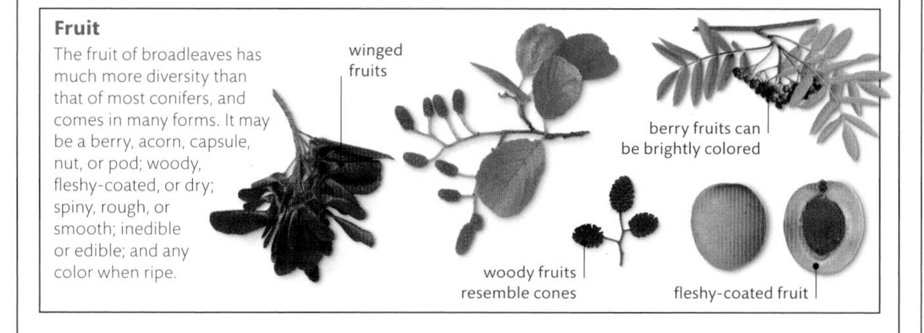

TREE IDENTIFICATION KEY

THE KEY ON pages 18 to 33 uses leaf characteristics to help you to identify the trees that are described in this book. Stage 1 (see right) establishes whether your tree is a conifer, broadleaf, or palm. Stage 2 divides conifers and broadleaves into groups, according to leaf type. Stage 3 divides each of these groups into more detailed groups that each contain two or more genera.

STAGE 1

WHICH GROUP?

The trees are divided into two major groups: Conifers and Broadleaves (including Palms). Conifer features are described on page 16. Broadleaf features are described on page 17. Palm features are described on page 19.

Conifer

Broadleaf

Palm

STAGE 2

CONIFERS—DECIDUOUS OR EVERGREEN?

Only a few conifer species in this book are deciduous; most are evergreen. Deciduous species lose their leaves in fall. In spring, their pale young leaves are clearly visible. Evergreens keep their leaves in winter, so they are easy to distinguish. In spring, look for pale young leaves along with dark old leaves. If your tree is deciduous, turn to pages 20–21. If it is evergreen, decide whether your leaf is not scalelike or scalelike, then turn to pages 20–21 or 22–23.

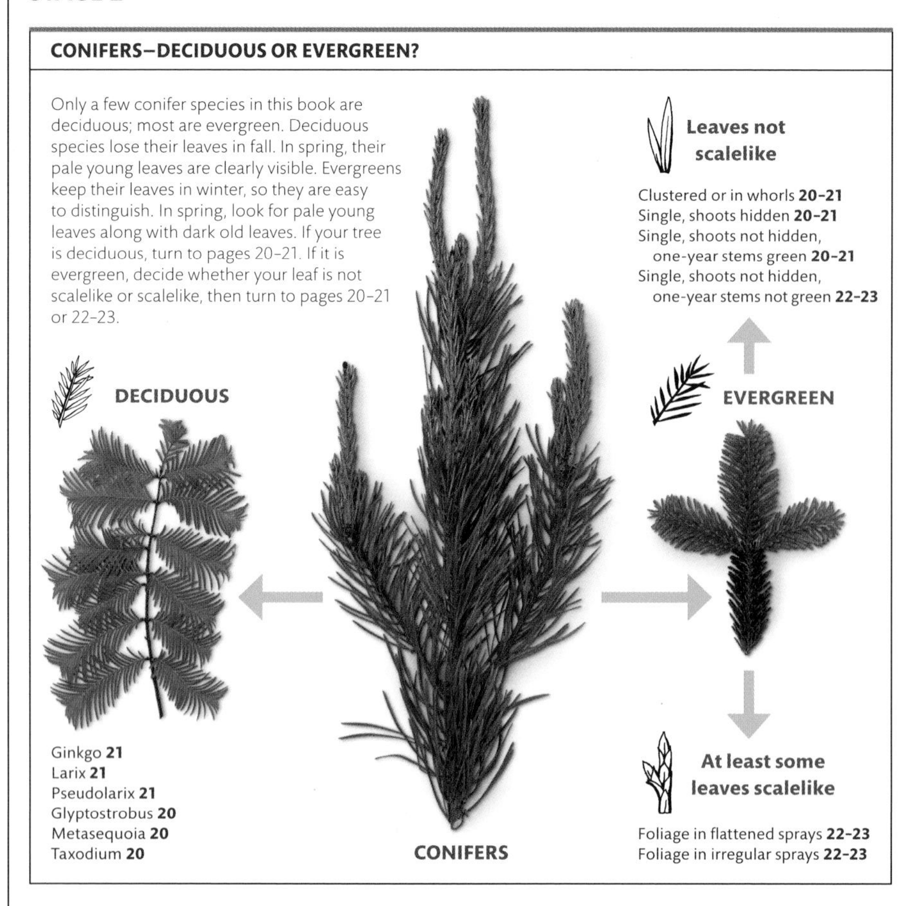

STAGE 2

BROADLEAVES—OPPOSITE OR ALTERNATE LEAVES?

All broadleaves have their leaves arranged in one of two ways: either opposite or alternate. Opposite leaves are borne in pairs or threes, one directly opposite the other, on either side of the stem. Alternate leaves are borne singly, staggered on alternate sides of the stem. Leaflets are opposite or alternate, too. If your leaf is opposite, turn to pages 22–25. If it is alternate, turn to pages 24–33.

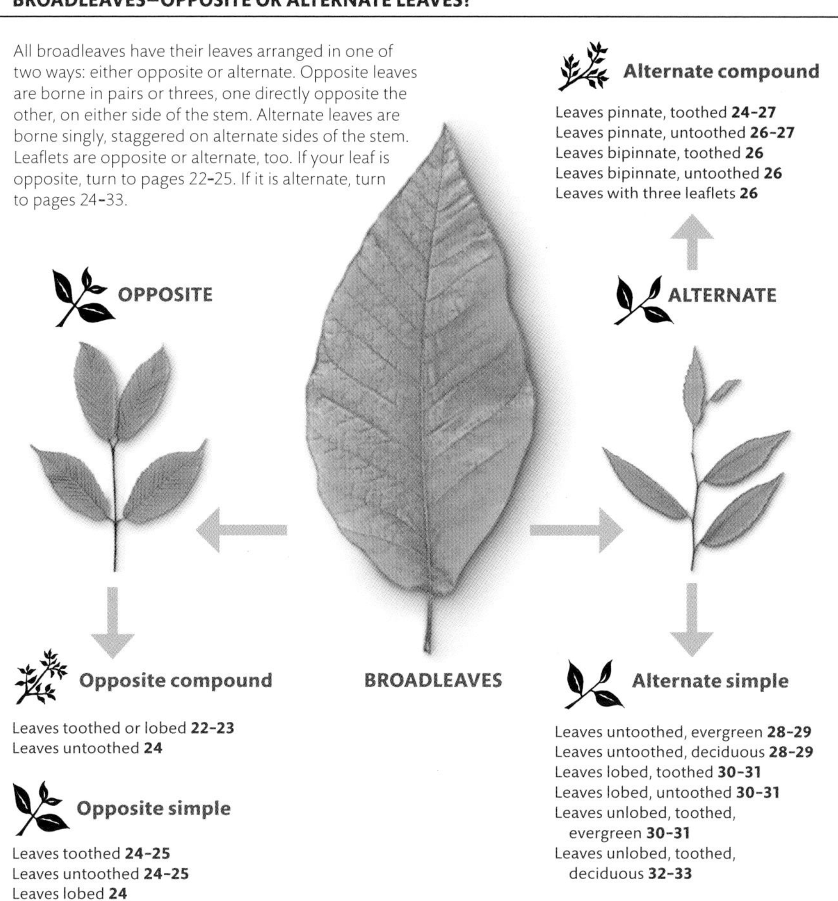

Opposite compound

Opposite simple

Alternate compound

Alternate simple

STAGE 2

PALMS

Palms are often treelike in habit, but are not true trees. They have a single, unbranched stem that does not increase in girth with age, and distinctively divided leaves. Most palms are native to warm regions, but some species grow in warm temperate regions, such as the Mediterranean and the southern US. Chusan palm (*Trachycarpus fortunei*), included in this book of largely temperate plants as an example of palms, is the hardiest species. If your leaf belongs to this palm, turn to page 30.

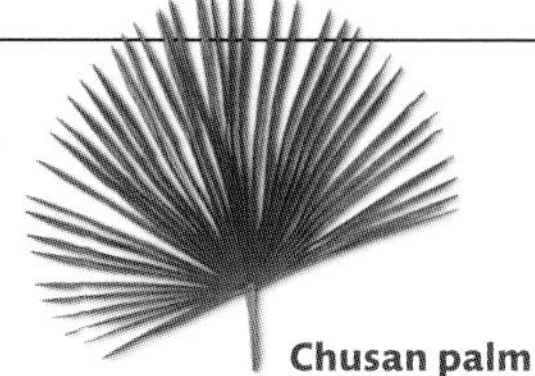

Chusan palm

STAGE 3

This final stage in the identification key will guide you quickly to the correct section of the book. If you have turned straight to this part of the key, go back to pages 16 and 17, where the main characteristics that distinguish conifers and their allies, and broadleaves, from each other are illustrated and described. Having noted these features, move on to pages 18 and 19 and read through Stages 1 and 2 of the key. Now you are all set to start Stage 3.

Each individual leaf in the key represents a genus. You have already decided which type of conifer leaf you have—whether it is deciduous or evergreen, not scalelike or scalelike. You will see

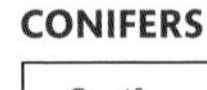

CONIFERS

Conifers	Leaf persistence: Deciduous	Leaf type: not scale-like

Leaves renewed annually

Glyptostrobus **44**

Metasequoia **49**

Taxodium **51**

Conifers	Leaf persistence: Evergreen	Leaf type: not scale-like

Leaves clustered or in whorls

Fitzroya **44**

Juniperus **45–49**

Cedrus **62–63**

Leaves single, young shoots hidden by leaves or leaf bases

Araucaria **34**

Wollemia **34**

Athrotaxis **35**

Cryptomeria **39**

Leaves single, young shoots not hidden, one-year stems green

Cunninghamia **39**

Prumnopitys **81**

Saxegothaea **81**

that each large group has been further divided into several smaller groups. These give you an additional layer of information, which points you to finer detail; for example, whether the leaves are borne in clusters or whorls, or singly. Compare your leaf carefully with the leaves shown in the bands of each section, and decide to which group your leaf belongs. Compare your leaf to the leaves in the final group, and find the individual leaf that it most closely resembles. The genus to which it belongs is written below the photograph of the leaf. Turn to the page(s) indicated beside the genus name to find the relevant species entry or entries.

Ginkgo **55**

Larix **64–65**

Pseudolarix **79**

Pinus **70–78**

Sciadopitys **82**

Sequoia **50**

Sequoiadendron **50**

Taiwania **51**

Cephalotaxus **82–83**

Taxus **83**

Torreya **83**

STAGE 3

CONIFERS

Leaves single, young shoots not hidden, one-year stems not green

Abies **56–61**

Picea **66–69**

Pinus monophylla **74**

Conifers	Leaf persistence: Evergreen	Leaf type: at least some leaves scalelike

Foliage in flattened sprays

Austrocedrus **35**

Calocedrus **36**

Chamaecyparis **37–38**

Cupressus cashmeriana **40**

Foliage in irregular sprays

Cupressus **40–42**

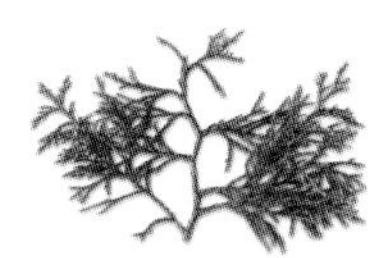
Juniperus **45–49**

STAGE 3

This final stage in the identification key will guide you quickly to the correct section of the book. If you have turned straight to this part of the key, go back to pages 16 and 17, where the main characteristics that distinguish conifers and their allies, and broadleaves, from each other are illustrated and described. Having noted these features, move on to pages 18 and 19 and read through Stages 1 and 2 of the key. Now you are all set to start Stage 3.

Each individual leaf in the key represents a genus. You have already decided which type of broadleaf leaf you have—whether it is opposite or alternate, compound or simple. You will see that

BROADLEAVES

Broadleaves	Leaf arrangement: Opposite	Leaf type: Compound

Leaflets toothed or lobed

Eucryphia **121–124**

Fraxinus **207–209**

Acer **275–296**

Pseudotsuga **79**

Tsuga **80**

x *Cuprocyparis* **43**

Thuja **52–53**

Thujopsis **54**

Xanthocyparis **54**

each large group has been further divided into several smaller groups. These give you an additional layer of information, which points you to finer detail; for example, whether the leaves are toothed, untoothed, or lobed, evergreen or deciduous. Compare your leaf carefully with the leaves shown in the bands of each section, and decide to which group your leaf belongs. Compare your leaf to those in the final group, and find the individual leaf that it most closely resembles. The genus to which it belongs is written below the leaf photograph. Turn to the page(s) indicated beside the genus name to find the relevant entry or entries.

Aesculus **297–299**

STAGE 3

BROADLEAVES

Leaflets untoothed

Phellodendron **262**

Tetradium **263**

Broadleaves	Leaf arrangement: Opposite	Leaf type: Simple

Leaves toothed

Euonymus **115**

Cercidiphyllum **116**

Eucryphia **121–124**

Chionanthus **206–207**

Leaves untoothed

Catalpa **111–113**

Buxus **113**

Cornus **117–121**

Eucryphia **121–124**

Leaves lobed

Catalpa **111–113**

Paulownia **211**

Acer **275–297**

Broadleaves	Leaf arrangement: Alternate	Leaf type: Compound

Leaves pinnate, leaflets toothed

Rhus **86–87**

Gleditsia **137**

Carya **166–167**

Juglans **167–169**

Phillyrea **210**

Rhamnus cathartica **216**

Acer **275–296**

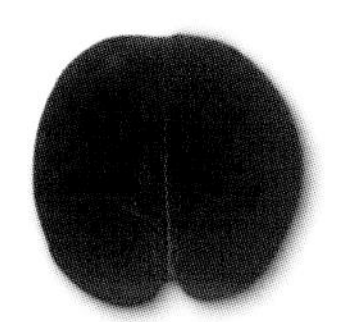
Eucalyptus **197–200**

Luma **200**

Chionanthus **206–207**

Ligustrum **210**

Platycarya **169**

Pterocarya **170–171**

Toona **193**

Cormus **219**

Sorbus **256–261**

STAGE 3

BROADLEAVES

Zanthoxylum **264**

Koelreuteria **300**

Xanthoceras **300**

Leaves pinnate, leaflets untoothed

Toxicodendron **87**

Cladrastis **136**

Maackia **140**

Robinia **141**

Leaves bipinnate, leaflets toothed

Aralia **95**

Gleditsia **137**

Leaves bipinnate, leaflets untoothed

Acacia **132–133**

Albizia **134**

Gymnocladus **137**

Leaves with three leaflets

Eucryphia **121–124**

+ *Laburnocytisus* **138**

Laburnum **139–140**

Acer **275–296**

Ailanthus **301**

Sophora **142**

Styphnolobium **142**

Juglans regia **169**

Ptelea **263**

STAGE 3

BROADLEAVES

Broadleaves	Leaf arrangement: Alternate	Leaf type: Simple

Leaves untoothed, evergreen

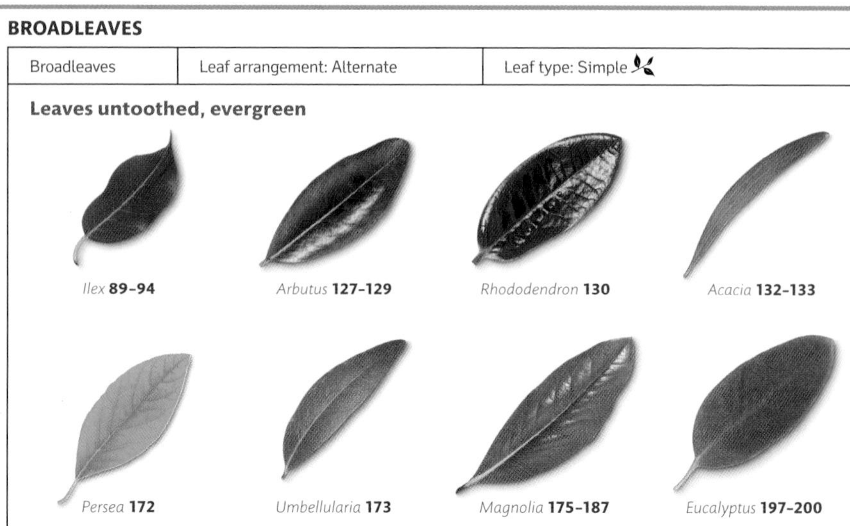

Ilex **89–94** *Arbutus* **127–129** *Rhododendron* **130** *Acacia* **132–133**

Persea **172** *Umbellularia* **173** *Magnolia* **175–187** *Eucalyptus* **197–200**

Leaves untoothed, deciduous

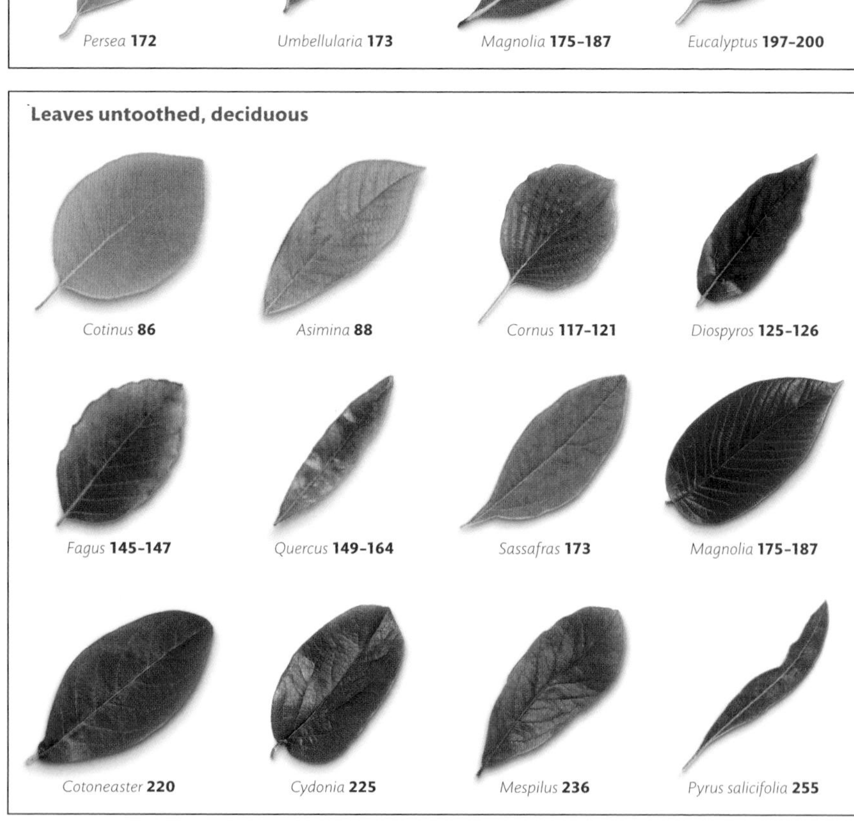

Cotinus **86** *Asimina* **88** *Cornus* **117–121** *Diospyros* **125–126**

Fagus **145–147** *Quercus* **149–164** *Sassafras* **173** *Magnolia* **175–187**

Cotoneaster **220** *Cydonia* **225** *Mespilus* **236** *Pyrus salicifolia* **255**

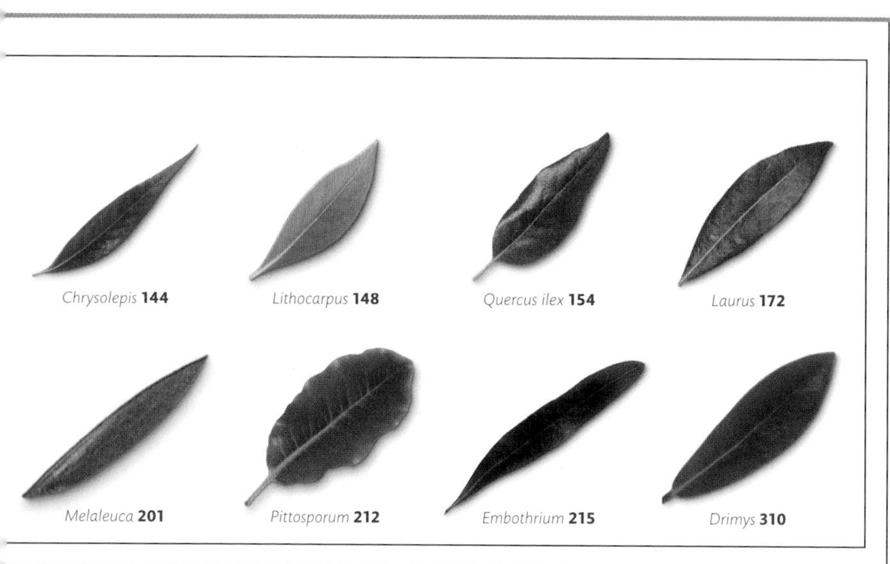

Chrysolepis **144**

Lithocarpus **148**

Quercus ilex **154**

Laurus **172**

Melaleuca **201**

Pittosporum **212**

Embothrium **215**

Drimys **310**

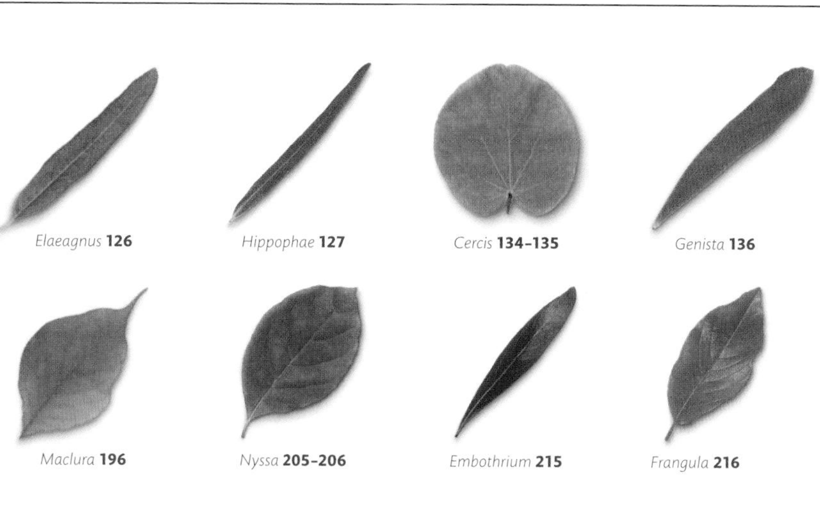

Elaeagnus **126**

Hippophae **127**

Cercis **134–135**

Genista **136**

Maclura **196**

Nyssa **205–206**

Embothrium **215**

Frangula **216**

STAGE 3

BROADLEAVES

Leaves lobed, toothed

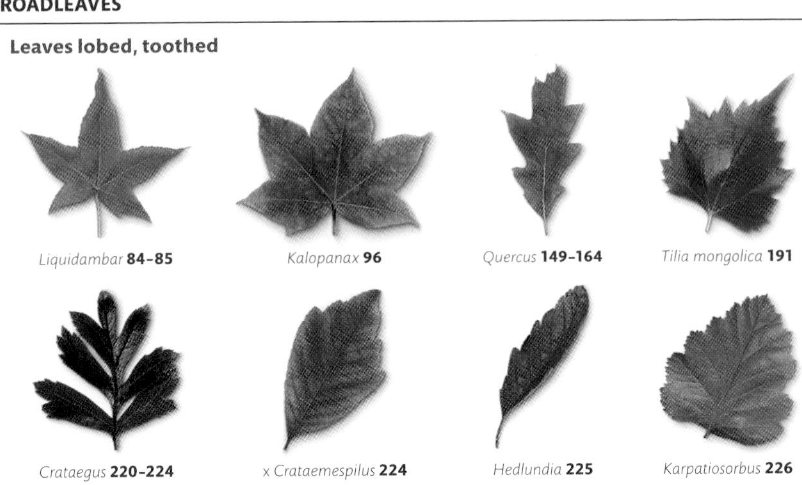

Liquidambar **84–85** | *Kalopanax* **96** | *Quercus* **149–164** | *Tilia mongolica* **191**

Crataegus **220–224** | x *Crataemespilus* **224** | *Hedlundia* **225** | *Karpatiosorbus* **226**

Leaves lobed, untoothed

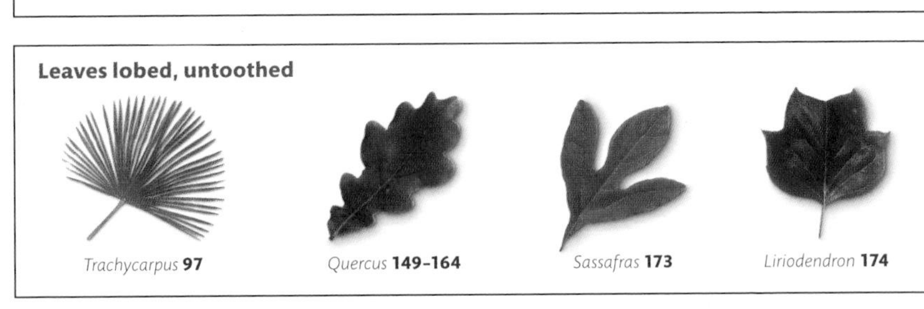

Trachycarpus **97** | *Quercus* **149–164** | *Sassafras* **173** | *Liriodendron* **174**

Leaves unlobed, toothed, evergreen

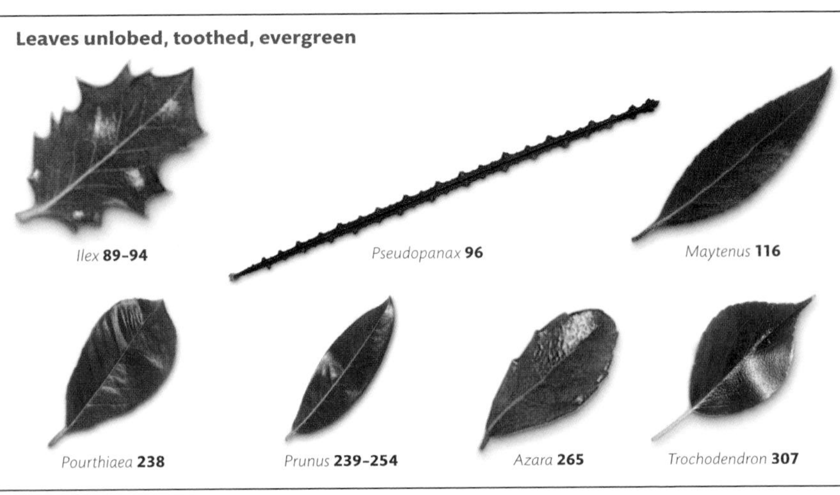

Ilex **89–94** | *Pseudopanax* **96** | *Maytenus* **116**

Pourthiaea **238** | *Prunus* **239–254** | *Azara* **265** | *Trochodendron* **307**

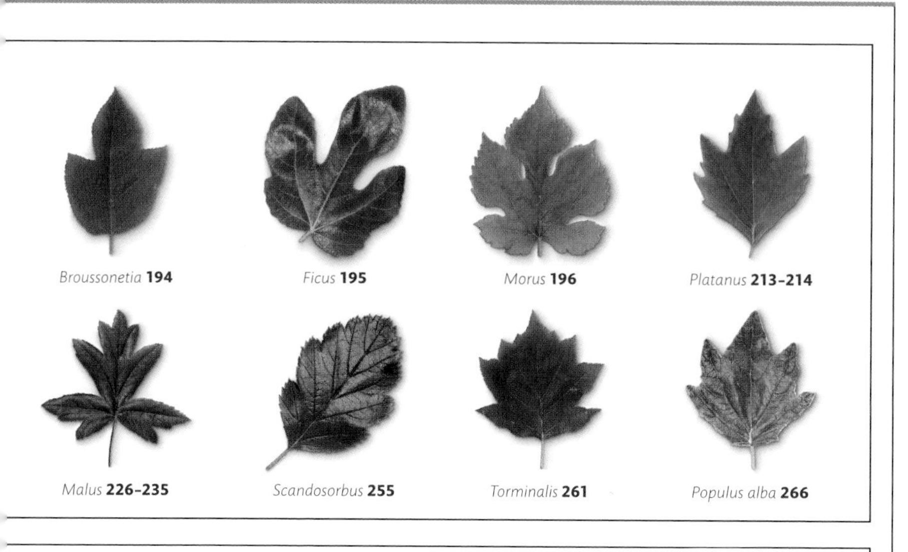

Broussonetia **194**

Ficus **195**

Morus **196**

Platanus **213–214**

Malus **226–235**

Scandosorbus **255**

Torminalis **261**

Populus alba **266**

Arbutus **127–129**

Quercus **149–164**

Nothofagus **202–204**

STAGE 3

BROADLEAVES

Leaves unlobed, toothed, deciduous

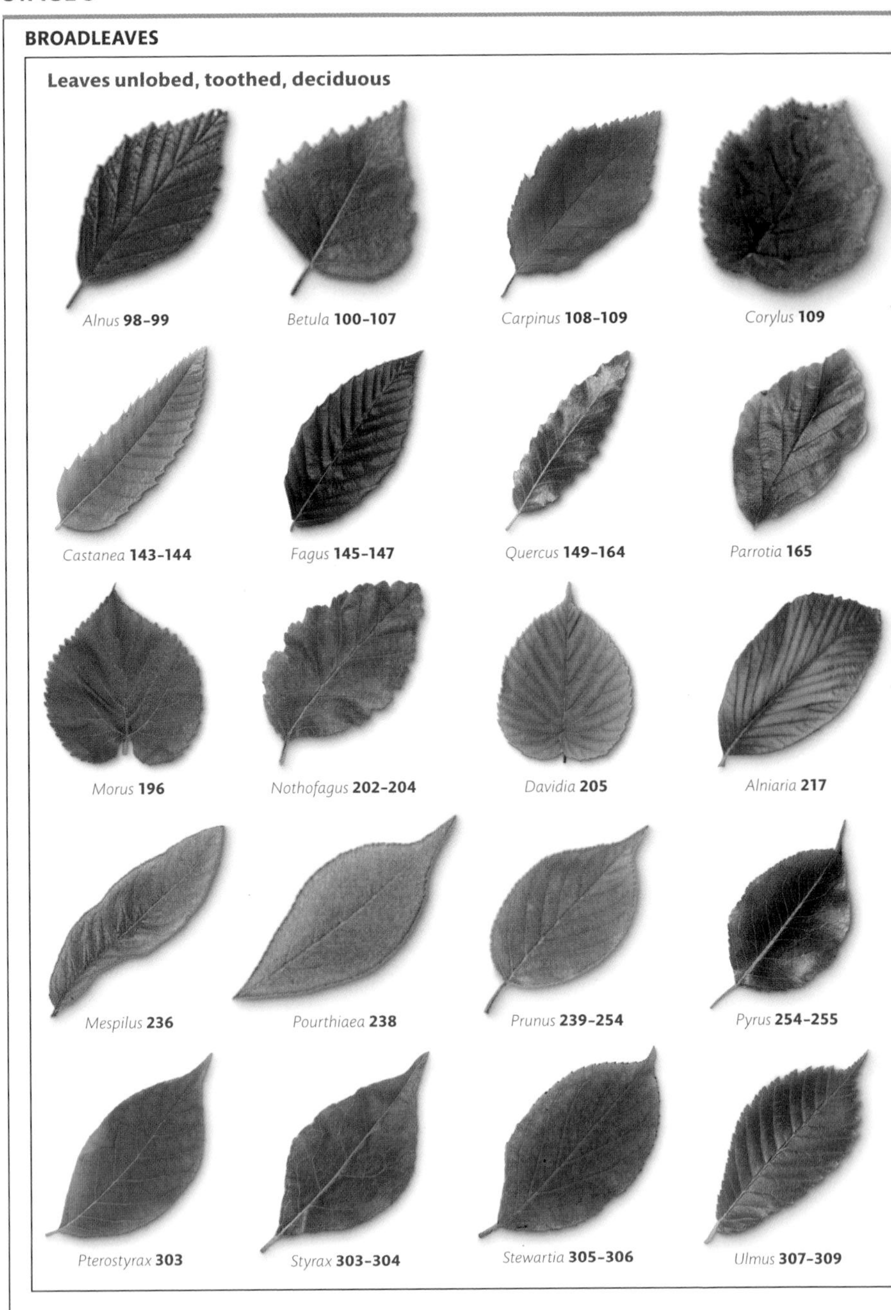

Alnus **98–99**
Betula **100–107**
Carpinus **108–109**
Corylus **109**
Castanea **143–144**
Fagus **145–147**
Quercus **149–164**
Parrotia **165**
Morus **196**
Nothofagus **202–204**
Davidia **205**
Alniaria **217**
Mespilus **236**
Pourthiaea **238**
Prunus **239–254**
Pyrus **254–255**
Pterostyrax **303**
Styrax **303–304**
Stewartia **305–306**
Ulmus **307–309**

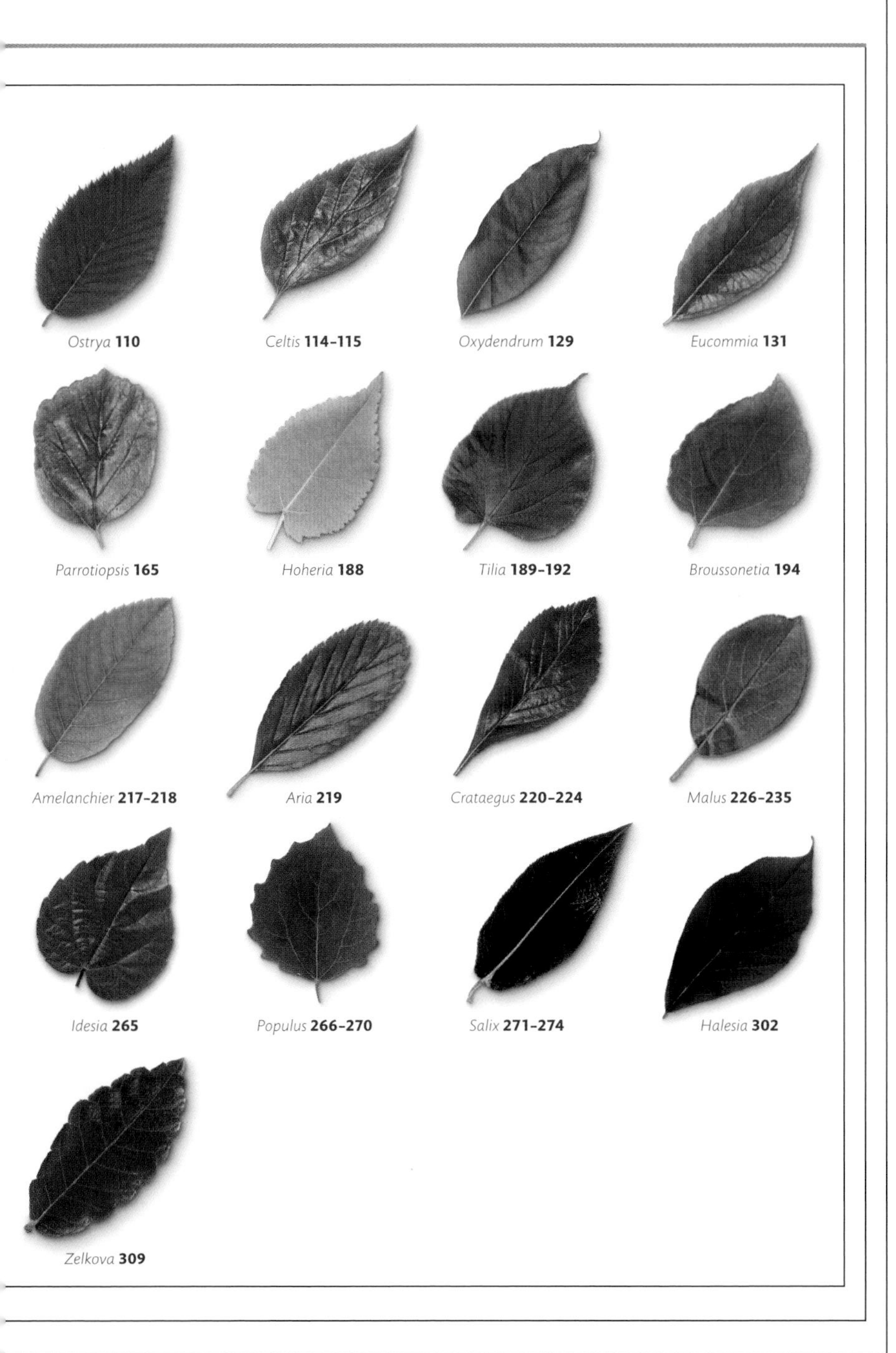
Ostrya **110**
Celtis **114–115**
Oxydendrum **129**
Eucommia **131**
Parrotiopsis **165**
Hoheria **188**
Tilia **189–192**
Broussonetia **194**
Amelanchier **217–218**
Aria **219**
Crataegus **220–224**
Malus **226–235**
Idesia **265**
Populus **266–270**
Salix **271–274**
Halesia **302**
Zelkova **309**

CONIFERS

AND THEIR ALLIES

ARAUCARIACEAE

THREE GENERA AND ABOUT 38 species of large, evergreen trees belong to this family. In the main, they are native to the southern hemisphere, but extend into Southeast Asia. Many are important timber trees. The monkey puzzle (*Araucaria araucana*) is the most well-known member of the family.

Family: Araucariaceae	Species: *Araucaria araucana*	Author: (Molina) K. Koch

Monkey Puzzle

Leaves Ovate, to 2in (5cm) long and ¾in (2cm) wide, broad at the base, with a spiny tip, glossy dark green, overlapping, all around the shoot. ***Bark*** Gray, wrinkled. ***Flowers*** 4in (10cm) long, males brown, clustered, females green-brown, singly, on separate plants in summer. ***Fruit*** An ovoid, brown cone, to 6in (15cm) long.

NATIVE REGION Argentina, Chile.
HABITAT Mountains.

Height: 164ft (50m)	Shape: Unique	Leaf persistence: Evergreen	Leaf type:

Family: Araucariaceae	Species: *Wollemia nobilis*	Author: W.G. Jones, K.D. Hill & J.M. Allen

Wollemi Pine

Leaves Linear, to 3¼in (8cm) long and 3/16in (5mm) wide with a blunt tip, dark green above, paler beneath, on juvenile branches in two rows, on adult branches shorter and in four rows. ***Bark*** Red-brown and spongy with bubblelike nodules on young trees, peeling in mature trees. ***Flowers*** Males and females borne at ends of branches, separately on the same tree, males red-brown 4in (10cm) long and ¾in (2cm) wide, females green and rounded. ***Fruit*** A rounded brown cone to 4¾in (12cm) long.

NATIVE REGION New South Wales.
HABITAT A single sandstone gorge.
REMARK A rare species discovered in 1994 with ancient fossil relatives; it has since been propagated and is grown in many gardens worldwide. Its name derives from the Wollemi National Park where it is found, while *nobilis* means "noble" in Latin and commemorates its discoverer David Noble. It is not related to the true pines (*Pinus*).

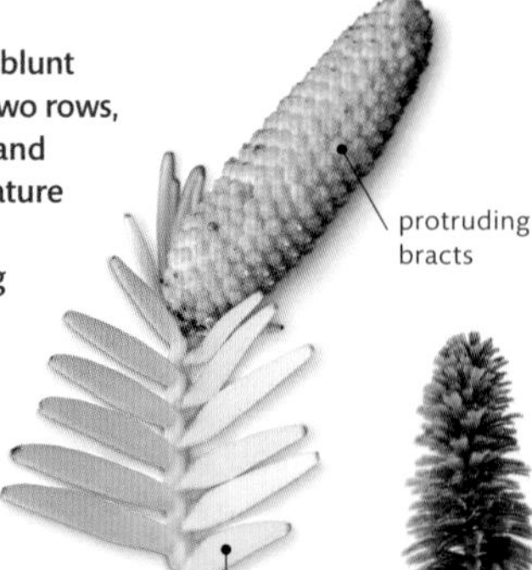

Height: 130ft (40m)	Habit: Narrowly columnar	Leaf persistence: Evergreen	Leaf type: 

CUPRESSACEAE

THIS FAMILY HAS ABOUT 30 genera, with more than 165 species of mainly evergreen trees and shrubs, including the cypresses (*Cupressus*, see pp.40–42) and junipers (*Juniperus*, see pp.45–49), found worldwide. The small leaves are usually needlelike in young plants, but scalelike in mature trees; some juniper species bear both types. Male and female flowers are separate, on the same or different plants. The fruit is a cone, but is berrylike in junipers.

Family: Cupressaceae	Species: *Athrotaxis* x *laxifolia*	Author: Hook.

Summit Cedar

Leaves Small, to ¼in (6mm) long, with sharp, free, spreading tips, yellowish becoming dark green. ***Bark*** Red-brown, peeling vertically. ***Flowers*** Males and females both yellow-brown, in separate clusters on the same plant in early spring. ***Fruit*** A rounded cone, ¾in (2cm) across, pale green ripening to red-brown, with spine-tipped scales.

NATIVE REGION Tasmania.
HABITAT Mountains.
REMARK A hybrid of *Athrotaxis cupressoides* and *Athrotaxis selaginoides*.

Height: 33ft (10m)	Shape: Broadly conical	Leaf persistence: Evergreen	Leaf type: 

Family: Cupressaceae	Species: *Austrocedrus chilensis*	Author: (D. Don) Pic. Serm. & Bizzarri

Chilean Cedar

Leaves Scalelike, to 3⁄16in (5mm) long, flattened, with a blunt point, glossy dark green sometimes marked with white above, with a conspicuous white band beneath, borne in flattened sprays; on upper and lower sides of shoot much smaller. ***Bark*** Gray-brown, scaly. ***Flowers*** Males and females both very small, males yellowish, females green, in small clusters at the tips of the shoots in early spring. ***Fruit*** An oblong cone, ⅜in (1cm) long, green ripening to brown, with four overlapping scales.

NATIVE REGION Argentina, Chile.
HABITAT Mountains.
REMARK Also known as *Libocedrus chilensis*. It is closely related to the incense cedar (*Calocedrus decurrens*, see p.36).

Height: 80ft (25m)	Shape: Narrowly conical	Leaf persistence: Evergreen	Leaf type: 

Family: Cupressaceae	Species: *Calocedrus decurrens*	Author: (Torr.) Florin

Incense Cedar

Leaves Scalelike, to about ½in (3mm) long, in sets of two pairs together, with a triangular, sharp-pointed tip, glossy dark green, borne in flattened, aromatic sprays; upper and lower leaves largest. ***Bark*** Red-brown and scaly. ***Flowers*** Males and females both very small, males yellow, females green, in small clusters at the tips of the shoots in winter. ***Fruit*** An oblong, yellow-brown cone, 1in (2.5cm) long, with six overlapping scales.

NATIVE REGION W. US, N.W. Mexico.
HABITAT Forests on mountain slopes.
REMARK Also known as *Libocedrus decurrens*. In the wild, old plants eventually become more open in shape. It produces a useful, very aromatic wood.

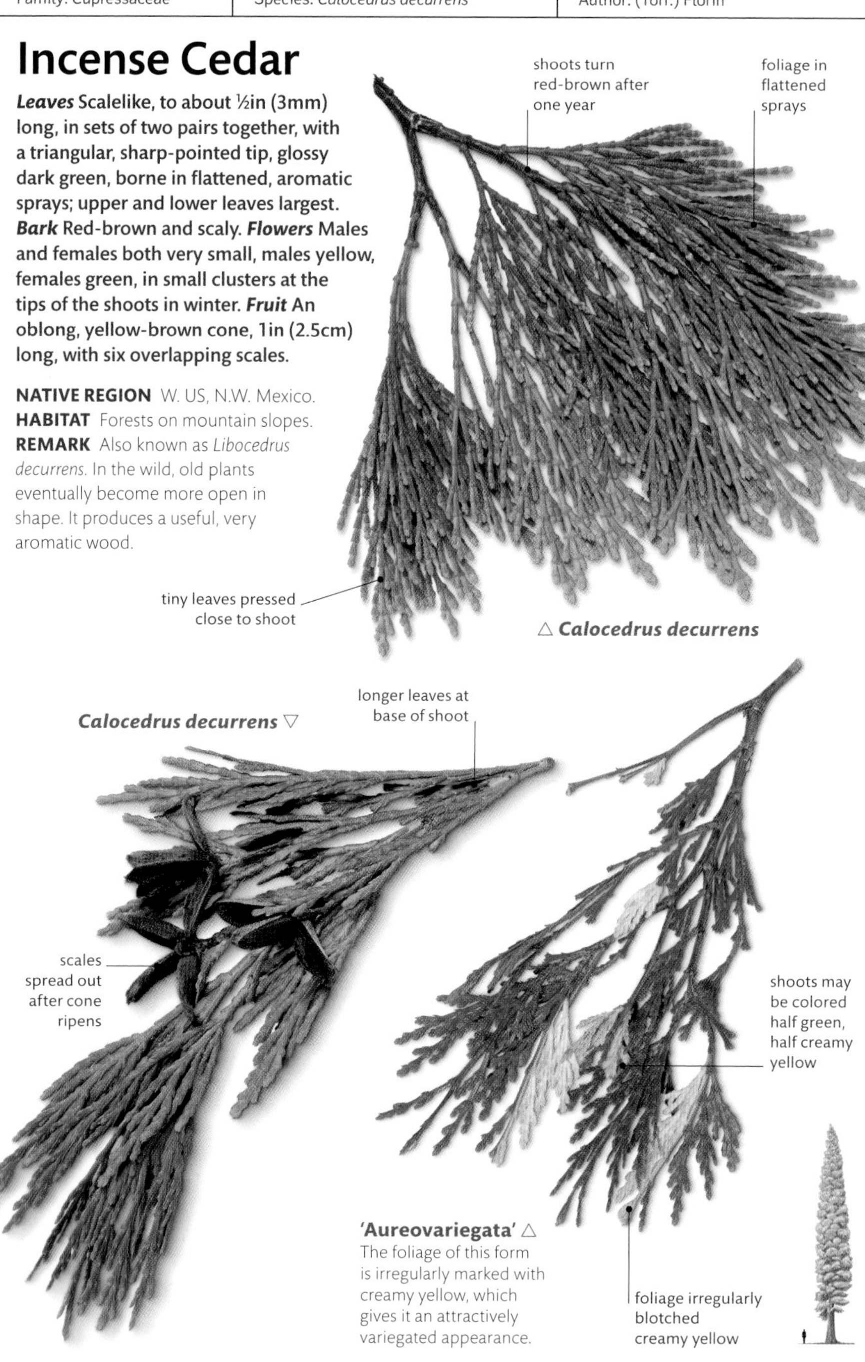

△ ***Calocedrus decurrens***

Calocedrus decurrens ▽

'Aureovariegata' △
The foliage of this form is irregularly marked with creamy yellow, which gives it an attractively variegated appearance.

Height: 130ft (40m)	Shape: Narrowly columnar	Leaf persistence: Evergreen	Leaf type:

Family: Cupressaceae	Species: *Chamaecyparis lawsoniana*	Author: (A. Murray bis) Parl.

Lawson Cypress

Leaves **Scalelike, very small, pointed, the tip often slightly free from the shoot, dark green above, paler with white X-shaped marks where the leaves meet beneath, borne in flattened sprays. *Bark* Purple-brown and flaking. *Flowers* Males red, females bluish, in clusters at the tips of the shoots in early spring. *Fruit* A rounded cone, $\frac{5}{16}$in (8mm) across, with eight scales.**

NATIVE REGION US: N.W. California, S.W. Oregon.
HABITAT Mountain slopes and canyons.

▽ ***Chamaecyparis lawsoniana***

cones ripen from blue-green to brown in one year

aromatic foliage

blue-green foliage

△ **'Grayswood Pillar'**
Ascending branches give this form a compact, columnar shape.

'Hillieri' ▽
The golden yellow leaves of this very ornamental form are borne in large, flattened sprays.

'Albospica' △
This slow-growing selection forms a broadly conical tree.

Height: 164ft (50m)	Shape: Narrowly conical	Leaf persistence: Evergreen	Leaf type:

Family: Cupressaceae	Species: *Chamaecyparis obtusa*	Author: (Siebold & Zucc.) Endl.

Hinoki Cypress

Leaves **Scalelike, very small, blunt at the tip, dark green above, with bright white X- or Y-shaped marks where the leaves meet beneath, in flattened, aromatic sprays. *Bark* Red-brown and soft, peeling in thin strips. *Flowers* Males reddish yellow, females pale brown, in small clusters at the tips of the shoots in spring. *Fruit* A rounded cone, to ½in (1.2cm) across, green ripening to brown.**

NATIVE REGION Japan.
HABITAT Usually mountain slopes.
REMARK The cultivated forms include some of dwarf habit.

tiny leaves end in blunt tip

cones have 8 to 10 scales

inner foliage remains green

△ ***Chamaecyparis obtusa***

'Crippsii' ▷
The bright golden-yellow coloration of this ornamental form appears only on the outermost branches.

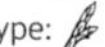

Height: 130ft (40m)	Shape: Narrowly conical	Leaf persistence: Evergreen	Leaf type:

Family: Cupressaceae	Species: *Chamaecyparis pisifera*	Author: (Siebold & Zucc.) Endl.

Sawara Cypress

Leaves **Scalelike, very small, with free, pointed tips, glossy green above, with conspicuous white marks beneath, in flattened, aromatic sprays; leaves at side of shoot slightly larger than those above and below.** ***Bark*** **Red-brown, peeling in narrow strips.** ***Flowers*** **Males brownish, females pale brown, in small clusters at the tips of the shoots in spring.** ***Fruit*** **A rounded cone, 5/16in (8mm) across, green ripening to brown.**

NATIVE REGION Japan.
HABITAT Stream banks in mountains.
REMARK The specific element of the scientific name, *pisifera*, refers to the diminutive, pea-sized cones. Young seedlings have narrow leaves, to ¼in (6mm) long, a feature that is retained in some cultivated forms. The plant pictured in the traditional blue and white "willow pattern" design on pottery and porcelain represents this species.

Height: 164ft (50m)	Shape: Broadly conical	Leaf persistence: Evergreen	Leaf type:

Family: Cupressaceae	Species: *Chamaecyparis thyoides*	Author: (L.) Britton, Sterns & Poggenb.

White Cypress

Leaves **Scalelike and very small, pointed at the tip, green to gray-green above, often with a tiny speck of resin, with bright white marks beneath, on slender shoots, in small, flattened, aromatic sprays; leaves at side of shoot slightly larger than those above.** ***Bark*** **Gray to brown, fibrous, peeling in strips.** ***Flowers*** **Males brownish, females green, in small clusters at the tips of the shoots in spring.** ***Fruit*** **A rounded cone, ¼in (6mm) across, glaucous ripening to brown, with six pointed scales.**

NATIVE REGION E. US.
HABITAT Usually swamps, wet ground, and moist places.
REMARK Also known as Atlantic white cedar, swamp cedar.

very small, pointed leaves

semi-ripe cone still whitish brown

△ ***Chamaecyparis thyoides***

'Glauca' ▷
This form is distinguished by its foliage, which is noticeably bluish white to blue-gray. The cones are also more bloomy.

'Variegata' ▷
As the cultivar name indicates, this plant is a variegated form of the species. Its foliage sprays are blotched more or less pale yellow.

Height: 80ft (25m)	Shape: Narrowly columnar	Leaf persistence: Evergreen	Leaf type: 

Family: Cupressaceae	Species: *Cryptomeria japonica*	Author: (Thunb. ex L. f.) D. Don

Japanese Cedar

Leaves **Slender, to ⅝in (1.5cm) long, flattened at the base, taper-pointed, bright green, curved forward along the shoots.** ***Bark*** **Orange-brown, soft, thick, peeling vertically.** ***Flowers*** **Males yellow-brown, in the leaf axils, females green, at the tips of the shoots, in separate clusters on the same plant in early spring.** ***Fruit*** **A rounded, brown cone, 2cm (¾in) across.**

NATIVE REGION Japan.
HABITAT Forests.

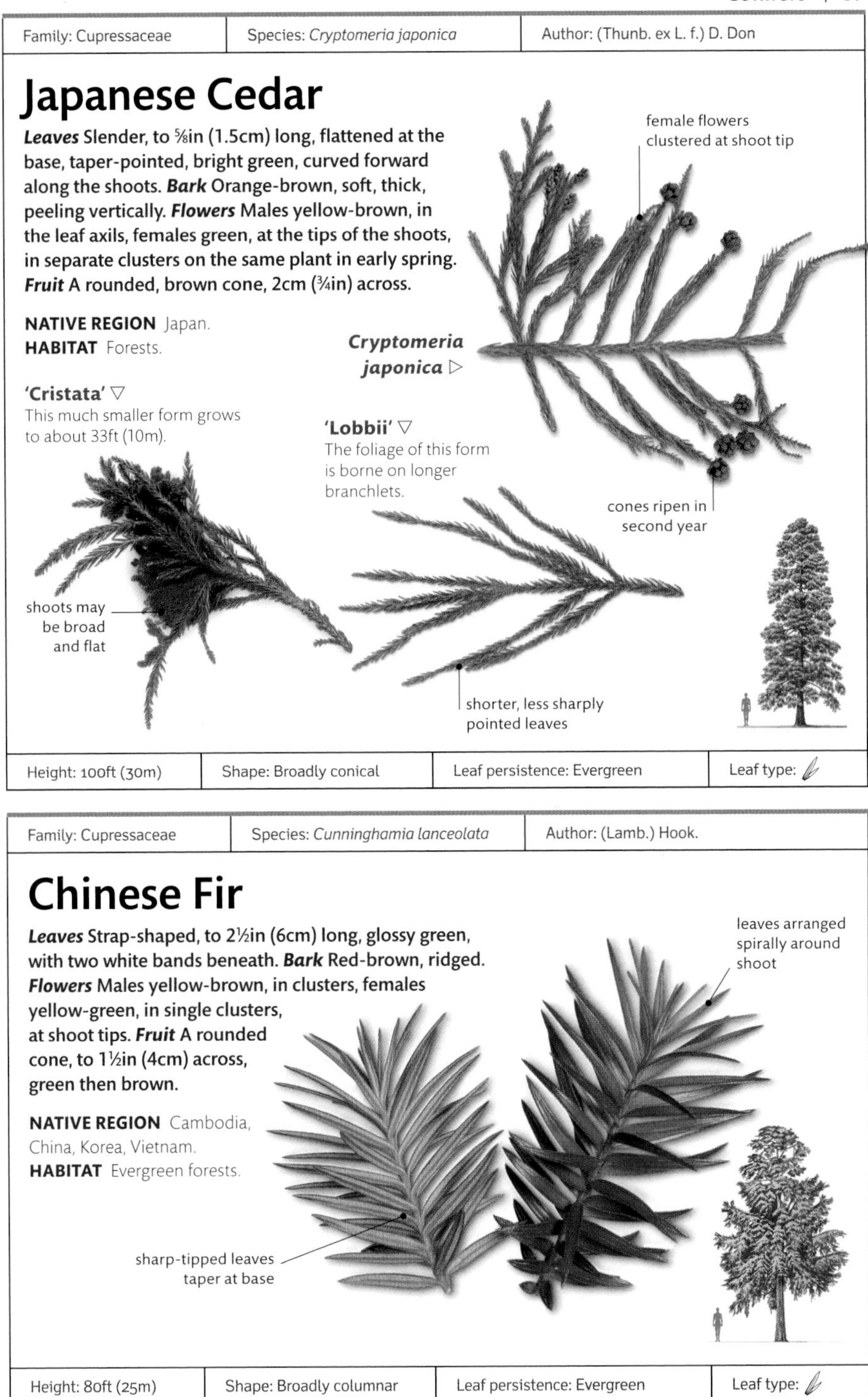

Height: 100ft (30m)	Shape: Broadly conical	Leaf persistence: Evergreen	Leaf type:

Family: Cupressaceae	Species: *Cunninghamia lanceolata*	Author: (Lamb.) Hook.

Chinese Fir

Leaves **Strap-shaped, to 2½in (6cm) long, glossy green, with two white bands beneath.** ***Bark*** **Red-brown, ridged.** ***Flowers*** **Males yellow-brown, in clusters, females yellow-green, in single clusters, at shoot tips.** ***Fruit*** **A rounded cone, to 1½in (4cm) across, green then brown.**

NATIVE REGION Cambodia, China, Korea, Vietnam.
HABITAT Evergreen forests.

Height: 80ft (25m)	Shape: Broadly columnar	Leaf persistence: Evergreen	Leaf type:

Family: Cupressaceae	Species: *Cupressus cashmeriana*	Author: Royle ex Carrière

Kashmir Cypress

Leaves **Scalelike and very small, but with free, spreading tips making the foliage rough to the touch, borne in glaucous, drooping, flattened sprays.** ***Bark*** **Red-brown, peeling in vertical strips.** ***Flowers*** **Males and females both inconspicuous, in separate clusters on the same plant in early to midwinter.** ***Fruit*** **A rounded cone, ½in (1.2cm) across, blue-green becoming greenish yellow ripening to brown, the scales each with a hooked point.**

NATIVE REGION Bhutan, N.E. India.
HABITAT Evergreen mountain forests.
REMARK A particularly elegant tree, of small to medium height. The habit becomes more spreading as it ages.

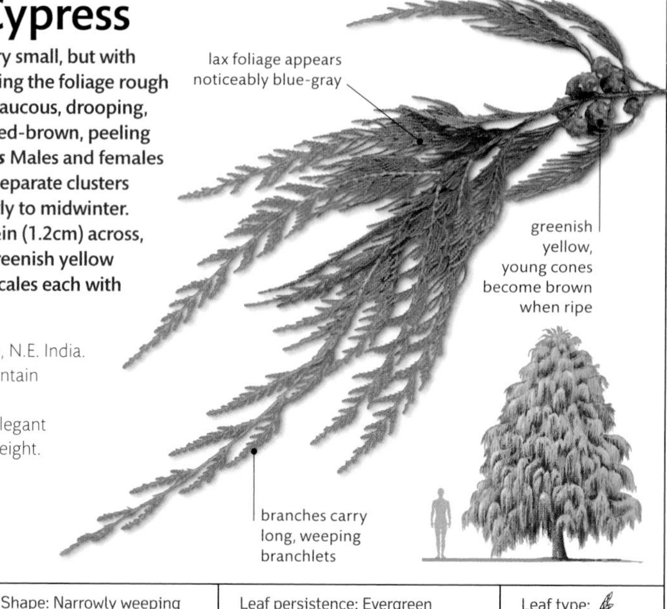

Height: 65ft (20m)	Shape: Narrowly weeping	Leaf persistence: Evergreen	Leaf type:

Family: Cupressaceae	Species: *Cupressus glabra*	Author: Sudw.

Smooth Arizona Cypress

Leaves **Scalelike and very small, with a pointed tip, blue-gray, with a minute fleck of white resin in the center on the underside, closely pressed to the stem, borne in irregular, aromatic sprays on reddish shoots.** ***Bark*** **Red-brown and red-purple, flaking in round patches.** ***Flowers*** **Males yellow and conspicuous, females green, in small clusters at the tips of the shoots, on the same plant in mid- to late winter.** ***Fruit*** **A rounded, gray-brown cone, to 1in (2.5cm) across, persisting on the branches for several years.**

NATIVE REGION US: Arizona.
HABITAT Rocky mountain slopes.
REMARK This species is commonly cultivated, and is usually found in the form 'Pyramidalis,' with silvery blue foliage and a dense habit. It is often found under the name of the similar, but much rarer, species *Cupressus arizonica*.

Height: 65ft (20m)	Shape: Narrowly conical	Leaf persistence: Evergreen	Leaf type: 

Family: Cupressaceae	Species: *Cupressus lusitanica*	Author: Mill.

Cedar of Goa

Leaves **Scalelike and very small, with free, pointed tips, gray-green, borne in irregular, slightly aromatic sprays.** ***Bark*** **Brown, peeling in vertical, fibrous strips.** ***Flowers*** **Males yellow-brown, females glaucous, in small clusters at the tips of the shoots in early spring.** ***Fruit*** **A rounded cone, ⅝in (1.5cm) across, glaucous-blue becoming glossy brown, each scale with a pointed projection, ripe in two years.**

NATIVE REGION C. America, Mexico.
HABITAT Mountains.
REMARK Also known as Mexican cypress. It was once thought to be native to Portugal.

△ ***Cupressus lusitanica***

◁ **'Glauca Pendula'**
Weeping shoots, bearing blue-gray foliage, distinguish this form of the species.

Height: 100ft (30m)	Shape: Narrowly conical	Leaf persistence: Evergreen	Leaf type:

Family: Cupressaceae	Species: *Cupressus macrocarpa*	Author: Hartw.

Monterey Cypress

Leaves **Scalelike and very small, with pointed tips, closely pressed to the shoot, borne in irregular, aromatic sprays.** ***Bark*** **Red-brown, with shallow ridges.** ***Flowers*** **Males yellow, females green, in small clusters at the tips of the shoots in spring to early summer.** ***Fruit*** **A rounded cone, to 1½in (4cm) across, each scale with a short, blunt projection.**

NATIVE REGION US: California.
HABITAT Evergreen forests near the coast.
REMARK A rare tree, found around Monterey. The shape becomes spreading with age.

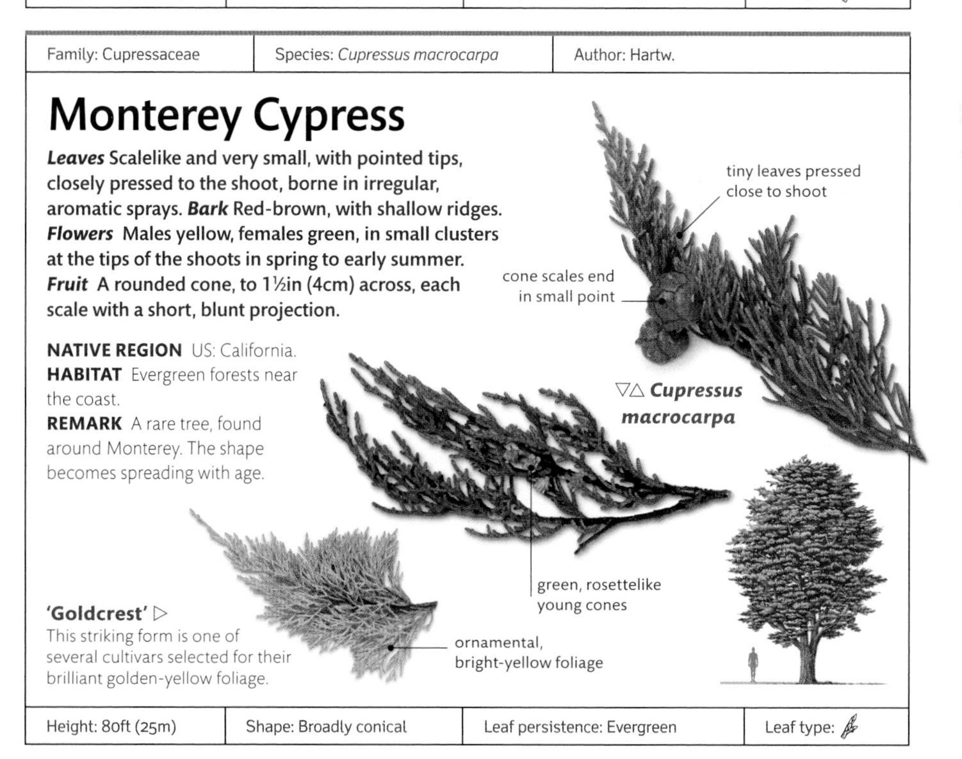

▽△ ***Cupressus macrocarpa***

'Goldcrest' ▷
This striking form is one of several cultivars selected for their brilliant golden-yellow foliage.

Height: 80ft (25m)	Shape: Broadly conical	Leaf persistence: Evergreen	Leaf type:

Family: Cupressaceae	Species: *Cupressus sempervirens*	Author: L.

Italian Cypress

Leaves **Scalelike and very small, with blunt tips, very dark green, with no white marks beneath, only slightly aromatic or with no scent, borne in irregular sprays, closely pressed to the shoots.** ***Bark*** **Gray-brown, with shallow, spiral ridges.** ***Flowers*** **Males yellow-brown, females green, in small clusters at the tips of the shoots in spring.** ***Fruit*** **An egg-shaped to rounded cone, to 1½in (4cm) long, green ripening to brown, the scales overlapping, each scale with a small projection.**

NATIVE REGION S.W. Asia, E. Mediterranean.
HABITAT Rocky places in mountains.
REMARK The narrow form known as 'Stricta' is so commonly planted in the Mediterranean that it forms a characteristic feature of the landscape.

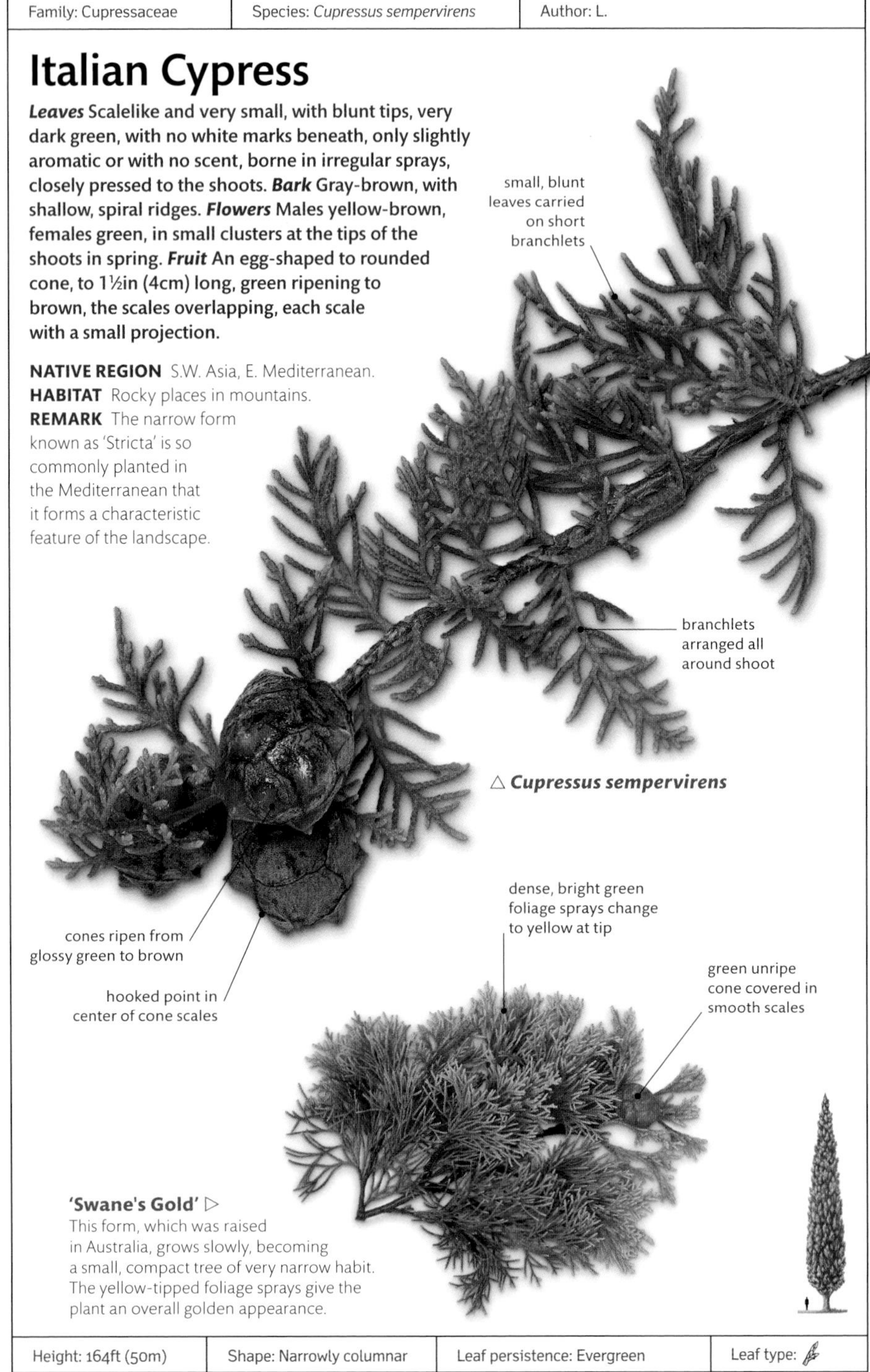

△ ***Cupressus sempervirens***

'Swane's Gold' ▷
This form, which was raised in Australia, grows slowly, becoming a small, compact tree of very narrow habit. The yellow-tipped foliage sprays give the plant an overall golden appearance.

Height: 164ft (50m)	Shape: Narrowly columnar	Leaf persistence: Evergreen	Leaf type:

Family: Cupressaceae	Species: x *Cuprocyparis leylandii*	Author: (A.B. Jacks. & Dallim.) Farjon

Leyland Cypress

Leaves Scalelike and very small, with pointed tips, dark green above, paler beneath, arranged at various angles to the shoot, borne in flattened sprays; leaves at side of and above shoot similar in size. ***Bark*** Red-brown, with shallow ridges. ***Flowers*** Males yellow, females green, in small clusters at the tips of the shoots in early spring. ***Fruit*** A rounded cone, to ¾in (2cm) across, blue-green ripening to glossy brown.

NATIVE REGION Of garden origin.
REMARK A hybrid between Nootka cypress (*Xanthocyparis nootkatensis*, see p.54) and Monterey cypress (*Cupressus macrocarpa*, see p.41). 'Haggerston Gray,' which has dull green foliage, is the form most commonly grown.

△ **'Haggerston Gray'**

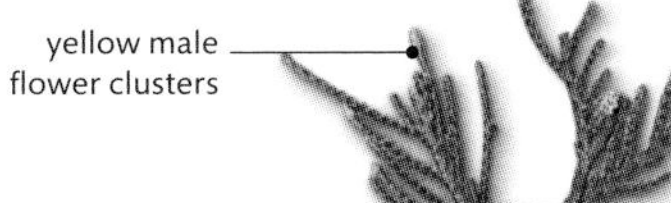

△ **'Castlewellan'**
Young specimens of this form exhibit bright yellow foliage. On older, mature plants, the color deepens to reddish bronze-yellow.

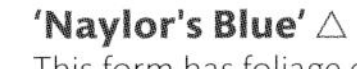

'Naylor's Blue' △
This form has foliage colored blue-gray to grayish green. It grows to a very narrowly columnar tree.

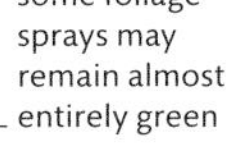

'Silver Dust' ▷
This form originated in the United States, at the U.S. National Arboretum, Washington, D.C.

Height: 100ft (30m)	Shape: Narrowly columnar	Leaf persistence: Evergreen	Leaf type:

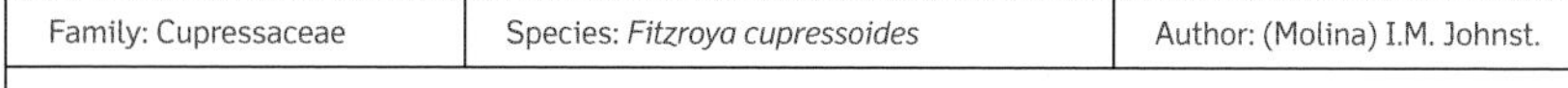

Family: Cupressaceae	Species: *Fitzroya cupressoides*	Author: (Molina) I.M. Johnst.

Patagonian Cypress

Leaves **Oblong and thick, to ⅛in (3mm) long, bluntly pointed, in whorls of three, dark green, with two white bands on each side, on slender, pendulous shoots.** ***Bark*** **Red-brown, peeling in long, vertical strips.** ***Flowers*** **Males yellow, females yellow-green, borne in small clusters at the tips of the shoots in spring.** ***Fruit*** **A rounded, brown cone, 5/16in (8mm) across.**

NATIVE REGION Argentina, Chile.
HABITAT Mountains.
REMARK Also known as alerce. Scientifically named after Captain Fitzroy, in whose ship, The Beagle, Charles Darwin voyaged to South America.

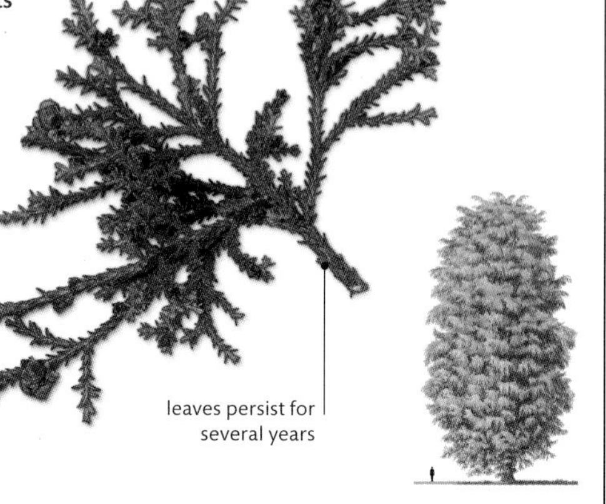

Height: 164ft (50m)	Shape: Broadly columnar	Leaf persistence: Evergreen	Leaf type:

Family: Cupressaceae	Species: *Glyptostrobus pensilis*	Author: (D. Don) K. Koch

Chinese Swamp Cypress

Leaves **Linear, scalelike, small, to ⅝in (1.5cm) long, blue-green, spreading either side of deciduous side shoots, arranged spirally on persistent shoots, turning red in late autumn when they fall.** ***Bark*** **Gray-brown, with shallow fissures.** ***Flowers*** **Males and females inconspicuous.** ***Fruit*** **A rounded to egg-shaped, rough, green cone, 1in (2.5cm) long.**

NATIVE REGION S. China, Laos, Vietnam.
HABITAT Swamps and riverbanks.
REMARK This species is now seen only rarely in the wild.

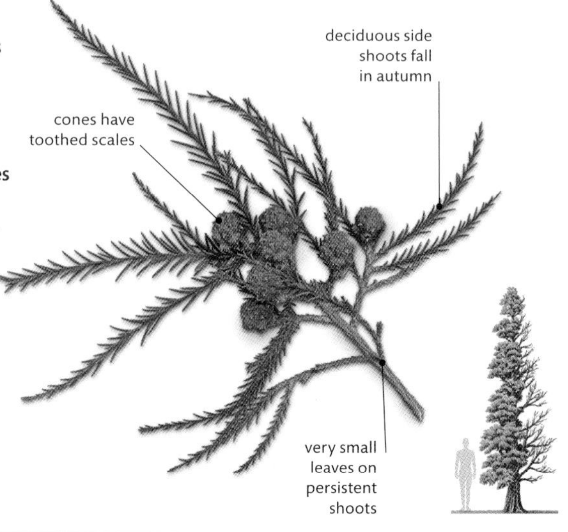

Height: 33ft (10m)	Shape: Narrowly conical	Leaf persistence: Deciduous	Leaf type: 

Family: Cupressaceae	Species: *Juniperus chinensis*	Author: L.

Chinese Juniper

Leaves **Adults scalelike and very small, with blunt tips, in irregular, aromatic sprays, closely pressed to the shoot; juveniles needlelike, to 5/16in (8mm) long, sharp-pointed, opposite or in whorls of three, green, with two glaucous bands on the upper surface, at the base of the shoots.** ***Bark*** **Red-brown, peeling in vertical strips.** ***Flowers*** **Males yellow, females small and purple-green, in small clusters at the tips of the shoots, on separate plants in spring.** ***Fruit*** **A berrylike, glaucous cone, to 5/16in (8mm) long.**

sharp-pointed juvenile leaves

△▽ ***Juniperus chinensis***

adult foliage has scalelike leaves

NATIVE REGION China, Japan.
HABITAT Hills and mountains.
REMARK Although both adult and juvenile foliage are usually present on individual plants, some trees may have either one type or the other. The species can be shrubby. It has many cultivated forms.

'Aurea' ▷
This form, known as Young's golden juniper, has golden-yellow foliage.

Height: 80ft (25m)	Shape: Narrowly conical	Leaf persistence: Evergreen	Leaf type:

Family: Cupressaceae	Species: *Juniperus communis*	Author: L.

Common Juniper

Leaves **Needlelike and slender, to ½in (1.2cm) long, in whorls of three, sharp-pointed, glossy green, with a broad white band on the upper surface.** ***Bark*** **Red-brown, peeling in thin, vertical strips.** ***Flowers*** **Males yellow, females small and green, in small clusters in the leaf axils, on separate plants in spring.** ***Fruit*** **A berrylike cone, ¼in (6mm) long, green becoming glaucous-bloomed ripening to glossy black.**

NATIVE REGION Temperate zones of the northern hemisphere.
HABITAT Open places, from coastal rocks to high mountains.
REMARK The species is variable: it can be a prostrate and creeping plant, a bushy shrub, or sometimes a tree. The berries give gin its characteristic taste. They are also used as a culinary flavoring.

Height: 20ft (6m)	Shape: Narrowly conical	Leaf persistence: Evergreen	Leaf type: 

Family: Cupressaceae	Species: *Juniperus coxii*	Author: A.B. Jacks.

Drooping Juniper

Leaves **Needlelike and slender, to ¼in (6mm) long, in whorls of three, sharp-pointed, matte gray-green above, with two white bands beneath, dry and papery to the touch, pointing forward along drooping shoots.** ***Bark*** **Red-brown, peeling in vertical strips.** ***Flowers*** **Males yellow, females green, borne in small clusters at the tips of the shoots, on the same plant in spring.** ***Fruit*** **A berrylike, glossy, blue-black cone, to 5⁄16in (8mm) long.**

NATIVE REGION S.W. China, Himalayas.
HABITAT High mountains.
REMARK Previously known as *Juniperus recurva* var. *coxii.*

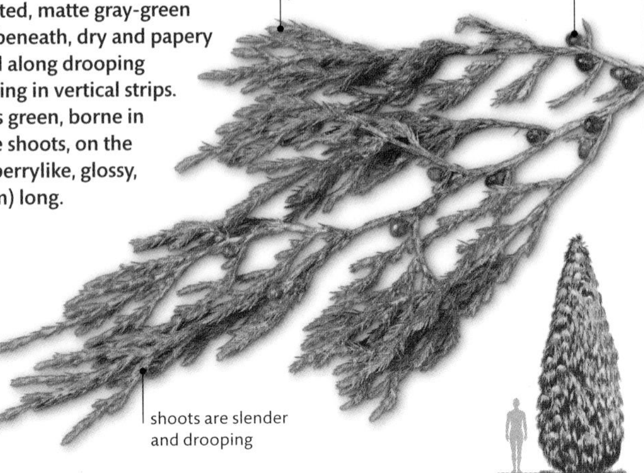

Height: 50ft (15m)	Shape: Narrowly conical	Leaf persistence: Evergreen	Leaf type:

Family: Cupressaceae	Species: *Juniperus deppeana*	Author: Steud.

Alligator Juniper

Leaves **Scalelike and small, to ⅛in (3mm) long, bright green to blue-gray, with a conspicuous speck of white resin on the back and two white bands toward the base, pressed to the shoot at the base, free at the tip and ending in a sharp point, making the foliage rough to the touch, aromatic when crushed.** ***Bark*** **Dark gray, deeply cut into small, oblong plates.** ***Flowers*** **Inconspicuous.** ***Fruit*** **A berrylike, rounded, red-brown, bloomy cone, to ⅝in (1.5cm) across.**

NATIVE REGION Mexico, S.W. US.
HABITAT Rocky slopes in high mountains.
REMARK Also known as *Juniperus deppeana* var. *pachyphlaea.* It is easily distinguished by its characteristically checkered bark.

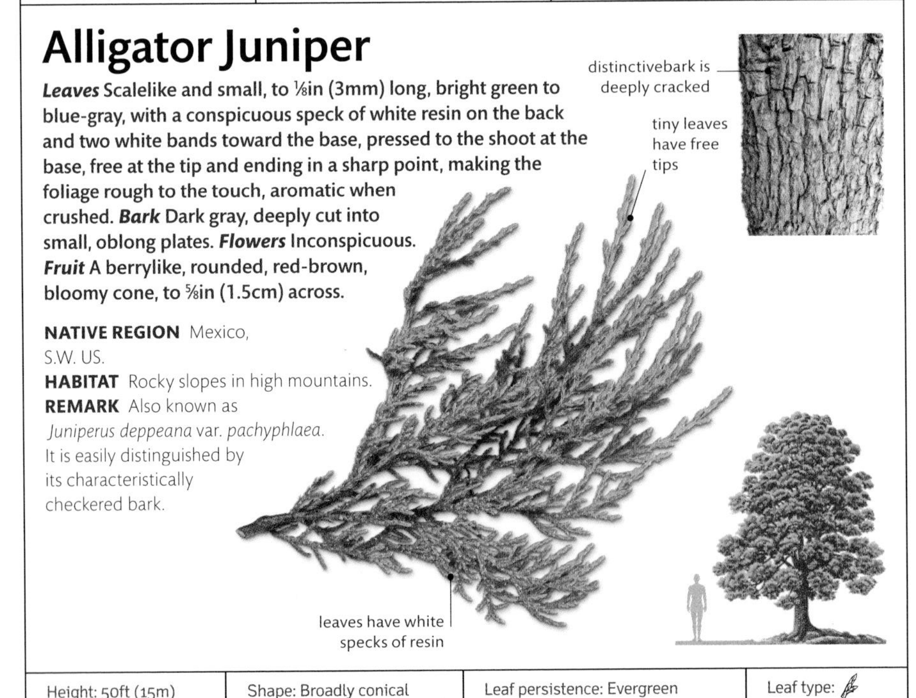

Height: 50ft (15m)	Shape: Broadly conical	Leaf persistence: Evergreen	Leaf type:

Family: Cupressaceae	Species: *Juniperus drupacea*	Author: Labill.

Syrian Juniper

Leaves Needlelike, rigid, and slender, to 1in (1in) long, in whorls of three, sharp-pointed, marked with two broad, whitish bands above with a green midrib and margin, glossy green and ridged beneath, spreading from three-angled shoots. ***Bark*** Orange-brown, peeling in thin, vertical strips. ***Flowers*** Males yellow, females very small and green, borne in small clusters at the tips of short, leafy shoots, on separate plants in spring. ***Fruit*** A rather large, berrylike, bloomy cone, 1in (2.5cm) long, blue-green at first becoming brown ripening to blackish purple, the triangular scales ending in a pointed tip.

NATIVE REGION S.W. Asia, Greece.
HABITAT Mountain forests.
REMARK The species is easily distinguished by its leaves, which are broader than those of any other juniper. The large cones are seen only rarely in cultivated plants.

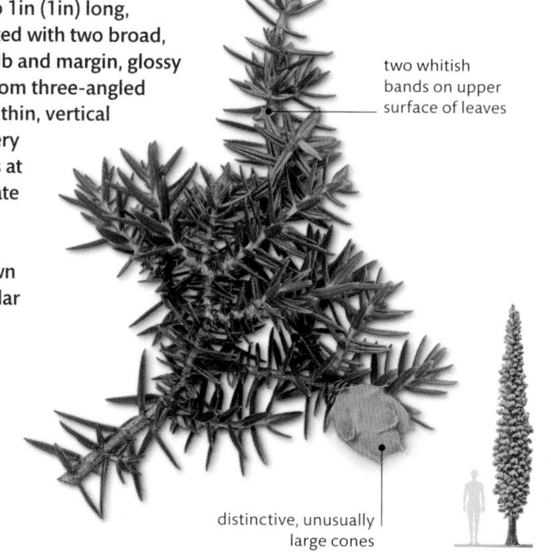

Height: 33ft (10m)	Shape: Narrowly columnar	Leaf persistence: Evergreen	Leaf type:

Family: Cupressaceae	Species: *Juniperus occidentalis*	Author: Hook.

Western Juniper

Leaves Scalelike and small, in threes, minutely toothed, gray-green, with a small gland beneath, closely pressed to stout shoots; on vigorous shoots sharp-pointed and free. ***Bark*** Red-brown, furrowed, and flaking. ***Flowers*** Males yellow, females green, in small clusters at the tips of the shoots, usually on separate plants in spring. ***Fruit*** A rounded to egg-shaped, berrylike, bloomy, blue-black cone, to ⅜in (1cm) long, ripe in two years.

NATIVE REGION W. US.
HABITAT Rocky slopes and dry soil in mountains.
REMARK The toothed leaf margin can be seen only under magnification. In the Sierra Nevada mountain range in California, specimens of the species more than 2,000 years old can be found growing out of solid rock.

Height: 65ft (20m)	Shape: Broadly conical	Leaf persistence: Evergreen	Leaf type: 

Family: Cupressaceae	Species: *Juniperus oxycedrus*	Author: L.

Prickly Juniper

Leaves **Needlelike and slender, to 1in (2.5cm) long, spreading in whorls of three, sharp-pointed, green above, with two glaucous bands beneath.** ***Bark*** **Purple-brown, flaking in vertical strips.** ***Flowers*** **Males yellow, females green, borne in small clusters in the leaf axils, on separate plants in spring.** ***Fruit*** **A berrylike cone, ½in (1.2cm) across, bloomy at first ripening red to purple.**

NATIVE REGION S.W. Asia, S. Europe.
HABITAT Dry hills and woods.
REMARK Also known as cade. Oil of cade, traditionally used to treat skin ailments, is obtained from the wood. In the Balearic Islands, where the common juniper (*Juniperus communis*, see p.45) does not grow, prickly juniper berries are used instead as a substitute for flavoring gin.

Height: 33ft (10m)	Shape: Broadly conical	Leaf persistence: Evergreen	Leaf type:

Family: Cupressaceae	Species: *Juniperus scopulorum*	Author: Sarg.

Rocky Mountain Juniper

Leaves **Scalelike, very small, green to gray-blue, closely pressed to the shoot.** ***Bark*** **Red-brown, peeling in thin strips.** ***Flowers*** **Males yellow, females green, in small clusters at the tips of the shoots, usually on the same plant in spring.** ***Fruit*** **A berrylike cone, ¼in (6mm) across, blue-black with a glaucous bloom, ripe in two years.**

NATIVE REGION W. North America.
HABITAT Woods and rocky soil in mountains.
REMARK Also known as Colorado red cedar, river juniper, Rocky Mountain red cedar. 'Skyrocket,' shown here, is the best-known cultivated garden form. This species, which resembles a cypress, gives its name to Cypress Island, in Washington State, where it grows abundantly.

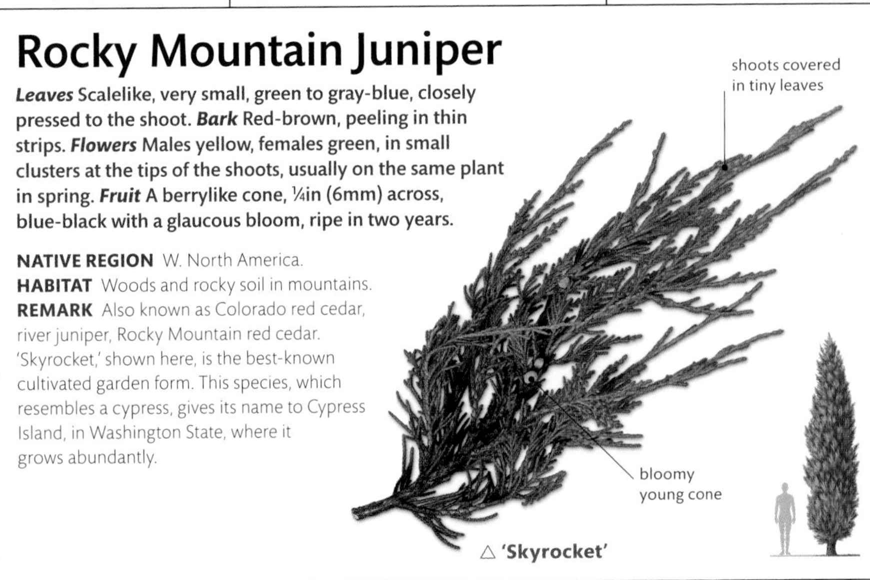

△ **'Skyrocket'**

Height: 40ft (12m)	Shape: Narrowly conical	Leaf persistence: Evergreen	Leaf type:

Family: Cupressaceae	Species: *Juniperus virginiana*	Author: L.

Pencil Cedar

Leaves Both juvenile and adult foliage usually present; adult leaves scalelike and very small, pointed, usually green to blue-green, closely pressed to the shoot; juvenile leaves needlelike, to ¼in (6mm) long, usually in pairs, sharp-pointed, gray-green above, glaucous beneath, at the tips of the shoots. ***Bark*** Red-brown, peeling in vertical strips. ***Flowers*** Males yellow, females green, in small clusters at the tips of the shoots, usually on separate plants in spring. ***Fruit*** A berrylike, glaucous, bloomy cone, ¼in (6mm) long, ripe in one year.

NATIVE REGION E. North America.
HABITAT Woods and rocky slopes.
REMARK Also known as eastern red cedar and red cedar. Widely distributed and planted. Its wood is used to make pencils.

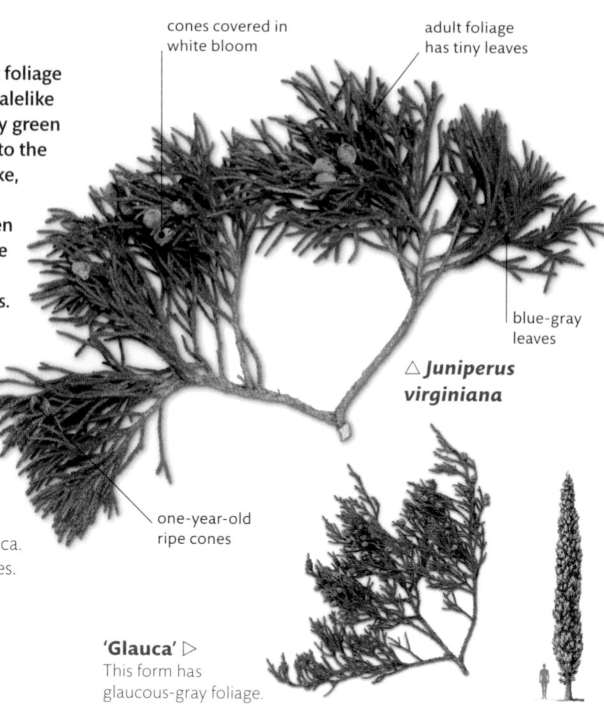

△ ***Juniperus virginiana***

'Glauca' ▷
This form has glaucous-gray foliage.

Height: 100ft (30m)	Shape: Narrowly columnar	Leaf persistence: Evergreen	Leaf type:

Family: Cupressaceae	Species: *Metasequoia glyptostroboides*	Author: Hu & W.C. Cheng

Dawn Redwood

Leaves Linear, to 1in (2.5cm) long, soft, flattened, emerging early and pale green becoming dark green, arranged opposite on short, deciduous side shoots, spirally on persistent shoots, turning yellow, pink, or red in fall. ***Bark*** Orange-brown to red-brown, peeling vertically in stringy flakes. ***Flowers*** Males yellow, females greenish, in separate clusters on young shoots, on the same plant in spring. ***Fruit*** A rounded cone, 1in (2.5cm) across, green ripening to brown.

NATIVE REGION S.W. China.
HABITAT Moist ground and riverbanks.
REMARK This species is rare in the wild but is commonly grown in yards. It can be confused with swamp cypress (*Taxodium distichum*, see p.51) but the opposite shoots easily distinguish it.

Height: 130ft (40m)	Shape: Narrowly conical	Leaf persistence: Deciduous	Leaf type:

Family: Cupressaceae	Species: *Sequoia sempervirens*	Author: (D. Don) Endl.

California Redwood

Leaves Linear, to ¾in (2cm) long, pointed at the tip, dark green above, with two white bands beneath, spreading either side of the shoot. ***Bark*** Red-brown, soft and fibrous, very thick, with broad ridges. ***Flowers*** Males yellow-brown, females green, in separate clusters on the same plant in late winter to early spring. ***Fruit*** A barrel-shaped to rounded, red-brown cone, to 1¼in (3cm) long, ripe in one year.

NATIVE REGION US: S. Oregon, California.
HABITAT Low slopes in coastal regions.
REMARKS A California Redwood holds the record of being the tallest tree in the world. They can live for up to 2,000 years or more.

Height: 330ft (100m)	Shape: Narrowly conical	Leaf persistence: Evergreen	Leaf type:

Family: Cupressaceae	Species: *Sequoiadendron giganteum*	Author: (Lindl.) J. Buchholz

Wellingtonia

Leaves To 5/16in (8mm) long, sharp-pointed, with spreading tips, deep blue-green, all around the shoot. ***Bark*** Red-brown, soft, fibrous, very thick. ***Flowers*** Males yellow, at the ends of the shoots, females green, in separate clusters in early spring. ***Fruit*** A barrel-shaped cone, to 3in (7.5cm) long, green ripening to brown in two years, often persisting for years.

NATIVE REGION US: California.
HABITAT West-facing mountain slopes.
REMARKS This tree is also known as giant redwood. The thick bark protects trees of this species from all but the most severe fires.

tiny, pointed leaves make foliage rough to the touch

one-year-old cone still green

male flower buds open in early spring

Height: 295ft (90m)	Shape: Narrowly conical	Leaf persistence: Evergreen	Leaf type:

Family: Cupressaceae	Species: *Taiwania cryptomerioides*	Author: Hayata

Coffin Tree

Leaves **Slender, to ¾in (2cm) long, broad and flattened at the base, with a sharp, spiny point at the tip, blue-green, curved forward along the shoots; on coning shoots much smaller.** ***Bark*** **Red-brown, peeling in vertical strips.** ***Flowers*** **Males in several clusters together, females in single clusters, borne separately at the ends of the shoots, on the same plant in spring.** ***Fruit*** **A rounded cone, to ½in (1.2cm) across, green ripening to brown.**

NATIVE REGION East Asia.
HABITAT Mountain forests.

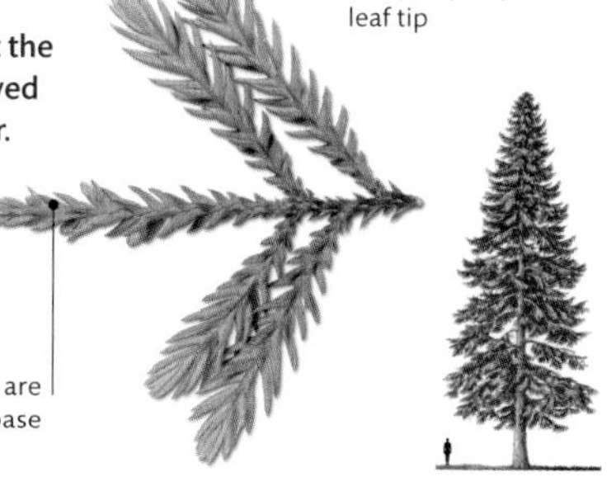

Height: 200ft (60m)	Shape: Broadly conical	Leaf persistence: Evergreen	Leaf type:

Family: Cupressaceae	Species: *Taxodium distichum*	Author: (L.) Rich.

Swamp Cypress

Leaves **Linear, to ¾in (2cm) long, mid- to yellowish green, soft and flattened, arranged spreading or spirally, emerging late.** ***Bark*** **Gray-brown, thin, rough, often fluted and buttressed at the base.** ***Flowers*** **Males yellow-green, in hanging catkins to 8in (20cm) long, females green, in small clusters at the base of the male catkins, on the same plant, forming in fall but opening in spring.** ***Fruit*** **A rounded cone, to 1¼in (3cm) across, green ripening to brown.**

NATIVE REGION S.E. US.
HABITAT Swamps, stream banks.
REMARKS Also known as bald cypress. Var. *imbricarium* (pond cypress, also known as *Taxodium ascendens*) is a narrower tree with the leaves closely pressed against upright shoots.

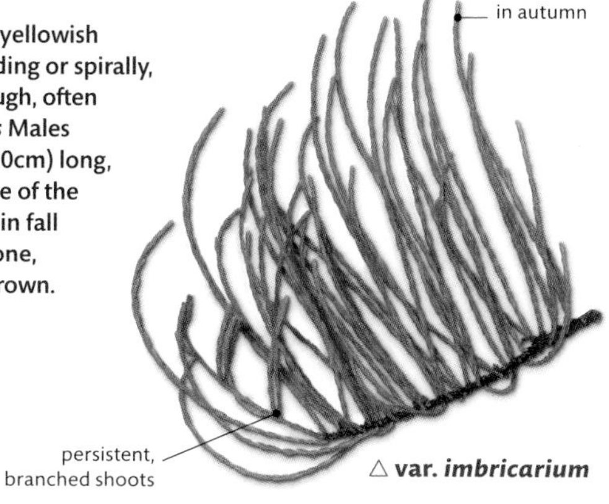

△ **var. *imbricarium***

◁△ ***Taxodium distichum***

Height: 130ft (40m)	Shape: Broadly conical	Leaf persistence: Deciduous	Leaf type:

Family: Cupressaceae	Species: *Thuja koraiensis*	Author: Nakai

Korean Arbor-vitae

Leaves **Scalelike and small, bright green above, with bright silvery marks beneath, in flattened sprays, aromatic when crushed.** ***Bark*** **Red-brown, peeling in thin scales.** ***Flowers*** **Males green, with black tips, females green, in separate clusters at the ends of the shoots, on the same plant in spring.** ***Fruit*** **An oblong, upright cone, ⅜in (1cm) long, yellow-green ripening to brown, with eight scales.**

NATIVE REGION
N.E. China, Korea.
HABITAT Mountain woods.
REMARK This species can be either a small tree or a dense shrub.

bright green leaf upperside

bright white markings on leaf underside

small gland on leaf surface contains aromatic oil

Height: 33ft (10m)	Shape: Narrowly conical	Leaf persistence: Evergreen	Leaf type:

Family: Cupressaceae	Species: *Thuja occidentalis*	Author: L.

American Arbor-vitae

Leaves **Scalelike and very small, glossy yellowish green above, paler with no white marks beneath, borne in flattened, aromatic sprays, on flat shoots.** ***Bark*** **Orange-brown, peeling in vertical strips.** ***Flowers*** **Males red, females yellow-brown, in separate clusters at the ends of the shoots, on the same plant in spring.** ***Fruit*** **An oblong, upright cone, ⅜in (1cm) long, yellow-green ripening to brown, with 8 to 10 scales.**

NATIVE REGION E. North America.
HABITAT Rocky mountain slopes, often on limestone, and swamps.
REMARK Also known as white cedar. The species was one of the first North American trees to be grown in Europe. In cultivation, it has given rise to innumerable selections, including ornamental forms with colored foliage, and many of dwarf habit.

Height: 65ft (20m)	Shape: Narrowly conical	Leaf persistence: Evergreen	Leaf type:

Family: Cupressaceae	Species: *Thuja plicata*	Author: Donn ex D. Don

Western Red Cedar

Leaves Scalelike, very small, glossy green above, with white marks beneath, in flattened, aromatic sprays. ***Bark*** Purplish brown, peeling vertically. ***Flowers*** Males red-black opening yellow, females yellow-green, in separate clusters at the ends of the shoots, on the same plant in spring. ***Fruit*** An ovoid, upright cone, ½in (1.2cm) long, yellow-green ripening to brown.

NATIVE REGION N.W. North America.
HABITAT Mountains.

white, X-shaped marks on underside of leaves

larger branchlets have slightly longer leaves

each tiny cone has about 10 scales

△ ***Thuja plicata***

stripy yellow and green foliage

◁ **'Zebrina'**
Alternate bands of green and yellow foliage give this form a variegated appearance.

Height: 164ft (50m)	Shape: Narrowly conical	Leaf persistence: Evergreen	Leaf type:

Family: Cupressaceae	Species: *Thuja standishii*	Author: (Gordon) Carrière

Japanese Arbor-vitae

Leaves Scalelike and very small, bluntly pointed at the tip, yellow-green above, paler with small, whitish marks beneath, in flattened, drooping, aromatic sprays, on flat shoots. ***Bark*** Red-brown, peeling in strips and plates. ***Flowers*** Males blackish red opening yellow, females greenish, in separate clusters at the tips of the shoots, on the same plant in spring. ***Fruit*** An oblong, upright cone, ⅜in (1cm) long, green ripening to red-brown, with about 10 scales.

NATIVE REGION Japan.
HABITAT Rocky mountain ridges and moors.
REMARK When crushed, the foliage has a particularly sweet scent.

bright yellowish green upperside of leaves

very small brown cones at tip of shoots

paler green, whitish underside of leaves

Height: 65ft (20m)	Shape: Broadly conical	Leaf persistence: Evergreen	Leaf type: 

Family: Cupressaceae	Species: *Thujopsis dolabrata*	Author: (L. f.) Siebold & Zucc.

Hiba

Leaves Scalelike, to ¼in (6mm) long, glossy dark green to yellow-green above, in flattened sprays, on broad, flat shoots. ***Bark*** Purple-brown, flaking in thin, vertical strips. ***Flowers*** Males blackish green, females blue-gray, borne in separate clusters at the ends of the shoots, on the same plant in spring. ***Fruit*** A brown, bloomy cone, ½in (1.2cm) long.

NATIVE REGION Japan.
HABITAT Moist mountain forests.

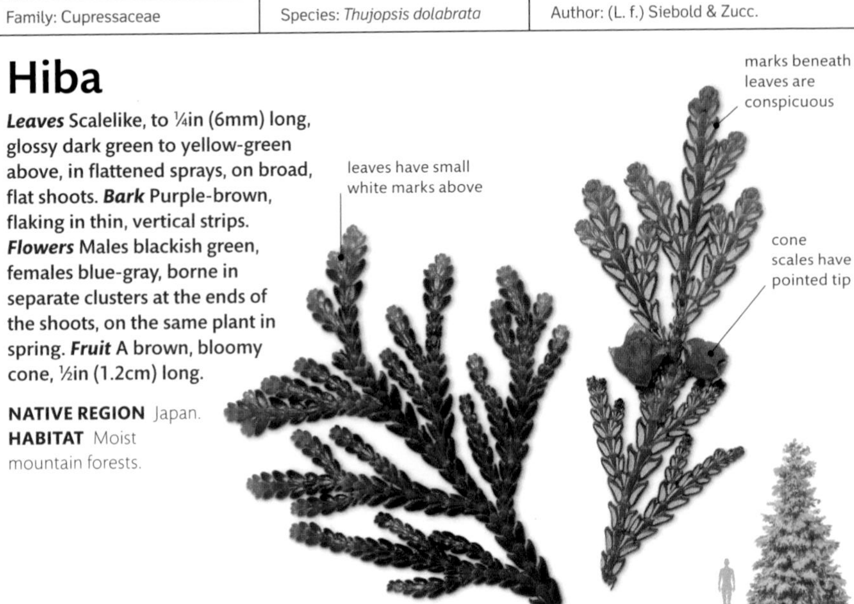

Height: 65ft (20m)	Shape: Broadly conical	Leaf persistence: Evergreen	Leaf type:

Family: Cupressaceae	Species: *Xanthocyparis nootkatensis*	Author: (D. Don) Farjon & D.K. Harder

Nootka Cypress

Leaves Scalelike, very small, with free, pointed tips, keeled, dark green above, paler beneath, in flattened, aromatic sprays. ***Bark*** Gray-brown to orange-brown, stringy. ***Flowers*** Males yellow, females blue, in clusters at the tips of the shoots in early spring. ***Fruit*** A rounded cone, ⅜in (1cm) across, ripe in two years.

NATIVE REGION N.W. North America.
HABITAT Coastal mountains.

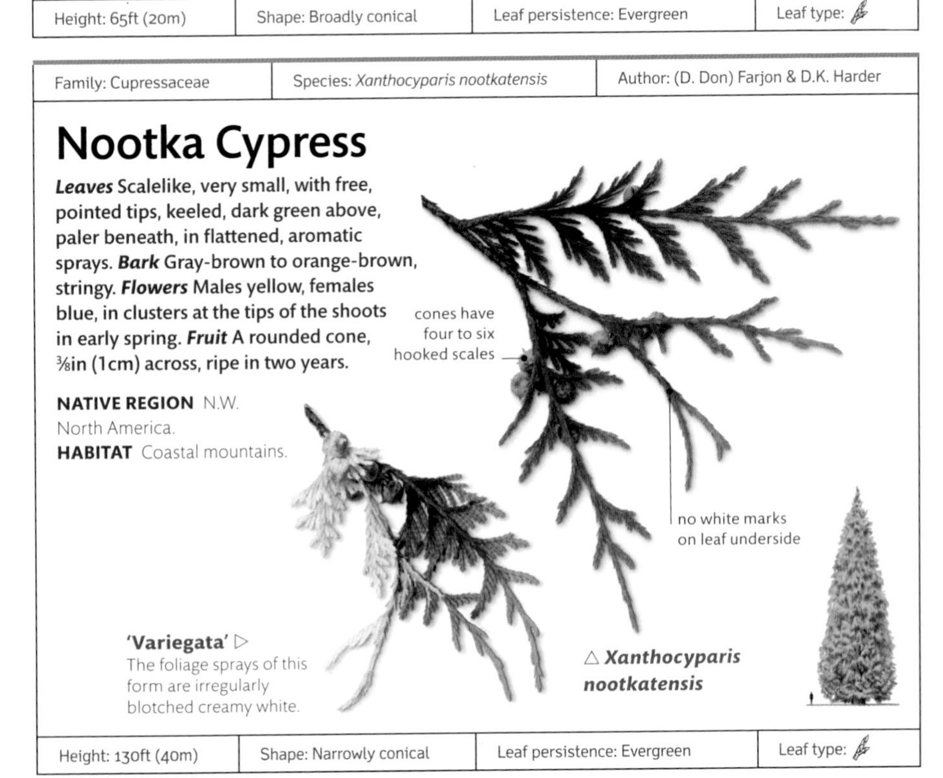

'Variegata' ▷ The foliage sprays of this form are irregularly blotched creamy white.

△ ***Xanthocyparis nootkatensis***

Height: 130ft (40m)	Shape: Narrowly conical	Leaf persistence: Evergreen	Leaf type:

GINKGOACEAE

ALTHOUGH THIS FAMILY HAS only a single member, with no closely related species, fossil records show that similar plants were at one time—between approximately 150 and 200 million years ago—widely distributed in all parts of the world. The species, usually classed as a conifer, is in fact the sole survivor of a group of plants more primitive than the true conifers and was once thought to be extinct in the wild.

Family: Ginkgoaceae	Species: *Ginkgo biloba*	Author: L.

Maidenhair Tree

Leaves Fan-shaped, about 3in (7.5cm) long, often variously notched and with numerous veins diverging from the base, matte green, turning bright yellow in fall, carried singly on long shoots, clustered on short side shoots. ***Bark*** Gray-brown, ridged and fissured. ***Flowers*** Males and females both small and yellow-green, males in catkinlike clusters, females singly or in pairs on a short stalk, on separate plants in spring. ***Fruit*** A fleshy, plumlike seed, yellow-green ripening to orange-brown, the kernel edible.

NATIVE REGION China.
HABITAT Cliffs, rocky slopes.
REMARK The rotting fruit has a particularly unpleasant smell.

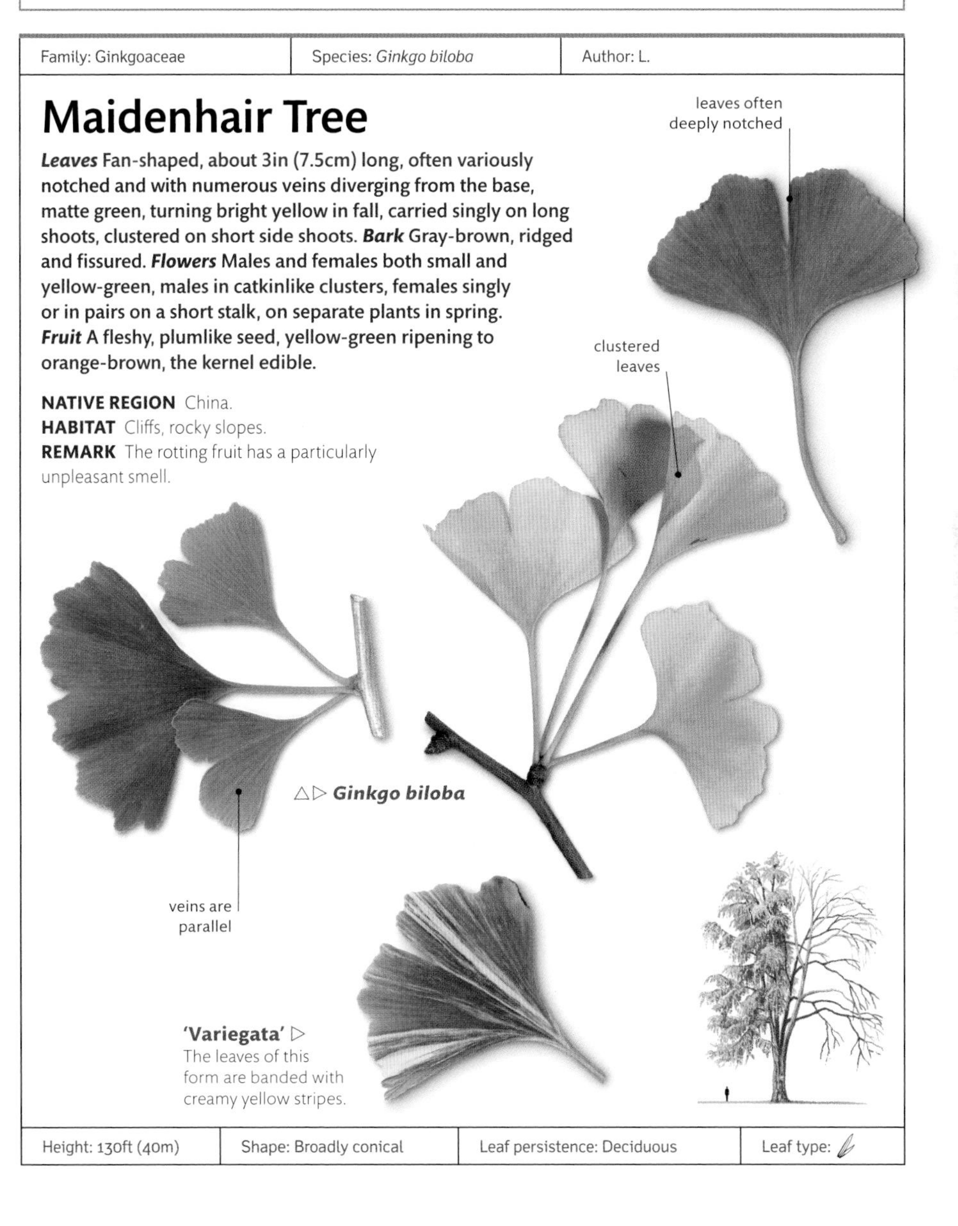

△▷ ***Ginkgo biloba***

'Variegata' ▷
The leaves of this form are banded with creamy yellow stripes.

Height: 130ft (40m)	Shape: Broadly conical	Leaf persistence: Deciduous	Leaf type:

PINACEAE

THIS FAMILY INCLUDES THE silver firs (*Abies*, see pp.56–61), larches (*Larix*, see pp.64–65), and pines (*Pinus*, see pp.70–78). About 225 species of trees and shrubs, in 11 genera, grow mainly in northern temperate regions. The species of larch and *Pseudolarix* (see p.79) are deciduous. The flowers are borne separately on the same plant: females develop into a woody cone.

Family: Pinaceae	Species: *Abies alba*	Author: Mill.

European Silver Fir

Leaves Linear, to 1¼in (3cm) long, with a notched tip, glossy dark green above, with two whitish bands beneath, spreading either side of the shoot, shorter and pointing forward above. ***Bark*** Gray and smooth, cracking into small plates with age. ***Flowers*** Males yellow, beneath the shoot, females green, upright, borne in separate clusters on the same plant in spring. ***Fruit*** A cylindrical, upright cone, to 6in (15cm) long, green at first ripening to brown, with protruding, down-turned bracts.

NATIVE REGION Europe.
HABITAT Mountain forests.
REMARK Also known as silver fir. Cones usually grow only high on the tree. This species is widely used as a Christmas tree in many parts of Europe.

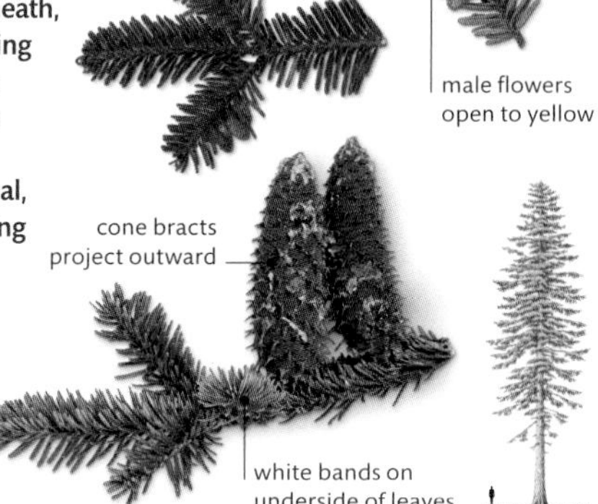

Height: 130ft (40m)	Shape: Narrowly conical	Leaf persistence: Evergreen	Leaf type:

Family: Pinaceae	Species: *Abies bracteata*	Author: (D. Don) Poit.

Santa Lucia Fir

Leaves Needlelike and rigid, to 2in (5cm) long, ending in a very sharp point, glossy dark green above, with two white bands beneath, spreading either side of the shoot. ***Bark*** Dark gray and smooth. ***Flowers*** Males yellowish, beneath the shoot, females green, upright, borne in separate clusters on the same plant in spring. ***Fruit*** An egg shaped, upright cone, to 4in (10cm) long, green ripening to brown, with conspicuously long, bristly bracts.

NATIVE REGION US: California.
HABITAT Evergreen forests on mountain slopes.
REMARK Also known as bristlecone fir. It is the rarest native North American fir.

Height: 115ft (35m)	Shape: Narrowly conical	Leaf persistence: Evergreen	Leaf type:

Family: Pinaceae	Species: *Abies cephalonica*	Author: Loudon

Greek Fir

Leaves Linear and rigid, to 1¼in (3cm) long, sharp-pointed, glossy dark green above, with two white bands beneath, all around the shoot. ***Bark*** Dark gray, cracking into small, square plates. ***Flowers*** Males reddish opening yellow, beneath the shoot, females green, upright, in separate clusters on the same plant in spring. ***Fruit*** A brown, upright cone, to 6in (15cm) long, cylindrical narrowing at either end, with protruding, down-turned bracts.

NATIVE REGION S.E. Europe.
HABITAT Mountains.

leaves end in sharp point

two white bands on underside of leaves

Height: 100ft (30m)	Shape: Narrowly conical	Leaf persistence: Evergreen	Leaf type:

Family: Pinaceae	Species: *Abies concolor*	Author: (Gordon & Glend.) Lindl. ex Hildebr.

Colorado Fir

Leaves Linear, to 2½in (6cm) long, with a blunt tip, blue-gray or gray-green, spreading beneath the shoot, upswept above. ***Bark*** Gray and smooth, becoming scaly with age. ***Flowers*** Males yellow, beneath the shoot, females greenish-yellow, upright, in separate clusters on the same plant in spring. ***Fruit*** A cylindrical, upright cone, to 4in (10cm) long, green to purple ripening to brown.

NATIVE REGION W. US.
HABITAT Mountain slopes.
REMARK Also known as white fir.

male flower clusters hang under shoot

same color on both sides of leaves

Height: 130ft (40m)	Shape: Narrowly conical	Leaf persistence: Evergreen	Leaf type:

Family: Pinaceae	Species: *Abies forrestii*	Author: Coltm.-Rog.

Forrest's Fir

Leaves Linear, to 1½in (4cm) long, with a notched tip, very dark green above, with two bright white bands beneath, spreading beneath the shoot, densely arranged above. ***Bark*** Gray, smooth. ***Flowers*** Males purple opening yellow, beneath the shoot, females purple, upright, in separate clusters on the same plant in spring. ***Fruit*** An upright cone, to 4in (10cm) long, broadly cylindrical with a flat top, deep purple ripening to purple-brown, with small, protruding, down-turned bracts.

NATIVE REGION W. China.
HABITAT High mountains.

Height: 65ft (20m)	Shape: Narrowly conical	Leaf persistence: Evergreen	Leaf type: 

Family: Pinaceae	Species: *Abies grandis*	Author: (Douglas ex D. Don) Lindl.

Giant Fir

Leaves Linear and slender, to 2in (5cm) long, with a notched tip, bright green above, with two white bands beneath, spreading either side of the shoot. ***Bark*** Gray-brown, smooth, cracking with age. ***Flowers*** Males reddish opening yellow, females green, upright, in separate clusters on the same plant in spring. ***Fruit*** A cylindrical, upright cone, to 4in (10cm) long, green ripening to brown.

NATIVE REGION W. North America.
HABITAT Evergreen forests on low mountain slopes.

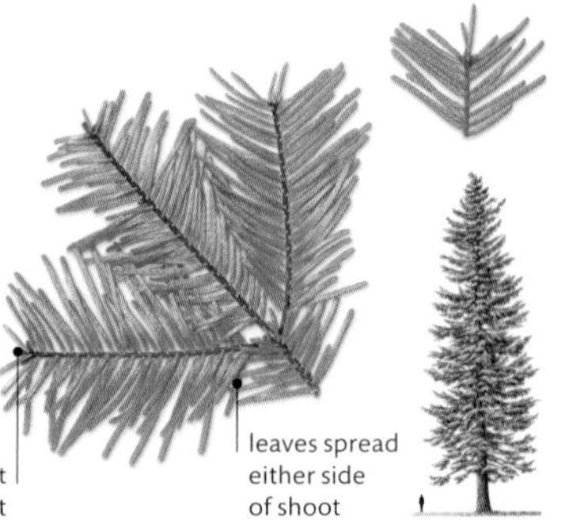

Height: 164ft (50m)	Shape: Narrowly conical	Leaf persistence: Evergreen	Leaf type:

Family: Pinaceae	Species: *Abies homolepis*	Author: Siebold & Zucc.

Nikko Fir

Leaves Linear, to 1¼in (3cm) long, with a notched tip, glossy dark green and bloomy at least when young above, with two broad white bands beneath, spreading either side of the shoot. ***Bark*** Gray, tinged pink, scaly with age. ***Flowers*** Males reddish opening yellow-green, beneath the shoot, females purplish red, upright, in separate clusters on the same plant in spring. ***Fruit*** A cylindrical, upright cone, to 4in (10cm) long, purple-blue ripening to brown.

NATIVE REGION Japan.
HABITAT Mountain forests.

notch at tip of leaves

underside of leaves

Height: 100ft (30m)	Shape: Narrowly conical	Leaf persistence: Evergreen	Leaf type:

Family: Pinaceae	Species: *Abies koreana*	Author: E.H. Wilson

Korean Fir

Leaves Linear, to ¾in (2cm) long, rounded to notched at the tip, dark green above, with two white bands or all white beneath, densely arranged above the shoot, spreading beneath. ***Bark*** Dark gray-brown. ***Flowers*** Males yellow, beneath the shoot, females reddish purple, upright, in separate clusters on the same plant in spring. ***Fruit*** A cylindrical, upright cone, to 3in (7.5cm) long, with protruding, down-curved bracts.

NATIVE REGION S. Korea.
HABITAT Mountains.

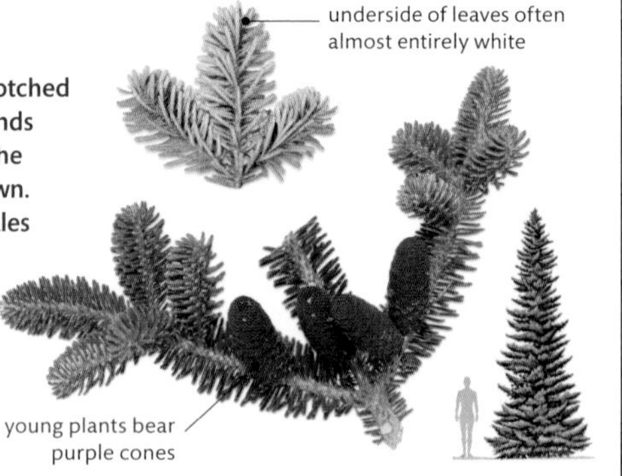

Height: 50ft (15m)	Shape: Narrowly conical	Leaf persistence: Evergreen	Leaf type:

Family: Pinaceae	Species: *Abies lasiocarpa*	Author: (Hook.) Nutt.

Subalpine Fir

Leaves **Linear, to 1½in (4cm) long, with a notched tip, gray-green above, with two white bands beneath, arranged upright above the shoot, the central leaves pointing forward, spreading beneath.** ***Bark*** **Gray-white, smooth, with resin blisters.** ***Flowers*** **Males tinged red opening yellow, beneath the shoot, females purple, upright, in separate clusters on the same plant in spring.** ***Fruit*** **A cylindrical, upright cone, to 4in (10cm) long, deep purple ripening to brown.**

NATIVE REGION W. North America.
HABITAT From sea level to the mountains.

Abies lasiocarpa ▷

two narrow, white bands on underside of leaves

var. *arizonica* ▷
This form, commonly known as the corkbark fir, comes from the south of the region. It is distinguished by its bluer leaves and corky bark.

Height: 100ft (30m)	Shape: Narrowly conical	Leaf persistence: Evergreen	Leaf type:

Family: Pinaceae	Species: *Abies magnifica*	Author: A. Murray

California Red Fir

Leaves **Linear, to 1½in (4cm) long, bluntly pointed, gray-green, arranged upright above the shoot, spreading to upswept beneath.** ***Bark*** **Gray, rough, corky; red in very old plants.** ***Flowers*** **Males purple-red, beneath the shoot, females red, upright, in separate clusters on the same plant in spring.** ***Fruit*** **A broadly cylindrical, upright cone, 8in (20cm) or more long, purple at first becoming yellow-green ripening to brown.**

NATIVE REGION US: California, S. Oregon.
HABITAT Dry mountain slopes and ridges.
REMARK Also known as red fir.

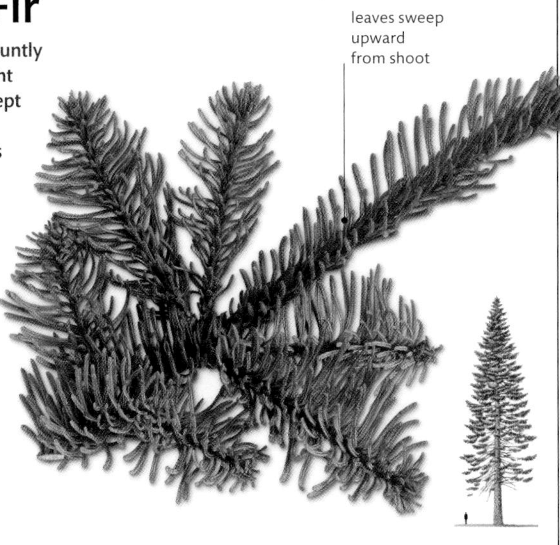

leaves sweep upward from shoot

Height: 130ft (40m)	Shape: Narrowly conical	Leaf persistence: Evergreen	Leaf type: 

Family: Pinaceae	Species: *Abies nordmanniana*	Author: (Steven) Spach

Caucasian Fir

Leaves Linear, to 1½in (4cm) long, with a notched tip, glossy bright green above, with two white bands beneath, dense above the shoot, spreading beneath. ***Bark*** Gray and smooth, cracking into small, square plates with age. ***Flowers*** Males reddish, beneath the shoot, females green, upright, in separate clusters on the same plant in spring. ***Fruit*** A broadly cylindrical, upright cone, to 6in (15cm) long, green ripening to purple-brown, with protruding, down-curved bracts.

male flower clusters open yellow

NATIVE REGION Caucasus, N.E. Turkey.
HABITAT Mountain forests.

Height: 164ft (50m)	Shape: Broadly conical	Leaf persistence: Evergreen	Leaf type:

Family: Pinaceae	Species: *Abies numidica*	Author: de Lannoy ex Carrière

Algerian Fir

Leaves Linear and rigid, to ¾in (2cm) long, rounded or notched at the tip, dark gray-green above, with a small whitish patch toward the tip, with two white bands beneath, densely arranged all around the shoot, upright above, spreading beneath. ***Bark*** Gray-purple, smooth, flaking with age. ***Flowers*** Males tinged red opening yellow, beneath the shoot, females green, upright, in separate clusters on the same plant in spring. ***Fruit*** A cylindrical, upright cone, to 7¼in (18cm) long, purple-green ripening to brown, ending in an abrupt point.

green female flower clusters

cones end in blunt tip

NATIVE REGION Algeria.
HABITAT Mountains near the coast.
REMARK A rare species in the wild. It is closely related to the Spanish fir (*Abies pinsapo*, see p.61).

purplish green young cones ripen to brown

short, stubby, blunt-pointed leaves

conspicuous white bands on underside of leaves

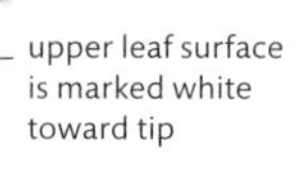

Height: 80ft (25m)	Shape: Narrowly conical	Leaf persistence: Evergreen	Leaf type:

Family: Pinaceae	Species: *Abies pinsapo*	Author: Boiss.

Spanish Fir

Leaves Linear and rigid, to ¾in (2cm) long, bluntly pointed, gray-green to gray-blue, densely arranged and standing out all around the shoot. ***Bark*** Dark gray, cracking into small, square plates with age. ***Flowers*** Males red opening yellow, beneath the shoot, females green, upright, borne in separate clusters on the same plant in spring. ***Fruit*** A cylindrical, upright cone, to 6in (15cm) long, green ripening to brown.

NATIVE REGION S. Spain.
HABITAT Dry mountain slopes.

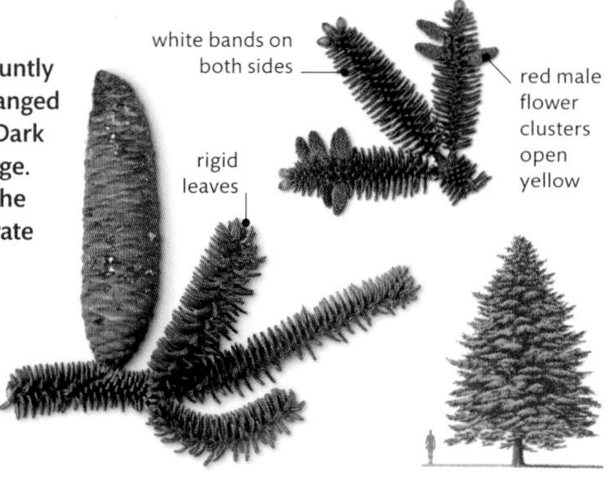

Height: 80ft (25m)	Shape: Broadly conical	Leaf persistence: Evergreen	Leaf type:

Family: Pinaceae	Species: *Abies procera*	Author: Rehder

Noble Fir

Leaves Linear, to 1¼in (3cm) long, bluntly pointed, grooved above, gray-green to gray-blue. ***Bark*** Pale silvery gray or purplish, shallowly fissured with age. ***Flowers*** Males red tinged yellow, beneath the shoot, females reddish or green, upright, in separate clusters on the same plant in spring. ***Fruit*** A broadly cylindrical, purple-brown, upright cone, to 10in (25cm) long, with protruding, down-curved bracts.

NATIVE REGION W. US.
HABITAT West-facing mountain slopes.

whitish bands on both sides of leaves

Height: 164ft (50m)	Shape: Narrowly conical	Leaf persistence: Evergreen	Leaf type: 

Family: Pinaceae	Species: *Abies veitchii*	Author: Lindl.

Veitch's Fir

Leaves Linear, to 1¼in (3cm) long, with a notched tip, glossy dark green above, with two bright blue-white bands beneath, dense and pointing forward along the shoot, spreading beneath. ***Bark*** Gray and smooth, scaly with age. ***Flowers*** Males reddish opening yellow, beneath the shoot, females red-purple, upright, in separate clusters on the same plant in late spring. ***Fruit*** A cylindrical, upright cone, to 3in (7.5cm) long, blue-purple ripening to brown.

NATIVE REGION Japan.
HABITAT Evergreen mountain forests.

bright bands on underside of leaves

bracts are paler brown at tip

Height: 80ft (25m)	Shape: Narrowly conical	Leaf persistence: Evergreen	Leaf type: 

Family: Pinaceae	Species: *Cedrus atlantica*	Author: (Endl.) Manetti ex Carrière

Atlas Cedar

Leaves **Needlelike and slender, to ¾in (2cm) long, borne singly on long shoots, in dense whorls on very slow-growing, shorter side shoots, sharp-pointed, gray-green to dark green, on hairy shoots.** ***Bark*** **Dark gray on old trees fissured into scaly plates.** ***Flowers*** **Males yellow, females green, both carried upright, in separate clusters on the same plant in fall.** ***Fruit*** **A barrel-shaped, upright cone, to 3in (7.5cm) long, green-purple when young becoming purple-brown ripening to brown, ripe in two to three years, breaking up before falling.**

NATIVE REGION Algeria, Morocco.
HABITAT Forests.
REMARK The species is sometimes listed as a geographical subspecies of the cedar of Lebanon (*Cedrus libani*, see p.63), from which it is usually most easily distinguished by its habit. In the wild, it is found only in the North African Atlas Mountains, a mountain range that lies between the Mediterranean and the Sahara.

male flower clusters open in fall

leaves borne singly on long shoots

△▽ ***Cedrus atlantica***

cones break up before falling

leaves whorled on side shoots

△ **Glauca Group**
The blue cedar is the form most commonly seen in yards. It has bright gray-blue foliage.

Height: 130ft (40m)	Shape: Broadly conical	Leaf persistence: Evergreen	Leaf type:

Family: Pinaceae	Species: *Cedrus brevifolia*	Author: (Hook. f.) Elwes & A. Henry

Cyprian Cedar

Leaves **Needlelike, to ¾in (2cm) long, borne singly on long shoots, in dense whorls on slow-growing side shoots, dark green.** ***Bark*** **Dark gray, cracking into vertical plates.** ***Flowers*** **Males blue-green, females green, both carried upright, in separate clusters on the same plant in fall.** ***Fruit*** **A cylindrical, upright cone, to 2¾in (7cm) long, purple-green at first ripening to brown.**

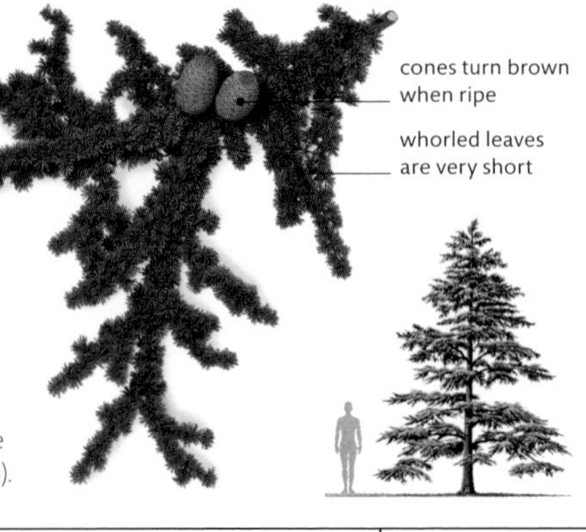

NATIVE REGION Cyprus.
HABITAT Mountains.
REMARK Short leaves distinguish this species from the closely related cedar of Lebanon (*Cedrus libani*, see p.63).

Height: 65ft (20m)	Shape: Broadly conical	Leaf persistence: Evergreen	Leaf type:

Family: Pinaceae	Species: *Cedrus deodara*	Author: (Roxb. ex D. Don) G. Don

Deodar

Leaves **Needlelike, to 1½in (4cm) long, borne singly on long shoots, in dense whorls on slow-growing side shoots, green to gray-green, the shoots drooping conspicuously at the tip.** ***Bark*** **Dark gray, cracking vertically with age.** ***Flowers*** **Males purple opening yellow, upright, females green, upright, borne in separate clusters on the same plant in fall.** ***Fruit*** **A barrel-shaped, upright cone, to 4¾in (12cm) long, green ripening to purple-brown.**

NATIVE REGION W. Himalayas.
HABITAT Mountain forests.
REMARK Also known as Himalayan cedar.

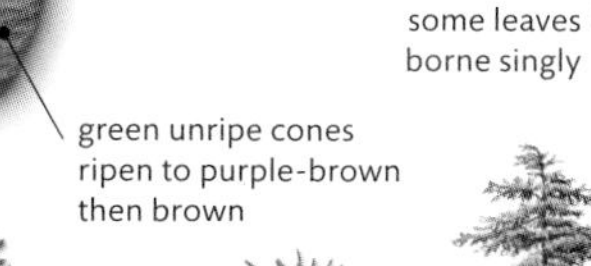

Height: 164ft (50m)	Shape: Broadly conical	Leaf persistence: Evergreen	Leaf type:

Family: Pinaceae	Species: *Cedrus libani*	Author: A. Rich.

Cedar of Lebanon

Leaves **Needlelike, to 1¼in (3cm) long, borne singly on long shoots, in dense whorls on slow-growing side shoots, dark green to gray-blue.** ***Bark*** **Dark gray, cracking into vertical plates.** ***Flowers*** **Males blue-green opening yellow, upright, females green, upright, borne in separate clusters on the same plant in fall.** ***Fruit*** **A barrel-shaped, upright cone, to 4¾in (12cm) long, purple-green ripening to brown.**

NATIVE REGION Lebanon, S.W. Turkey.
HABITAT Mountain forests.
REMARK Old plants of this species have a distinctive characteristic: the foliage is carried in broad, flattened sprays of branches, and is held on several massive stems.

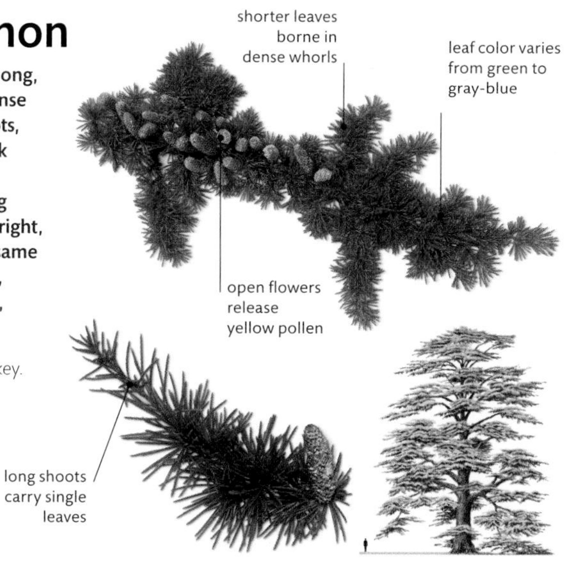

Height: 130ft (40m)	Shape: Broadly columnar	Leaf persistence: Evergreen	Leaf type: 

Family: Pinaceae	Species: *Larix decidua*	Author: Mill.

European Larch

Leaves Needlelike and soft, to 1½in (4cm) long, singly on long shoots, in dense whorls on side shoots, bright green, turning yellow in fall. ***Bark*** Gray becoming red-brown, fissured and scaly. ***Flowers*** Males yellow, drooping, females red, upright, borne in separate clusters on the same plant in spring. ***Fruit*** An egg-shaped, brown, upright cone, about 1½in (4cm) long.

NATIVE REGION Europe.
HABITAT Mountains.

cones develop from female flowers

yellow male flower clusters

cones have upright scales

Height: 130ft (40m)	Shape: Narrowly conical	Leaf persistence: Deciduous	Leaf type:

Family: Pinaceae	Species: *Larix kaempferi*	Author: (Lamb.) Carrière

Japanese Larch

Leaves Needlelike and soft, to 1½in (4cm) long, singly on long shoots, whorled on side shoots, gray-green to blue-green. ***Bark*** Reddish brown, scaly. ***Flowers*** Males yellow, drooping, females creamy or pinkish, upright, borne in separate clusters on the same plant in spring. ***Fruit*** An egg-shaped, upright cone, to 1¼in (3cm).

NATIVE REGION C. Japan.
HABITAT Mountains.

cone scales turn outward

female flowers borne in larger clusters

variable leaves may be blue-green

male flower clusters

Height: 100ft (30m)	Shape: Broadly conical	Leaf persistence: Deciduous	Leaf type:

Family: Pinaceae	Species: *Larix laricina*	Author: (Du Roi) K. Koch

Tamarack

small cones covered with few scales

Leaves **Needlelike and soft, to 1¼in (3cm) long, borne singly on long shoots, in dense whorls on slow-growing side shoots, blue-green, turning yellow in fall.** ***Bark*** **Pinkish to reddish brown, scaly.** ***Flowers*** **Males yellow, drooping beneath the shoot, females red, upright, borne in separate clusters on the same plant in spring.** ***Fruit*** **An egg-shaped, brown, upright cone, to ¾in (2cm) long, with relatively few straight scales.**

NATIVE REGION Canada, N.E. US.
HABITAT Woods and swamps.
REMARK Also known as American larch. Widely distributed in Canada and the northeast United States, growing as far north as the Arctic Circle.

red female flower clusters

Height: 65ft (20m)	Shape: Narrowly conical	Leaf persistence: Deciduous	Leaf type:

Family: Pinaceae	Species: *Larix* x *marschlinsii*	Author: Coaz

Dunkeld Larch

red female flower clusters

Leaves **Needlelike, soft, gray-green to green.** ***Bark*** **Reddish brown, scaly.** ***Flowers*** **Males yellow, drooping, females red, upright, in separate clusters on the same plant in spring.** ***Fruit*** **An egg-shaped, brown, upright cone, to 1¼in (3cm) long.**

NATIVE REGION Of garden origin.
REMARK A hybrid between the European larch (*Larix decidua*, see p.64) and the Japanese larch (*Larix kaempferi*, see p.64).

orange-brown shoots

cone scales spread slightly

Height: 115ft (35m)	Shape: Broadly conical	Leaf persistence: Deciduous	Leaf type:

Family: Pinaceae	Species: *Larix occidentalis*	Author: Nutt.

Western Larch

Leaves **Needlelike, soft, to 1½in (4cm) long, borne singly on long shoots, in dense whorls on slow-growing side shoots, bright green, turning yellow in fall.** ***Bark*** **Reddish-brown, thick and scaly.** ***Flowers*** **Males yellow, drooping beneath the shoot, females red, upright, borne in separate clusters on the same plant in spring.** ***Fruit*** **An egg-shaped, brown, upright cone, to 1½in (4cm) long, with bracts protruding from between the scales.**

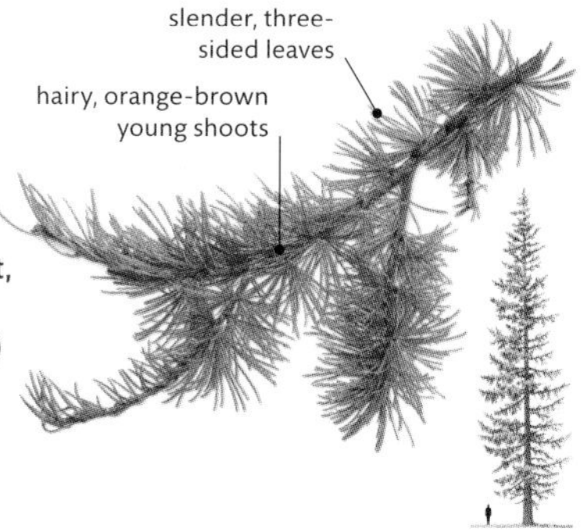

NATIVE REGION W. North America.
HABITAT Mountains.

Height: 164ft (50m)	Shape: Narrowly conical	Leaf persistence: Deciduous	Leaf type:

Family: Pinaceae	Species: *Picea abies*	Author: (L.) H. Karst.

Norway Spruce

Leaves Needlelike, slender, and rigid, to ¾in (2cm) long, four-sided, with a sharp point at the tip, dark green, spreading beneath smooth, brown shoots. ***Bark*** Red-brown to gray, peeling in thin strips. ***Flowers*** Males red opening yellowish, females red, borne in separate, upright clusters on the same plant in spring. ***Fruit*** A cylindrical, brown, hanging cone, to 6in (15cm) long.

NATIVE REGION Europe.
HABITAT Mountain forests, on damp soil.
REMARK This important species has many cultivars, such as dwarf forms. It is widely planted for the commercial value of its timber.

pointed, four-sided leaves

cone scales have cut-off or toothed tip

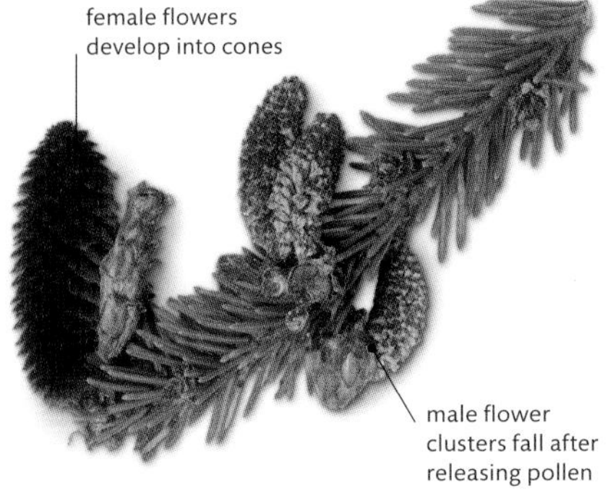

leaves dark green on all sides

Height: 164ft (50m)	Shape: Narrowly conical	Leaf persistence: Evergreen	Leaf type:

Family: Pinaceae	Species: *Picea breweriana*	Author: S. Watson

Brewer Spruce

Leaves Needlelike, slender, often curved, to 1¼in (3cm) long, flattened, blunt, dark green, with two whitish bands beneath, arranged all around the shoot. ***Bark*** Gray-purple, scaly with age. ***Flowers*** Males red opening yellowish, females red or green, in separate clusters on the same plant in spring. ***Fruit*** A narrowly cylindrical, brown, hanging one, to 4¾in (12cm) long.

NATIVE REGION US: N. California, S. Oregon.
HABITAT Mountains.

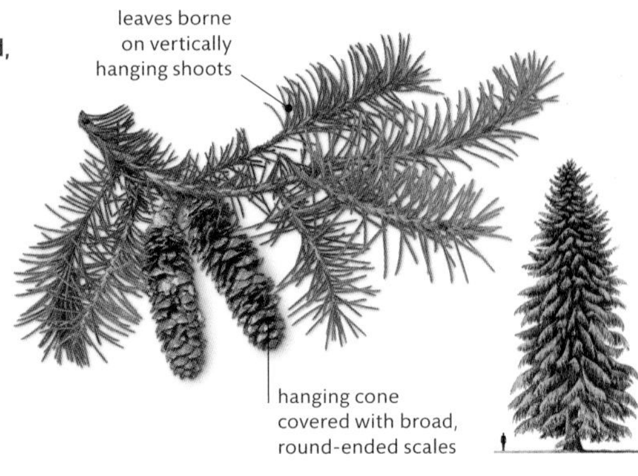

Height: 115ft (35m)	Shape: Narrowly weeping	Leaf persistence: Evergreen	Leaf type:

Family: Pinaceae	Species: *Picea glauca*	Author: (Moench) Voss

White Spruce

Leaves Needlelike, slender, and rigid, to ⅝in (1.5cm) long, four-sided, blue-green, with white bands, densely arranged pointing forward above smooth, nearly white shoots. ***Bark*** Gray-brown and scaly. ***Flowers*** Males red opening yellow, females purple-red, borne in separate clusters on the same plant in spring. ***Fruit*** A cylindrical, pale brown, hanging cone, to 2½in (6cm) long.

NATIVE REGION Canada, N.E. US.
HABITAT Woods.

glossy cones

both sides of leaves banded with white

Height: 100ft (30m)	Shape: Narrowly conical	Leaf persistence: Evergreen	Leaf type:

Family: Pinaceae	Species: *Picea jezoensis*	Author: (Siebold & Zucc.) Carrière

Yezo Spruce

Leaves Needlelike and slender, to ⅝in (1.5cm) long, flattened, dark green above, with two broad, white bands beneath, pointing forward above smooth, pale shoots, spreading beneath. ***Bark*** Gray-brown, flaking and deeply fissured. ***Flowers*** Males reddish, females purple red, in separate clusters on the same plant in spring. ***Fruit*** A cylindrical, red-brown, hanging cone, to 3in (7.5cm) long.

NATIVE REGION N.E. Asia, Japan.
HABITAT Subalpine forests on steep slopes and dry plateaux.

▽ var. ***hondoensis***

female flowers

wavy-margined cone scales

green unripe cone

Height: 164ft (50m)	Shape: Narrowly conical	Leaf persistence: Evergreen	Leaf type: 

Family: Pinaceae	Species: *Picea likiangensis*	Author: (Franch.) E. Pritz.

Lijiang Spruce

Leaves Needlelike and slender, to ⅝in (1.5cm) long, sharp at the tip, blue-green above, blue-white beneath, pointing forward above usually hairy, pale brown shoots, spreading beneath. ***Bark*** Pale gray and scaly, fissured with age. ***Flowers*** Males and females both profuse, males red opening yellowish, females bright red, in separate clusters on the same plant in spring. ***Fruit*** A cylindrical, hanging cone, to 4in (10cm) long, purple ripening to pale brown.

NATIVE REGION W. China.
HABITAT Mountain woods.

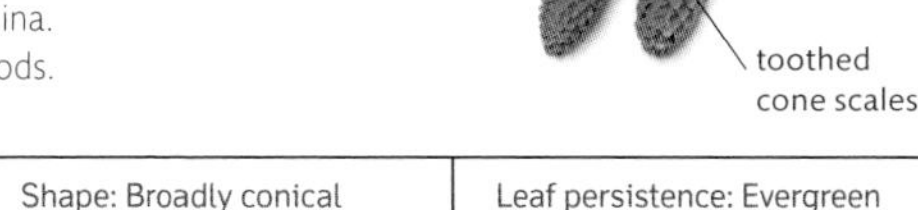

Height: 100ft (30m)	Shape: Broadly conical	Leaf persistence: Evergreen	Leaf type:

Family: Pinaceae	Species: *Picea mariana*	Author: (Mill.) Britton, Sterns & Poggenb.

Black Spruce

Leaves Needlelike, slender, to ⅝in (1.5cm) long, four-sided, bluntly pointed, blue-green above, blue-white beneath, borne all around hairy, yellow-brown shoots. ***Bark*** Gray-brown and flaking. ***Flowers*** Males and females both red, in separate clusters on the same plant in spring. ***Fruit*** An egg-shaped, red-brown, hanging cone, to 1½in (4cm) long.

NATIVE REGION Canada, N.E. US.
HABITAT Mountain slopes and bogs.

rigid leaves are four-sided

unusually short cones

Height: 100ft (30m)	Shape: Narrowly conical	Leaf persistence: Evergreen	Leaf type:

Family: Pinaceae	Species: *Picea omorika*	Author: (Pancic) Purk.

Serbian Spruce

Leaves Needlelike and slender, to ¾in (2cm) long, flattened, glossy dark green above, most lying above but some all around hairy, pale brown shoots. ***Bark*** Purple-brown, cracking into square plates. ***Flowers*** Males and females both red, borne in separate clusters on the same plant in spring. ***Fruit*** A narrowly egg-shaped, purple-brown, hanging cone, to 2½in (6cm) long.

NATIVE REGION Bosnia and Herzegovina, Serbia.
HABITAT Near River Drina, on limestone.

leaves spread out from shoots

bluish white bands on underside of leaves

Height: 30m (100ft)	Shape: Narrowly conical	Leaf persistence: Evergreen	Leaf type:

Family: Pinaceae	Species: *Picea orientalis*	Author: (L.) Peterm.

Oriental Spruce

Leaves Needlelike, to 5/16in (8mm) long, four-sided, bluntly pointed at the tip, glossy dark green, pointing forward all around hairy; whitish to pale brown shoots. ***Bark*** Pinkish brown, flaking in small plates. ***Flowers*** Males red opening yellow, females red, in separate clusters on the same plant in spring. ***Fruit*** A cylindrical, hanging cone, to 4in (10cm) long, purple ripening to brown.

NATIVE REGION Caucasus, N.E. Turkey.
HABITAT Mountain forests.

Picea orientalis ▷

◁ **'Aurea'**
A form with bright yellow young foliage.

Height: 164ft (50m)	Shape: Narrowly conical	Leaf persistence: Evergreen	Leaf type:

Family: Pinaceae	Species: *Picea pungens*	Author: Engelm.

Colorado Spruce

Leaves Needlelike, to 1¼in (3cm) long, spine-tipped, gray-green to blue-gray, arranged all around pale brown shoots. ***Bark*** Purple-gray, scaly. ***Flowers*** Males reddish, females green, in separate clusters on the same plant in late spring. ***Fruit*** A pale brown, hanging cone, to 4in (10cm) long.

NATIVE REGION W. US.
HABITAT High mountains, on dry slopes and stream banks.

△ **'Koster'** This form has bright silvery blue foliage.

Height: 115ft (35m)	Shape: Narrowly conical	Leaf persistence: Evergreen	Leaf type:

Family: Pinaceae	Species: *Picea sitchensis*	Author: (Bong.) Carrière

Sitka Spruce

Leaves Needlelike and slender, to 1¼in (3cm) long, sharp-pointed, bright green above, with two white bands beneath, arranged all around whitish to pale brown shoots, parted beneath. ***Bark*** Gray and purple-gray, flaking in large scales. ***Flowers*** Males reddish, females green, borne in separate clusters on the same plant in spring. ***Fruit*** A cylindrical, pale brown, hanging cone, to 4in (10cm) long.

NATIVE REGION W. North America.
HABITAT Coastal, moist lowland.

Height: 164ft (50m)	Shape: Narrowly conical	Leaf persistence: Evergreen	Leaf type:

Family: Pinaceae	Species: *Picea smithiana*	Author: (Wall.) Boiss.

West Himalayan Spruce

Leaves Needlelike, long, and slender, to 1½in (4cm) long, four-sided, dark green, arranged all around smooth, glossy, pale brown, hanging shoots. ***Bark*** Purple-gray, flaking in scales. ***Flowers*** Males yellow-green, hanging, at the tips of the shoots, females green, upright, in separate clusters on the same plant in late spring to early summer. ***Fruit*** A hanging cone, to 8in (20cm) long, green ripening to glossy brown.

NATIVE REGION W. Himalayas.
HABITAT High evergreen forests.

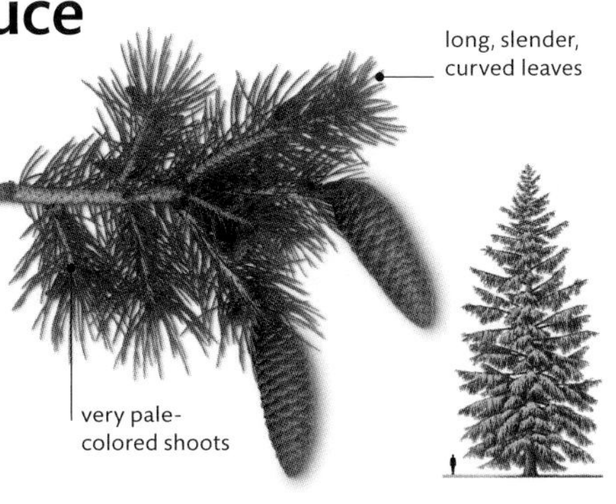

Height: 130ft (40m)	Shape: Narrowly weeping	Leaf persistence: Evergreen	Leaf type:

Family: Pinaceae	Species: *Pinus ayacahuite*	Author: Ehrenb. ex Schltdl.

Mexican White Pine

Leaves Needlelike and slender, to 6in (15cm) long, in clusters of five, blue-green, borne on finely hairy, yellow-brown shoots. ***Bark*** Gray, rough and coarsely fissured. ***Flowers*** Males yellow, females red, in separate clusters on the young shoots in early summer. ***Fruit*** A cylindrical, yellow-brown, resinous, hanging cone, to 18in (45cm) long, with purple-tipped scales.

NATIVE REGION N. Guatemala, Mexico.
HABITAT Mountain slopes.

long, often curved leaves droop on shoots

△ **var. *veitchii***

Height: 115ft (35m)	Shape: Broadly conical	Leaf persistence: Evergreen	Leaf type:

Family: Pinaceae	Species: *Pinus bungeana*	Author: Zucc. ex Endl.

Lace-bark Pine

Leaves Needlelike and rigid, to 3in (7.5cm) long, in clusters of three, with a sharp point at the tip, yellow-green, borne on smooth, gray-green shoots. ***Bark*** Gray-green and creamy white, flaking in small patches. ***Flowers*** Males yellow, females green, borne in separate clusters on the young shoots in early summer. ***Fruit*** An egg-shaped, yellow-brown cone, to 2¾in (7cm) long, with spine-tipped scales.

NATIVE REGION N. China.
HABITAT Mainly steep mountain slopes, on shale.

sparsely arranged clusters of three leaves

small, squat cones

Height: 65ft (20m)	Shape: Broadly conical	Leaf persistence: Evergreen	Leaf type:

Family: Pinaceae	Species: *Pinus cembra*	Author: L.

Arolla Pine

Leaves Needlelike, to 3½in (9cm) long, in clusters of five, glossy green on the outer surface, blue-gray on the inner, on greenish shoots, the shoots covered in orange-brown hairs. ***Bark*** Gray-brown and scaly. ***Flowers*** Males purple opening yellow, females red, in separate clusters on the young shoots in late spring. ***Fruit*** An egg-shaped cone, to 3in (7.5cm) long, blue-purple ripening to red-brown, never opening fully.

NATIVE REGION N. Asia, Europe.
HABITAT Mountains.
REMARK Also known as Swiss stone pine.

densely bunched leaf clusters

Height: 65ft (20m)	Shape: Narrowly columnar	Leaf persistence: Evergreen	Leaf type:

Family: Pinaceae	Species: *Pinus contorta*	Author: Douglas ex Loudon

Beach Pine

Leaves Needlelike and twisted, to 2in (5cm) long, in pairs, densely arranged, dark green or yellow-green, on smooth, green-brown shoots. ***Bark*** Red-brown, fissured into small squares. ***Flowers*** Males yellow, females red, in separate clusters on the young shoots in late spring. ***Fruit*** An egg-shaped, pale brown cone, pointing backward along the shoot, to 2in (5cm) long, the scales with slender spines.

NATIVE REGION W. North America.
HABITAT Coastal dunes and bogs.
REMARK Also known as shore pine. Widely distributed from Alaska to Mexico. The lodgepole pine, var. *latifolia*, can reach 100ft (30m) in mountain habitats.

Pinus contorta △▽

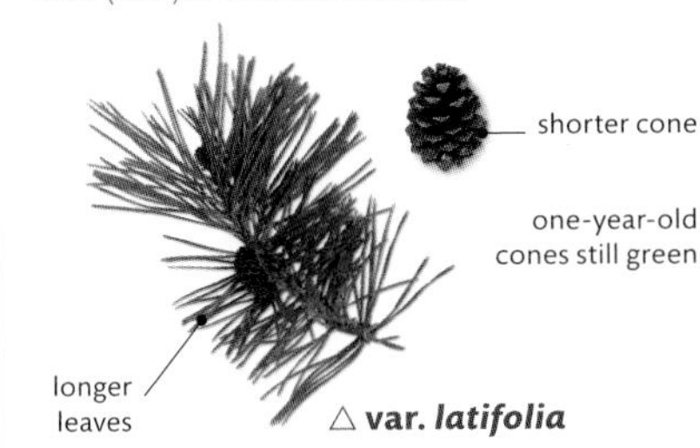

△ **var. *latifolia***

Height: 33ft (10m)	Shape: Broadly conical	Leaf persistence: Evergreen	Leaf type:

Family: Pinaceae	Species: *Pinus coulteri*	Author: D. Don

Big-cone Pine

Leaves Needlelike and stiff, to 12in (30cm) long, in clusters of three, gray-green, on very stout, bloomy shoots. ***Bark*** Purple-brown, scaly, deeply fissured. ***Flowers*** Males purple opening yellow, females red, borne in separate clusters on the young shoots in late spring to early summer. ***Fruit*** An egg-shaped, yellow-brown, resinous cone, to 12in (30cm) long, the scales ending in hooked spines, usually remaining closed for many years.

NATIVE REGION US: California.
HABITAT Dry, rocky slopes in the mountains.

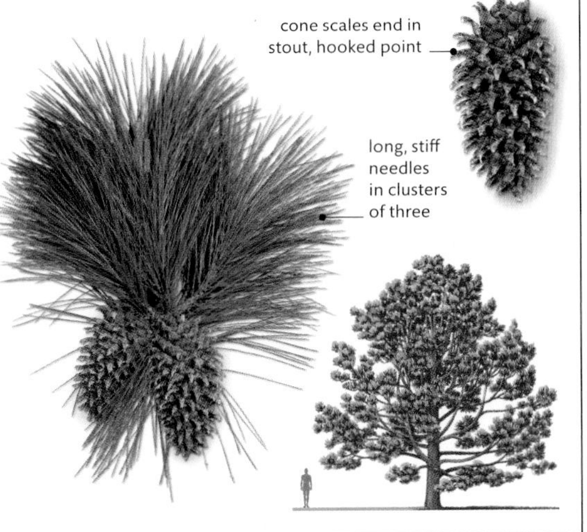

Height: 80ft (25m)	Shape: Broadly spreading	Leaf persistence: Evergreen	Leaf type:

Family: Pinaceae	Species: *Pinus densiflora*	Author: Siebold & Zucc.

Japanese Red Pine

Leaves Needlelike and slender, to 4in (10cm) long, in pairs, bright green, pointing forward, on smooth, green shoots. ***Bark*** Reddish-brown becoming gray-red, cracking into irregular plates with age. ***Flowers*** Males yellow-brown, females red, in separate clusters on the young shoots in late spring. ***Fruit*** A conical, pale brown cone, to 2in (5cm) long, ripe in two years.

NATIVE REGION N.E. China, Japan, Korea.
HABITAT Sea level to mountains.

Height: 115ft (35m)	Shape: Broadly spreading	Leaf persistence: Evergreen	Leaf type:

Family: Pinaceae	Species: *Pinus engelmannii*	Author: Carrière

Apache Pine

Leaves Needlelike, to 18in (45cm) long, usually in clusters of three, minutely toothed and slightly rough at the margin, dark green, drooping in brushlike clusters, on stout, rough, dark brown shoots. ***Bark*** Dark brown, thick and deeply furrowed. ***Flowers*** Males purple opening yellow, females red, in separate clusters on the young shoots in early summer. ***Fruit*** A conical to egg-shaped, sometimes curved, cone to 5½in (14cm) long, blue-purple ripening to light brown, borne singly or in clusters.

NATIVE REGION S.W. US, N. Mexico.
HABITAT Mountains.

Height: 65ft (20m)	Shape: Broadly spreading	Leaf persistence: Evergreen	Leaf type:

Family: Pinaceae	Species: *Pinus heldreichii*	Author: Christ

Bosnian Pine

Leaves Needlelike and rigid, to 3½in (9cm) long, in pairs, sharp-pointed at the tip, dark green, densely clustered and pointing forward, on bloomy shoots. ***Bark*** Gray, cracking into small, square plates. ***Flowers*** Males yellow, females purple-red, at the tips of the shoots, borne in separate clusters on the same plant in early summer. ***Fruit*** An egg-shaped cone, to 4in (10cm) long, deep blue at first ripening to yellow-brown in two years.

NATIVE REGION S.E. Europe.
HABITAT Mountains, usually on limestone.

Height: 80ft (25m)	Shape: Narrowly conical	Leaf persistence: Evergreen	Leaf type:

Family: Pinaceae	Species: *Pinus* x *holfordiana*	Author: A.B. Jacks.

Holford Pine

Leaves Needlelike and slender, to 7¼in (18cm) long, in clusters of five, the outer surface bright green, the inner surface blue-gray, borne on hairy, green shoots. ***Bark*** Gray and fissured. ***Flowers*** Males yellow, females red, in separate clusters on the young shoots in early summer. ***Fruit*** A resinous, orange-brown, hanging cone, to 12in (30cm) long.

resinous cone scales darken toward tip

leaves borne five together

NATIVE REGION Of garden origin.
REMARK A hybrid between Mexican white pine (*Pinus ayacahuite* var. *veitchii*, see p.70) and Himalayan pine (*Pinus wallichiana*, see p.78).

Height: 80ft (25m)	Shape: Broadly conical	Leaf persistence: Evergreen	Leaf type:

Family: Pinaceae	Species: *Pinus jeffreyi*	Author: Balf.

Jeffrey Pine

Leaves Needlelike and rigid, to 10in (25cm) long, in clusters of three, blue-green, borne on stout, smooth, bloomy shoots. ***Bark*** Dark gray-brown, with deep, narrow fissures. ***Flowers*** Males red opening yellow, females red-purple, in separate clusters on the young shoots in early summer. ***Fruit*** A conical, yellow-brown cone, to 12in (30cm) long, the scales each with a slender, curved spine.

NATIVE REGION W. US.
HABITAT Dry slopes on high mountains.
REMARK Closely related to western yellow pine (*Pinus ponderosa*, see p.76).

Height: 130ft (40m)	Shape: Broadly conical	Leaf persistence: Evergreen	Leaf type:

Family: Pinaceae	Species: *Pinus koraiensis*	Author: Siebold & Zucc.

Korean Pine

Leaves Needlelike and slender, to 4¾in (12cm) long, in dense clusters of five, glossy green on the outer surface, blue-white on the inner. ***Bark*** Dark gray, thick, flaking. ***Flowers*** Males red opening yellow, females red, in separate clusters on the young shoots in early summer. ***Fruit*** A conical, purple-brown cone, to 4¾in (12cm) long.

NATIVE REGION N.E. Asia, Japan, Korea.
HABITAT River valleys and low mountain slopes.

Height: 115ft (35m)	Shape: Broadly conical	Leaf persistence: Evergreen	Leaf type:

Family: Pinaceae	Species: *Pinus monophylla*	Author: Torr. & Frém.

One-leaved Nut Pine

Leaves Needlelike, curved, and rigid, to 2in (5cm) long, tapered to a sharp point, borne singly, gray-green to blue-green, on stout, orange shoots. ***Bark*** Gray, with narrow ridges. ***Flowers*** Males yellow, females red, in separate clusters on the young shoots in early summer. ***Fruit*** A cone, to 2¼in (5.5cm) long, green ripening to gray-brown.

NATIVE REGION N. Mexico, S.W. US.
HABITAT Dry, rocky, mountain slopes and ridges.
REMARK Also known as *P. cembroides* var. *monophylla*. Easily distinguished by its singly borne needles: most pines bear their needles in clusters of two or more.

cone scales have four-angled sides

brownish mature cone

Height: 50ft (15m)	Shape: Broadly conical	Leaf persistence: Evergreen	Leaf type:

Family: Pinaceae	Species: *Pinus muricata*	Author: D. Don

Bishop Pine

Leaves Needlelike and stiff, to 6in (15cm) long, in pairs, gray-green or blue-green, on orange-brown shoots. ***Bark*** Purple-brown, thick, furrowed and ridged. ***Flowers*** Males yellow, females red, in separate clusters on the young shoots in early summer. ***Fruit*** An egg-shaped, red-brown cone, to 3¼in (8cm) long, oblique at the base, borne in whorls, persisting for many years.

NATIVE REGION US: California.
HABITAT Low hills in coastal areas.

paired leaves spread in untidy clusters

prickle-tipped cone scales

Height: 80ft (25m)	Shape: Broadly columnar	Leaf persistence: Evergreen	Leaf type:

Family: Pinaceae	Species: *Pinus nigra*	Author: J.F. Arnold

Austrian Pine

Leaves Needlelike and stiff, to 6in (15cm) long, in pairs, sharp-pointed, very dark green, on stout, glossy brown shoots. ***Bark*** Nearly black, scaly, ridged. ***Flowers*** Males yellow, females red, in separate clusters on the young shoots in late spring to early summer. ***Fruit*** An egg-shaped, brown cone, to 3¼in (8cm) long.

NATIVE REGION C. and S.E. Europe.
HABITAT Mountains and hills, often on limestone.

cones may be borne singly or in clusters

△ ***Pinus nigra***

◁ **subsp. *laricio***
Also known as var. *maritima*, the Corsican pine has gray-green leaves.

Height: 130ft (40m)	Shape: Broadly columnar	Leaf persistence: Evergreen	Leaf type:

Family: Pinaceae	Species: *Pinus parviflora*	Author: Siebold & Zucc.

Japanese White Pine

Leaves Needlelike, slightly twisted, to 2½in (6cm) l ong, in clusters of five, the outer surface green or blue-green, the inner surface blue-white, on greenish shoots. ***Bark*** Gray, scaly, with deep fissures. ***Flowers*** Males purple-red opening yellow, females red, in separate clusters on the young shoots in early summer. ***Fruit*** An egg-shaped cone, to 2¾in (7cm) long, green ripening to red-brown, with leathery scales.

NATIVE REGION Japan.
HABITAT Mountains, on stony soil.

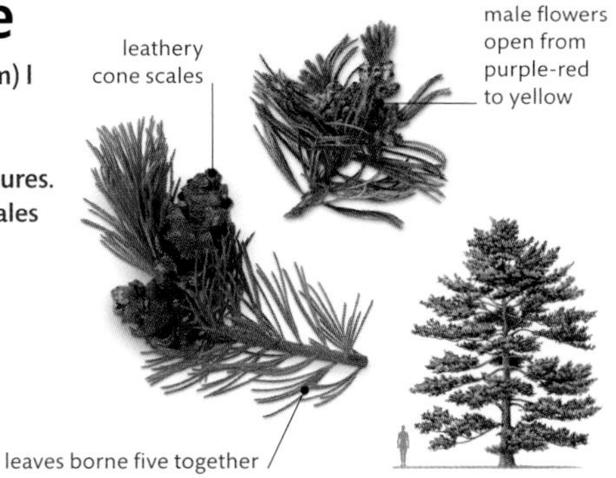

Height: 80ft (25m)	Shape: Broadly columnar	Leaf persistence: Evergreen	Leaf type:

Family: Pinaceae	Species: *Pinus peuce*	Author: Griseb.

Macedonian Pine

Leaves Needlelike and stiff, to 4in (10cm) long, in dense clusters of five, blue-green, pointing forward on smooth, bloomy, green shoots. ***Bark*** Purple-brown, fissured and cracked into plates. ***Flowers*** Males yellow, females red, in separate clusters on the young shoots in early summer. ***Fruit*** A cylindrical to conical, resinous, drooping cone, to 6in (15cm) long, green at first ripening to brown.

NATIVE REGION S.E. Europe.
HABITAT Mountains.

female flowers
slender leaves in clusters of five

Height: 100ft (30m)	Shape: Narrowly columnar	Leaf persistence: Evergreen	Leaf type:

Family: Pinaceae	Species: *Pinus pinaster*	Author: Aiton

Maritime Pine

Leaves Needlelike and stiff, to 8in (20cm) long, in pairs, sharp-pointed, gray-green becoming dark green, borne on stout shoots. ***Bark*** Purple-brown, ridged, deeply fissured. ***Flowers*** Males yellow, females red, in separate clusters on the young shoots in early summer. ***Fruit*** A conical, glossy brown cone, to 8in (20cm) long, the scales with sharp prickles, persisting for many years.

NATIVE REGION N. Africa, S.W. Europe.
HABITAT Sandy soil.

Height: 115ft (35m)	Shape: Broadly columnar	Leaf persistence: Evergreen	Leaf type:

Family: Pinaceae	Species: *Pinus pinea*	Author: L.

Stone Pine

Leaves Needlelike and stout, to 4¾in (12cm) long, in pairs, gray-green, on smooth, orange-brown shoots; on young plants, singly, bright blue-gray. ***Bark*** Orange-brown, deeply fissured. ***Flowers*** Males yellow, females green, borne in separate clusters on the young shoots in early summer. ***Fruit*** A nearly rounded, heavy, glossy brown cone, to 4¾in (12cm) long.

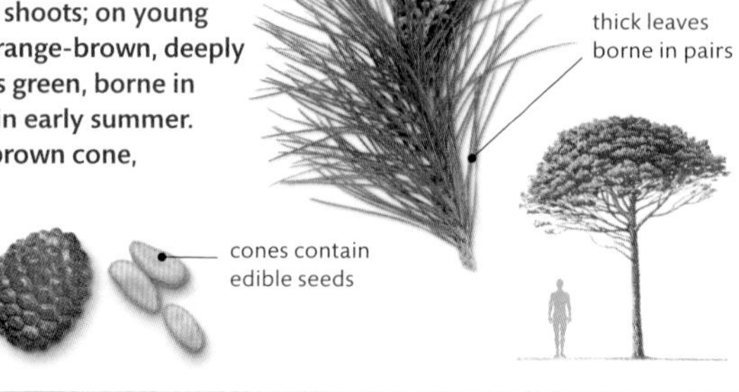

NATIVE REGION Mediterranean.
HABITAT Sandy soil near the coast.

Height: 65ft (20m)	Shape: Broadly spreading	Leaf persistence: Evergreen	Leaf type:

Family: Pinaceae	Species: *Pinus ponderosa*	Author: Douglas ex C. Lawson

Western Yellow Pine

purple male flowers

long leaves in threes

Leaves Needlelike and rigid, to 10in (25cm) long, in clusters of three, dark gray-green, pointing forward, on stout, smooth, yellow- to red-brown shoots. ***Bark*** Yellow-brown or reddish, thick, in large plates. ***Flowers*** Males deep purple, females red, borne in separate clusters on the young shoots in late spring. ***Fruit*** An egg-shaped cone, to 4in (10cm) or more long, purple ripening to glossy red-brown.

cone scales have spiny tip

NATIVE REGION W. North America.
HABITAT Mountain slopes.

Height: 164ft (50m)	Shape: Broadly conical	Leaf persistence: Evergreen	Leaf type:

Family: Pinaceae	Species: *Pinus radiata*	Author: D. Don

Monterey Pine

male flowers in dense clusters

leaves in threes

red-purple female flowers borne on vigorous shoots

Leaves Needlelike and slender, to 6in (15cm) long, in clusters of three, bright green, on gray-green shoots. ***Bark*** Dark gray, deeply fissured. ***Flowers*** Males yellow-brown, females red-purple, in separate clusters on the young shoots in early summer. ***Fruit*** A brown cone, to 4¾in (12cm) long, persisting for years.

NATIVE REGION US: California.
HABITAT Dry slopes near coast.

cones ripen from green to brown

Height: 100ft (30m)	Shape: Broadly conical	Leaf persistence: Evergreen	Leaf type: 

Family: Pinaceae	Species: *Pinus strobus*	Author: L.

Weymouth Pine

Leaves Needlelike and slender, to 4¾in (12cm) long, in clusters of five, the outer surface gray-green, the inner surface gray-white, densely set. ***Bark*** Dark gray and smooth, becoming deeply fissured. ***Flowers*** Males yellow, females pink, in separate clusters on the young shoots in early summer. ***Fruit*** A cylindrical, curved, hanging cone, to 6in (15cm) or more long, green ripening to pale brown.

NATIVE REGION E. North America.
HABITAT Woods at low altitudes.

bright yellow male flowers

leaves in fives

slender cone often marked with white resin

nearly smooth, olive-brown shoots

Height: 164ft (50m)	Shape: Narrowly conical	Leaf persistence: Evergreen	Leaf type: 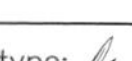

Family: Pinaceae	Species: *Pinus sylvestris*	Author: L.

Scots Pine

Leaves Needlelike, stout, and twisted, to 2¾in (7cm) long, in pairs, blue-green to blue-gray. ***Bark*** Purple-gray, peeling in irregular plates; orange and flaking toward the top of the plant. ***Flowers*** Males yellow, females red, in separate clusters on the young shoots in late spring to early summer. ***Fruit*** An egg-shaped cone, to 3in (7.5cm) long, green ripening to brown.

NATIVE REGION Asia, Europe.
HABITAT Mountains, on sandy or gravelly soil.

female flowers borne at end of shoots

male flowers borne at base of shoots

paired, usually twisted, leaves

Height: 115ft (35m)	Shape: Broadly spreading	Leaf persistence: Evergreen	Leaf type:

Family: Pinaceae	Species: *Pinus tabuliformis*	Author: L.

Chinese Pine

Leaves Needlelike, to 6in (15cm) long, usually in pairs but sometimes in clusters of three, green to gray-green, on yellow-brown shoots; young shoots bloomy. ***Bark*** Gray, fissured; tinged with orange or pink toward the top of the plant. ***Flowers*** Males pale yellow, females red-purple, in separate clusters on the young shoots in early summer. ***Fruit*** An egg-shaped, brown cone, to 2½in (6cm) long, the scales each with a small spine at the tip, long-persistent on the shoots.

NATIVE REGION China, Korea.
HABITAT Mountains.

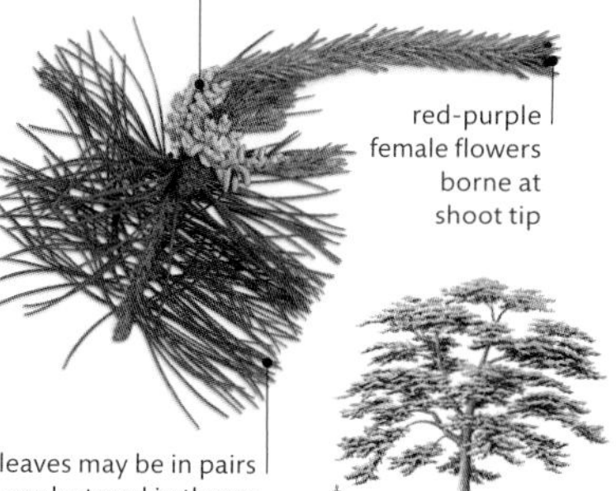

Height: 80ft (25m)	Shape: Broadly spreading	Leaf persistence: Evergreen	Leaf type:

Family: Pinaceae	Species: *Pinus thunbergii*	Author: Parl.

Japanese Black Pine

Leaves Needlelike and rigid, to 4in (10cm) long, in pairs, sharp-pointed, densely set, pointing forward, on smooth, yellow-brown shoots. ***Bark*** Gray, cracking into irregular plates. ***Flowers*** Males yellowish, females purple-red, in separate clusters on the young shoots in early summer. ***Fruit*** An egg-shaped cone, to 2¾in (7cm) long, purple or green ripening to gray-brown.

NATIVE REGION N.E. China, Japan, Korea.
HABITAT Near coastline.
REMARK This species is related to the Austrian pine (*Pinus nigra*, see p.74). In winter, it is easily distinguished by its white-hairy leaf buds.

Height: 100ft (30m)	Shape: Broadly conical	Leaf persistence: Evergreen	Leaf type:

Family: Pinaceae	Species: *Pinus wallichiana*	Author: A.B. Jacks.

Himalayan Pine

Leaves Needlelike and slender, often kinked at first, flexible, to 8in (20cm) long, in clusters of five, the outer surface green, the inner surface blue-white, on smooth, green, bloomy shoots. ***Bark*** Gray and smooth, becoming dark gray and fissured. ***Flowers*** Males yellow, females blue-green and pink, in separate clusters on the young shoots in early summer. ***Fruit*** A curved, resinous, hanging cone, to 12in (30cm) long, green ripening to pale brown.

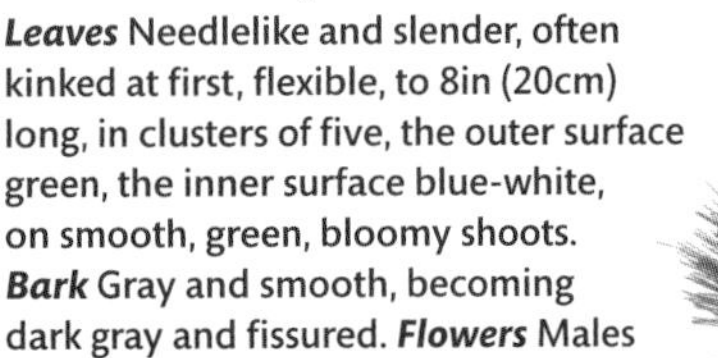

NATIVE REGION Himalayas.
HABITAT Mountain forests.
REMARK Also known as Bhutan pine, blue pine. The first name should be reserved for *Pinus bhutanica*, a recently described species from Bhutan, S. Asia.

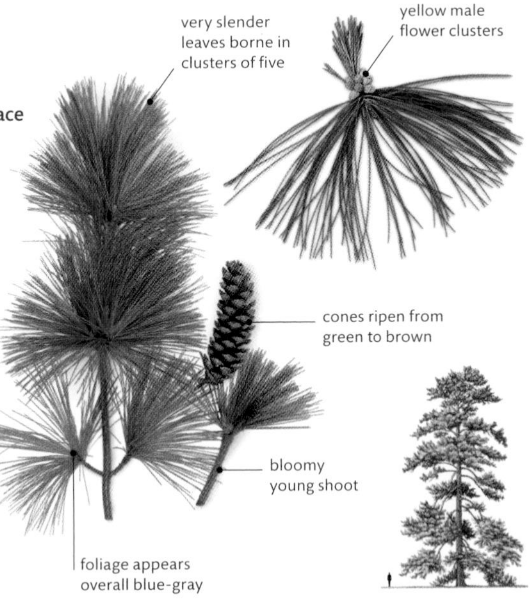

Height: 130ft (40m)	Shape: Broadly conical	Leaf persistence: Evergreen	Leaf type:

Family: Pinaceae	Species: *Pseudolarix amabilis*	Author: (J. Nelson) Rehder

Golden Larch

Leaves **Linear and slender, to 2in (5cm) long, borne singly on long shoots, in dense whorls on upcurved, short shoots, turning golden yellow in fall.** ***Bark*** **Gray-brown, cracking into small, square plates.** ***Flowers*** **Males and females both yellow, in separate clusters at the ends of short shoots, on the same plant in late spring or early summer.** ***Fruit*** **An egg-shaped cone, to 2in (5cm) long, green ripening to brown, breaking up before falling.**

NATIVE REGION E. China.
HABITAT Mountain forests.
REMARK A relative of the larches (*Larix*, see pp.64–65).

Height: 130ft (40m)	Shape: Broadly conical	Leaf persistence: Deciduous	Leaf type:

Family: Pinaceae	Species: *Pseudotsuga menziesii*	Author: (Mirb.) Franco

Douglas Fir

Leaves **Linear, to 1¼in (3cm) long, rounded and blunt at the tip, green above, with two white bands beneath, aromatic, arranged all around the shoot or spreading above.** ***Bark*** **Purple-brown, thick, with red-brown fissures.** ***Flowers*** **Males yellow, beneath the shoot, females green flushed pink, at the tip, in separate clusters on the same plant in spring.** ***Fruit*** **A red-brown, hanging cone, to 4in (10cm) long, with three-pronged bracts projecting from between the scales.**

NATIVE REGION W. North America.
HABITAT Evergreen forests on moist mountain slopes.
REMARK The common name commemorates the 19th-century Scottish plant hunter, David Douglas. Also known as Oregon fir, Oregon pine.

Height: 200ft (60m)	Shape: Narrowly conical	Leaf persistence: Evergreen	Leaf type: 

Family: Pinaceae	Species: *Tsuga canadensis*	Author: (L.) Carrière

Eastern Hemlock

Leaves Linear, to ½in (1.2cm) long, dark green above, with two white bands beneath. ***Bark*** Purple-gray, with scaly ridges. ***Flowers*** Males yellow, beneath the shoot, females resembling small, green cones, at the tip, in separate clusters in late spring. ***Fruit*** An egg-shaped, pale brown, hanging cone, to ¾in (2cm) long.

NATIVE REGION E. North America.
HABITAT Hilly or rocky woods.

Height: 100ft (30m)	Shape: Broadly conical	Leaf persistence: Evergreen	Leaf type:

Family: Pinaceae	Species: *Tsuga caroliniana*	Author: Engelm.

Carolina Hemlock

Leaves Linear, to ¾in (2cm) long, dark green above, with two white bands beneath. ***Bark*** Red-brown, furrowed and ridged with age. ***Flowers*** Males and females both reddish, males below the shoot, females at the tip, in separate clusters in late spring. ***Fruit*** An egg-shaped, pale brown, hanging cone, 1in (2.5cm) long.

NATIVE REGION S.E. US.
HABITAT Mountain slopes.

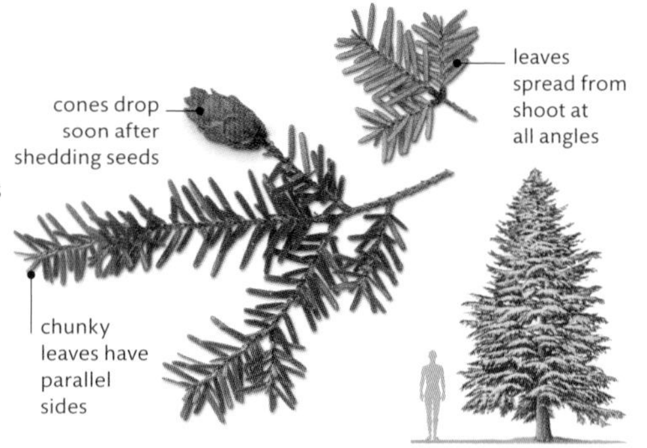

Height: 65ft (20m)	Shape: Broadly conical	Leaf persistence: Evergreen	Leaf type:

Family: Pinaceae	Species: *Tsuga heterophylla*	Author: (Raf.) Sarg.

Western Hemlock

Leaves Linear, to ¾in (2cm) long, with parallel sides, dark green above, with two white bands beneath. ***Bark*** Purple-brown, ridged, flaking. ***Flowers*** Both reddish, males beneath the shoot, females at the tip, in separate clusters on the same plant in spring. ***Fruit*** An egg-shaped, brown, hanging cone, ¾in (2cm) long.

NATIVE REGION
W. North America.
HABITAT Forests.

purplish red young cone
leaves spread either side of shoot
mature cone has slightly opened scales

Height: 200ft (60m)	Shape: Narrowly conical	Leaf persistence: Evergreen	Leaf type: 

PODOCARPACEAE

OVER 175 SPECIES in 20 genera of evergreen trees and shrubs, mainly in the genus *Podocarpus*, belong to this family; most grow in warm regions of the southern hemisphere. Male and female flowers are usually on separate plants, the males in catkinlike clusters. Females develop into a fleshy cone or seed.

Family: Podocarpaceae	Species: *Prumnopitys andina*	Author: (Poepp. ex Endl.) de Laub.

Plum-fruited Yew

Leaves Linear, to 1in (2.5cm) long, abruptly short-pointed, deep blue-green above, with two whitish bands beneath, all around the shoot. ***Bark*** Dark gray and smooth. ***Flowers*** Males yellow, in branched clusters 1in (2.5cm) long, females small, green, on separate plants in early summer. ***Fruit*** Fleshy, plumlike, edible, green ripening to yellow, with a single seed.

NATIVE REGION Argentina, S. Chile.
HABITAT Mountains.

flattened leaves

two paler bands on underside of leaves

fruit matures to yellow

Height: 50ft (15m)	Shape: Broadly conical	Leaf persistence: Evergreen	Leaf type:

Family: Podocarpaceae	Species: *Saxegothaea conspicua*	Author: Lindl.

Prince Albert's Yew

Leaves Linear, usually curved, to 1¼in (3cm) long, with a fine, sharp point at the tip, dark green above, with two whitish bands beneath, loosely arranged in two ranks either side of the shoot or spreading all around it. ***Bark*** Purple-brown, smooth, peeling in strips. ***Flowers*** Males purplish, in the leaf axils, beneath the shoot, females blue-green, at the tip of the shoot, in separate clusters on the same plant in late spring to early summer. ***Fruit*** A rounded, fleshy cone, ¾in (2cm) across, with prickly, blue-green scales.

NATIVE REGION Chile.
HABITAT Forests.

tiny, purplish male flower clusters

leaves end in a small, sharp point at tip

sharp-pointed cone scales

Height: 40ft (12m)	Shape: Broadly conical	Leaf persistence: Evergreen	Leaf type: 

SCIADOPITYACEAE

THIS FAMILY CONSISTS OF a single living species described here but fossil evidence indicates that the genus was once widespread in Europe and Asia. It was previously included in the family Taxodiaceae.

Family: Sciadopityaceae	Species: *Sciadopitys verticillata*	Author: (Thunb.) Siebold & Zuccarini

Umbrella Pine

Leaves Needlelike, to 4¾in (12cm) long, deeply grooved on both sides, deep green above, yellow-green beneath. ***Bark*** Red-brown, peeling in long, vertical strips. ***Flowers*** Males yellow, in many clusters, females green, at the ends of the shoots, on the same plant in spring. ***Fruit*** An egg-shaped cone, to 3in (7.5cm) long, green ripening to red-brown in two years.

NATIVE REGION Japan.
HABITAT Mountains.

slender leaves borne in umbrella-like clusters

mature cone has loose scales

male flower clusters open yellow

Height: 80ft (25m)	Shape: Narrowly conical	Leaf persistence: Evergreen	Leaf type:

TAXACEAE

THIS FAMILY WAS often classed apart from the true conifers because its members do not bear their seeds in cones. The six genera contain about 35 species of evergreen trees and shrubs. Male and female flowers are usually on separate plants. Females mature to a single seed surrounded by a fleshy aril.

Family: Taxaceae	Species: *Cephalotaxus fortunei*	Author: Hook.

Chinese Plum Yew

Leaves Linear, to 4in (10cm) long and about ⅛in (3mm) across, pointed, glossy green above, with two whitish bands beneath, spreading either side of the shoot. ***Bark*** Red-brown and flaking. ***Flowers*** Males and females creamy yellow, on separate plants in spring. ***Fruit*** Oval, fleshy-coated, purple-brown, 1in (2.5cm) long.

NATIVE REGION
C. and E. China.
HABITAT Mountain forests.

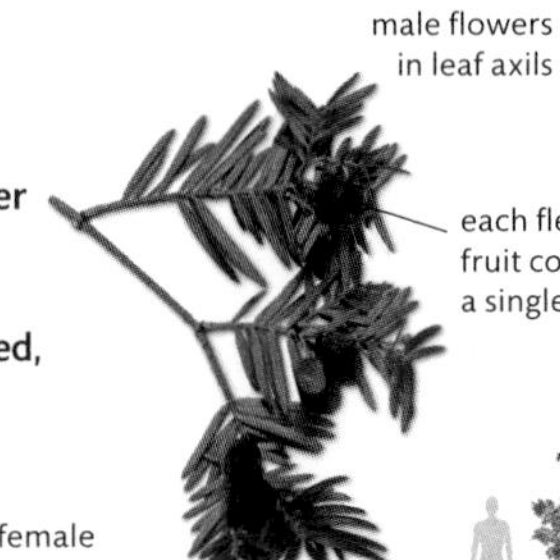

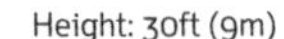

Height: 30ft (9m)	Shape: Broadly spreading	Leaf persistence: Evergreen	Leaf type:

Family: Taxaceae	Species: *Cephalotaxus harringtonia*	Author: (Knight ex J. Forbes) K. Koch

Cowtail Pine

Leaves **Linear, to 2in (5cm) long and ⅛in (3mm) across, pointed, glossy dark green above, with two bands beneath, spreading either side of the shoot. *Bark* Brown, flaking. *Flowers* Creamy white, males in the leaf axils, females at the shoot tips, on separate plants in spring. *Fruit* An oval, fleshy-coated seed, 1in (2.5cm) long, blue-green ripening to purple-brown.**

female flowers

two whitish bands

underside of leaves

NATIVE REGION Japan, Korea, China.
HABITAT An understory forest tree.
REMARK Originally described from a backyard plant, the wild Japanese form previously known as var. *drupacea* has shorter leaves.

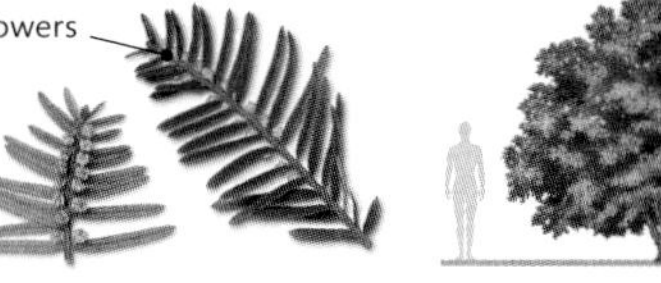

Height: 20ft (6m)	Shape: Broadly spreading	Leaf persistence: Evergreen	Leaf type:

Family: Taxaceae	Species: *Taxus baccata*	Author: Linnaeus

Common Yew

Leaves **Linear, to 1¼in (3cm) long, pointed at the tip, dark green above, with two paler green bands beneath, mainly spreading in two ranks either side of the shoot. *Bark* Purple-brown, smooth and flaking. *Flowers* Males and females both small, males pale yellow, in clusters in the leaf axils, beneath the shoot, females singly, at the end of the shoot, on separate plants in spring. *Fruit* A single seed, enclosed in a fleshy, usually red, aril, the whole ¾in (1cm) long, open at the top, exposing the green seed.**

△ ***Taxus baccata***

NATIVE REGION N. Africa, S.W. Asia, Europe.
HABITAT Limey soil.
REMARK All parts are poisonous, except the aril.

'Lutea' ▷
The yellow-berried yew is named for the color of its fruits.

yellow aril

Height: 65ft (20m)	Shape: Broadly conical	Leaf persistence: Evergreen	Leaf type:

Family: Taxaceae	Species: *Torreya californica*	Author: Torrey

California Nutmeg

Leaves **Needlelike, to 2½in (6cm) long, pointed, glossy dark green above, with two whitish bands beneath. *Bark* Gray-brown, with vertical ridges. *Flowers* Males cream, in the leaf axils, females green, on separate plants in spring to early summer. *Fruit* A seed, enclosed in a green, purple-flushed aril, about 1½in (4cm) long.**

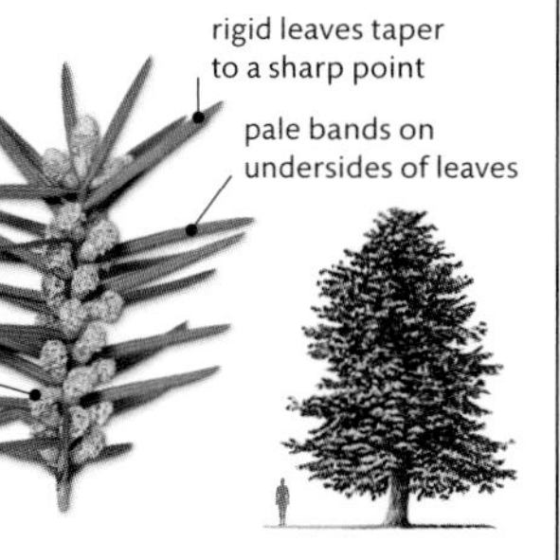

NATIVE REGION US: California.
HABITAT Cool slopes and canyons in coastal regions and mountains.

Height: 100ft (30m)	Shape: Broadly conical	Leaf persistence: Evergreen	Leaf type:

BROADLEAVES

ALTINGIACEAE

THIS IS A FAMILY of a single genus and 15 species of evergreen and deciduous trees found in the Americas, Turkey, and E. Asia that usually have palmately lobed leaves. The species below were previously included in the Hamamelidaceae family.

Family: Altingiaceae	Species: *Liquidambar formosana*	Author: Hance

Liquidambar formosana

Leaves Palmately lobed, to 5in (13cm) long and 6in (15cm) across, heart-shaped at the base, usually with three taper-pointed, toothed lobes, purple when young becoming dark green, turning red to purple in fall, carried on red-tinged stalks. ***Bark*** Gray-white, darker and fissured with age. ***Flowers*** Males and females small, yellow-green, without petals, borne in separate, rounded heads on the same plant in spring at the same time as the leaves emerge. ***Fruit*** Small, brown, in rounded, hanging clusters, 1½in (4cm) across.

NATIVE REGION China, Korea, Vietnam.
HABITAT Woods and thickets in mountainous areas.

leaves are occasionally five-lobed

reddish base of veins

Height: 130ft (40m)	Shape: Broadly conical	Leaf persistence: Deciduous	Leaf type:

Family: Altingiaceae	Species: *Liquidambar orientalis*	Author: Mill.

Liquidambar orientalis

Leaves Palmately lobed, to 3in (7.5cm) long and across, matte green above, smooth on both sides, turning orange in fall. ***Bark*** Orange-brown and thick, cracking into small plates. ***Flowers*** Males and females both very small and yellow-green, without petals, borne in separate, rounded heads on the same plant in spring as the young leaves emerge. ***Fruit*** Small and brown, in rounded, hanging clusters, 1in (2.5cm) across.

NATIVE REGION S.W. Turkey, Rhodes.
HABITAT Moist woods, floodplains, and streamsides.

Height: 25m (80ft)	Shape: Broadly conical	Leaf persistence: Deciduous	Leaf type: 

Family: Altingiaceae	Species: *Liquidambar styraciflua*	Author: L.

Sweet Gum

Leaves Palmately lobed, to 6in (15cm) long and across, with five or seven taper-pointed, finely toothed lobes, glossy green above, turning orange to red or purple in fall, borne on often corky-winged shoots. ***Bark*** Dark gray-brown, deeply furrowed, with narrow ridges. ***Flowers*** Males and females both very small and yellow-green, without petals, borne in separate, rounded heads in late spring as the leaves emerge. ***Fruit*** Individually small and brown, borne in rounded, hanging clusters, 1½in (4cm) across.

NATIVE REGION C. America, Mexico, E. US.
HABITAT Moist woods.
REMARK Easily distinguished from the maples (*Acer*, see pp.275–296) by its alternate, rather than opposite, leaves.

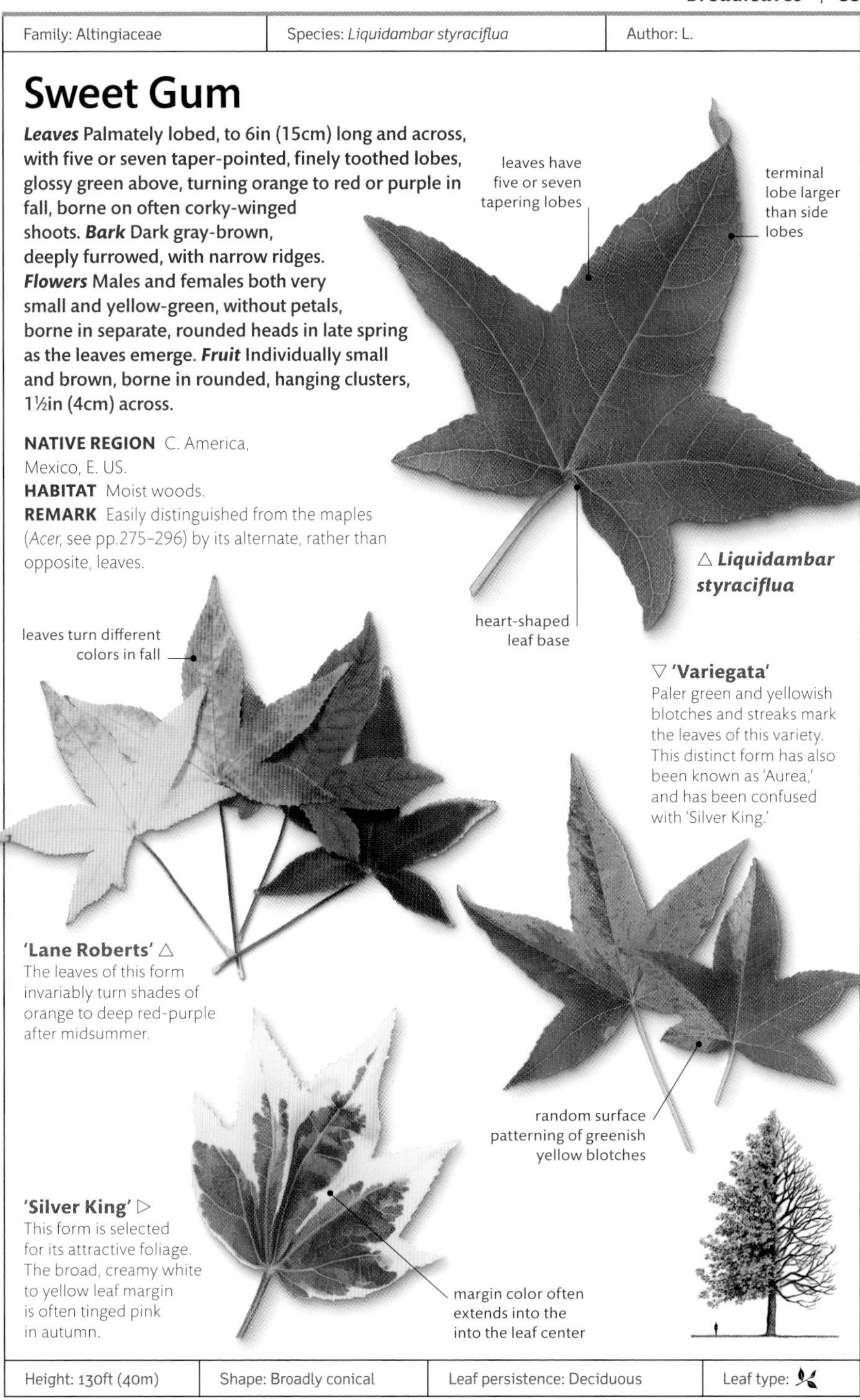

△ ***Liquidambar styraciflua***

▽ **'Variegata'**
Paler green and yellowish blotches and streaks mark the leaves of this variety. This distinct form has also been known as 'Aurea,' and has been confused with 'Silver King.'

'Lane Roberts' △
The leaves of this form invariably turn shades of orange to deep red-purple after midsummer.

'Silver King' ▷
This form is selected for its attractive foliage. The broad, creamy white to yellow leaf margin is often tinged pink in autumn.

Height: 130ft (40m)	Shape: Broadly conical	Leaf persistence: Deciduous	Leaf type:

ANACARDIACEAE

WITH A WIDE DISTRIBUTION in the warm regions of the world, this family contains over 850 species of evergreen and deciduous trees, shrubs, and climbing plants, collected in 80 genera. The leaves are nearly always alternate, and are pinnate or simple. Small male and female flowers are sometimes borne on separate plants. The foliage often contains a skin-irritating resin. Other family members include the cashew nut (*Anacardium occidentale*), mango (*Mangifera indica*), and poison ivy (*Toxicodendron radicans*).

Family: Anacardiaceae	Species: *Cotinus obovatus*	Author: Raf.

Chittamwood

Leaves Obovate, to 6in (15cm) long and 3in (7.5cm) across, rather thin, untoothed, bronze when young becoming blue-green, smooth above, hairy beneath, turning brilliant yellow to orange and red in fall. ***Bark*** Gray-brown, becoming scaly with age. ***Flowers*** Males and females both small and yellow, in long, conical clusters at the ends of the shoots, usually on separate plants in early summer. ***Fruit*** Individually small, clustered together, with numerous, slender, feathery flower stalks.

NATIVE REGION C. and S. US.
HABITAT Rocky hills.

tiny flowers borne in large panicles

bronzy young leaves

leaves have untoothed margin

brilliant fall color

Height: 33ft (10m)	Shape: Broadly conical	Leaf persistence: Deciduous	Leaf type:

Family: Anacardiaceae	Species: *Rhus copallinum*	Author: L.

Dwarf Sumac

Leaves Pinnate, to 14in (35cm) long, with up to 23 oblong, narrow, usually untoothed leaflets, to 4in (10cm) long and ¾in (2cm) across, downy becoming glossy dark green above, paler and hairy beneath, turning bright red in fall. ***Bark*** Dark gray, thinly scaly. ***Flowers*** Small, yellowish, in dense, conical clusters at the ends of the shoots in summer. ***Fruit*** Small, densely packed into a conical, bright red cluster, to 8in (20cm) long.

NATIVE REGION S. Canada, E. US, Cuba, Mexico.
HABITAT Mountains, woods, and scrub, on dry soil.

Height: 33ft (10m)	Shape: Broadly spreading	Leaf persistence: Deciduous	Leaf type:

Family: Anacardiaceae	Species: *Rhus typhina*	Author: L.

Staghorn Sumac

Leaves To 60cm (24in) long, with up to 27 lanceolate to oblong, sharply toothed leaflets, to 12cm (4¾in) long and 5cm (2in) across, dark green above, blue-green beneath, downy on both sides when young becoming nearly smooth, turning bright orange and red in autumn, on stout, velvety shoots. ***Bark*** Dark brown and smooth. ***Flowers*** Males and females both small and green, borne in dense, conical clusters at the ends of the shoots, on the same plant or on separate plants in summer. ***Fruit*** Small, bright red, in a dense, conical cluster, to 20cm (8in) long.

NATIVE REGION E. North America.
HABITAT Meadows, scrub, and wood margins, often on dry, rocky soil.

leaves color brilliantly in fall

Rhus typhina △▽

lobed leaflets

flowers are green

◁ **'Dissecta'**
This ornamental form has finely cut leaflets.

Height: 33ft (10m)	Shape: Broadly spreading	Leaf persistence: Deciduous	Leaf type:

Family: Anacardiaceae	Species: *Toxicodendron trichocarpum*	Author: (Miq.) Kuntze

Toxicodendron trichocarpum

Leaves To 20in (50cm) long, with up to 17 ovate, taper-pointed leaflets, to 4in (10cm) long and 1½in (4cm) across, reddish at first becoming matte dark green, downy, turning orange-red in fall. ***Bark*** Pale gray-brown, with conspicuous lenticels. ***Flowers*** Very small, yellowish, in conical panicles in the leaf axils in summer. ***Fruit*** Small, brownish yellow.

NATIVE REGION China, Japan, Korea.
HABITAT Mountain and roadside thickets.

Height: 26ft (8m)	Shape: Broadly spreading	Leaf persistence: Deciduous	Leaf type: 

ANNONACEAE

A MAINLY TROPICAL FAMILY, with more than 2,000 species in over 100 genera, related to the magnolias (*Magnolia*, see pp.175–187). The trees typically have simple, alternate leaves, and flowers with the petals arranged in whorls of three. Custard apples (*Annona*) are well-known members of the family.

Family: Annonaceae	Species: *Asimina triloba*	Author: (L.) Dunal

Pawpaw

Leaves Oblong to obovate, to 10in (25cm) long, taper-pointed at the tip, untoothed, rather pale green, downy when young becoming smooth beneath, turning yellow in fall. ***Bark*** Gray-brown, becoming somewhat rough and scaly with age. ***Flowers*** To 1½in (4cm) across, green at first becoming purple-brown, with six petals, the inner three upright, the outer three larger and spreading, borne singly on short, stout stalks on the old shoots in late spring as the young leaves emerge. ***Fruit*** Fleshy and edible, to 6in (15cm) long, green at first becoming yellow-brown when ripe.

NATIVE REGION E. North America.
HABITAT Rich, moist woods.
REMARK The flavor of the unusual fruits may be likened to that of bananas. This species is often confused with *Carica papaya*, a tropical tree grown for its edible fruits, and also known by the common name, pawpaw.

leaves end in short point

leaves taper to base

green young fruits turn yellow-brown when ripe

mature flowers are purple-brown

green young flowers darken as they age

Height: 30ft (9m)	Shape: Broadly spreading	Leaf persistence: Deciduous	Leaf type:

AQUIFOLIACEAE

A FAMILY OF WIDE DISTRIBUTION in temperate and tropical regions, comprising over 500 evergreen and deciduous species in a single genus (*Ilex*), which includes the hollies. The trees and shrubs usually have alternate leaves. Male and female flowers are small, white or pink, borne on separate plants; in the fall, females develop into yellow, red, orange, or black berries. The leaves of *Ilex paraguariensis*, a South American species, are used for yerba maté tea.

Family: Aquifoliaceae	Species: *Ilex* x *altaclerensis*	Author: (hort. ex Loud.) Dallim.

Highclere Holly

Leaves **Variable in size and shape, oblong to ovate or nearly rounded, to 5in (13cm) or more long and 3in (7.5cm) across, spine-tipped and often with a spiny margin, glossy dark green above.** ***Bark*** **Gray and smooth.** ***Flowers*** **Males and females both small and white, usually tinged purple, fragrant, in clusters in the leaf axils, borne on separate plants in spring.** ***Fruit*** **A large, fleshy, red berry.**

NATIVE REGION Of garden origin.
REMARK A hybrid between the common holly (*Ilex aquifolium*, see p.90) and *Ilex perado*, a species native to the Canary Islands, Madeira, and the Azores. This hybrid is recognized mainly as named cultivars, and is represented in gardens and backyards by many ornamental forms.

◁ **'Belgica Aurea'**
The long leaves of this female plant have few spines.

reddish purple leaf stalks

△ **'Camelliifolia'**
This female plant has nearly spineless leaves, which are purple when young.

creamy yellow leaf margin

deeply veined leaves

△ **'Golden King'**
The broad, thick leaves of this female plant have a bold, yellow margin.

red-tinged buds open into white flowers

△ **'Hodginsii'**
This male plant has large, few-spined, dark green leaves and purple shoots.

glossy, dark leaves

△ **'Wilsonii'**
This female plant has large leaves.

irregularly blotched yellow and green marks on leaves

△ **'Lawsoniana'**
The yellow-splashed leaves of this female plant have a nearly spineless margin.

Height: 65ft (20m)	Shape: Broadly columnar	Leaf persistence: Evergreen	Leaf type: 

Family: Aquifoliaceae	Species: *Ilex aquifolium*	Author: L.

Common Holly

Leaves **Variable, elliptic to ovate, to 4in (10cm) long and 2in (5cm) across, spine-tipped, juveniles on lower part of plant with a very spiny margin, adults with a more or less spineless margin, glossy dark green above. *Bark* Pale gray and smooth. *Flowers* Males and females both small and white or purple-tinged, fragrant, borne in clusters in the leaf axils, usually on separate plants in late spring. *Fruit* A usually red berry, to 3/8in (1cm) across.**

NATIVE REGION W. Asia, Europe, N. Africa.
HABITAT Woods, particularly those of beech and oak.
REMARK This species has given rise to numerous variations in both leaf and fruit.

male flowers

female flowers have prominent green ovary

leaves both with and without spines

◁△▽ *Ilex aquifolium*

'Crispa Aurea Picta' ▷
The thick, often twisted, leaves of this male form are spineless, except at the tip, and have a central yellow and pale green blotch.

spine emerges from indented leaf tip

▽ 'Argentea Marginata'
This female plant has pink young leaves, green shoots, and red berries.

red, densely clustered berries

berries borne abundantly

spiny leaves have creamy white margin

◁ 'Ferox'
The spines on the upper surface of the leaves give this male plant its common name, hedgehog holly.

'Bacciflava' △
This handsome cultivar bears yellow berries, and has spiny leaves.

pale spines on upper leaf surface

Height: 65ft (20m)	Shape: Broadly columnar	Leaf persistence: Evergreen	Leaf type:

'Flavescens' ▽
The moonlight holly, a female plant, has leaves flushed yellow. The leaf stalk and midrib are also yellow.

△ 'Ferox Argentea'
The leaves of this male cultivar have a creamy yellow to white margin. The tree is commonly known as silver hedgehog holly.

△ 'Handsworth New Silver'
Purple stems, white-margined leaves, and small red berries characterize this female form.

△ 'J.C. van Tol'
This plant is both male and female. Its thick leaves are glossy dark green and smooth above, and have few spines or none at all.

Family: Aquifoliaceae	Species: *Ilex aquifolium*	Author: L.

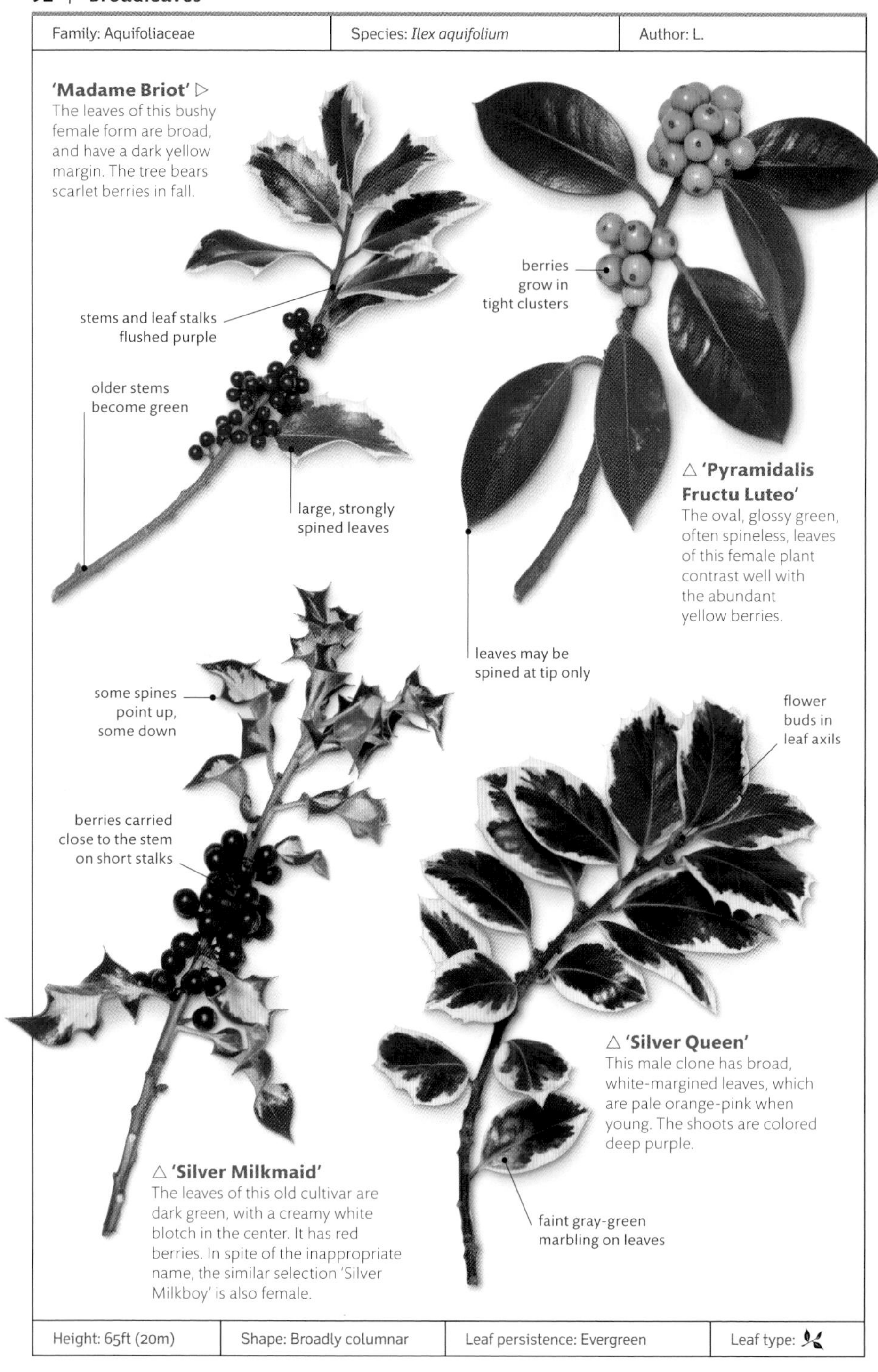

'Madame Briot' ▷
The leaves of this bushy female form are broad, and have a dark yellow margin. The tree bears scarlet berries in fall.

△ **'Pyramidalis Fructu Luteo'**
The oval, glossy green, often spineless, leaves of this female plant contrast well with the abundant yellow berries.

△ **'Silver Milkmaid'**
The leaves of this old cultivar are dark green, with a creamy white blotch in the center. It has red berries. In spite of the inappropriate name, the similar selection 'Silver Milkboy' is also female.

△ **'Silver Queen'**
This male clone has broad, white-margined leaves, which are pale orange-pink when young. The shoots are colored deep purple.

Height: 65ft (20m)	Shape: Broadly columnar	Leaf persistence: Evergreen	Leaf type:

Family: Aquifoliaceae	Species: *Ilex* x *koehneana*	Author: L.

Ilex x koehneana

Leaves **Elliptic to oblong, to 6in (15cm) long, very spiny at the margin, often bronze when young becoming glossy dark green, the young shoots flushed purple.**
Bark **Gray and smooth.**
Flowers **Males and females both small and greenish white, borne in clusters in the leaf axils, on separate plants in spring.**
Fruit **A red berry, 5/16in (8mm) across.**

NATIVE REGION Of garden origin.
REMARK A hybrid, first reported in Florence, Italy, between common holly (*Ilex aquifolium*, see p.90) and tarajo holly (*Ilex latifolia*, see below). The large leaves show the influence of the latter parent.

green ovary visible on female flowers

bronzy young leaves have strong, lateral veining on underside

numerous spines spaced regularly apart

△ ***Ilex x koehneana***

elongated, leathery, yellowish green leaves

'Chestnut Leaf' ▷
This form originated in France. It has strongly spined leaves, and bears small, brilliant red berries.

Height: 20ft (6m)	Shape: Broadly conical	Leaf persistence: Evergreen	Leaf type:

Family: Aquifoliaceae	Species: *Ilex latifolia*	Author: Thunb.

Tarajo Holly

Leaves **Oblong, to 8in (20cm) long and 3in (7.5cm) across, very thick, with coarse but not spiny teeth, glossy dark green above, yellow-green beneath, borne on stout shoots; young branches olive-green.** ***Bark*** **Gray, fissured with age.**
Flowers **Males and females both small and yellow-green, fragrant, in clusters in the leaf axils, on separate plants in late spring.**
Fruit **A red-orange berry, 5/16in (8mm) across, in abundant clusters, ripe in late fall.**

NATIVE REGION E. China, Japan.
HABITAT Warm regions.
REMARK The exceedingly large leaves make the species unique among hollies of temperate origin. In Japan, it is often planted near temples.

Height: 65ft (20m)	Shape: Broadly conical	Leaf persistence: Evergreen	Leaf type: 

Family: Aquifoliaceae	Species: *Ilex opaca*	Author: Aiton

American Holly

Leaves Elliptic, to 4in (10cm) long and 2in (5cm) across, spiny at the tip and margin, matt dark green or yellow-green above, yellow-green beneath. ***Bark*** Gray and smooth. ***Flowers*** Males and females small, dull white, in the leaf axils, usually on separate plants in late spring. ***Fruit*** A berry, to ⅜in (1cm) across, usually red.

NATIVE REGION E. US.
HABITAT Sandy soil near the coast and moist woods.

smooth, matte upper leaf surface

female flowers

Height: 50ft (15m)	Shape: Broadly conical	Leaf persistence: Evergreen	Leaf type:

Family: Aquifoliaceae	Species: *Ilex pedunculosa*	Author: Miq.

Ilex pedunculosa

Leaves Ovate to elliptic, to 3in (7.5cm) long and 1¼in (3cm) across, taper-pointed, untoothed, glossy dark green above. ***Bark*** Gray-green, smooth. ***Flowers*** Males and females small, white, in the leaf axils and on the shoots, on separate plants in summer. ***Fruit*** A bright red berry, to 5⁄16in (8mm) across.

NATIVE REGION China, Japan.
HABITAT Woods and thickets.

leaf margin turns bronze in winter

male flowers borne in clusters

long fruit stalks

Height: 33ft (10m)	Shape: Broadly conical	Leaf persistence: Evergreen	Leaf type:

Family: Aquifoliaceae	Species: *Ilex purpurea*	Author: Hassk.

Chinese Holly

Leaves Elliptic-lanceolate, to 4¾in (12cm) long and 1½in (4cm) across, tapered, toothed, glossy dark green above, paler beneath, smooth. ***Bark*** Gray, smooth. ***Flowers*** Males and females deep reddish lilac, the corona with four reflexed lobes, in the leaf axils and on the shoots, on separate plants in early to midsummer. ***Fruit*** A red berry, 5⁄16in (8mm) long.

NATIVE REGION China, Japan.
HABITAT Mountain woods.

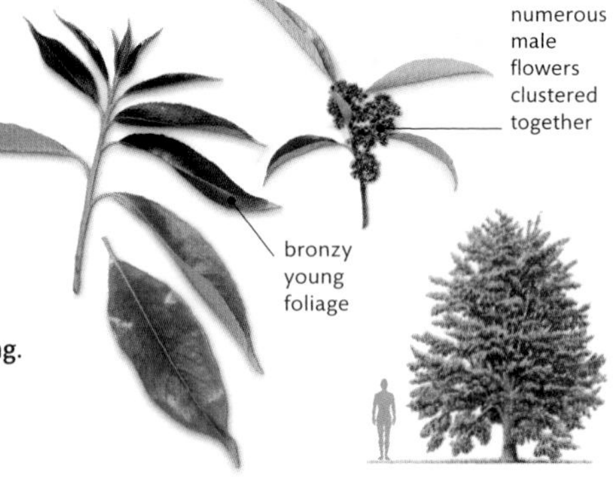

Height: 42ft (13m)	Shape: Broadly conical	Leaf persistence: Evergreen	Leaf type:

ARALIACEAE

WITH MORE THAN 40 GENERA, and about 1,450 species, this family of evergreen and deciduous trees, shrubs, and herbaceous plants is found all over the world, particularly in the tropics. The leaves are usually compound or lobed, and the small, greenish white or white flowers are borne in clusters.

Family: Araliaceae	Species: *Aralia spinosa*	Author: L.

Devil's Walking Stick

Leaves Bipinnate and very large, to 39in (1m) or more long, with numerous ovate, taper-pointed, toothed leaflets, to 3in (7.5cm) long and 1½in (4cm) across, bronze when young becoming dark green above, paler beneath, hairy on both sides, turning yellow to purple in fall, with a prickly stalk, carried on very stout, spiny shoots. ***Bark*** Gray, with stout prickles. ***Flowers*** Small and white, in small, rounded clusters, the clusters forming large heads, borne on a single main axis in late summer. ***Fruit*** Rounded and purple-black, ¼in (6mm) long.

NATIVE REGION E. US.
HABITAT Riverbanks and moist woods.
REMARK Also known as angelica tree, Hercules' club.

small, blackish fruits carried on red stalks

Aralia spinosa △▽

large leaves composed of numerous leaflets

▽ ***Aralia elata***
Commonly known as Japanese angelica tree, this similar species from Northeast Asia and Japan flowers in fall, when *Aralia spinosa* is in fruit.

flower clusters borne from one central stalk

flowers have exserted, yellow anthers

flower clusters borne on several main stalks that arise from a short stem

Height: 33ft (10m)	Shape: Broadly spreading	Leaf persistence: Deciduous	Leaf type:

Family: Araliaceae	Species: *Kalopanax septemlobus*	Author: (Thunb.) Koidz.

Castor Aralia

Leaves **Palmately lobed, with five to seven toothed lobes, to 10in (25cm) or more long and across, glossy dark green and smooth above, downy when young beneath, on long stalks.** ***Bark*** **Black-brown, spiny, deeply fissured.** ***Flowers*** **Individually small and white, numerous, with slender stalks, borne in large, rounded clusters in late summer.** ***Fruit*** **Rounded, blue-black, about 3/16in (5mm) long.**

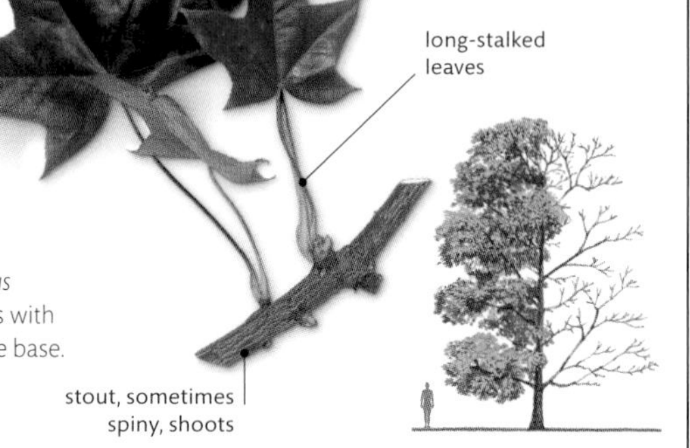

NATIVE REGION China, Eastern Russian Federation, Japan, Korea.
HABITAT Riverbanks and other moist places in forests.
REMARK The young leaves of this species are edible when cooked. The name *Kalopanax pictus* var. *maximowiczii* was previously used for plants with deeply lobed leaves cut more than halfway to the base.

Height: 25m (80ft)	Shape: Broadly columnar	Leaf persistence: Deciduous	Leaf type:

Family: Araliaceae	Species: *Pseudopanax ferox*	Author: Kirk

Toothed Lancewood

Leaves **On young plants narrow and rigid, to 18in (45cm) long, with sharp, hooked teeth at the margin, dark purple-green, with an orange midrib, pointing down; on mature plants to 6in (15cm) long, bluntly toothed or untoothed, carried upright to spreading.** ***Bark*** **Gray and smooth.** ***Flowers*** **Produced on mature plants only, small and greenish, borne in rounded heads at the ends of the shoots in summer.** ***Fruit*** **Oblong, black, 5/16in (8mm) across.**

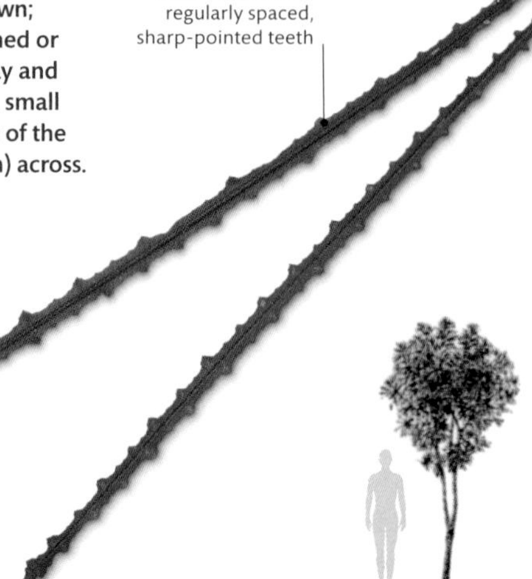

NATIVE REGION New Zealand.
HABITAT Forests and scrub.
REMARK The tree remains unbranched for many years, passing through several stages of growth, and slowly developing the small, rounded head of a mature plant. The related *Pseudopanax crassifolius* is commoner in the wild. This New Zealand native has even longer juvenile leaves, which may reach 39in (1m) or more.

Height: 17ft (5m)	Shape: Unique	Leaf persistence: Evergreen	Leaf type:

ARECACEAE

THE PALMS FORM A distinct group of about 180 genera and nearly 2,500 species of mainly tropical distribution. In the US, they are native to the southern States and California alone; Europe has two native species, in the western Mediterranean and in Crete.

Palms are trees or shrubs, sometimes climbing, that differ from other trees in several ways. With few exceptions, they have a single, unbranched stem which, once formed, does not increase in girth. The often very large leaves are mainly one of two types, either palmately divided, as in the fan palms (eg *Trachycarpus*), or pinnately divided, as in the feather palms (eg *Phoenix*). The small flowers have three sepals and three petals, and are often carried in very large, heavy clusters, males and females sometimes on separate plants.

Family: Arecaceae	Species: *Trachycarpus fortunei*	Author: (Hook.) H. Wendl.

Chusan Palm

Leaves Fan-shaped, to 4ft (120cm) across, segmented, dark green above, blue-green beneath. ***Bark*** Densely covered with brown, fibrous remnants of old leaves. ***Flowers*** Very small and yellow, fragrant, in large, drooping panicles, males and females, on separate plants in early summer. ***Fruit*** A rounded to kidney-shaped, three-lobed, blue-black berry, ½in (1.2cm) across.

NATIVE REGION C. and S. China, Myanmar.
HABITAT Mountain slopes.

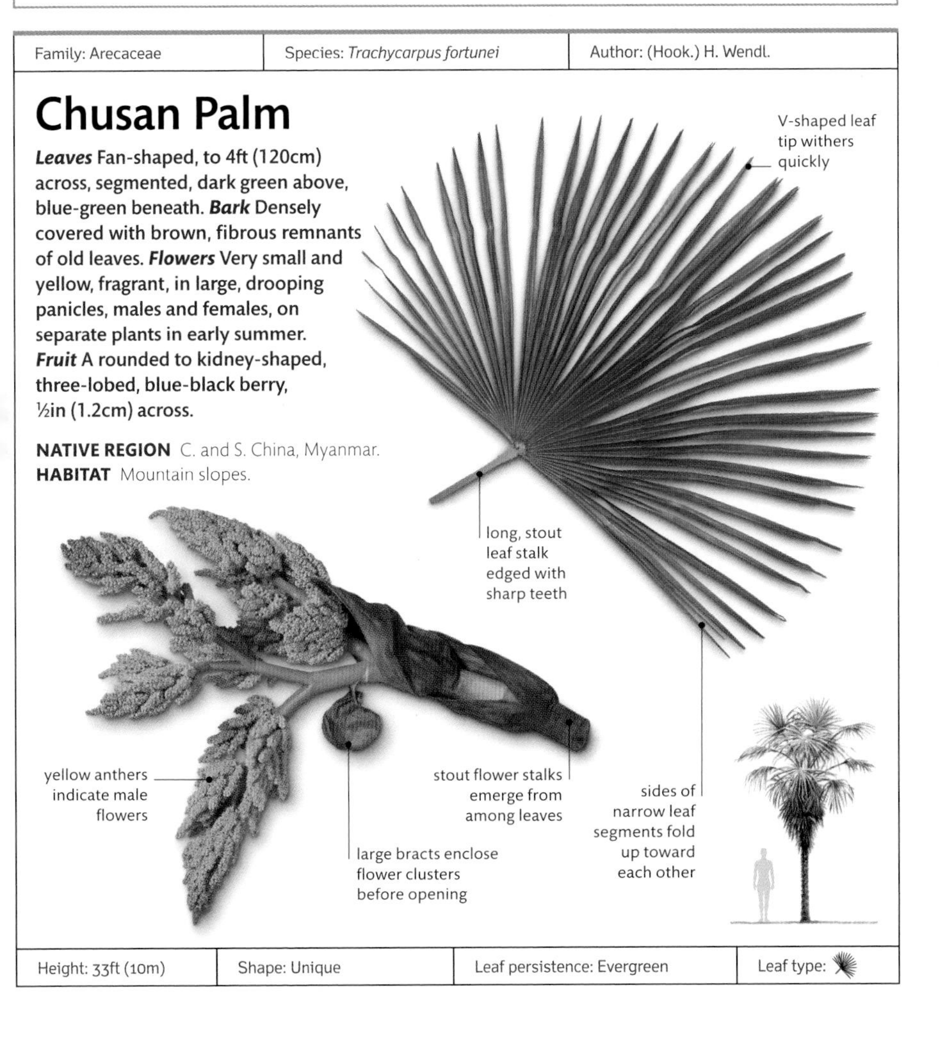

Height: 33ft (10m)	Shape: Unique	Leaf persistence: Evergreen	Leaf type:

BETULACEAE

SOME OF THE MOST WELL-KNOWN catkin-bearing plants belong to the birch family, which also includes the hazels (*Corylus*, see p.109). Its six genera and about 130 species of deciduous trees and shrubs grow wild mainly in northern temperate regions; alders (*Alnus*, see pp.98–99) extend to the Andes. The leaves are alternate. Male and female flowers are borne in separate catkins on the same plant, but only the males are conspicuous.

Family: Betulaceae	Species: *Alnus cordata*	Author: (Loisel.) Duby

Italian Alder

Leaves Rounded, to 4in (10cm) long and across, toothed, glossy dark green and smooth above, paler with hairs in the vein axils beneath. ***Bark*** Gray and smooth, shallowly fissured with age. ***Flowers*** In catkins, males to 3in (7.5cm) long, yellow, females small, red, upright, on the same plant in early spring. ***Fruit*** Woody, 1¼in (3cm) long, green ripening to brown.

NATIVE REGION Corsica, C. and S. Italy.
HABITAT Deciduous woods in mountains.

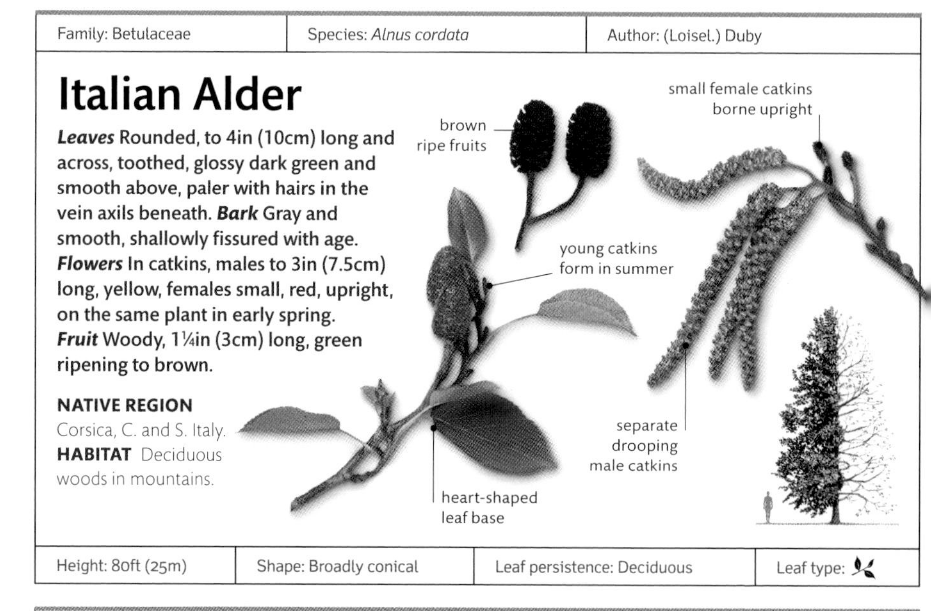

Height: 80ft (25m)	Shape: Broadly conical	Leaf persistence: Deciduous	Leaf type:

Family: Betulaceae	Species: *Alnus glutinosa*	Author: (L.) Gaertn.

Common Alder

Leaves Obovate, to 4in (10cm) long and about 3in (7.5cm) across, toothed, dark green and smooth above, with tufts of hairs in the vein axils beneath. ***Bark*** Dark gray and fissured. ***Flowers*** In catkins, males to 4in (10cm) long, yellow-green, drooping, females small, red, upright, separately on the same plant in early spring. ***Fruit*** Woody, dark brown, ¾in (2cm) long.

NATIVE REGION N. Africa, W. Asia, Europe.
HABITAT By rivers.

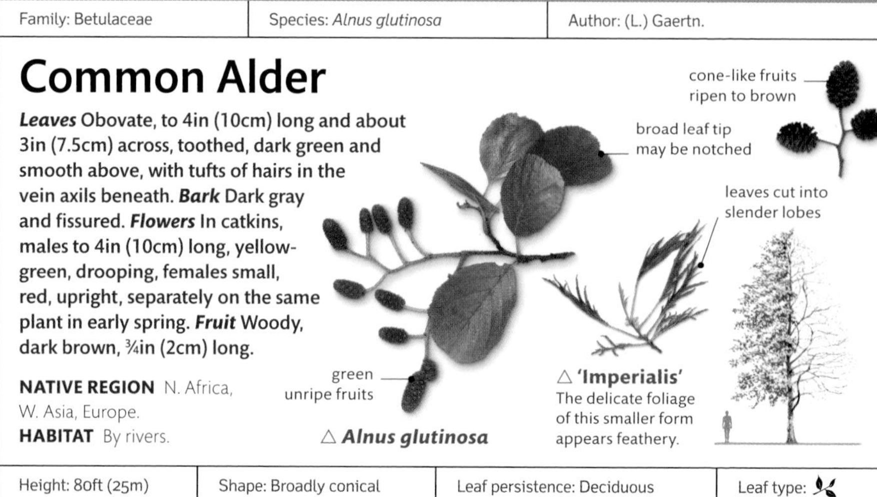

△ ***Alnus glutinosa***

△ **'Imperialis'**
The delicate foliage of this smaller form appears feathery.

Height: 80ft (25m)	Shape: Broadly conical	Leaf persistence: Deciduous	Leaf type:

Family: Betulaceae	Species: *Alnus incana*	Author: (L.) Moench

Gray Alder

Leaves Ovate, to 4in (10cm) long and 2in (5cm) across, with a pointed tip, double-toothed and sometimes shallowly lobed at the margin, dull dark green above and hairy at first, gray and downy beneath. ***Bark*** Dark gray, smooth. ***Flowers*** In catkins, males to 4in (10cm) long, reddish, drooping, females small, red, upright, borne separately on the same plant in late winter to early spring. ***Fruit*** Conelike, woody, to ¾in (2cm) long, green ripening to brown.

NATIVE REGION Caucasus, Europe.
HABITAT Mountains.

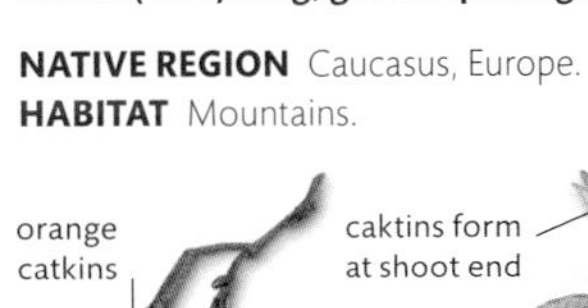

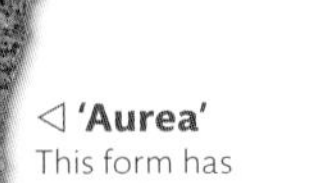

◁ **'Aurea'**
This form has yellow foliage and orange shoots

◁△ ***Alnus incana***

Height: 65ft (20m)	Shape: Broadly conical	Leaf persistence: Deciduous	Leaf type:

Family: Betulaceae	Species: *Alnus rubra*	Author: Bong.

Red Alder

Leaves Ovate to elliptic, to 4in (10cm) or more long and 3in (7.5cm) across, narrowed at the base, pointed at the tip, dark green and smooth or nearly so above, downy becoming blue-green and nearly smooth except for hair along the veins beneath. ***Bark*** Pale gray, rough and warty. ***Flowers*** In catkins, males to 6in (15cm) long, yellow-orange, drooping, females small, red, and upright, borne separately on the same plant in early spring. ***Fruit*** Conelike, woody, to 1in (2.5cm) long.

NATIVE REGION W. North America.
HABITAT Riverbanks and canyons in mountains and along the coast.
REMARK Resembles pale-barked birch species when seen from a distance.

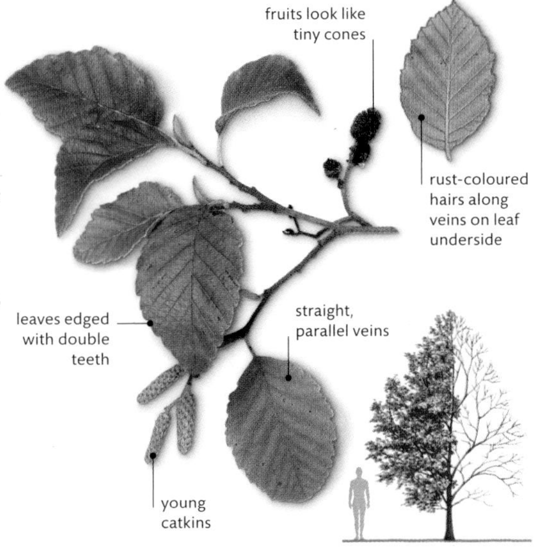

Height: 50ft (15m)	Shape: Broadly conical	Leaf persistence: Deciduous	Leaf type:

Family: Betulaceae	Species: *Betula alleghaniensis*	Author: Britton

Yellow Birch

Leaves Ovate-oblong, to 4in (10cm) or more long and 2in (5cm) across, pointed, toothed, becoming matte deep green above, paler beneath, turning yellow in fall, on aromatic shoots. ***Bark*** Yellow-brown, peeling horizontally. ***Flowers*** In catkins, males to 4in (10cm) long, yellow, females reddish green, on the same plant in spring. ***Fruit*** A stout, erect catkin, breaking up when ripe.

NATIVE REGION E. North America.
HABITAT Moist woods.

Height: 100ft (30m)	Shape: Broadly columnar	Leaf persistence: Deciduous	Leaf type:

Family: Betulaceae	Species: *Betula ermanii*	Author: Cham.

Gold Birch

Leaves Ovate, to 3in (7.5cm) long and 2in (5cm) across, pointed, toothed, glossy green and smooth above, with hairy veins beneath, turning yellow in fall. ***Bark*** Creamy white, with horizontal lenticels, peeling in papery strips. ***Flowers*** In catkins, males to 4in (10cm) long, yellowish, drooping, females green, upright, separately on the same plant in spring. ***Fruit*** A catkin, breaking up when ripe.

coarsely toothed
leaf margin

NATIVE REGION N.E. Asia, Japan.
HABITAT Mountain forests.

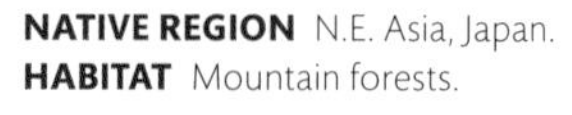

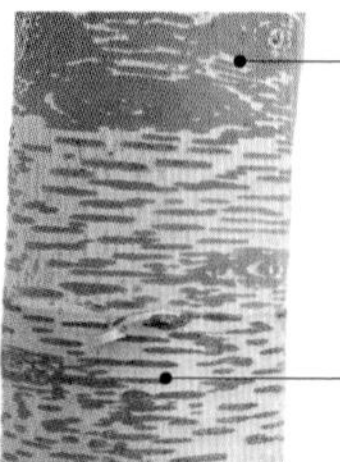

Height: 80ft (25m)	Shape: Broadly conical	Leaf persistence: Deciduous	Leaf type:

Family: Betulaceae	Species: *Betula grossa*	Author: Siebold & Zucc.

Japanese Cherry Birch

Leaves **Ovate, to 4in (10cm) long and 2in (5cm) across, taper-pointed at the tip, usually heart-shaped at the base, coarsely toothed, dark green above, silky-hairy on the veins beneath, turning yellow in fall, on aromatic shoots.** ***Bark*** **Reddish, with horizontal bands, becoming dark gray with age.** ***Flowers*** **In catkins, males to 1in (2.5cm) long, yellow, drooping, females green, upright, separately on the same plant in spring.** ***Fruit*** **An erect catkin, breaking up when ripe.**

NATIVE REGION Japan.
HABITAT Mountain forests.
REMARK The species is closely related to the North American cherry birch (*Betula lenta*, see below), which has similar bark and aromatic shoots.

Height: 65ft (20m)	Shape: Broadly conical	Leaf persistence: Deciduous	Leaf type:

Family: Betulaceae	Species: *Betula lenta*	Author: L.

Cherry Birch

Leaves **Ovate, to 4¾in (12cm) long and 2½in (6cm) across, taper-pointed, sharply toothed, glossy dark green above, paler and silky-hairy beneath, at least when young, turning yellow in fall, carried on aromatic shoots.** ***Bark*** **Red-brown, with pale, horizontal lenticels, becoming dark and furrowed.** ***Flowers*** **In catkins, males to 3in (7.5cm) long, yellow, drooping, females green, upright, separately on the same plant in spring.** ***Fruit*** **An erect catkin, breaking up when ripe.**

NATIVE REGION E. North America.
HABITAT Moist woods at low altitude in the north to mountains in the south of its native region.
REMARK Also known as black birch, sweet birch.

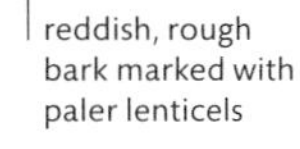

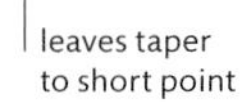

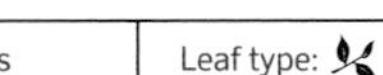

Height: 80ft (25m)	Shape: Broadly spreading	Leaf persistence: Deciduous	Leaf type:

Family: Betulaceae	Species: *Betula maximowicziana*	Author: Regel

Monarch Birch

Leaves **Broadly ovate, to 6in (15cm) long and 4¾in (12cm) across, deeply heart-shaped at the base, taper-pointed at the tip, sharply and doubly toothed, dark green and smooth above, turning yellow in fall, carried on warty shoots.** ***Bark*** **Reddish brown at first becoming grayish white tinged orange-yellow and pink, with horizontal lenticels, peeling in papery strips.** ***Flowers*** **In catkins, males to 4in (10cm) long, yellow-brown, drooping, females green, clustered together, spreading to drooping, borne separately on the same plant in late winter.** ***Fruit*** **A pendulous catkin, breaking up when ripe.**

NATIVE REGION C. and N. Japan.
HABITAT Woods.
REMARK Also known as Japanese red birch. The leaves are larger than those of any other birch.

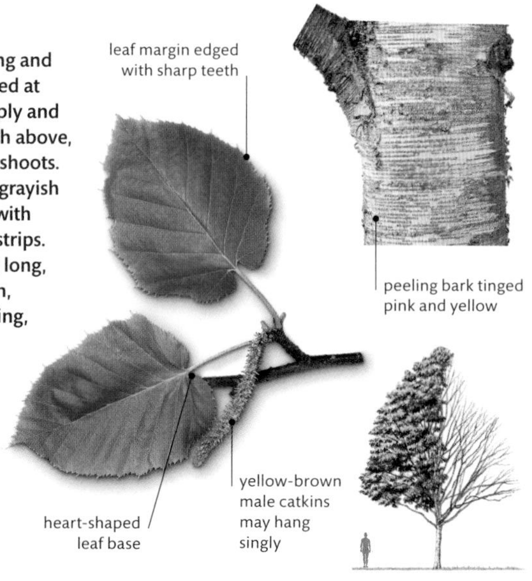

Height: 80ft (25m)	Shape: Broadly conical	Leaf persistence: Deciduous	Leaf type:

Family: Betulaceae	Species: *Betula nigra*	Author: L.

River Birch

Leaves **To 4in (10cm) long, tapered at the base, pointed at the tip, double-toothed, deep blue-green and smooth above, blue-gray with hairs on the veins beneath.** ***Bark*** **Pink-gray, peeling, dark brown and ridged with age.** ***Flowers*** **In catkins, males to 3in (7.5cm) long, yellow-brown, females green, on the same plant in spring.** ***Fruit*** **A catkin, breaking up when ripe.**

NATIVE REGION E. US.
HABITAT Wet woods and by streams.

Height: 100ft (30m)	Shape: Broadly spreading	Leaf persistence: Deciduous	Leaf type: 

Family: Betulaceae	Species: *Betula papyrifera*	Author: Marshall

Paper Birch

Leaves Ovate, to 4in (10cm) long and 7.5cm (3in) across, taper-pointed, toothed, dark green above, paler and with hairs on the veins beneath, at least when young, turning yellow to orange in fall. ***Bark*** White, with conspicuous dark lenticels, peeling in thin layers; pale pinkish orange when freshly exposed. ***Flowers*** In catkins, males to 4in (10cm) long, yellow, drooping, females slender, green, spreading or drooping, borne separately on the same plant in spring. ***Fruit*** A catkin, breaking up when ripe.

NATIVE REGION North America.
HABITAT Woods in northerly latitudes and on mountains.
REMARK Also known as canoe birch. The bark was used by Native Americans to make canoes, which gives the alternative common name. This most widespread of the American birches occurs from Labrador to Alaska and in the northern United States.

smooth leaf upperside

green fruiting catkins droop

leaf margin edged with small teeth

male catkins hang down from shoot tip

leaves turn from green to yellow and orange in fall

bark spotted with dark, horizontal lenticels

paler leaf underside has hairy veins

female catkins hang at an angle

peeling bark reveals orange-pink layer beneath

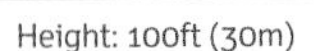

Height: 100ft (30m)	Shape: Broadly conical	Leaf persistence: Deciduous	Leaf type:

Family: Betulaceae	Species: *Betula pendula*	Author: Roth

Silver Birch

Leaves **Ovate to triangular, to 2½in (6cm) long and 1½in (4cm) across, taper-pointed, coarsely double-toothed, glossy dark green above, turning yellow in fall, carried on slender, hairless, warty, pendulous shoots. *Bark* White, developing dark, rugged cracks at the base with age. *Flowers* In catkins, males to 2½in (6cm) long, yellow, drooping, females green, upright or drooping, borne separately on the same plant in early spring. *Fruit* A catkin, breaking up when ripe.**

NATIVE REGION N. Asia, Europe.
HABITAT Light, especially sandy, soil.
REMARK Also known as European white birch. Forms extensive woods in its habitat.

pendulous male catkins

female catkins may be erect or drooping

leaves edged with large, double teeth

◁△▽ ***Betula pendula***

bark at base of trunk develops dark cracks

fruiting catkins droop

'Laciniata' ▷
The small, slender leaves of the Swedish birch are cut into tapered, finely toothed lobes.

deeply cut leaves

leaves carried on red stalks

'Purpurea' △
This ornamental form is selected for its deep purple foliage and red leaf stalks. The bark also develops a purple tinge.

Height: 100ft (30m)	Shape: Narrowly weeping	Leaf persistence: Deciduous	Leaf type:

Family: Betulaceae	Species: *Betula populifolia*	Author: Marshall

Gray Birch

Leaves **Ovate to triangular, to 3in (7.5cm) long, ending in a long, tapered point, sharply toothed, glossy dark green and slightly rough above, turning yellow in fall.** ***Bark*** **White, with black marks under the branches, not peeling, becoming black at the base with age.** ***Flowers*** **In catkins, males to 3in (7.5cm) long, yellow-brown, drooping, females green, upright, borne separately on the same plant in spring.** ***Fruit*** **A catkin, breaking up when ripe.**

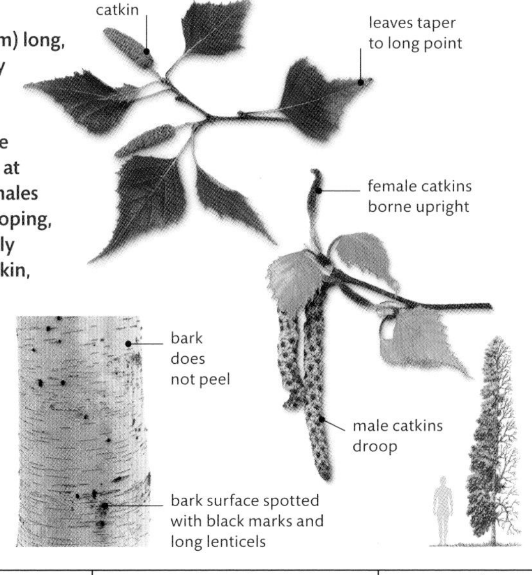

NATIVE REGION E. North America.
HABITAT Mountain woods.
REMARK Also known as white birch. Grows in the wild from Nova Scotia, Canada to N. Carolina, US. The trees are often branched from the base, and are usually fast-growing, small, and short-lived.

Height: 33ft (10m)	Shape: Narrowly conical	Leaf persistence: Deciduous	Leaf type:

Family: Betulaceae	Species: *Betula pubescens*	Author: Ehrh.

Downy Birch

Leaves **Rounded to ovate, to 2½in (6cm) long and 2in (5cm) across, pointed, with regular, single teeth, dark green and downy at least when young above and on the veins beneath, turning yellow in fall, carried on downy shoots.** ***Bark*** **White to the base.** ***Flowers*** **In catkins, males to 2½in (6cm) long, yellow, drooping, females green, upright, borne separately on the same plant in spring.** ***Fruit*** **A catkin, breaking up when ripe.**

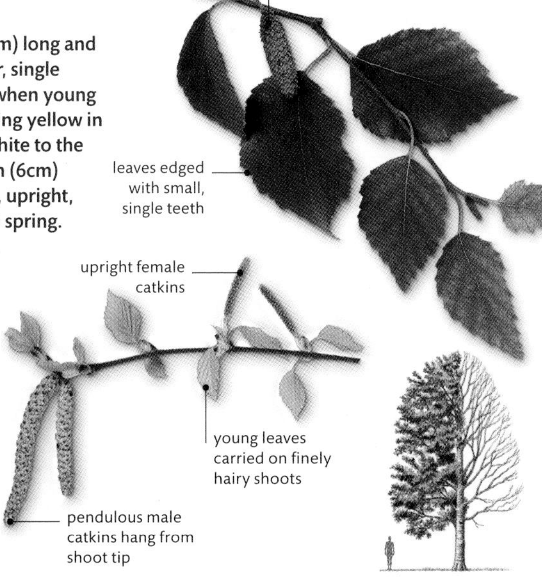

NATIVE REGION N. Asia, Europe.
HABITAT Woods.
REMARK Also known as white birch. The species is related to the silver birch (*Betula pendula*, see p.104), but is easily distinguished by its shoots, which are hairy and not pendulous. In its habitat, it especially favors poor soil and wet ground.

Height: 80ft (25m)	Shape: Broadly conical	Leaf persistence: Deciduous	Leaf type: 

Family: Betulaceae	Species: *Betula utilis*	Author: D. Don

Himalayan Birch

Leaves **Ovate, to 4in (10cm) long and 2½in (6cm) across, taper-pointed, toothed, dark sometimes glossy green above, downy on the veins beneath, turning a rich, golden yellow in fall, on downy shoots. *Bark* Very variable, glossy orange-brown or dark copper-brown to pinkish or pure white, paper-thin and peeling. *Flowers* In catkins, males yellow and drooping, to 4¾in (12cm) or more long, females green and upright, in spring. *Fruit* A catkin, green ripening to brown, breaking up when ripe.**

NATIVE REGION China, Himalayas.
HABITAT High mountain forests.
REMARK Subsp. *albosinensis*, from W. China, was previously known as *Betula albosinensis*. It has orange-red to coppery red bark peeling in thin strips, cream when freshly exposed.

△ ***Betula utilis***

◁▽ ***Betula utilis***

△ **subsp. *jacquemontii***
This subspecies, also known as *Betula jacquemontii*, occurs in the Himalayas from Nepal to Afghanistan, and has white bark. The leaves vary, and three different selections are shown.

subsp. *jacquemontii* 'Silver Shadow' ▷
A form with large and drooping, dark green leaves.

◁ **subsp. *jacquemontii* 'Grayswood Ghost'**
Very glossy leaves distinguish this attractive form.

◁ **subsp. *jacquemontii* 'Jermyns'**
This vigorous variety has broad leaves.

Height: 80ft (25m)	Shape: Broadly conical	Leaf persistence: Deciduous	Leaf type:

◁△ *Betula albosinensis* var. *septentrionalis*
This form is distinguished by its matte, rather than glossy, green leaves, and coppery to gray-pink bark.

Family: Betulaceae	Species: *Carpinus betulus*	Author: L.

Hornbeam

Leaves **Ovate-oblong, to 4in (10cm) long and 2½in (6cm) across, pointed, double-toothed, with conspicuous veins, dark green and smooth above, downy on the veins beneath, turning yellow in fall. *Bark* Pale gray, fluted, fissured with age. *Flowers* In catkins, males to 2in (5cm) long, yellowish, drooping, females small, green, at the tips of the shoots, borne separately on the same plant in spring. *Fruit* A nut, with three-lobed bracts, the bracts green turning yellowish brown, clustered in pendulous catkins, to 3in (7.5cm) long.**

NATIVE REGION S.W. Asia, Europe.
HABITAT Hedgerows and broadleaf woods.
REMARK A common hedging plant.

leaf margin edged with double teeth

fruit bracts colored green in summer

three-lobed, usually untoothed, bract surrounds each fruit

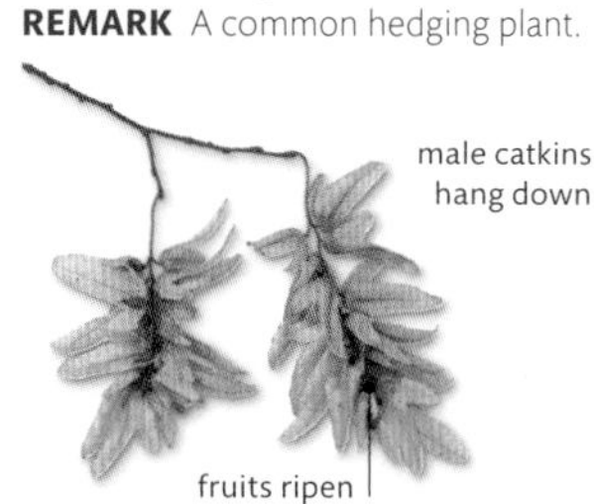

male catkins hang down

female catkins at shoot tip

Height: 100ft (30m)	Shape: Broadly spreading	Leaf persistence: Deciduous	Leaf type:

Family: Betulaceae	Species: *Carpinus caroliniana*	Author: Walter

American Hornbeam

Leaves **Ovate, to 4in (10cm) long, taper-pointed at the tip, double-toothed, dark green, turning orange to red in autumn, on slender shoots. *Bark* Gray, smooth, and fluted. *Flowers* In catkins, males to 1½in (4cm) long, yellowish, drooping, females small, green, at the tips of the shoots, borne separately on the same plant in spring. *Fruit* A nut, with two- or three-lobed, green bracts, clustered in pendulous catkins, to 3in (7.5cm) long.**

NATIVE REGION Mexico, E. North America.
HABITAT Moist woods, riverbanks, and swamps.
REMARK Also known as blue beech, water beech. Similar to beech (*Fagus*, see pp.145-147), but distinguished by its fruit.

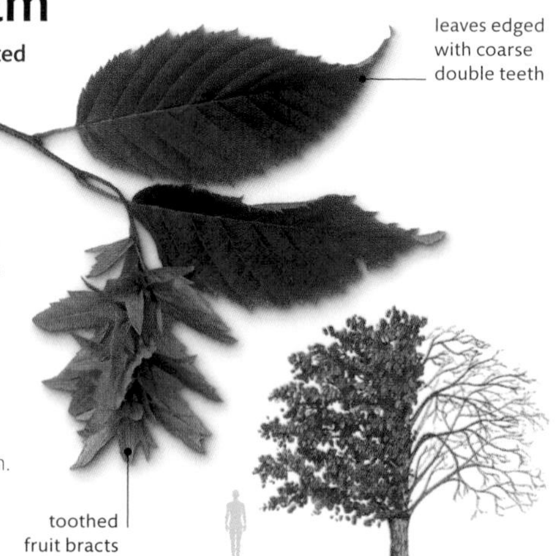

Height: 33ft (10m)	Shape: Broadly spreading	Leaf persistence: Deciduous	Leaf type:

Family: Betulaceae	Species: *Carpinus cordata*	Author: Blume

Sawa Hornbeam

Leaves Oblong-ovate, to 4¾in (12cm) long and 3in (7.5cm) across, heart-shaped at the base, pointed, toothed, deep green above, smooth. ***Bark*** Gray-brown, smooth, furrowed and scaly with age. ***Flowers*** In catkins, males to 2in (5cm) long, yellowish, females small, green, at the tips of the shoots, separately on the same plant in spring. ***Fruit*** A nut, with green bracts, in hanging catkins, to 4in (10cm) long.

NATIVE REGION Japan.
HABITAT Mountain woods.

female catkin
male catkin
overlapping, toothed fruit bracts

Height: 50ft (15m)	Shape: Broadly columnar	Leaf persistence: Deciduous	Leaf type:

Family: Betulaceae	Species: *Carpinus japonica*	Author: Blume

Japanese Hornbeam

Leaves Ovate-oblong, to 4in (10cm) long and 1½in (4cm) across, pointed, toothed, dark green and smooth above, turning yellow in fall. ***Bark*** Gray, smooth, dark brown, and scaly with age. ***Flowers*** In catkins, males to 2in (5cm) long, yellowish, females small, green, at the tips of the shoots, on the same plant in spring. ***Fruit*** A nut, with toothed bracts, in catkins, to 2½in (6cm) long.

NATIVE REGION Japan.
HABITAT Woods and thickets.

numerous parallel veins either side of midrib
hairy leaf underside
male catkins
unlobed, toothed fruit bracts

Height: 50ft (15m)	Shape: Broadly spreading	Leaf persistence: Deciduous	Leaf type:

Family: Betulaceae	Species: *Corylus colurna*	Author: L.

Turkish Hazel

Leaves Broadly oval, to 6in (15cm) long and 4in (10cm) across, heart-shaped at the base, coarsely double-toothed, dark green and nearly smooth above, downy on the veins beneath, turning yellow in fall. ***Bark*** Gray and corky. ***Flowers*** In catkins, males to 3in (7.5cm) long, yellow, drooping, females very small, red, separately on the same plant in late winter to early spring. ***Fruit*** An edible nut, enclosed in a deeply lobed husk.

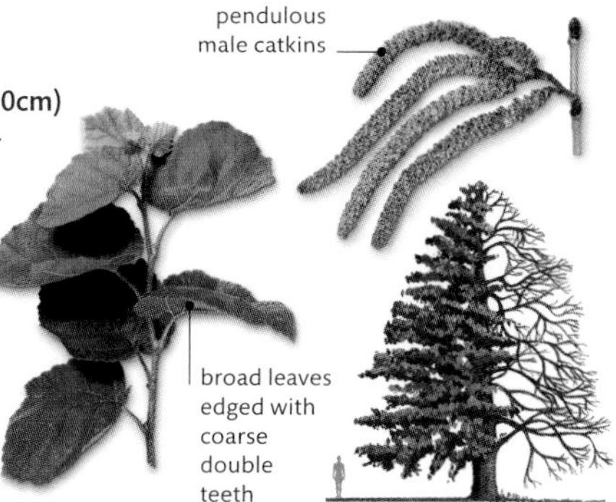

NATIVE REGION S.W. Asia, S.E. Europe.
HABITAT Shady mountain forests.

Height: 80ft (25m)	Shape: Broadly conical	Leaf persistence: Deciduous	Leaf type:

Family: Betulaceae	Species: *Ostrya carpinifolia*	Author: Scop.

Hop Hornbeam

Leaves Ovate, to 4in (10cm) long and 2in (5cm) across, pointed, double-toothed, dark green above, sparsely hairy on both sides. ***Bark*** Gray and smooth, becoming brown and flaking with age. ***Flowers*** In catkins, males to 3in (7.5cm) long, yellow, drooping, females small, green, borne separately on the same plant in spring. ***Fruit*** A nut, enclosed in a bladderlike, creamy husk, in pendulous clusters, to 2in (5cm) long.

NATIVE REGION W. Asia, S. Europe.
HABITAT Low forests in mountains.

hairy leaf underside
double-toothed leaf margin
fruit clusters look like hops
drooping male catkins

Height: 65ft (20m)	Shape: Broadly conical	Leaf persistence: Deciduous	Leaf type:

Family: Betulaceae	Species: *Ostrya japonica*	Author: Sarg.

Japanese Hop Hornbeam

Leaves Ovate, to 4¾in (12cm) long and 2in (5cm) across, taper-pointed, sharply toothed, dark green above, softly hairy on both sides. ***Bark*** Gray-brown and scaly. ***Flowers*** In catkins, males to 3in (7.5cm) long, yellow, drooping, females very small, green, borne separately on the same plant in spring. ***Fruit*** A nut, enclosed in a bladderlike, creamy husk, borne in pendulous clusters, to 2in (5cm) long.

NATIVE REGION China, Japan, Korea.
HABITAT Mountain woods.

fruit husk turns brown before falling
male catkins
female catkins

Height: 80ft (25m)	Shape: Broadly conical	Leaf persistence: Deciduous	Leaf type:

Family: Betulaceae	Species: *Ostrya virginiana*	Author: (Mill.) K. Koch

Ironwood

Leaves Ovate, to 4¾in (12cm) long and 2in (5cm) across, pointed, toothed, dark green and smooth above, with tufts of hair in the vein axils beneath. ***Bark*** Gray-brown and scaly. ***Flowers*** In catkins, males to 2in (5cm) long, yellow, drooping, females small, green, borne separately on the same plant in spring. ***Fruit*** A nut, enclosed in a bladderlike, creamy husk, borne in hanging clusters, to 2½in (6cm) long.

NATIVE REGION E. North America to C. America.
HABITAT Woods.
REMARK Also known as American hop hornbeam.

husk opens to release small nut
leaf margin edged with coarse teeth

 Height: 65ft (20m)	Shape: Broadly conical	Leaf persistence: Deciduous	Leaf type: 

BIGNONIACEAE

THIS IS A LARGELY TROPICAL family, with evergreen and deciduous trees, shrubs, a few herbaceous plants, and many climbers. It comprises about 80 genera and nearly 800 species, widely distributed, found particularly in South America. The leaves are often compound, and are arranged in whorls or in opposite pairs. The tubular flowers end in an often frilly petalled, flared bell.

Family: Bignoniaceae	Species: *Catalpa bignonioides*	Author: Walter

Indian Bean Tree

Leaves Broadly ovate, to 10in (25cm) long and 8in (20cm) across, heart-shaped at the base, short-pointed at the tip, occasionally lobed, untoothed, tinged purple and downy when young becoming light green and smooth above, paler and downy beneath, carried on long stalks. ***Bark*** Gray-brown and scaly. ***Flowers*** Bell-shaped, 2in (5cm) long, two-lipped, white, with yellow and purple spots, borne in large panicles in mid- to late summer. ***Fruit*** A slender, beanlike, hanging pod, to 16in (40cm) long, with inedible seeds, long-persistent.

NATIVE REGION S.E. US.
HABITAT Stream banks and low woods.
REMARK Also known as southern catalpa.

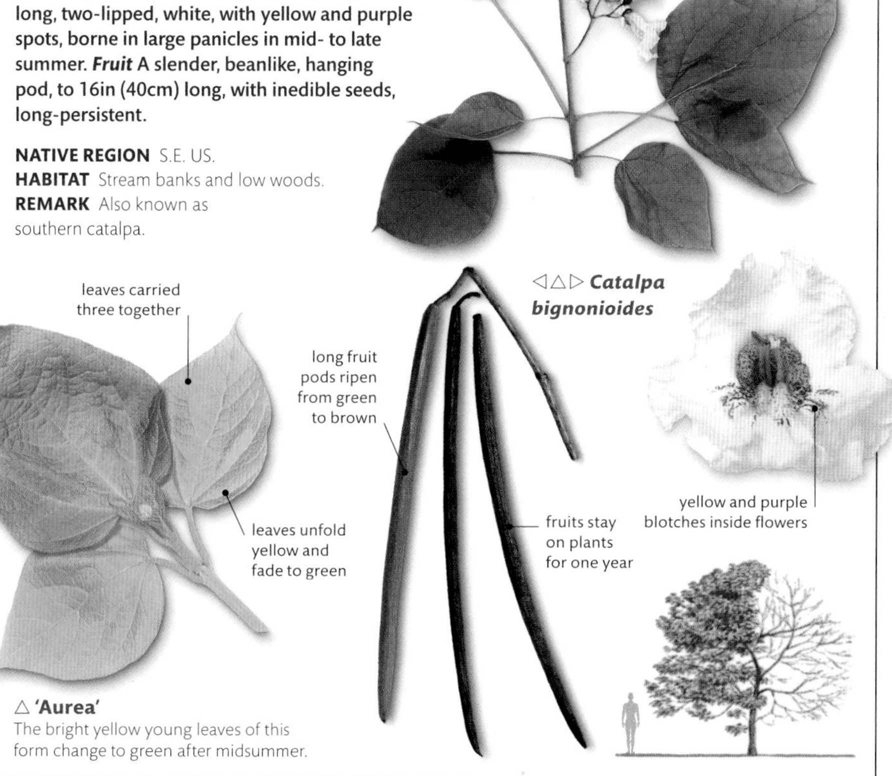

◁△▷ ***Catalpa bignonioides***

△ **'Aurea'**
The bright yellow young leaves of this form change to green after midsummer.

Height: 50ft (15m)	Shape: Broadly spreading	Leaf persistence: Deciduous	Leaf type: 

Family: Bignoniaceae	Species: *Catalpa bungei*	Author: C.A. Mey.

Bunge's Catalpa

Leaves **Broadly ovate, to 6in (15cm) long and 4¾in (12cm) across, sometimes with one or two taper-pointed side lobes, bronze when young becoming rather glossy green, usually downy beneath.** ***Bark*** **Dark gray, peeling in rectangular places; pale gray-pink when freshly exposed.** ***Flowers*** **Bell-shaped, 2in (5cm) long, pink, with purple spots and a yellow blotch, in clusters in midsummer.** ***Fruit*** **A beanlike, hanging pod, to 18in (45cm) long.**

NATIVE REGION China.
HABITAT Open situations in mountains.
REMARK Also known as *Catalpa fargesii.*

pink flowers borne in dense clusters

very long, slender point at leaf tip

leaves may have one or two side lobes

Height: 65ft (20m)	Shape: Broadly columnar	Leaf persistence: Deciduous	Leaf type:

Family: Bignoniaceae	Species: *Catalpa* x *erubescens*	Author: Carrière

Catalpa x erubescens

Leaves **Three-lobed, to 12in (30cm) long and 10in (25cm) or more across, untoothed, bronze becoming light green.** ***Bark*** **Gray-brown, with scaly ridges.** ***Flowers*** **Bell-shaped, 1½in (4cm) long, white, with yellow and purple spots, fragrant, in large panicles in late summer.** ***Fruit*** **A bean-like, hanging pod, to 16in (40cm) long.**

NATIVE REGION Of garden origin.
REMARK A hybrid between Indian bean tree (*Catalpa bignonioides*, see p.111) and the Chinese *Catalpa ovata*. 'Purpurea,' shown here, has black-purple young foliage.

leaves cut into three shallow lobes

flower petals splashed yellow and purple

ripe pods split open to release seeds

◁△ **'Purpurea'**

flower clusters form at end of shoots

deep purple young leaves mature to dark green

Height: 50ft (15m) 	Shape: Broadly spreading	Leaf persistence: Deciduous	Leaf type: 

Family: Bignoniaceae	Species: *Catalpa speciosa*	Author: Teas

Western Catalpa

Leaves Broadly ovate, to 12in (30cm) long and 8in (20cm) across, with a long, tapering point at the tip, glossy dark green and downy when young becoming smooth above, downy beneath, carried on long stalks. ***Bark*** Gray, scaly and fissured. ***Flowers*** Bell-shaped, 2in (5cm) long, white, spotted with yellow and some purple, borne in large panicles in summer. ***Fruit*** Slender, beanlike, and hanging, to 18in (45cm) long, persisting on the plant until the following year.

NATIVE REGION US.
HABITAT Riverbanks, damp woods, and swamps.

each cluster has few flowers

fruits ripen in late summer, but fall next year

long-stalked leaves can be opposite or in threes

Height: 130ft (40m)	Shape: Broadly columnar	Leaf persistence: Deciduous	Leaf type: 

BUXACEAE

THE PLANT KNOWN AS the common box (*Buxus sempervirens*) is the most familiar tree in this family, which contains six genera, with more than 130 species of evergreen trees, shrubs, and the occasional herbaceous plant. They usually have opposite leaves, and small flowers borne in clusters.

Family: Buxaceae	Species: *Buxus sempervirens*	Author: L.

Common Box

Leaves Ovate to oblong, to 1in (2.5cm) long and ⅜in (1cm) across, notched at the tip, glossy dark green above, paler beneath, on four-angled shoots. ***Bark*** Gray and smooth, cracking into small squares with age. ***Flowers*** Males and females both small and green, males with conspicuous, yellow anthers, separate but in the same cluster, in the leaf axils in early spring. ***Fruit*** A small, woody, green capsule, to ⁵⁄₁₆in (8mm) long.

NATIVE REGION N. Africa, S.W. Asia, Europe.
HABITAT Usually alkaline soil.
REMARK Can be either a small tree or a large shrub, producing very hard, close-grained, yellow wood. In cultivation, it is traditionally used as a hedging plant, and for topiary.

stigma become horns on fruit

male flowers have yellow anthers

female flowers have three stigmas

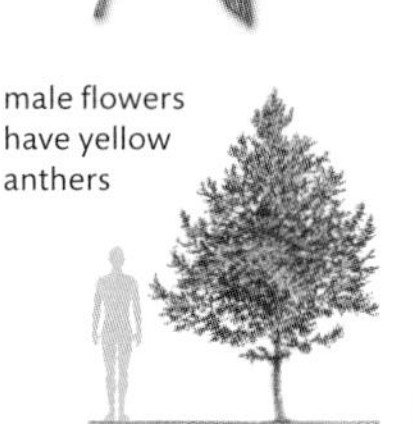

Height: 20ft (6m)	Shape: Broadly conical	Leaf persistence: Evergreen	Leaf type: 

CANNABACEAE

THE NINE GENERA and more than 100 species of deciduous and evergreen trees and shrubs and herbaceous plants in this family are widely distributed in temperate and tropical regions. The flowers are usually small, males and females sometimes separate, on the same or different plants. The family contains the well-known herbaceous plants hop (*Humulus lupulus*) and hemp (*Cannabis sativa*). The species below were previously included in the family Ulmaceae.

Family: Cannabaceae	Species: *Celtis australis*	Author: L.

Southern Nettle Tree

Leaves Lanceolate to ovate, to 6in (15cm) long and 2in (5cm) across, slender-pointed at the tip, light to dark green and roughly hairy above, gray-green and softly hairy beneath. ***Bark*** Pale gray, smooth. ***Flowers*** Males and females both small and green, without petals, either singly or in small clusters in the leaf axils, separately on the same plant in spring. ***Fruit*** Rounded, berrylike, about ⅜in (1cm) across, nearly black when ripe.

NATIVE REGION S.W. Asia, S. Europe, N. Africa.
HABITAT Warm, dry, rocky slopes.

rough upper leaf surface

base of leaf is three-veined

leaves edged with sharp teeth

Height: 65ft (20m)	Shape: Broadly columnar	Leaf persistence: Deciduous	Leaf type:

Family: Cannabaceae	Species: *Celtis laevigata*	Author: Willd.

Mississippi Hackberry

Leaves Narrrowly ovate, to 4in (10cm) long and 1½in (4cm) across, with three veins, often oblique at the base, taper-pointed at the tip, untoothed or with few teeth, rather pale green, smooth. ***Bark*** Pale gray, smooth, with corky lenticels. ***Flowers*** Males and females both small and green, without petals, either singly or in small clusters in the leaf axils, separately on the same plant in spring. ***Fruit*** Rounded, berrylike, edible, and orange-red to purple, about 5⁄16in (8mm) across.

NATIVE REGION N. Mexico, S. US.
HABITAT Moist flood plains and woods.
REMARK The form shown was regarded as var. *smallii*, with more prominently toothed leaves.

leaves taper to fine point

leaves are smooth on both sides

Height: 80ft (25m)	Shape: Broadly columnar	Leaf persistence: Deciduous	Leaf type:

Family: Cannabaceae	Species: *Celtis occidentalis*	Author: L.

Hackberry

Leaves **Ovate, to 4¾in (12cm) long and 2½in (6cm) across, with three veins, often oblique at the base, taper-pointed, toothed, mid- to dark green, smooth or rough above, hairy beneath.** ***Bark*** **Gray and smooth, with corky warts, furrowed and scaly with age.** ***Flowers*** **Males and females both small and green, without petals, singly or in small clusters in the leaf axils, separately on the same plant in spring.** ***Fruit*** **Rounded, berrylike, edible, and orange-red to purple, about ⅜in (1cm) across.**

glossy upper leaf surface

NATIVE REGION E. Canada, E. US.
HABITAT Rich woods and hill slopes.
REMARK Can be either a tree or a shrub.

lower half of leaves is untoothed

base of leaf has three veins

Height: 80ft (25m)	Shape: Broadly columnar	Leaf persistence: Deciduous	Leaf type:

CELASTRACEAE

THIS WIDESPREAD FAMILY contains nearly 100 genera and over 1,000 species of evergreen and deciduous trees, shrubs, herbs, and climbing plants. The leaves are opposite or alternate, and the flowers usually small and greenish.

Family: Celastraceae	Species: *Euonymus europaeus*	Author: L.

Spindle Tree

Leaves **Elliptic to ovate or lanceolate, to 3¼in (8cm) long and 1¼in (3cm) across, taper-pointed, finely toothed, dark green above, paler beneath, usually turning red in fall.** ***Bark*** **Gray and smooth.** ***Flowers*** **Males and females both small and greenish white, with four petals, borne in clusters of up to 10 in the leaf axils, sometimes on separate plants in late spring to early summer.** ***Fruit*** **Bright pink, about ½in (1.2cm) across, the four lobes opening to reveal bright orange-coated seeds.**

NATIVE REGION W. Asia, Europe.
HABITAT Woods, thickets, and hedgerows.

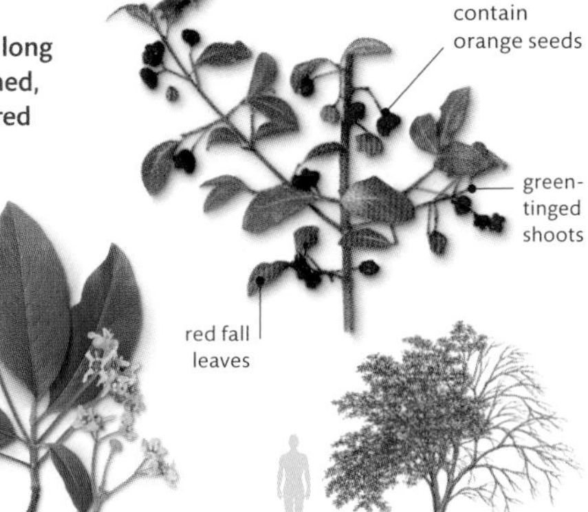

Height: 20ft (6m)	Shape: Broadly spreading	Leaf persistence: Deciduous	Leaf type: 

Family: Celastraceae	Species: *Maytenus boaria*	Author: Molina

Maiten

Leaves Narrowly elliptic to lanceolate, to 2in (5cm) long and ¾in (2cm) across, pointed at the tip, finely toothed, pale green becoming glossy dark green above, paler beneath, on drooping shoots. ***Bark*** Gray and smooth, with narrow vertical fissures, peeling at the base; orange when freshly exposed. ***Flowers*** Very small and pale green, with yellow anthers, borne in clusters in the leaf axils in mid- to late spring. ***Fruit*** A small, orange-red capsule.

NATIVE REGION South America.
HABITAT Open situations in mountains.
REMARK In its native regions the leaves are eaten by cattle.

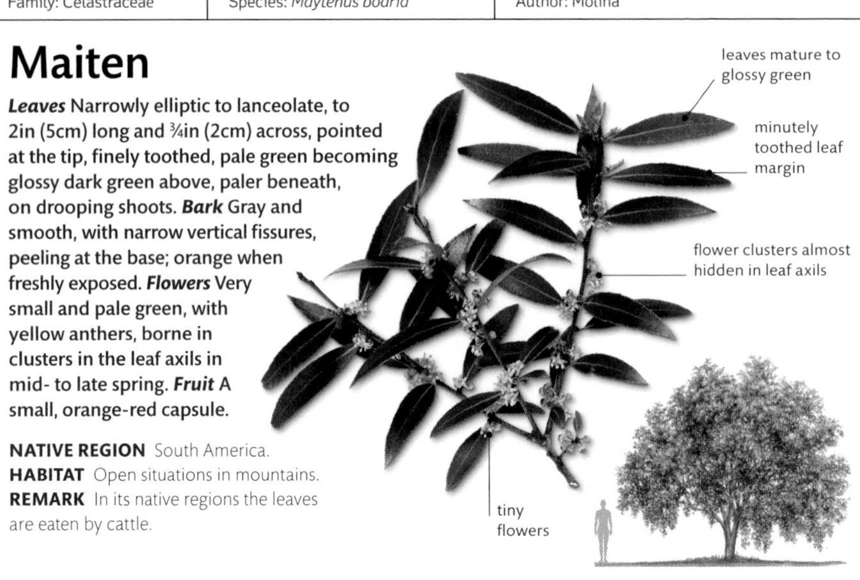

Height: 65ft (20m)	Shape: Broadly weeping	Leaf persistence: Evergreen	Leaf type: 

CERCIDIPHYLLACEAE

THERE ARE ONLY two species and one genus in this family. The species were once thought to be related to the magnolias (*Magnolia*, see pp.175–187), and were classified with them, but are now regarded as plants of primitive origin, and more closely related to the Hamamelidaceae (see p.165).

Family: Cercidiphyllaceae	Species: *Cercidiphyllum japonicum*	Author: J.J. Hoffm. & J.H. Schult. Bis

Katsura Tree

Leaves Rounded, to 3in (7.5cm) long and across, heart-shaped at the base, with rounded teeth, bronzy becoming blue-green and smooth, turning yellow, pink, or purple in fall. ***Bark*** Gray-brown, furrowed, flaking. ***Flowers*** Small and without petals, males with numerous red stamens, females with four to six red styles, in the leaf axils, on separate plants in early spring. ***Fruit*** A small, curved, green pod.

NATIVE REGION Himalayas to Japan.
HABITAT Mountain forests.

Height: 100ft (30m)	Shape: Broadly spreading	Leaf persistence: Deciduous	Leaf type:

CORNACEAE

THIS FAMILY HAS TWO GENERA and 100 species of evergreen and deciduous trees and shrubs, and includes the dogwoods (*Cornus*, see pp.117–121); most grow in northern temperate regions. Leaves are usually opposite. The small flowers may be surrounded by conspicuous bracts.

Family: Cornaceae	Species: *Cornus alternifolia*	Author: L. f.

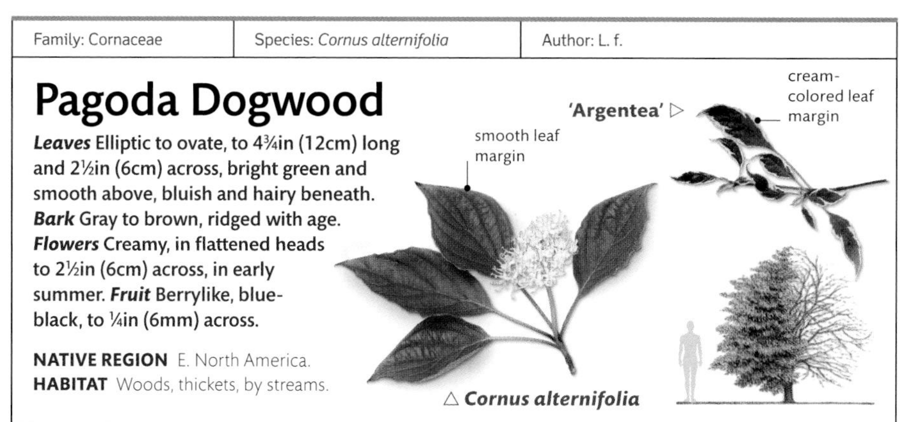

Pagoda Dogwood

Leaves Elliptic to ovate, to 4¾in (12cm) long and 2½in (6cm) across, bright green and smooth above, bluish and hairy beneath. ***Bark*** Gray to brown, ridged with age. ***Flowers*** Creamy, in flattened heads to 2½in (6cm) across, in early summer. ***Fruit*** Berrylike, blue-black, to ¼in (6mm) across.

NATIVE REGION E. North America.
HABITAT Woods, thickets, by streams.

'Argentea' ▷

△ ***Cornus alternifolia***

Height: 20ft (6m)	Shape: Broadly spreading	Leaf persistence: Deciduous	Leaf type:

Family: Cornaceae	Species: *Cornus controversa*	Author: Hemsl.

Giant Dogwood

Leaves Ovate to elliptic, to 6in (15cm) long and 3in (7.5cm) across, taper-pointed, untoothed, glossy dark green and smooth above, blue-green beneath, turning purple in fall, carried on long, slender stalks, clustered at the tips of the shoots. ***Bark*** Smooth, gray, becoming fissured with age. ***Flowers*** Small and creamy white, with four petals, borne in flattened heads to 6in (15cm) across, along distinctly layered branches in early to midsummer. ***Fruit*** A small, rounded, blue-black berry.

NATIVE REGION E. Asia.
HABITAT Woods and thickets.
REMARK This species and the much smaller *Cornus alternifolia* (see above) are the only two dogwoods that bear their leaves alternately, rather than opposite. In Japan, wooden dolls are often made from the wood of this tree.

small flowers clustered in large heads

bluish leaf underside

Cornus controversa △

broad, white leaf margin

△ **'Variegata'**
The leaves of this slower-growing form are strikingly variegated.

Height: 65ft (20m)	Shape: Broadly spreading	Leaf persistence: Deciduous	Leaf type:

Family: Cornaceae	Species: *Cornus* 'Eddie's White Wonder'	Author: None

Cornus 'Eddie's White Wonder'

Leaves Broadly elliptic, to 12cm (4¾in) long, with an abruptly pointed tip, slightly glossy dark green above, gray and hairy beneath, turning orange, red, and purple in fall. ***Bark*** Gray and smooth, with few slender, pale stripes. ***Flowers*** Individually small and greenish, numerous, borne in dense, hemispherical clusters, each cluster surrounded by four white or slightly pink-tinged bracts, the bracts not joined at the tip at first, emerging in late spring at the same time as the young leaves. ***Fruit*** Individually small and red, in hemispherical clusters, the fruits separating when ripe.

NATIVE REGION Of garden and backyard origin.
REMARK A hybrid between the flowering dogwood (*Cornus florida*, see below) and the Pacific dogwood (*Cornus nuttallii*, see p.120). Individual specimens do not always produce fruit.

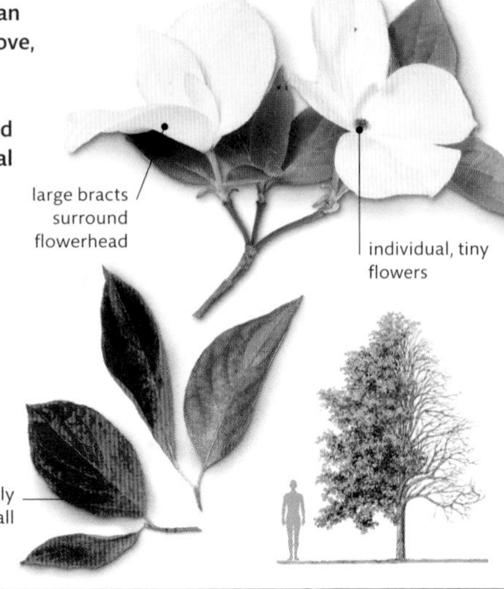

Height: 40ft (12m)	Shape: Broadly conical	Leaf persistence: Deciduous	Leaf type:

Family: Cornaceae	Species: *Cornus florida*	Author: L.

Flowering Dogwood

Leaves Ovate to elliptic, to 4in (10cm) long and 2½in (6cm) across, taper-pointed, untoothed, dark green and smooth above, whitish and softly hairy beneath, turning red in fall, carried on bloomy shoots. ***Bark*** Red-brown to blackish, deeply cracked into small, square plates. ***Flowers*** Small and greenish, numerous, in dense, hemispherical clusters, each cluster surrounded by four white to deep pink bracts, each bract notched at the tip, visible in bud during winter, opening in late spring before or with the young leaves. ***Fruit*** Individually small, red, in clusters, the fruits separating when ripe.

NATIVE REGION E. North America.
HABITAT Acid soil in woods.

notch at tip where bracts were once joined

large, pure white bracts

untoothed leaf margin

'White Cloud' ▷ This selected form is distinguished by the broad, white bracts that surround the green flowers.

▽ **'Cherokee Chief'** The deep pink bracts of this form fade at the base to pinkish white.

◁▷ ***Cornus florida***

bloomy shoots

Height: 40ft (12m)	Shape: Broadly spreading	Leaf persistence: Deciduous	Leaf type: 

Family: Cornaceae	Species: *Cornus kousa*	Author: Hance

Japanese Strawberry Tree

Leaves Ovate, to 3in (7.5cm) long and 2in (5cm) across, taper-pointed, with a wavy margin, untoothed, smooth and dark green above, smooth beneath, with tufts of brown hairs in the vein axils. ***Bark*** Red-brown, peeling in irregular plates with age. ***Flowers*** Tiny, yellow-white or greenish, numerous, in dense, hemispherical, long-stalked, upright clusters, each cluster surrounded by four creamy white or pink-tinged, taper-pointed bracts, in early summer. ***Fruit*** Individually small, clustered together in a fleshy, strawberry-like, edible, red, pendulous head.

NATIVE REGION Japan, with a subspecies in China.
HABITAT Mountain woods.

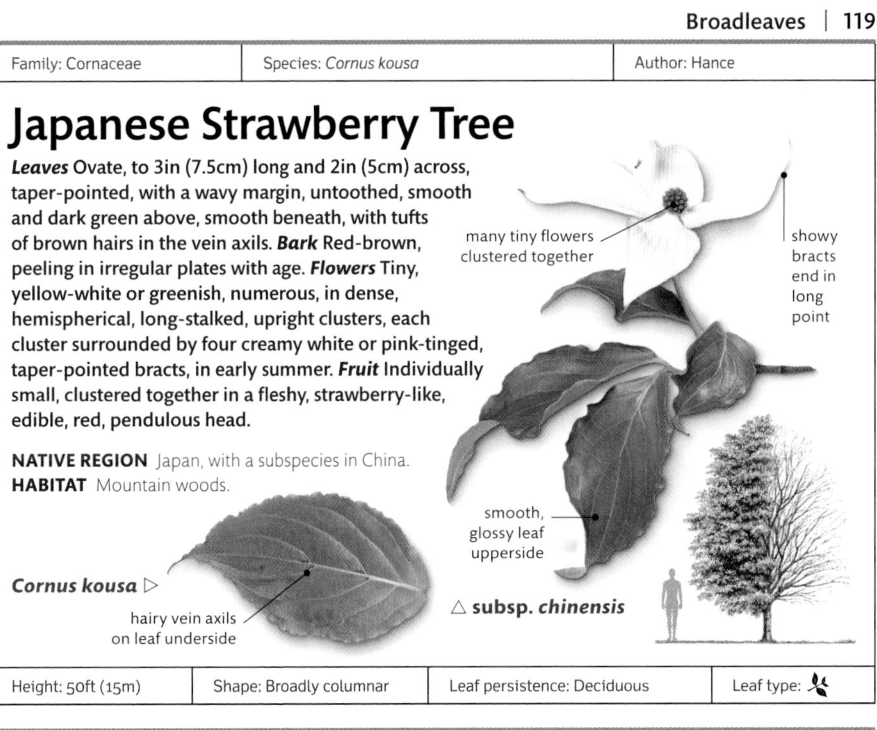

Cornus kousa ▷

△ **subsp. *chinensis***

Height: 50ft (15m)	Shape: Broadly columnar	Leaf persistence: Deciduous	Leaf type:

Family: Cornaceae	Species: *Cornus macrophylla*	Author: Wall.

Cornus macrophylla

Leaves Ovate, to 6in (15cm) long and 3in (7.5cm) across, tapering to a slender tip, with a wavy margin, untoothed, glossy dark green and smooth above, with up to eight pairs of veins either side of the midrib, bluish-green and thinly hairy beneath. ***Bark*** Dark gray, becoming fissured with age. ***Flowers*** Small and creamy white, with four petals, borne in loose, flattened heads to 6in (15cm) across, in mid- to late summer. ***Fruit*** Small, rounded, and berrylike, ripening from green to reddish purple and finally to blue-black, to ¼in (6mm) across.

NATIVE REGION China, Himalayas, Japan.
HABITAT Forests and thickets.
REMARK A handsome tree, little known even in cultivation.

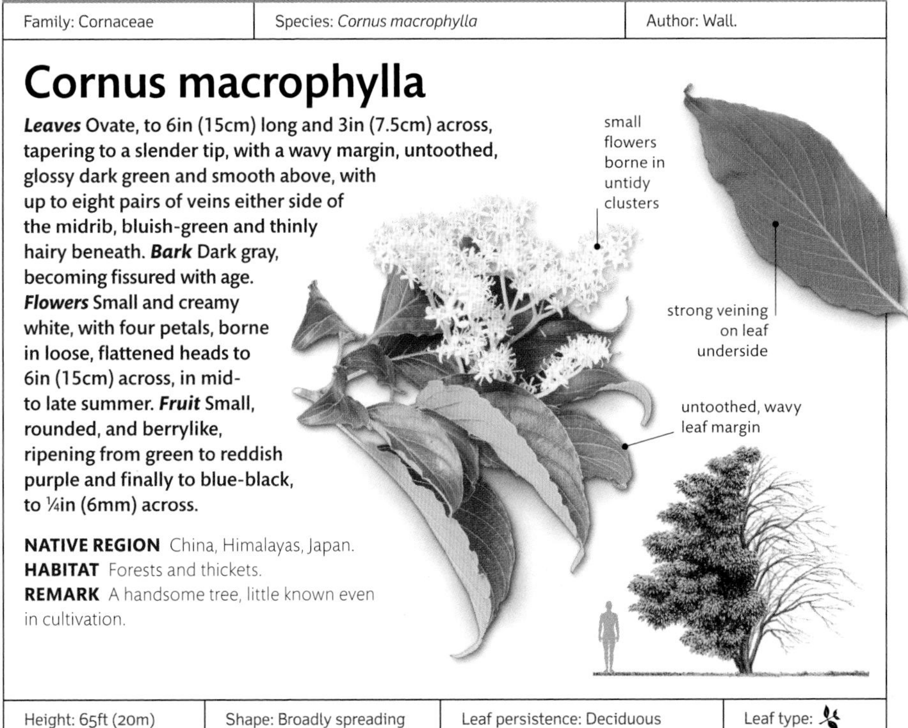

Height: 65ft (20m)	Shape: Broadly spreading	Leaf persistence: Deciduous	Leaf type:

Family: Cornaceae	Species: *Cornus nuttallii*	Author: Audubon ex Torr. & A. Gray

Pacific Dogwood

Leaves Elliptic to obovate, to 6in (15cm) long and 3in (7.5cm) across, pointed, untoothed, dark green, and nearly smooth above, hairy beneath when young, often turning yellow and occasionally red in fall. ***Bark*** Gray and smooth, with few slender, pale stripes, slightly fluted at the base. ***Flowers*** Tiny and greenish, numerous, borne in dense, hemispherical, upright clusters, each cluster surrounded by four to seven large bracts to 3in (7.5cm) long, creamy white at first becoming white or white flushed pink, in late spring. ***Fruit*** Small, red, in hemispherical clusters, the fruits separating when ripe.

NATIVE REGION W. North America.
HABITAT Lowland forests, and on mountains in the south of its native region.

up to seven large bracts

many greenish flowers

leaves emerge at flowering time

leaves may turn red in fall

Height: 80ft (25m)	Shape: Broadly conical	Leaf persistence: Deciduous	Leaf type:

Family: Cornaceae	Species: *Cornus* 'Porlock'	Author: None

Cornus 'Porlock'

Leaves Elliptic, to 3in (7.5cm) long, bronze-green becoming pale green above, gray-green beneath, some turning pinkish in fall, others persisting over winter. ***Bark*** Gray and smooth, with shallow orange fissures, flaking at the base, leaving pale brown and pale gray patches. ***Flowers*** Tiny, yellow-white, numerous, in dense, hemispherical, long-stalked, upright clusters, each cluster surrounded by four taper-pointed bracts, creamy white becoming deep pink, in early summer. ***Fruit*** Individually small, clustered in a fleshy, strawberry-like, edible, red, pendulous head.

NATIVE REGION Of garden origin.
REMARK A hybrid between *Cornus capitata* and *Cornus kousa* (see p.119).

taper-pointed leaves

flowerheads carried at first on upright stalks

fruit clusters hang down

creamy bracts

leaves can persist during winter

Height: 26ft (8m)	Shape: Broadly spreading	Leaf persistence: Deciduous	Leaf type:

Family: Cornaceae	Species: *Cornus walteri*	Author: Wangerin

Walter's Dogwood

Leaves Elliptic, to 4in (10cm) long and 2in (5cm) across, tapered at the tip, untoothed, slightly glossy dark green above, thinly hairy beneath. ***Bark*** Pale gray-brown, deeply fissured, with narrow, rather corky, ridges. ***Flowers*** Individually small and creamy white, with four petals, borne in flattened heads 3in (7.5cm) across, in midsummer. ***Fruit*** Small, rounded, and black.

NATIVE REGION China.
HABITAT Mountain woods.
REMARK The species can be either a shrub or a small tree. It is uncommon in the wild, and little known even in cultivation. In winter, the upperside of shoots exposed to the sun is purplish pink.

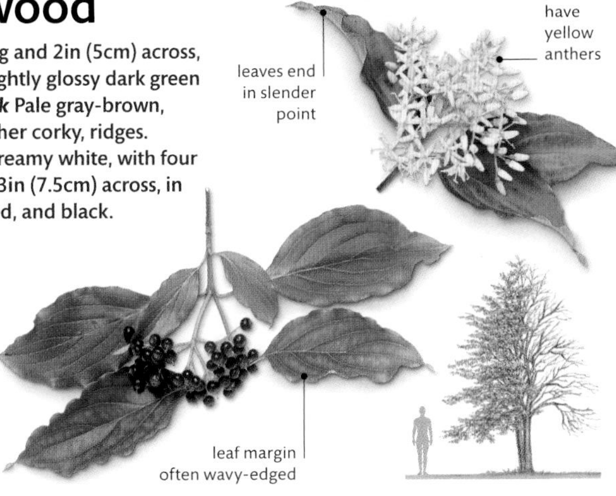

Height: 40ft (12m)	Shape: Broadly conical	Leaf persistence: Deciduous	Leaf type:

CUNONIACEAE

THIS IS A largely tropical family occurring particularly in the southern hemisphere and comprising about 27 genera and 300 species of mainly evergreen trees and shrubs that have opposite, often pinnate leaves. The species listed here were previously included in their own family—Eucryphiaceae.

Family: Cunoniaceae	Species: *Eucryphia cordifolia*	Author: Cav.

Ulmo

Leaves Oblong, to 3in (7.5cm) long and 2in (5cm) across, heart-shaped at the base, toothed, dark green above, gray and hairy beneath. ***Bark*** Gray and smooth. ***Flowers*** 2in (5cm) across, white, with four petals, the numerous stamens turning from pink to orange, fragrant, borne singly in the leaf axils in late summer. ***Fruit*** A small, woody capsule.

NATIVE REGION Chile.
HABITAT Rain forests.
REMARK At high altitudes, this species is a large shrub.

Height: 130ft (40m)	Shape: Narrowly columnar	Leaf persistence: Evergreen	Leaf type: 

Family: Cunoniaceae	Species: *Eucryphia glutinosa*	Author: (Poepp. & Endl.) Baill.

Ñirre

Leaves Pinnate, with three to five leaflets, to 2½in (6cm) long and 1¼in (3cm) across, toothed, glossy dark green above, paler beneath, hairy on both sides, at least when young. ***Bark*** Gray and smooth. ***Flowers*** 2in (5cm) across, white, with four petals and numerous pink-tipped stamens, fragrant, borne singly in the leaf axils in late summer. ***Fruit*** A small, woody capsule.

NATIVE REGION Chile.
HABITAT Forests and riverbanks.
REMARK Cultivated plants of the species are semi-evergreen or deciduous, with most leaves turning orange-red in autumn before falling.

Plena Group ▷
This selected form has double flowers.

anthers colored deep pink at first

flowers have eight or more petals

prominently toothed, glossy leaflets

△ ***Eucryphia glutinosa***

Height: 33ft (10m)	Shape: Narrowly columnar	Leaf persistence: Evergreen	Leaf type:

Family: Cunoniaceae	Species: *Eucryphia* x *intermedia*	Author: J. Bausch

Eucryphia x intermedia

Leaves Variable, either simple and oblong, to 2½in (6cm) long and 1in (2.5cm) across, or with three leaflets, the central leaflet largest, both types untoothed or with a few teeth toward the tip, glossy dark green above, gray-green beneath. ***Bark*** Gray, smooth. ***Flowers*** 2in (5cm) across, white, with four petals and numerous dark-tipped stamens, fragrant, borne singly in the leaf axils in late summer to fall. ***Fruit*** A small, woody capsule.

NATIVE REGION Of garden origin.
REMARK A hybrid between *Eucryphia glutinosa* (see above) and *Eucryphia lucida* (see p.123), first raised at Rostrevor in Northern Ireland, the garden of the late Sir John Ross of Blandenburg. The original and most common form, 'Rostrevor,' is shown here.

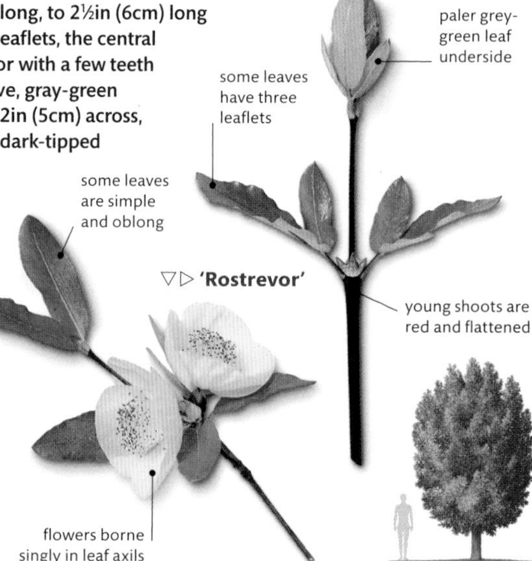

▽▷ **'Rostrevor'**

Height: 33ft (10m)	Shape: Broadly columnar	Leaf persistence: Evergreen	Leaf type:

Family: Cunoniaceae	Species: *Eucryphia lucida*	Author: (Labill.) Baill.

Leatherwood

Leaves Narrowly oblong, to 2in (5cm) long and ⅝in (1.5cm) across, on short stalks, untoothed, leathery, rounded to minutely notched at the tip, glossy dark green and thinly hairy above, blue-white and smooth beneath with a distinct network of veins; on vigorous shoots sometimes with three leaflets. ***Bark*** Gray, smooth. ***Flowers*** To 2in (5cm) across, white, with four rounded petals and numerous slender, dark-tipped stamens, fragrant, borne singly in the leaf axils in late summer, cup-shaped at first, opening flat. ***Fruit*** A small, woody capsule, splitting open when ripe.

NATIVE REGION Tasmania.
HABITAT Woods and riverbanks in mountainous areas.
REMARK Cultivated plants are smaller, usually reaching only about 50ft (15m). A pink-flowered form found in Tasmania has been named 'Pink Cloud.'

Height: 65ft (20m)	Shape: Narrowly columnar	Leaf persistence: Evergreen	Leaf type:

Family: Cunoniaceae	Species: *Eucryphia milliganii*	Author: Hook. f.

Dwarf Leatherwood

Leaves Oblong, to ¾in (2cm) long and 5⁄16in (8mm) across, untoothed, glossy dark green above, blue-white beneath. ***Bark*** Gray and smooth. ***Flowers*** To ¾in (2cm) across, white, with four petals and numerous pink-tipped stamens, fragrant, borne singly in the leaf axils in late summer. ***Fruit*** A small, woody capsule.

NATIVE REGION Tasmania.
HABITAT Woods and riverbanks in mountainous areas.
REMARK Can be a tree or a shrub.

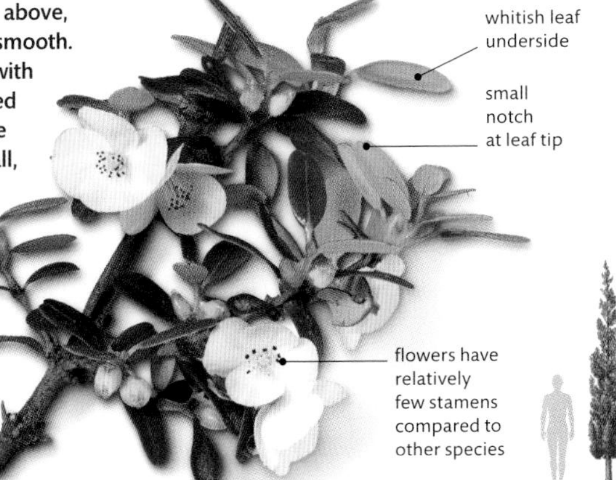

Height: 20ft (6m)	Shape: Narrowly columnar	Leaf persistence: Evergreen	Leaf type:

Family: Cunoniaceae	Species: *Eucryphia* x *nymansensis*	Author: J. Bausch

Nymans Eucryphia

Leaves Elliptic, to 2½in (6cm) long and 1¼in (3cm) across, or with three leaflets, toothed, glossy dark green above, paler beneath. ***Bark*** Gray and smooth. ***Flowers*** To 3in (7.5cm) across, white, with four petals and numerous pink-tipped stamens, in the leaf axils in late summer to fall. ***Fruit*** A small, woody capsule.

NATIVE REGION Chile.
REMARK A hybrid between ulmo (*Eucryphia cordifolia*, see p.121) and *Eucryphia glutinosa* (see p.122).

Height: 50ft (15m)	Shape: Narrowly columnar	Leaf persistence: Evergreen	Leaf type: 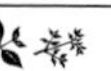

Family: Cunoniaceae	Species: *Eucryphia* 'Penwith'	Author: None

Eucryphia 'Penwith'

Leaves Oblong, to 2¾in (7cm) long and 1¼in (3cm) across, slightly heart-shaped at the base, untoothed, dark green and smooth above, blue-white and nearly smooth beneath. ***Bark*** Dark gray and smooth. ***Flowers*** To 2in (5cm) across, white, with four petals and numerous pink-tipped stamens, fragrant, in the leaf axils in late summer to fall. ***Fruit*** A small, woody capsule.

NATIVE REGION Of garden origin.
REMARK A hybrid between ulmo (*Eucryphia cordifolia*, see p.121) and *Eucryphia lucida* (see p.123).

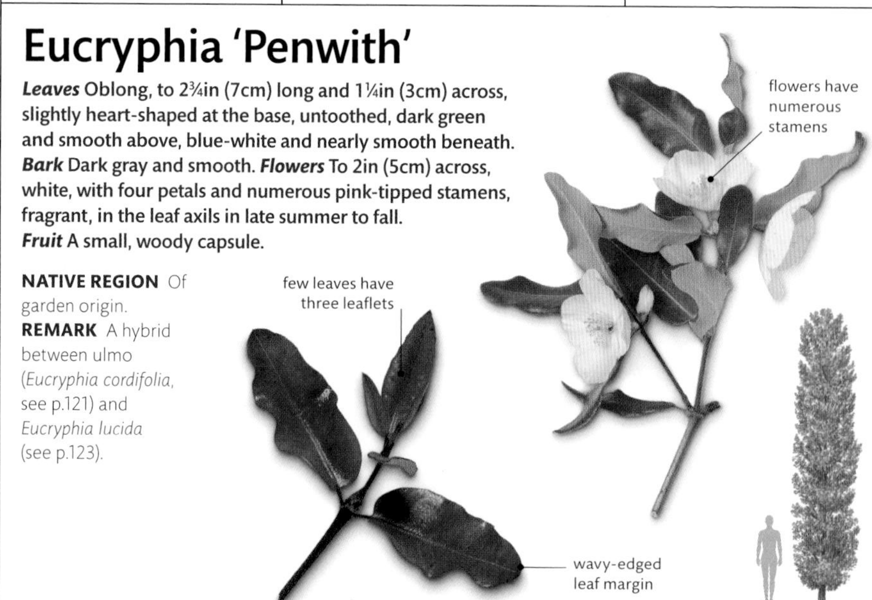

Height: 50ft (15m)	Shape: Narrowly columnar	Leaf persistence: Evergreen	Leaf type: 

EBENACEAE

ABOUT 750 SPECIES are included in the three genera of this family; nearly all are in the genus *Diospyros*. These evergreen and deciduous trees and shrubs, mainly of tropical origin, normally have alternate, untoothed leaves. Small male and female flowers are usually borne on separate plants.

Family: Ebenaceae	Species: *Diospyros kaki*	Author: L. f.

Chinese Persimmon

Leaves Ovate to obovate, to 6in (15cm) or more long and 3in (7.5cm) across, pointed at the tip, untoothed, glossy dark green and smooth or nearly so above, paler and usually hairy beneath, turning red or orange in fall. ***Bark*** Pale gray and scaly, peeling to furrowed. ***Flowers*** Males and females both small and bell-shaped, about ¾in (1.5cm) long, yellow, males in clusters together, females singly, on young shoots, on separate plants in midsummer. ***Fruit*** A large, juicy, yellow to orange or red berry, to 3in (7.5cm) across, edible when ripe.

paper-thin persistent calyx

flat, brown seed

large glossy, leaves

NATIVE REGION E. Asia.
HABITAT Forests and scrub on mountain slopes.
REMARK Fruits are also known as kaki.

Height: 46ft (14m)	Shape: Broadly spreading	Leaf persistence: Deciduous	Leaf type:

Family: Ebenaceae	Species: *Diospyros lotus*	Author: L.

Date Plum

Leaves Ovate to lanceolate, to 6in (15cm) long, pointed, untoothed, glossy dark green above, gray-green beneath, smooth or hairy on both sides. ***Bark*** Gray, smooth, fissured into square plates with age. ***Flowers*** Males and females both bell-shaped, about 3/16in (5mm) long, deep pink or orange-yellow, males in clusters, females singly, on the underside of the young shoots, on separate plants in midsummer. ***Fruit*** An edible berry, ¾in (2cm) across, green ripening to yellow-brown to blue-black, sometimes bloomy.

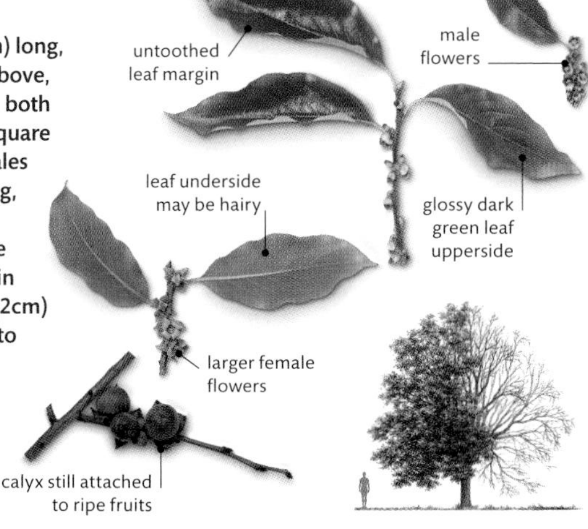

NATIVE REGION Turkey to E. Asia.
HABITAT Woods.
REMARK In its native region, the species is widely cultivated for its edible fruits.

Height: 80ft (25m)	Shape: Broadly spreading	Leaf persistence: Deciduous	Leaf type:

Family: Ebenaceae	Species: *Diospyros virginiana*	Author: L.

Persimmon

Leaves Ovate to oblong, to 4¾in (12cm) long and 3in (7.5cm) across, pointed, untoothed, dark often glossy green and smooth or nearly so above, gray-green and smooth or hairy beneath. ***Bark*** Dark brown to black, fissured into small, square plates. ***Flowers*** Males and females both bell-shaped, about ⅜in (1cm) long, yellow, males in clusters, females singly, along the young shoots, on separate plants in midsummer. ***Fruit*** An edible berry, to 1½in (4cm) across, green ripening to yellowish red or orange-red.

NATIVE REGION E. US.
HABITAT Woods and dry soil.
REMARK Also known as possumwood. The fruits are very bitter until they are fully ripe.

more or less glossy leaf upperside
leaves arranged alternately on shoot
calyx remains on fruits
fruits ripen from green to orange in the fall

Height: 100ft (30m)	Shape: Broadly spreading	Leaf persistence: Deciduous	Leaf type:

ELAEAGNACEAE

THE OLEASTER FAMILY has three genera, with some 100 species of evergreen and deciduous small trees and shrubs spreading to all temperate northern regions. The plants are often spiny. The untoothed, usually scaly, leaves are opposite or alternate. Small, petalless male and female flowers may be borne on separate plants; in several species they develop into edible fruits.

Family: Elaeagnaceae	Species: *Elaeagnus angustifolia*	Author: L.

Oleaster

Leaves Lanceolate to oblong, to 3in (7.5cm) long and ⅝in (1.5cm) across, untoothed, dark green above, silvery and scaly beneath, carried on silvery, often spiny, shoots. ***Bark*** Red-brown, rough and shredding. ***Flowers*** Small and yellow, fragrant, borne in clusters in the leaf axils in late spring to early summer. ***Fruit*** A sweet, edible, yellow berry, ⅜in (1cm) long, with silvery scales.

NATIVE REGION E. Europe to China.
HABITAT Coasts, riverbanks, dry riverbeds, and floodplains.
REMARK Also known as Russian olive. In its native region, this species has an important commercial value for its fruits and its timber.

Height: 40ft (12m)	Shape: Broadly conical	Leaf persistence: Deciduous	Leaf type:

Family: Elaeagnaceae	Species: *Hippophae rhamnoides*	Author: L.

Sea Buckthorn

Leaves Narrowly linear, to 2¾in (7cm) long and ⅝in (1.5cm) across, untoothed, silvery and scaly on both sides, on spiny shoots. ***Bark*** Green-brown to blackish, rough, vertically fissured. ***Flowers*** Males and females both very small and yellowish, borne in small clusters on separate plants in spring before the leaves. ***Fruit*** A bright orange berry, about 5⁄16in (8mm) long, borne in dense clusters on the shoots, usually persisting over winter.

gray-green, extremely slender leaves

orange berries remain on plant during winter

NATIVE REGION Asia, Europe.
HABITAT Coasts, riverbanks, sandy woods.
REMARK Can be a shrub. The edible but sour fruit is rich in vitamin C and has been used to make jam and sauces.

Height: 10ft (3m)	Shape: Broadly spreading	Leaf persistence: Deciduous	Leaf type:

ERICACEAE

THE HEATHER FAMILY, with about 120 genera and more than 4,000 species, occurs almost worldwide: it is of restricted distribution only in low, tropical regions. The plants are in the main evergreen and deciduous trees and shrubs, with usually alternate leaves. The flowers vary in shape and size, but normally have five petals, joined at least at the base. In all members of the family, a root-associated fungus assists the plant in absorbing nutrients.

Family: Ericaceae	Species: *Arbutus andrachne*	Author: L.

Greek Strawberry Tree

Leaves Elliptic to obovate, to 4in (10cm) long and 2in (5cm) across, usually entire but sometimes toothed, glossy dark green above, paler beneath, smooth. ***Bark*** Red-brown, peeling in thin strips. ***Flowers*** Urn-shaped to about ¼in (6mm) long, greenish at first opening white, in upright clusters to 4in (10cm) long and across, at the ends of the shoots in early spring. ***Fruit*** A nearly smooth, rounded, orange-red, berry, ⅜in (1cm) across.

green-tinged flower clusters open white in early spring

NATIVE REGION S.E. Europe to S.W. Asia.
HABITAT Woods, thickets, and rocky slopes.
REMARK Crosses with the strawberry tree (*Arbutus unedo*, see p.129) to produce the hybrid *Arbutus* x *andrachnoides* (see p.128).

old bark flakes freely

peeling bark reveals brightly colored layer beneath

leaves usually untoothed at margin

smooth young shoots

Height: 33ft (10m)	Shape: Broadly spreading	Leaf persistence: Evergreen	Leaf type:

Family: Ericaceae	Species: *Arbutus* x *andrachnoides*	Author: Link

Arbutus x andrachnoides

Leaves **Ovate to elliptic, to 4in (10cm) long and 2in (5cm) across, toothed, glossy dark green above, paler beneath, smooth on both sides.** ***Bark*** **Red-brown, peeling vertically in long, thin strips.** ***Flowers*** **Urn-shaped, small, and white, in drooping clusters at the ends of the shoots, over a long period between fall and spring.** ***Fruit*** **A strawberry-like, warty, red berry, ⅝in (1.5cm) across.**

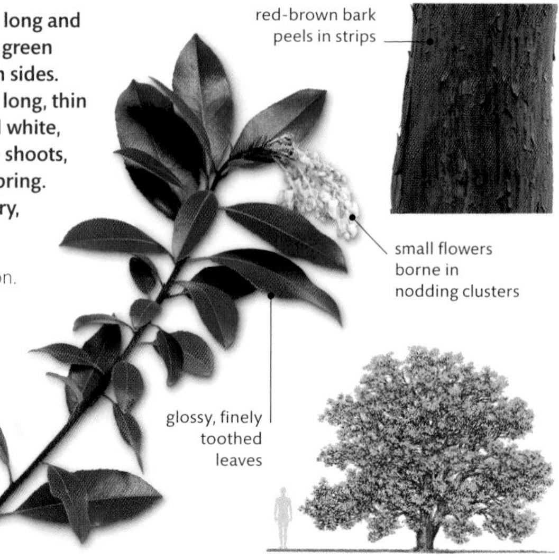

NATIVE REGION E. Mediterranean region.
HABITAT Woods and thickets.
REMARK A naturally occurring hybrid between the Greek strawberry tree (*Arbutus andrachne*, see p.127), whose attractive, peeling bark it inherits, and the strawberry tree (*Arbutus unedo*, see p.129), found in the wild where the parent plants grow together.

Height: 33ft (10m)	Shape: Broadly spreading	Leaf persistence: Evergreen	Leaf type:

Family: Ericaceae	Species: *Arbutus menziesii*	Author: Pursh

Madroña

Leaves **Elliptic, to 6in (15cm) long and 3in (7.5cm) across, usually untoothed, glossy dark green above, blue-white beneath, smooth.** ***Bark*** **Red-brown, smooth, peeling, becoming dark and fissured with age; green when freshly exposed.** ***Flowers*** **Urn-shaped, small, and white, or sometimes pink-tinged, borne upright, in large, upright clusters to 6in (15cm) long, at the ends of the shoots in late spring.** ***Fruit*** **A strawberry-like, rather rough, orange to red berry, ⅜in (1cm) across, covered in small warts.**

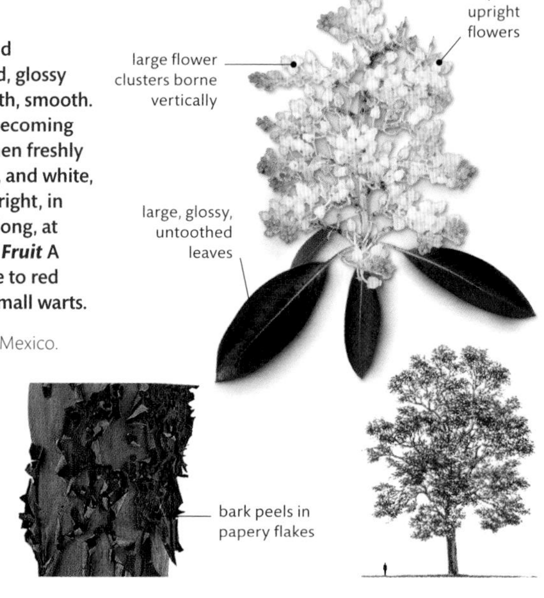

NATIVE REGION S.W. Canada to N.W. Mexico.
HABITAT Moist, wooded slopes, canyons in forests of oak and redwood, and coastal rocks and cliffs.
REMARK Also known as Pacific madrone. The fruits are edible in small quantities. During the fruiting season, trees attract many different bird species, which serve to distribute the seeds.

Height: 130ft (40m)	Shape: Broadly columnar	Leaf persistence: Evergreen	Leaf type: 

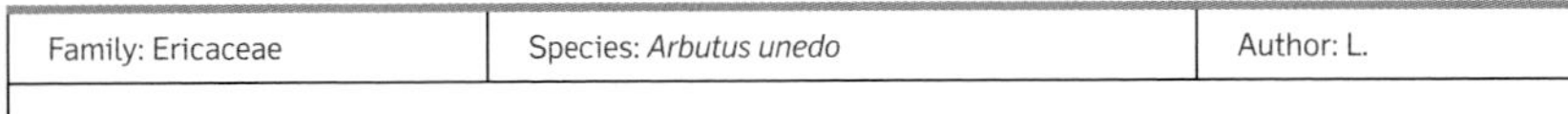

Family: Ericaceae	Species: *Arbutus unedo*	Author: L.

Strawberry Tree

Leaves **Elliptic to oblong or obovate, to 4in (10cm) long and 2in (5cm) across, toothed, very glossy dark green above, paler beneath, smooth on both sides.** ***Bark*** **Red-brown, rough and fissured, not peeling.** ***Flowers*** **Urn-shaped, small, and white, or sometimes pink, borne in drooping clusters about 2in (5cm) long, at the ends of the shoots in fall.** ***Fruit*** **A strawberry-like, roughly warty, red berry, ¾in (2cm) across, ripening in fall from flowers borne the previous year.**

NATIVE REGION W. Ireland, Mediterranean.
HABITAT Rocky places and thickets.
REMARK One of the few members of the family that grows on limey soil. With flowers and fruits borne at the same time, it is a particularly ornamental species.

Height: 33ft (10m)	Shape: Broadly spreading	Leaf persistence: Evergreen	Leaf type:

Family: Ericaceae	Species: *Oxydendrum arboreum*	Author: (L.) DC.

Sorrel Tree

Leaves **Elliptic to oblong, to 8in (20cm) long and 3in (7.5cm) across, taper-pointed, very finely toothed, glossy dark green and smooth above, slightly hairy beneath, turning red to yellow or purple in fall.** ***Bark*** **Gray-brown, thick, deeply furrowed, with scaly ridges.** ***Flowers*** **Urn-shaped, small, white, and numerous, fragrant, borne in large, upright clusters at the ends of the shoots in fall.** ***Fruit*** **A small, woody, brown capsule.**

NATIVE REGION E. North America.
HABITAT Woods and by streams.
REMARK Also known as sourwood. The species can be either a tree or a shrub. The leaves have a sharp, acid taste, somewhat similar to that of the herbaceous plant, sorrel, which gives the species its common name.

Height: 65ft (20m)	Shape: Broadly conical	Leaf persistence: Deciduous	Leaf type: 

Family: Ericaceae	Species: *Rhododendron arboreum*	Author: Sm.

Rhododendron arboreum

Leaves **Oblong to lanceolate, to 8in (20cm) long and 2in (5cm) across, thick and leathery, tapering to a pointed tip, glossy dark green and smooth with deeply impressed midrib and veins above, variably hairy from silvery to rusty and often shining beneath.** ***Bark*** **Red-brown, rough and shredding.** ***Flowers*** **Bell-shaped, to 2in (5cm) long, red, pink, or sometimes white, in dense clusters of up to 20 in late winter to mid-spring.** ***Fruit*** **A woody, brown capsule, splitting open to release numerous tiny seeds.**

NATIVE REGION Himalayas, with forms extending to S.W. China and Sri Lanka.
HABITAT Forests and thickets in hills and mountains.
REMARK In its native region and habitat, this species is a tree; in less favorable situations it may be only a large shrub. It was the first rhododendron to be introduced to Europe from the Himalayas. The young leaves are poisonous.

Height: 50ft (15m)	Shape: Broadly columnar	Leaf persistence: Evergreen	Leaf type: 

EUCOMMIACEAE

THE ONLY MEMBER of this family, *Eucommia ulmoides* is a vigorous and decorative plant when mature. It was thought to be related to the elms (*Ulmus*) but is now considered close to *Aucuba* and *Garrya*. If in doubt about its identity, the rubbery latex, which forms an integral part of the leaf structure, provides instant identification. However, the latex is present in quantities that are too small to make commercial extraction an economic proposition. This unique species is the only tree from temperate regions known to produce rubber.

Family: Eucommiaceae	Species: *Eucommia ulmoides*	Author: Oliv.

Gutta-percha Tree

Leaves Ovate to elliptic, to 5in (20cm) long and 3½in (9cm) across, leathery, taper-pointed at the tip, toothed, glossy dark green, with prominent lateral veining, drooping on thin shoots. ***Bark*** Pale dove-gray, deeply fissured. ***Flowers*** Males and females both very small, without petals, opening on the old shoots, on separate plants in late spring just before or as the young leaves emerge. ***Fruit*** Winged, green keys, 1½in (4cm) long, in clusters, each key containing a seed.

NATIVE REGION C. and S. China
HABITAT Forests on mountain slopes, valleys, and ridges.
REMARK This hardy tree was introduced to the West in about 1896, from plants propagated in China, where it is widely cultivated. In China, the bark is used for medicinal purposes.

leaves emerge at flowering time

male flowers may each have up to 10 stamens

thin strands of rubber join two halves of a torn leaf

Invisible rubber ▷
When a leaf is gently torn apart, and is held upside-down by its stalk, the two separate parts remain hanging together, connected almost invisibly by a network of gossamer-like latex fibers.

deeply impressed leaf veins

Height: 65ft (20m)	Shape: Broadly spreading	Leaf persistence: Deciduous	Leaf type:

FABACEAE

THE PEA FAMILY contains about 770 genera and nearly 20,000 species of trees, shrubs, and herbaceous plants, found worldwide. The leaves are often compound, and frequently pinnate or with three leaflets. Species that grow in cool temperate regions have pealike flowers. The fruit, usually a pod, splits open along both sides or breaks into portions to release its seeds.

Family: Fabaceae	Species: *Acacia dealbata*	Author: Link

Silver Wattle

Leaves Bipinnate, to 4¾in (12cm) long, with numerous linear leaflets, to 3⁄16in (5mm) long, the leaflets untoothed, blue-green, and finely hairy. ***Bark*** Smooth and green or blue-green, becoming nearly black with age. ***Flowers*** Very small, with bright yellow petals and numerous conspicuous stamens, fragrant, in panicles of small, rounded clusters in late winter to early spring. ***Fruit*** A flattened pod, to 3in (7.5cm) long, green becoming blue-white, ripening to brown.

NATIVE REGION S.E. Australia, Tasmania.
HABITAT Mainly mountain gullies and stream banks.

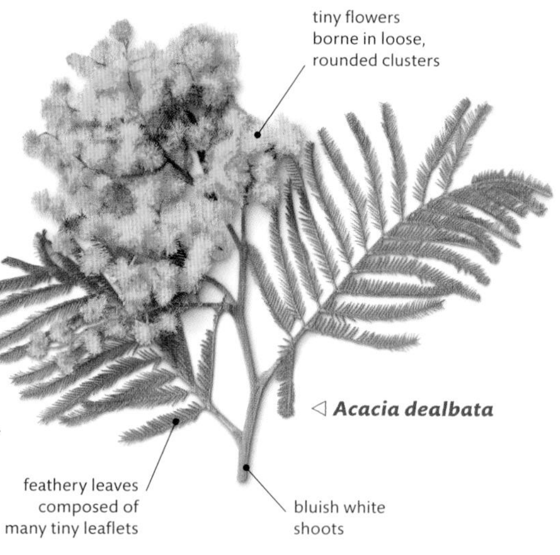

◁ ***Acacia dealbata***

◁ ***Acacia mearnsii***
This species, commonly known as black wattle, grows wild throughout east and south Australia.

Height: 65ft (20m)	Shape: Broadly conical	Leaf persistence: Evergreen	Leaf type:

Acacia falciformis ▷
Commonly known as pale hickory wattle, this species is found in Southeast Australia. The leaves are undivided. In spring, small, rounded heads of yellow flowers appear in large clusters.

△ ***Acacia glaucoptera***
The leaves of this western Australian species, commonly known as flat wattle, are arranged in one plane, forming a blue-green wing along the stem.

◁△ ***Acacia melanoxylon***
This species is commonly known as blackwood. All acacia species with usually undivided leaves produce compound leaves in seedlings, which give way to adult foliage as the plants age. The intermediate leaves of blackwood best illustrate this transition between the two different types of foliage.

Family: Fabaceae	Species: *Albizia julibrissin*	Author: Durazz.

Silk Tree

Leaves **Bipinnate, to 20in (50cm) long, with numerous small, taper-pointed, untoothed leaflets, about ⅜in (1cm) long, dark green and smooth on both sides.** ***Bark*** **Dark brown and smooth.** ***Flowers*** **Individually small, conspicuous by the numerous long, pink stamens, borne in dense, fluffy clusters, opening in late summer to early fall.** ***Fruit*** **A pod, to 6in (15cm) long.**

NATIVE REGION Iran to China and Japan.
HABITAT Woods and river margins.
REMARK Also known as Persian acacia, pink siris.

Height: 40ft (12m)	Shape: Broadly spreading	Leaf persistence: Deciduous	Leaf type:

Family: Fabaceae	Species: *Cercis canadensis*	Author: L.

Redbud

Leaves **Rounded, to 4in (10cm) long and 4¾in (12cm) across, heart-shaped at the base, untoothed, bronze becoming bright green and smooth above, smooth or hairy beneath, sometimes turning yellow in fall.** ***Bark*** **Dark gray-brown to black.** ***Flowers*** **Pealike, ⅜in (1cm) long, pink, borne in clusters along the old shoots, and often from the main branches and trunk, in spring to early summer before and as the young leaves emerge.** ***Fruit*** **A flattened pod, to 3in (7.5cm) long, green becoming pink, ripening to brown.**

NATIVE REGION E. and C. US, Mexico.
HABITAT Moist woods.

young leaves emerge at flowering time

bronzy young leaves

small flowers have slender stalks

◁△ ***Cercis canadensis***

leaves do not turn green

△ **'Forest Pansy'**
This form is selected for its gorgeous red-purple foliage.

several veins diverge from the heart-shaped leaf base

Height: 33ft (10m)	Shape: Broadly spreading	Leaf persistence: Deciduous	Leaf type:

Family: Fabaceae	Species: *Cercis racemosa*	Author: Oliv.

Cercis racemosa

Leaves Rounded, to 5in (13cm) long and 4in (10cm) across, rounded at the base, dark green above, hairy beneath. ***Bark*** Pale-gray, flaking with age. ***Flowers*** Pealike, ⅜in (1cm) long, pale pink, borne in racemes from the old shoots in mid- to late spring or early summer. ***Fruit*** A flattened pod, to 4in (10cm) long, green becoming pink-tinged, ripening to brown.

NATIVE REGION China.
HABITAT Woods and stream banks in mountains.
REMARK A rarely seen species, distinguished by its flowers borne in racemes.

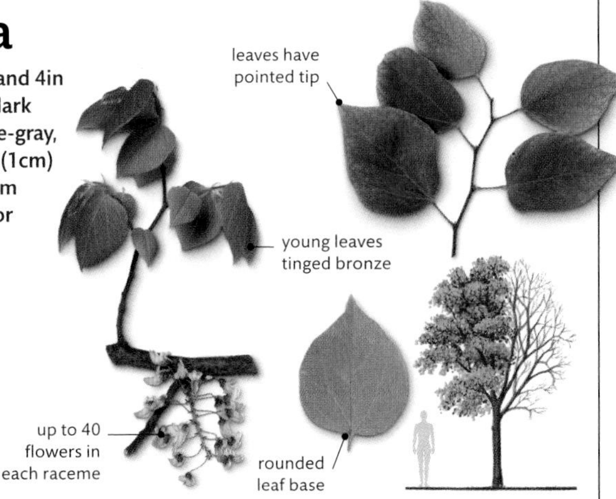

Height: 33ft (10m)	Shape: Broadly columnar	Leaf persistence: Deciduous	Leaf type:

Family: Fabaceae	Species: *Cercis siliquastrum*	Author: L.

Judas Tree

Leaves Rounded, to 4in (10cm) long and 4¾in (12cm) across, deeply heart-shaped at the base, untoothed, bronze when young becoming dark blue-green above, smooth. ***Bark*** Gray-brown, cracking into small, rectangular and square plates. ***Flowers*** Pealike, ¾in (2cm) long, pink, in clusters along the old shoots, and often from the main branches and trunk, in late spring to early summer before and with the leaves. ***Fruit*** A flattened pod, to 4in (10cm) long, green becoming pink, ripening to brown, often persisting after the leaves fall.

NATIVE REGION S. Europe, S.W. Asia.
HABITAT Dry, rocky places.

fruits ripen from green to brown

leaves fold up towards midrib

△ ***Cercis siliquastrum***

◁ **'Bodnant'** A form raised at the National Trust garden at Bodnant, UK.

Height: 33ft (10m)	Shape: Broadly spreading	Leaf persistence: Deciduous	Leaf type:

Family: Fabaceae	Species: *Cladrastis kentukea*	Author: (Dum.Cours.) Rudd

Yellow Wood

Leaves **Pinnate, with 7 to 11 elliptic to ovate, untoothed leaflets, to 4in (10cm) long, the terminal one largest, bright green above and smooth on both sides, turning bright yellow in fall, the stalk swollen at the base and enclosing the bud.** ***Bark*** **Gray and smooth, often horizontally wrinkled.** ***Flowers*** **Pealike, 1¼in (3cm) long, white, slightly fragrant, in large, hanging panicles to 18in (45cm) long, at the ends of the shoots in early summer.** ***Fruit*** **A flattened, brown pod, to 4in (10cm) long.**

NATIVE REGION S.E. US.
HABITAT Rich woods and rocky bluffs.
REMARK Also known as virgilia. This species is rare in the wild, with a restricted distribution in only a few states. The wood produces a yellow dye.

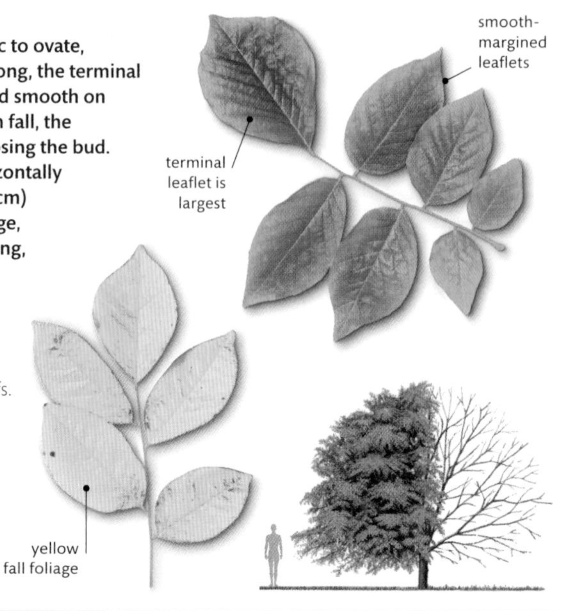

Height: 50ft (15m)	Shape: Broadly spreading	Leaf persistence: Deciduous	Leaf type:

Family: Fabaceae	Species: *Genista aetnensis*	Author: (Biv.) DC.

Mount Etna Broom

Leaves **Linear and small, ⅜in (1cm) long, borne sparsely on slender, bright green shoots; on mature plants usually absent by flowering time.** ***Bark*** **Gray-brown, deeply fissured at the base.** ***Flowers*** **Pealike, ⅝in (1.5cm) long, bright golden yellow, fragrant, profuse, borne singly along the new shoots in mid- to late summer.** ***Fruit*** **A small, blackish brown pod, about ⅜in (1cm) long, ending in a short, slender, pointed tip, and containing two or three seeds.**

NATIVE REGION Corsica, Sardinia, Sicily.
HABITAT Rocky slopes.
REMARK This species can be either a large shrub or a small tree. In the wild, it is found particularly on the slopes of Mount Etna, in Sicily, where it grows on old volcanic lava. The rushlike shoots take over the role of photosynthesis from the leaves. They are green even during winter, giving the tree an evergreen appearance.

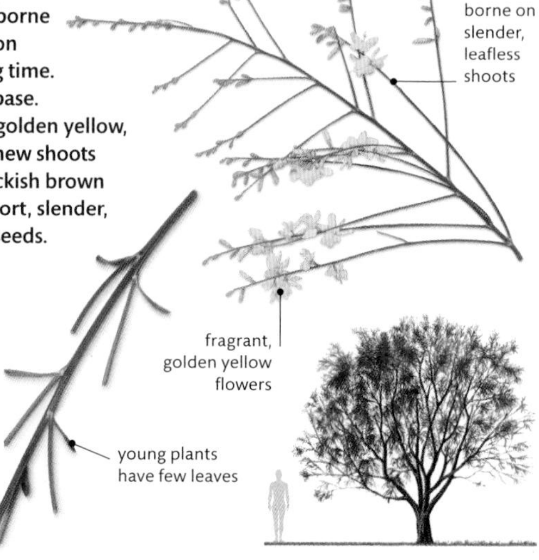

Height: 33ft (10m)	Shape: Broadly spreading	Leaf persistence: Deciduous	Leaf type:

Family: Fabaceae	Species: *Gleditsia triacanthos*	Author: L.

Honey Locust

Leaves First leaves from spurs on the old wood pinnate, later leaves on new shoots usually bipinnate, with numerous small leaflets, to 1½in (4cm) long, minutely toothed, bright green, turning yellow in fall; shoots usually spiny. ***Bark*** Dark gray, scaly, with clusters of branched spines. ***Flowers*** Males and females both very small and yellow-green, in separate small, cylindrical, mainly upright racemes to 2in (5cm) long, from the old shoots, on the same plant in early summer. ***Fruit*** A large, often twisted, brown, hanging pod, to 18in (45cm) long.

NATIVE REGION C. and E. US, N. Mexico.
HABITAT Rich, moist woods.
REMARK The fruits contain a sweet, edible flesh.

some leaves bipinnate

◁△ ***Gleditsia triacanthos***

some leaves pinnate

bright young leaves

'Sunburst' ▷
The foliage of this form matures from golden yellow to dark green.

Height: 100ft (30m)	Shape: Broadly spreading	Leaf persistence: Deciduous	Leaf type:

Family: Fabaceae	Species: *Gymnocladus dioicus*	Author: (L.) K. Koch

Kentucky Coffee Tree

Leaves Bipinnate and very large, to 39in (1m) long, with numerous ovate leaflets, to 3in (7.5cm) long, untoothed, bronze becoming dark green above, bluish beneath, becoming smooth on both sides, on very stout shoots. ***Bark*** Dark brown and rough, with scaly ridges. ***Flowers*** Whitish, fragrant, about 1in (2.5cm) across, in conical panicles, males to 4in (10cm) long, females to 12in (30cm) long, usually on separate plants in late spring to early summer. ***Fruit*** A large, leathery, red-brown, hanging pod, to 10in (25cm) long, persisting for some time.

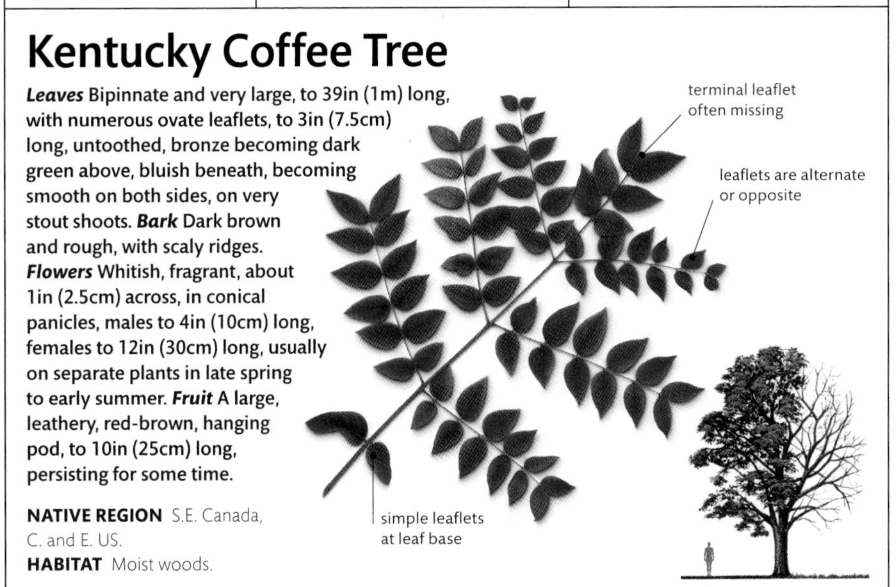

NATIVE REGION S.E. Canada, C. and E. US.
HABITAT Moist woods.

Height: 80ft (25m)	Shape: Broadly columnar	Leaf persistence: Deciduous	Leaf type: 

Family: Fabaceae	Species: + *Laburnocytisus adami*	Author: (Poit.) C.K. Schneid.

+ Laburnocytisus adami

Leaves **Variable, with three leaflets, resembling one parent or intermediate between both parents. *Bark* Dark gray, smooth, shallowly fissured with age. *Flowers* Pealike, of three sorts, either yellow laburnum or purple broom, resembling one parent, or between the two, the intermediate flowers pale purple-pink flushed yellow, borne in short, hanging racemes to 6in (15cm) long, in late spring to early summer. *Fruit* A brown pod, to 3in (7.5cm) long, hanging in clusters, with black seeds, produced from the yellow flowers.**

NATIVE REGION Of garden or backyard origin.
REMARK A chimera, or graft hybrid, between the common laburnum (*Laburnum anagyroides*, see p.139) and the shrubby purple broom (*Chamaecytisus purpureus*). A graft hybrid is not a true hybrid, because it contains a mixture of the tissues of the two genetically distinct parents. All parts of this tree are poisonous.

intermediate leaves are dark green above, paler beneath

intermediate flowers carried on most branches

△ **+ *Laburnocytisus adami***

laburnum leaves are dull gray-green

◁ ***Laburnum anagyroides***
Common laburnum (*Laburnum anagyroides*) forms the inner core of the + *Laburnocytisus adami* plant.

yellow laburnum flowers borne in drooping racemes

dense clusters of purple broom flowers borne on some branches

△ ***Chamaecytisus purpureus***
The outer envelope of the tree is formed by purple broom (*Chamaecytisus purpureus*).

purple broom leaves have tiny leaflets

Height: 20ft (6m)	Shape: Broadly spreading	Leaf persistence: Deciduous	Leaf type: 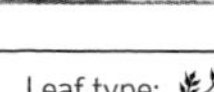

Family: Fabaceae	Species: *Laburnum alpinum*	Author: (Mill.) Bercht. & J. Presl

Scotch Laburnum

Leaves **Each with three separate, elliptic leaflets, to 4in (10cm) long, slightly pointed at the tip, shining deep green above, smooth, glossy, and nearly hairless when young beneath.** ***Bark*** **Dark gray and smooth, shallowly fissured with age.** ***Flowers*** **Pealike, ¾in (2cm) long, bright golden yellow, fragrant, borne in long, slender, hanging racemes to 18in (45cm) long, in early summer.** ***Fruit*** **A hairless, brown pod, to 3in (7.5cm) long, the upper margin flattened to a narrow wing, containing brown seeds.**

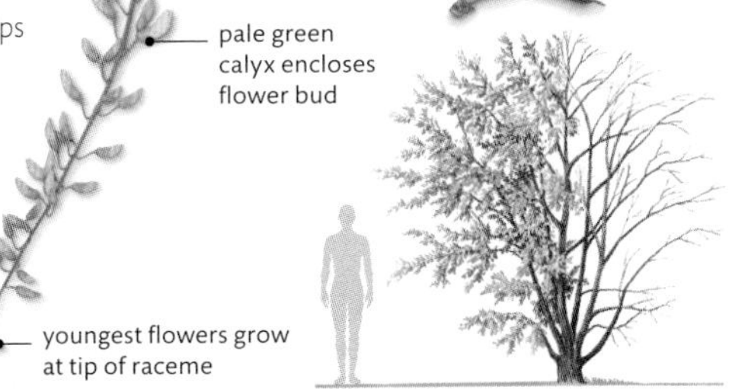

NATIVE REGION C. and S. Europe, from the Alps to the Czech Republic and the Balkans.
HABITAT Mountains.
REMARK This later-flowering laburnum can be a either a small tree or a shrub. The very long, delicate racemes of flowers are a particular feature of the species. All parts of the plant are poisonous if consumed, the seeds especially so.

Height: 20ft (6m)	Shape: Broadly spreading	Leaf persistence: Deciduous	Leaf type:

Family: Fabaceae	Species: *Laburnum anagyroides*	Author: Medik.

Common Laburnum

Leaves **Each with three elliptic leaflets, to 3½in (9cm) long, rounded at the tip, dull deep green above, gray-green and silky-hairy when young beneath.** ***Bark*** **Dark gray and smooth, shallowly fissured with age.** ***Flowers*** **Pealike, 1in (2.5cm) long, golden yellow, densely clustered, borne in hanging racemes to 10in (25cm) long, in late spring to early summer.** ***Fruit*** **A slightly rounded, hairy, brown pod, to 3in (7.5cm) long, the upper edge thickened, hanging in clusters, with black seeds.**

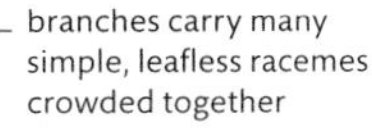

NATIVE REGION C. and S. Europe.
HABITAT Mountainous areas, woods, and thickets.
REMARK All parts of the plant contain a harmful alkaloid, and are poisonous if consumed. The immature seeds look like small, green peas.

Height: 23ft (7m)	Shape: Broadly spreading	Leaf persistence: Deciduous	Leaf type:

Family: Fabaceae	Species: *Laburnum* x *watereri*	Author: (A.C. Rosenthal & Bermann) Dippel

Laburnum x watereri

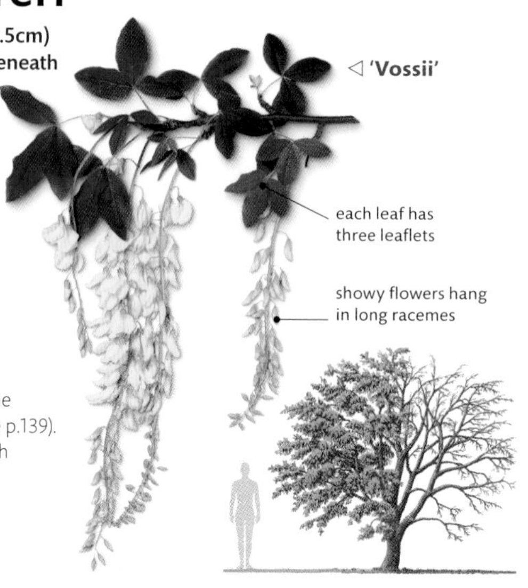

Leaves **With three elliptic leaflets, to 3in (7.5cm) long, deep green above, hairy but green beneath when young.** ***Bark*** **Dark gray and smooth, becoming shallowly fissured with age.** ***Flowers*** **Pealike, 1in (2.5cm) long, golden yellow, borne in dense, hanging racemes to 12in (30cm) long, in late spring to early summer.** ***Fruit*** **A brown pod, to 2½in (6cm) long, with few seeds, often sparsely produced.**

NATIVE REGION Austria, Switzerland.
HABITAT Mountains, with the parents.
REMARK A hybrid between the Scotch laburnum (*Laburnum alpinum*, see p.139) and the common laburnum (*Laburnum anagyroides*, see p.139). It combines the long racemes of the former with the large flowers of the latter. The form shown, 'Vossii,' is the most familiar. It bears its flowers in very long racemes, to 20in (50cm) or more.

Height: 23ft (7m)	Shape: Broadly spreading	Leaf persistence: Deciduous	Leaf type:

Family: Fabaceae	Species: *Maackia hupehensis*	Author: Takeda

Maackia hupehensis

Leaves **Pinnate, to 8in (20cm) long, with 9 to 13 elliptic to ovate, untoothed and shortly stalked leaflets, to 2½in (6cm) long and ¾in (2cm) across, silvery blue-gray when young becoming green above, downy beneath.** ***Bark*** **Gray-brown, marked with conspicuous lenticels.** ***Flowers*** **Pealike, ¾in (1cm) long, white, borne in dense, upright racemes, clustered at the ends of the shoots in mid-to late summer.** ***Fruit*** **A small pod, about 2in (5cm) long.**

NATIVE REGION C. and S. China.
HABITAT Woods and scrub in mountains.
REMARK This genus is related to *Cladrastis* (see p.136), but is distinguished by its flowers, which are borne in upright, rather than hanging, clusters.

Height: 50ft (15m)	Shape: Broadly spreading	Leaf persistence: Deciduous	Leaf type:

Family: Fabaceae	Species: *Robinia* x *holdtii*	Author: Beissn.

Robinia x holdtii

Leaves Pinnate, to 18in (45cm) long, with up to 21 oblong leaflets, to 2in (5cm) long and 1in (2.5cm) across, often indented at the tip with a very fine point, deep green above, gray-green beneath, thinly hairy on both sides. ***Bark*** Gray-brown, deeply furrowed, with scaly ridges. ***Flowers*** Pealike, ¾in (2cm) long, white flushed purplish pink, faintly fragrant, borne in hanging clusters over a long period in summer. ***Fruit*** A slightly sticky, bristly, red pod, about 2½in (6cm) long.

very long leaves with leaflets arranged in opposite pairs

flowers often produced into early fall

very fine point at tip of leaflet

NATIVE REGION W. US.
HABITAT This vigorous tree is a hybrid between the pink-flowered, often shrubby, *Robinia luxurians* and the black locust (*Robinia pseudoacacia*, see below). Of the two parent plants, it is most similar in appearance and habit to *Robinia pseudoacacia*, from which it is distinguished by the color of its flowers.

Height: 65ft (20m)	Shape: Broadly columnar	Leaf persistence: Deciduous	Leaf type:

Family: Fabaceae	Species: *Robinia pseudoacacia*	Author: L.

Black Locust

Leaves Pinnate, to 12in (30cm) long, with 11 to 21 elliptic to ovate, untoothed leaflets, to 2in (5cm) long, often indented and ending in a slender point, blue-green above, gray-green and thinly hairy becoming smooth beneath, the shoot often with two spines at the base of each leaf. ***Bark*** Gray-brown, deeply furrowed, with scaly ridges. ***Flowers*** Pealike, ¾in (2cm) long, white, with a yellow-green blotch, fragrant, in dense, hanging racemes to 8in (20cm) long, in early to midsummer. ***Fruit*** A smooth, dark brown, hanging pod, to 4in (10cm) long.

△ **'Frisia'**
This smaller form is less vigorous. It has golden yellow foliage from spring to early fall.

NATIVE REGION S.E. US.
HABITAT Woods and thickets.
REMARK Widely planted and naturalized in many countries.

Height: 80ft (25m)	Shape: Broadly columnar	Leaf persistence: Deciduous	Leaf type:

Family: Fabaceae	Species: *Sophora microphylla*	Author: Aiton

Kowhai

Leaves **Pinnate, to 6in (15cm) long, with numerous oblong, untoothed leaflets, to ⅜in (1cm) long, rounded or notched at the tip, dark green above, dull green beneath, silky-hairy when young, becoming smooth, on silky-hairy shoots.** ***Bark*** **Gray to gray-brown, smooth, with small lenticels.** ***Flowers*** **Pealike, to 2in (5cm) long, golden yellow, borne in hanging racemes in the leaf axils in late winter to spring.** ***Fruit*** **A winged, brown pod, to 6in (15cm) or more long, hairy when young.**

many small, paired leaflets

slender, exserted flower stamens

dull green underside of leaflets

NATIVE REGION New Zealand.
HABITAT Forests, open places, and riverbanks from sea level to the mountains.
REMARK Can be either a small tree or a large shrub and semi-evergreen or evergreen. It is closely related to the similar *Sophora tetraptera*, which is also known by the common name, kowhai. Seedlings go through an intricately branched juvenile phase, and take many years to flower.

Height: 33ft (10m)	Shape: Broadly spreading	Leaf persistence: Deciduous	Leaf type:

Family: Fabaceae	Species: *Styphnolobium japonicum*	Author: (L.) Schott

Pagoda Tree

Leaves **Pinnate, to 10in (25cm) long, with 7 to 17 ovate, pointed leaflets, to 2in (5cm) long, whitish becoming glossy dark green above, blue-green and hairy beneath, sometimes turning yellow in fall.** ***Bark*** **Gray-brown, with prominent ridges.** ***Flowers*** **Pealike, ⅝in (1.5cm) long, white, fragrant, borne in hanging panicles to 12in (30cm) long, at the ends of the shoots in late summer to early fall.** ***Fruit*** **A pod, to 3in (7.5cm) long, constricted between the seeds.**

NATIVE REGION China.
HABITAT Woods, thickets, and dry valleys in mountains.
REMARK Also known as Japanese pagoda tree.

some leaves turn yellow before falling

Height: 65ft (20m)	Shape: Broadly spreading	Leaf persistence: Deciduous	Leaf type:

FAGACEAE

SOME VERY FAMILIAR deciduous and evergreen trees belong to this family, which includes the chestnuts (*Castanea*, see pp.143–144), beeches (*Fagus*, see pp.145–147), and oaks (*Quercus*, see pp.149–164). Eight genera with about 1,000 species extend from northern temperate regions to parts of the southern hemisphere. Leaves are simple, and often lobed or toothed. The small male or female flowers are often borne in separate catkins, on the same plant. The fruit is a nut, surrounded by, or enclosed in, a cupule.

Family: Fagaceae	Species: *Castanea dentata*	Author: (Marshall) Borkh.

American Chestnut

Leaves Oblong, to 10in (25cm) long and 2in (5cm) across, narrowed at the base, taper-pointed at the tip, sharply toothed, matte dark green above, paler beneath, smooth on both sides. ***Bark*** Dark brown, shallowly fissured, with broad, scaly ridges. ***Flowers*** Males and females both small and creamy yellow, in catkins to 8in (20cm) long, separate but usually on the same spike in summer. ***Fruit*** A spiny husk, to 2½in (6cm) across, enclosing one to three edible, sweet, glossy red-brown nuts.

NATIVE REGION E. North America.
HABITAT Woods.
REMARK Increasingly rare in the wild.

matte green leaf upperside

leaf margin edged with numerous bristly teeth

leaves narrow toward base

Height: 100ft (30m)	Shape: Broadly columnar	Leaf persistence: Deciduous	Leaf type:

Family: Fagaceae	Species: *Castanea mollissima*	Author: Blume

Chinese Chestnut

Leaves Oblong to lanceolate, to 8in (20cm) long and 3in (7.5cm) across, usually rounded at the base, taper-pointed at the tip, coarsely toothed, glossy dark green and smooth above, softly hairy beneath, at least when young. ***Bark*** Dark gray, smooth, becoming gray-brown and deeply fissured with age. ***Flowers*** Males and females both small and creamy yellow, in catkins to 8in (20cm) long, separate but usually on the same spike in summer. ***Fruit*** A spiny, downy husk, to 2in (5cm) across, enclosing two to three edible, glossy red-brown nuts.

NATIVE REGION China, Korea.
HABITAT Mountain woods.
REMARK This species is grown in China for its nuts.

Height: 80ft (25m)	Shape: Broadly columnar	Leaf persistence: Deciduous	Leaf type:

Family: Fagaceae	Species: *Castanea sativa*	Author: Mill.

Sweet Chestnut

Leaves Oblong, to 8in (20cm) long and 3in (7.5cm) across, usually rounded or heart-shaped at the base, taper-pointed at the tip, toothed, glossy dark green and smooth above, paler becoming smooth beneath. ***Bark*** Gray and smooth, becoming brown and usually spirally ridged with age. ***Flowers*** Males and females both small and creamy yellow, in catkins to 10in (25cm) long, separate but usually on the same spike in summer. ***Fruit*** A spiny husk, to 2½in (6cm) across, enclosing one to three edible, glossy red-brown nuts.

NATIVE REGION N. Africa, S.W. Asia, S. Europe.
HABITAT Woods.

leaves edged with coarse, bristly teeth

green fruit husks

male and female flowers clustered on same spike

each prickly fruit husk contains up to three nuts

Height: 100ft (30m)	Shape: Broadly columnar	Leaf persistence: Deciduous	Leaf type: 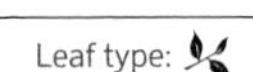

Family: Fagaceae	Species: *Chrysolepis chrysophylla*	Author: (Marshall) Borkh.

Golden Chinkapin

Leaves Oblong to lanceolate, to 4in (10cm) or more long and 1in (2.5cm) across, rigid, leathery, untoothed, glossy dark green above, hairy beneath. ***Bark*** Gray, furrowed. ***Flowers*** Males and females both creamy white, fragrant, in catkins to 1½in (4cm) long, separate but usually on the same spike in summer. ***Fruit*** A spiny husk, to 1½in (4cm) across, enclosing one to three edible, glossy brown nuts.

NATIVE REGION W. US.
HABITAT Woods and thickets in coastal mountains.

leaves taper to very long, slender point

nuts inside densely prickly husk ripen in two years

leaf underside covered in golden hairs

Height: 100ft (30m)	Shape: Broadly conical	Leaf persistence: Evergreen	Leaf type: 

Family: Fagaceae	Species: *Fagus grandifolia*	Author: Ehrh.

American Beech

Leaves Ovate to elliptic, to 4¾in (12cm) long and 2½in (6cm) across, taper-pointed, toothed, with 11 to 15 pairs of veins, silky-hairy becoming smooth or nearly so, glossy dark green above, paler beneath, turning yellow in fall. ***Bark*** Gray, smooth. ***Flowers*** Males and females both small, males yellow, females green, in separate clusters on the same plant in mid-spring. ***Fruit*** A husk, to ¾in (2cm) long, enclosing one to three small, edible nuts.

NATIVE REGION E. North America.
HABITAT Rich woods.

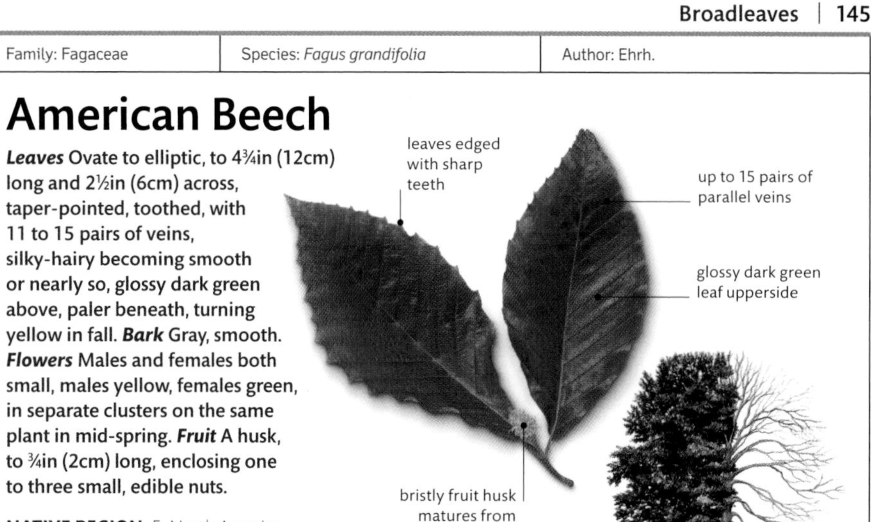

Height: 80ft (25m)	Shape: Broadly spreading	Leaf persistence: Deciduous	Leaf type:

Family: Fagaceae	Species: *Fagus orientalis*	Author: Lipsky

Oriental Beech

Leaves Elliptic to obovate, to 4¾in (12cm) long and 2½in (6cm) across, usually with a wavy margin, untoothed or slightly toothed, with up to 12 pairs of veins, dark green and smooth above, silky-hairy on the veins beneath, turning yellow in fall. ***Bark*** Gray and smooth, sometimes furrowed. ***Flowers*** Males and females both small, males yellow, females green, in separate clusters on the same plant in mid-spring. ***Fruit*** A bristly husk, to 1in (2.5cm) long, enclosing one to three small, edible nuts.

NATIVE REGION S.W. Asia, S.E. Europe.
HABITAT Hills and mountains.

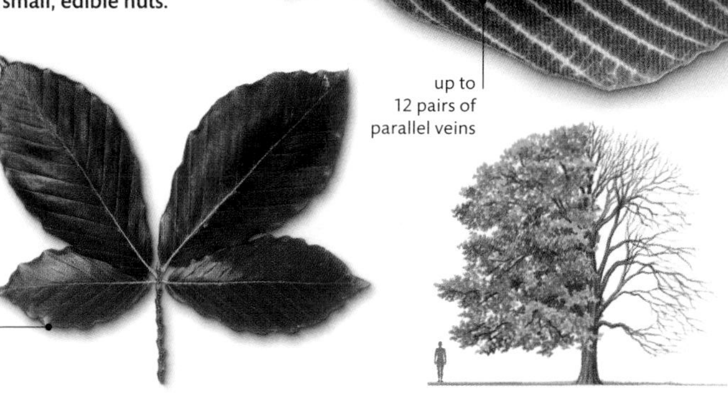

Height: 100ft (30m)	Shape: Broadly spreading	Leaf persistence: Deciduous	Leaf type:

Family: Fagaceae	Species: *Fagus sylvatica*	Author: L.

Common Beech

Leaves **Ovate to obovate, to 4in (10cm) long and 2½in (6cm) across, abruptly short-pointed, with a wavy margin, untoothed or edged with small teeth, with fewer than 10 pairs of veins, silky-hairy when unfolding becoming smooth, glossy dark green above, paler beneath, turning yellow in fall.** ***Bark*** **Gray, smooth.** ***Flowers*** **Small, males yellow, females green, borne in separate clusters on the same plant in mid-spring as the young, pale green leaves emerge.** ***Fruit*** **A bristly husk, to 1in (2.5cm) long, enclosing one to three small, edible nuts.**

NATIVE REGION Europe.
HABITAT Woods, particularly on chalk.

fruit husk covered in dense bristles

◁△ ***Fagus sylvatica***

wavy, untoothed or slightly toothed leaf margin

no more than 10 pairs of parallel veins

▽ **'Aspleniifolia'**
The slender leaves of the fern-leaved beech are deeply cut into long, narrow lobes.

leaves taper to long, fine point

△ **'Aurea Pendula'**
This slender tree has hanging branches, clothed from spring to fall with foliage that matures from golden yellow to green.

curiously contorted leaves

'Cristata' ▷
Clustered and seemingly misshapen leaves are a feature of this very unusual form.

Height: 130ft (40m)	Shape: Broadly spreading	Leaf persistence: Deciduous	Leaf type:

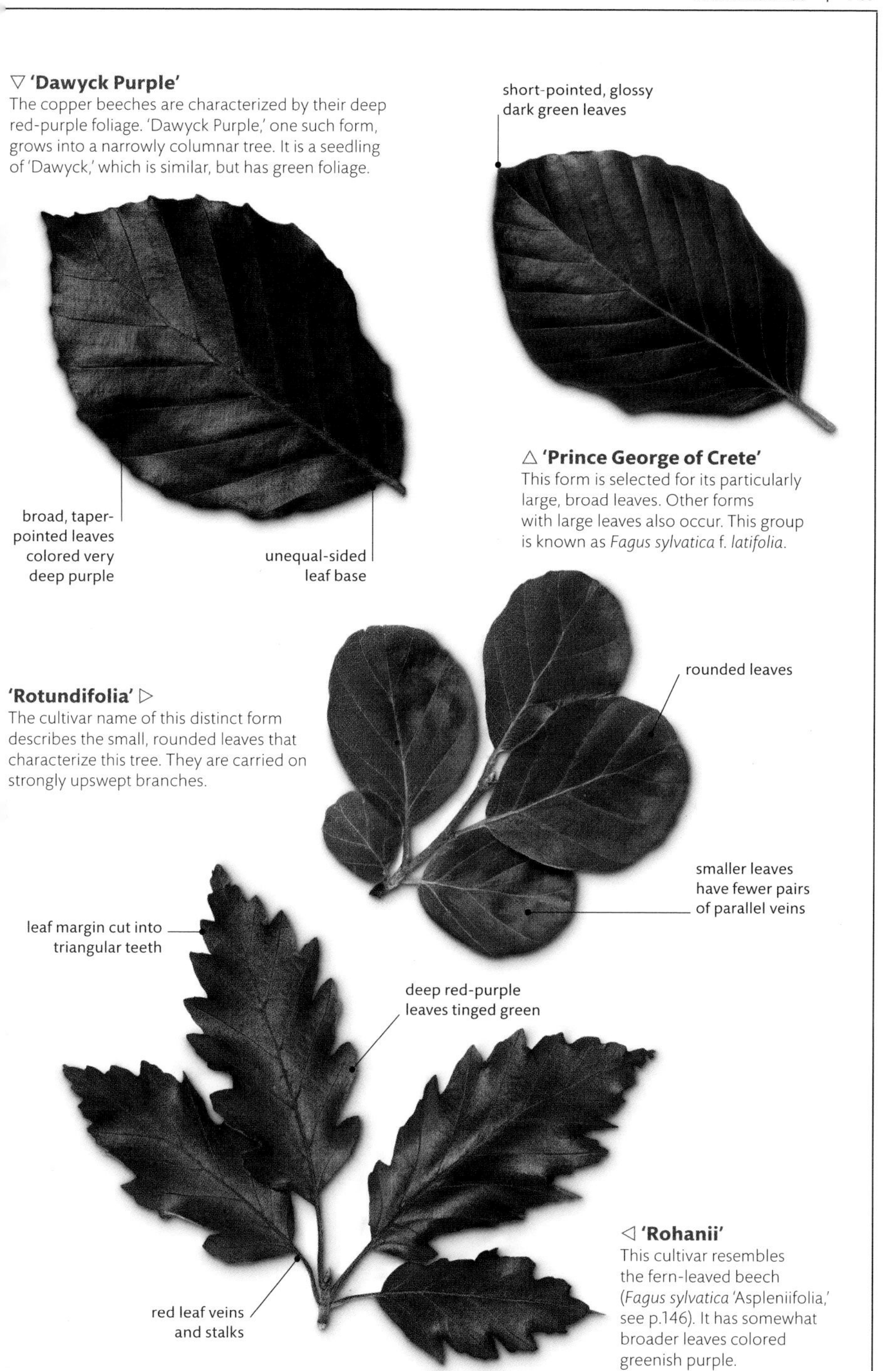

▽ 'Dawyck Purple'
The copper beeches are characterized by their deep red-purple foliage. 'Dawyck Purple,' one such form, grows into a narrowly columnar tree. It is a seedling of 'Dawyck,' which is similar, but has green foliage.

△ 'Prince George of Crete'
This form is selected for its particularly large, broad leaves. Other forms with large leaves also occur. This group is known as *Fagus sylvatica* f. *latifolia*.

'Rotundifolia' ▷
The cultivar name of this distinct form describes the small, rounded leaves that characterize this tree. They are carried on strongly upswept branches.

◁ 'Rohanii'
This cultivar resembles the fern-leaved beech (*Fagus sylvatica* 'Aspleniifolia,' see p.146). It has somewhat broader leaves colored greenish purple.

Family: Fagaceae	Species: *Lithocarpus edulis*	Author: (Makino) Nakai

Lithocarpus edulis

Leaves **Narrowly elliptic, to 6in (15cm) long and 2in (5cm) across, gradually tapered from the center of the leaf to the base, with a short, blunt point at the tip, untoothed, rigid and leathery, glossy pale green above, gray-green beneath, smooth.** ***Bark*** **Gray-brown, smooth.** ***Flowers*** **Males and females both very small and creamy white, in slender, upright catkins, males at the tip of the catkin, females at the base, in the leaf axils in late summer.** ***Fruit*** **A pointed acorn, to 1in (2.5cm) long, about one-third enclosed in a cup, in stalkless clusters, ripe in two years.**

NATIVE REGION Japan.
HABITAT Woods.
REMARK *Lithocarpus* species are closely related to the oaks (*Quercus*, see pp.149–164), but differ in their upright catkins.

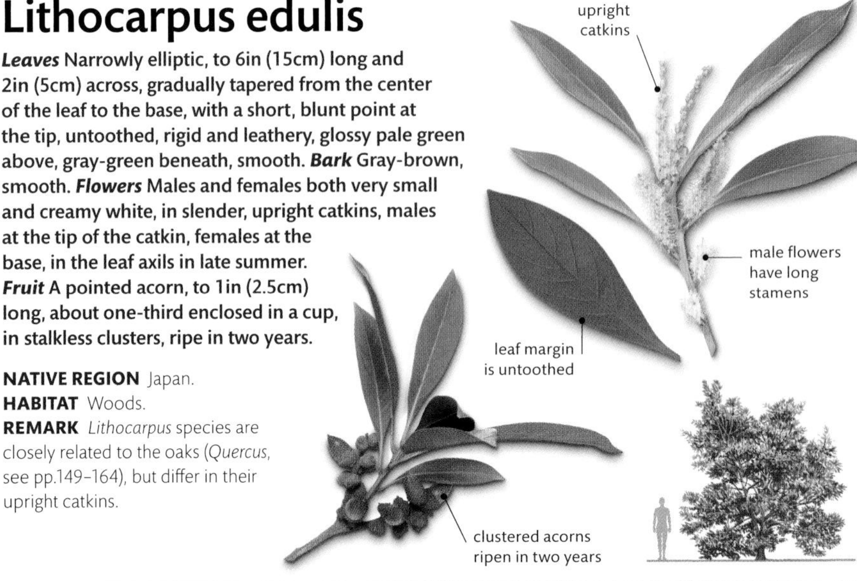

Height: 50ft (15m)	Shape: Broadly spreading	Leaf persistence: Evergreen	Leaf type:

Family: Fagaceae	Species: *Lithocarpus henryi*	Author: (Seemen) Rehder & E.H. Wilson

Lithocarpus henryi

Leaves **Elliptic to oblong or lanceolate, to 10in (25cm) long and 3in (7.5cm) across, tapered to a slender point at the tip, untoothed, pale green becoming dark and slightly glossy, whitish beneath when young, thinly hairy becoming smooth on both sides.** ***Bark*** **Gray, with pale gray lenticels, and shallow, orange-brown fissures at the base.** ***Flowers*** **Males and females both very small and creamy white, in slender, upright catkins, separately but on the same spike in late summer.** ***Fruit*** **A rounded acorn, about ¾in (2cm) long, enclosed in a shallow cup, borne in dense clusters.**

NATIVE REGION China.
HABITAT Woods in hills and mountains.
REMARK The bold, long-pointed leaves make the massed foliage a handsome sight.

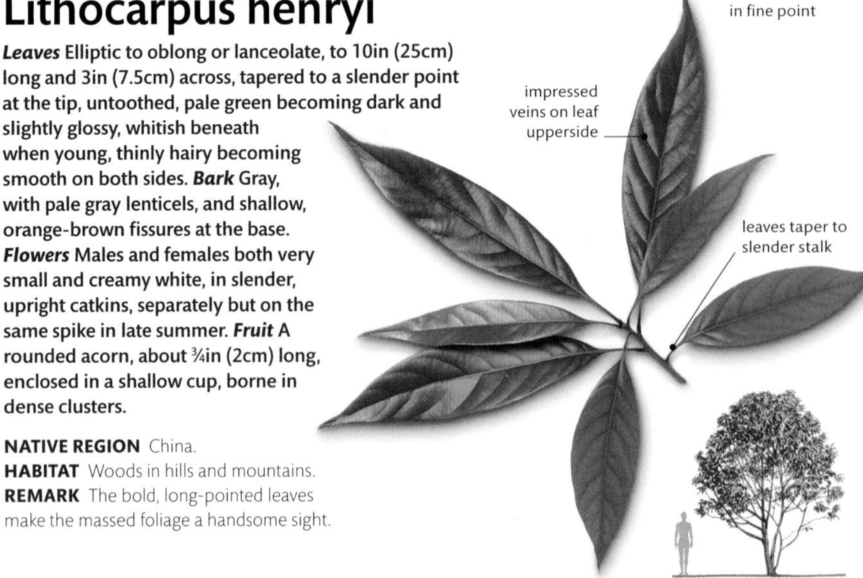

Height: 50ft (15m)	Shape: Broadly conical	Leaf persistence: Evergreen	Leaf type: 

Family: Fagaceae	Species: *Quercus acutissima*	Author: Carruth.

Asian Chestnut Oak

Leaves Oblong, to 8in (20cm) long and 2½in (6cm) across, with numerous veins ending in slender-tipped teeth, glossy green above, paler beneath, smooth on both sides. ***Bark*** Gray-brown, with deep fissures. ***Flowers*** Males in yellow-green, drooping catkins, females inconspicuous, borne separately on the same plant in late spring. ***Fruit*** A rounded acorn, to 1in (2.5cm) long, about two-thirds enclosed in a cup.

NATIVE REGION Himalayas to Japan.
HABITAT Woods.

acorn cup loosely covered with long, slender scales

leaves edged with bristlelike teeth

Height: 50ft (15m)	Shape: Broadly spreading	Leaf persistence: Deciduous	Leaf type: 

Family: Fagaceae	Species: *Quercus alba*	Author: L.

White Oak

Leaves Obovate, to 8in (20cm) long and 4in (10cm) across, tapered at the base, deeply cut into two to four lobes on each side, pink-tinged and white-hairy becoming bright green above, blue-green beneath, turning purple-red in fall. ***Bark*** Pale gray and scaly, fissured with age. ***Flowers*** Males in yellow-green, drooping catkins, females inconspicuous, borne separately on the same plant in late spring. ***Fruit*** An acorn, to 1in (2.5cm) long, one-quarter enclosed in a roughened cup.

NATIVE REGION E. North America.
HABITAT Dry woods.
REMARK In the US, the State tree of Connecticut, Illinois, and Maryland.

rough-textured, scaly acorn cup

untoothed leaf lobes

leaves color brilliantly in the fall

Height: 115ft (35m)	Shape: Broadly spreading	Leaf persistence: Deciduous	Leaf type:

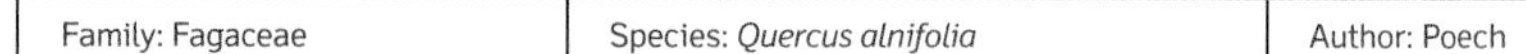

Family: Fagaceae	Species: *Quercus alnifolia*	Author: Poech

Golden Oak of Cyprus

Leaves **Rounded and convex, to 2in (5cm) long and across, leathery, edged with small teeth, glossy dark green and smooth above, covered in golden felt beneath.** ***Bark*** **Dark gray, with pale gray to orange-brown lenticels.** ***Flowers*** **Males in yellow-green, drooping catkins, females inconspicuous, borne separately on the same plant in late spring.** ***Fruit*** **An acorn, to 1¼in (3cm) long.**

NATIVE REGION Cyprus.
HABITAT Mountains.
REMARK Easily distinguished from most oaks by the felted leaf underside.

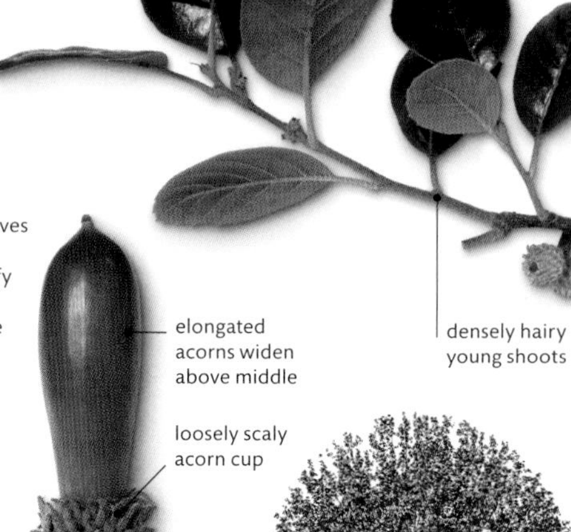

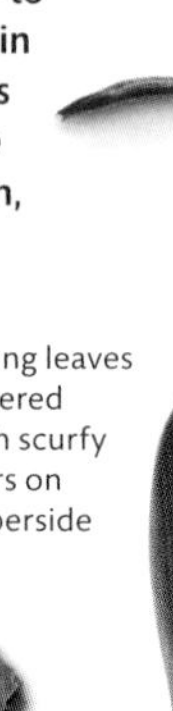

Height: 26ft (8m)	Shape: Broadly spreading	Leaf persistence: Evergreen	Leaf type:

Family: Fagaceae	Species: *Quercus canariensis*	Author: Willd.

Algerian Oak

Leaves **Obovate to elliptic, to 6in (15cm) long and 3in (7.5cm) across, with usually 8 to 12 prominent lobes, reddish and hairy becoming dark green and smooth above, paler beneath.** ***Bark*** **Dark gray and thick, with deep fissures.** ***Flowers*** **Males in yellow-green, drooping catkins, females inconspicuous, borne separately on the same plant in late spring.** ***Fruit*** **An acorn, to 1in (2.5cm) long, one-third enclosed in a cup.**

NATIVE REGION N. Africa, S.W. Europe.
HABITAT Woods.
REMARK The scientific name suggests that this species might be associated with the Canary Islands, but it is not native to these islands.

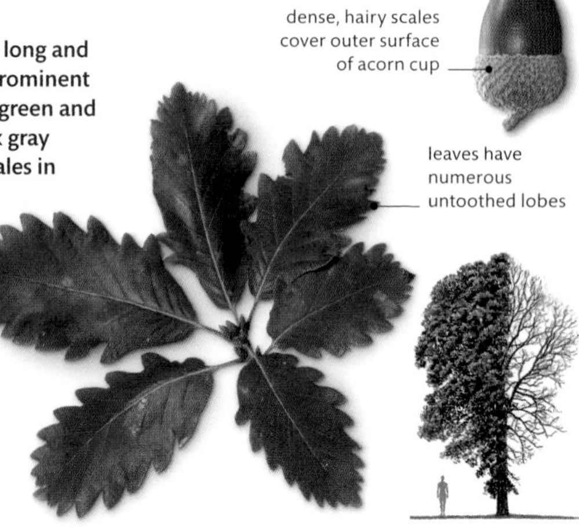

Height: 80ft (25m)	Shape: Broadly columnar	Leaf persistence: Deciduous	Leaf type:

Family: Fagaceae	Species: *Quercus castaneifolia*	Author: C.A. Mey.

Chestnut-leaved Oak

Leaves Oblong, to 8in (20cm) long and 3in (7.5cm) across, with 10 to 12 teeth on each side, glossy dark green and smooth above, blue-gray and thinly hairy beneath. ***Bark*** Gray and smooth. ***Flowers*** Males in yellow-green, drooping catkins, females inconspicuous, borne separately on the same plant in late spring. ***Fruit*** An acorn, to 1in (2.5cm) long, one-half enclosed in a cup, the cup covered in long scales.

NATIVE REGION Caucasus, N. Iran.
HABITAT Forests.

Height: 100ft (30m)	Shape: Broadly spreading	Leaf persistence: Deciduous	Leaf type:

Family: Fagaceae	Species: *Quercus cerris*	Author: L.

Turkey Oak

Leaves Elliptic to oblong, to 4¾in (12cm) long and 3in (7.5cm) across, deeply lobed, toothed, glossy dark green above, downy when young becoming smooth beneath. ***Bark*** Dark gray-brown, thick, rough, and deeply ridged. ***Flowers*** Males in yellow-green, drooping catkins, females inconspicuous, borne separately on the same plant in early summer. ***Fruit*** An acorn, to 1in (2.5cm) long, one-half enclosed in a cup, the cup covered in long, slender scales.

NATIVE REGION C. and S. Europe.
HABITAT Woods.

◁△ ***Quercus cerris***

◁ **'Argenteovariegata'**
The leaves of this form are margined yellow when they unfold, and creamy white as they mature.

 Height: 115ft (35m)	Shape: Broadly spreading	Leaf persistence: Deciduous	Leaf type: 

Family: Fagaceae	Species: *Quercus coccinea*	Author: Münchh.

Scarlet Oak

Leaves Elliptic, to 6in (15cm) long and 4in (10cm) across, deeply lobed, toothed, glossy dark green and smooth above, paler and glossy beneath, with small tufts of hairs in the vein axils, turning bright red in fall. ***Bark*** Dark gray-brown, smooth, shallowly ridged with age. ***Flowers*** Males in yellow-green, drooping catkins, females inconspicuous, borne separately on the same plant in late spring. ***Fruit*** An acorn, to 1in (2.5cm) long, up to one-half enclosed in a glossy cup.

NATIVE REGION E. North America.
HABITAT Woods and sandy soil.

△ ***Quercus coccinea***

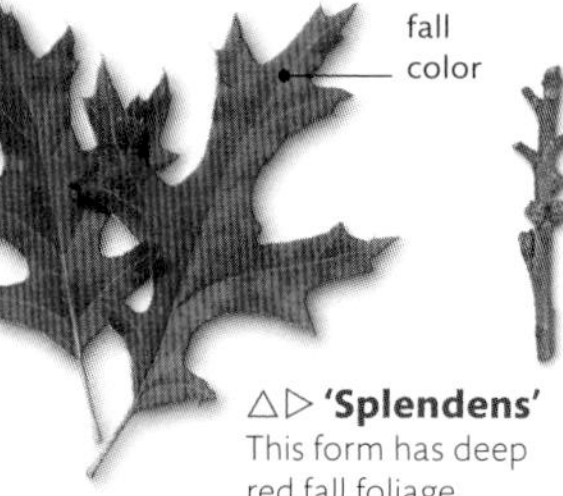

△▷ **'Splendens'**
This form has deep red fall foliage.

Height: 80ft (25m)	Shape: Broadly spreading	Leaf persistence: Deciduous	Leaf type:

Family: Fagaceae	Species: *Quercus* x *crenata*	Author: Lam.

Quercus x crenata

Leaves Ovate to elliptic or oblong, to 5in (13cm) long and 2in (5cm) across, toothed, glossy dark green above, gray and downy beneath. ***Bark*** Gray, corky. ***Flowers*** Males in yellow-green, drooping catkins, females inconspicuous, borne separately on the same plant in late spring. ***Fruit*** An acorn, to 1in (2.5cm) long, about one-third enclosed in a cup.

NATIVE REGION S.W. Europe.
HABITAT Woods, usually with both parents.
REMARK A hybrid between turkey oak (*Quercus cerris*, see p.151) and cork oak (*Quercus suber*, see p.163). Also known as *Quercus* x *hispanica*. Leaves can remain well into winter.

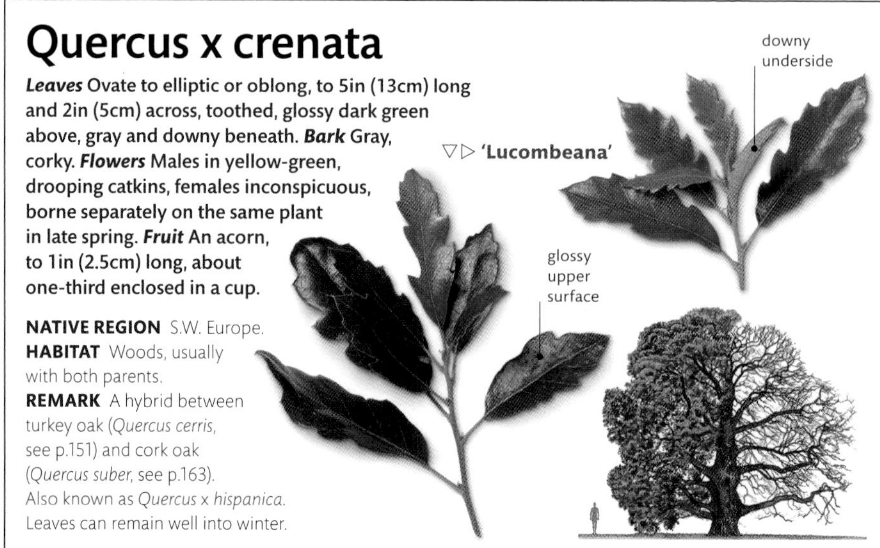

▽▷ **'Lucombeana'**

Height: 100ft (30m)	Shape: Broadly spreading	Leaf persistence: Deciduous	Leaf type:

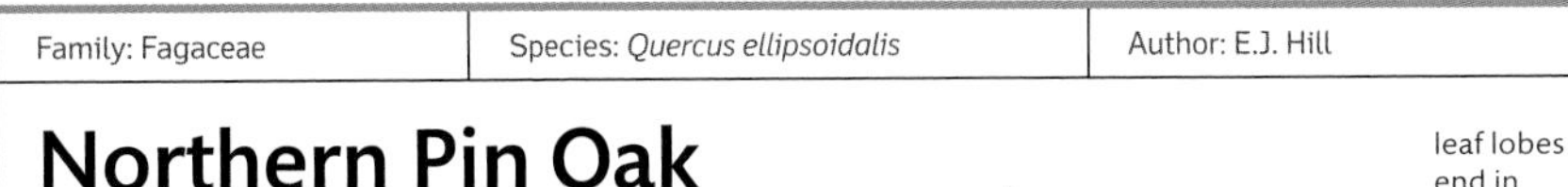

Family: Fagaceae	Species: *Quercus ellipsoidalis*	Author: E.J. Hill

Northern Pin Oak

Leaves Elliptic, to 5in (13cm) long and 4in (10cm) across, very deeply lobed, the lobes ending in slender-pointed teeth, glossy dark green and smooth above, paler and glossy with distinct tufts of brown hairs in the vein axils beneath, turning deep red-purple in fall.
Bark Gray, smooth or lightly furrowed.
Flowers Males in yellow-green, drooping catkins, females inconspicuous, borne separately on the same plant in late spring. ***Fruit*** An acorn, to ¾in (2cm) long, one-third to one-half enclosed in a grey cup.

NATIVE REGION
S. Canada, N. US.
HABITAT Woods, usually on dry soil.

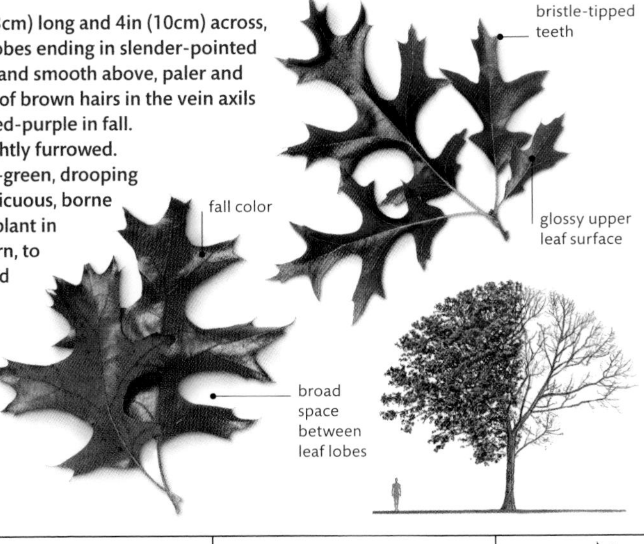

Height: 80ft (25m)	Shape: Broadly spreading	Leaf persistence: Deciduous	Leaf type:

Family: Fagaceae	Species: *Quercus falcata*	Author: Michx.

Spanish Oak

Leaves Elliptic to ovate, to 8in (20cm) long and 6in (15cm) across, deeply cut into bristle-tipped lobes, the terminal lobe often long and narrow, glossy dark green and smooth above, covered in brown or grayish hairs beneath. ***Bark*** Dark gray-brown, fissured into narrow ridges. ***Flowers*** Males in yellow-green, drooping catkins, females inconspicuous, borne separately on the same plant in late spring. ***Fruit*** An acorn, to ¾in (2cm) long, one-third to one-half enclosed in a broad, shallow cup.

NATIVE REGION
S.E. US.
HABITAT Dry woods from coast to mountains.

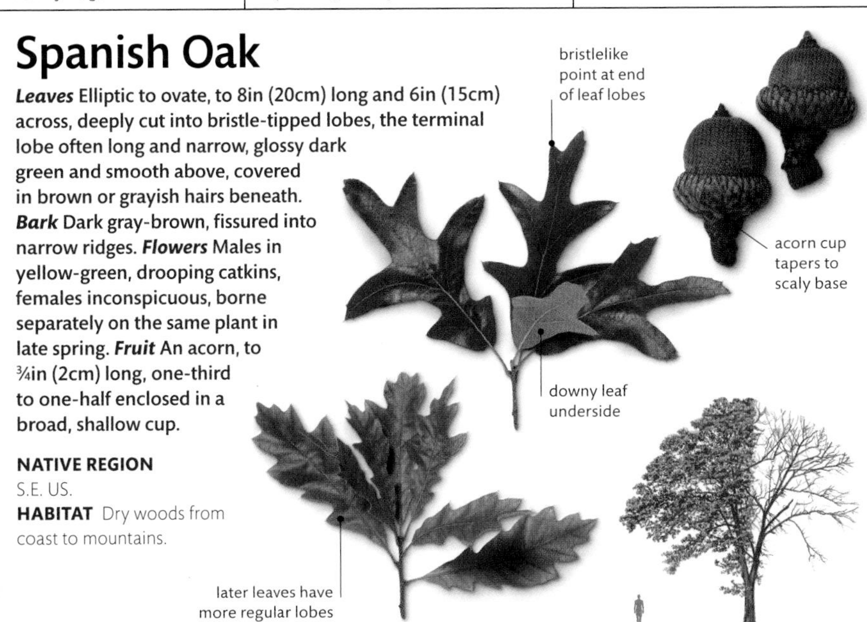

Height: 80ft (25m)	Shape: Broadly spreading	Leaf persistence: Deciduous	Leaf type: 

Family: Fagaceae	Species: *Quercus frainetto*	Author: Ten.

Hungarian Oak

Leaves Obovate to oblong, to 8in (20cm) long and 4in (10cm) across, with numerous lobes, deep green and hairy above, at least when young, gray-green and downy beneath. ***Bark*** Dark gray, rugged and fissured. ***Flowers*** Males in yellow-green, drooping catkins, females inconspicuous, borne separately on the same plant in late spring. ***Fruit*** An acorn, to ¾in (2cm) long, one-half enclosed in a cup.

NATIVE REGION Italy to Turkey.
HABITAT Woods.
REMARK The form shown, 'Hungarian Crown,' has branches that sweep up to make a broadly oval crown.

◁△ **'Hungarian Crown'**

Height: 100ft (30m)	Shape: Broadly spreading	Leaf persistence: Deciduous	Leaf type:

Family: Fagaceae	Species: *Quercus ilex*	Author: L.

Holm Oak

Leaves Elliptic to narrowly ovate, to 3in (7.5cm) long and 2in (5cm) across, rigid and leathery, taper-pointed, untoothed or with few small teeth, white-hairy when young becoming glossy dark green above, gray and hairy beneath; on young plants, variable in shape, with a spiny margin. ***Bark*** Nearly black, rough, cracking into small squares. ***Flowers*** Males in yellow, drooping catkins, females inconspicuous, borne separately on the same plant in early summer. ***Fruit*** An acorn, to ¾in (2cm) long, one-third enclosed in a cup.

NATIVE REGION Mediterranean.
HABITAT Hills, woods, scrub, and dry places.

Height: 100ft (30m)	Shape: Broadly spreading	Leaf persistence: Evergreen	Leaf type:

Family: Fagaceae	Species: *Quercus imbricaria*	Author: Michx.

Shingle Oak

Leaves Oblong to lanceolate, to 6in (15cm) long and 3in (7.5cm) across, ending in a fine tip, untoothed, yellow when young becoming glossy dark green and smooth above, gray-hairy beneath, often persisting far into winter. ***Bark*** Gray-brown, smooth at first becoming fissured with age. ***Flowers*** Males in yellow-green, drooping catkins, females inconspicuous, borne separately on the same plant in early summer. ***Fruit*** An acorn, to ¾in (2cm) long, one-third to one-half enclosed in a cup, the cup covered in broad, hairy scales.

NATIVE REGION C. and E. US.
HABITAT Rich woods and riverbanks.
REMARK Early settlers made roof shingles from the wood, giving this species its common name.

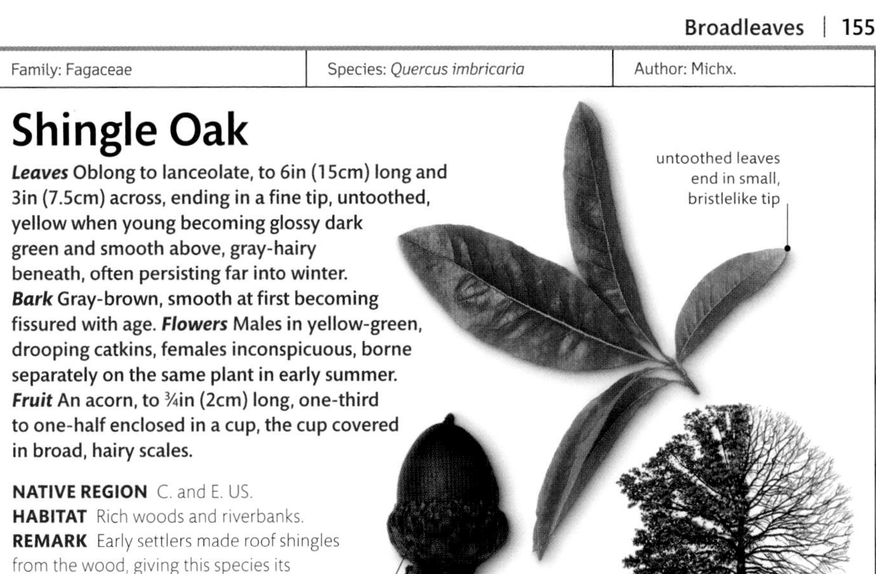

Height: 80ft (25m)	Shape: Broadly spreading	Leaf persistence: Deciduous	Leaf type:

Family: Fagaceae	Species: *Quercus laurifolia*	Author: Michx.

Laurel Oak

Leaves Oblanceolate to oblong, to 4in (10cm) long and 1½in (4cm) across, sometimes shallowly lobed, untoothed, glossy green, smooth on both sides. ***Bark*** Gray and scaly. ***Flowers*** Males in yellow-green, drooping catkins, females inconspicuous, borne separately on the same plant in early summer. ***Fruit*** An acorn, to ⅝in (1.5cm) long, one-third enclosed in a cup.

NATIVE REGION S.E. US.
HABITAT Woods, sandy soil, and swamp margins on coastal plains.
REMARK Also known as Darlington oak. The leaves look similar to those of the bay laurel (*Laurus nobilis*, see p.172). They persist through fall into winter, giving the tree a semi-evergreen appearance.

Height: 65ft (20m)	Shape: Broadly conical	Leaf persistence: Deciduous	Leaf type:

Family: Fagaceae	Species: *Quercus macranthera*	Author: Fisch. & C.A. Mey. ex Hohen.

Caucasian Oak

Leaves Obovate, to 6in (15cm) long and 4in (10cm) across, with 6 to 11 rounded lobes on each side, dark green above, paler and hairy beneath, carried on stout, densely hairy shoots. ***Bark*** Gray-brown, thick and fissured. ***Flowers*** Males in yellow-green, drooping catkins, females inconspicuous, borne separately on the same plant in early summer. ***Fruit*** An acorn, to 1in (2.5cm) long, one-half enclosed in a cup, the cup covered in hairy scales.

NATIVE REGION Caucasus, N. Iran.
HABITAT Forests on dry mountain slopes.

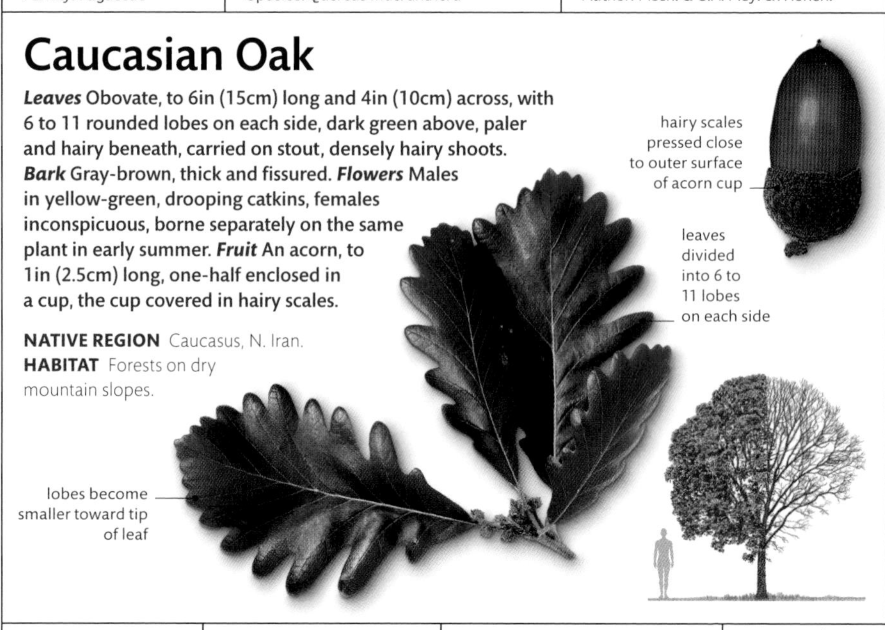

Height: 65ft (20m)	Shape: Broadly spreading	Leaf persistence: Deciduous	Leaf type:

Family: Fagaceae	Species: *Quercus macrocarpa*	Author: Michx.

Burr Oak

Leaves Obovate, to 10in (25cm) long and 4¾in (12cm) across, deeply cut into round-ended lobes, with a distinct, broad sinus toward the base, glossy green and smooth above, paler and hairy beneath. ***Bark*** Gray, rough, and deeply furrowed. ***Flowers*** Males in yellow, drooping catkins, females inconspicuous, borne separately on the same plant in early summer. ***Fruit*** An acorn, to 2in (5cm) long, one-half or more enclosed in a cup, the cup rimmed with a fringe of scales.

NATIVE REGION E. North America.
HABITAT Rich woods.
REMARK Also known as blue oak, mossy cup oak. The acorns are larger than any other oak in US.

Height: 130ft (40m)	Shape: Broadly spreading	Leaf persistence: Deciduous	Leaf type:

Family: Fagaceae	Species: *Quercus marilandica*	Author: Münchh.

Black Jack Oak

Leaves Triangular-obovate, to 10in (25cm) long and nearly the same across at the tip, tapered at the base, usually with three bristle-pointed lobes at the tip, glossy dark green above, paler beneath, thinly hairy becoming nearly smooth on both sides. ***Bark*** Blackish, cracking into small, square plates. ***Flowers*** Males in yellow-green, drooping catkins, females inconspicuous, borne separately on the same plant in early summer. ***Fruit*** An acorn, to ¾in (2cm) long, about one-half enclosed in a cup.

NATIVE REGION E. US.
HABITAT Woods and poor, often sandy, soil.

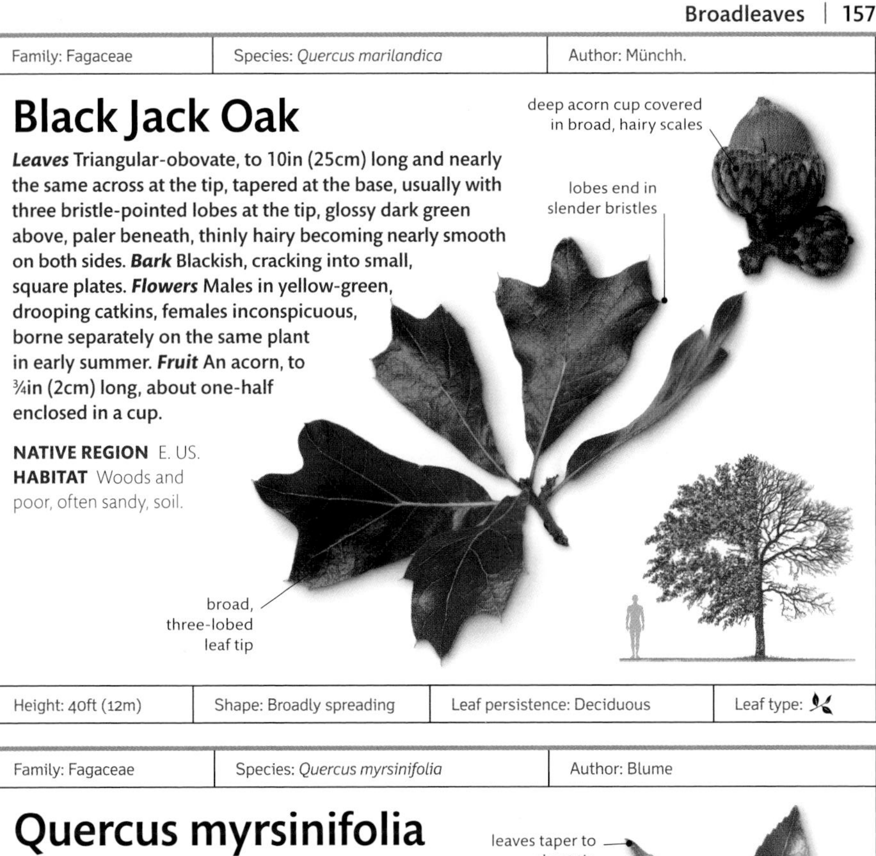

Height: 40ft (12m)	Shape: Broadly spreading	Leaf persistence: Deciduous	Leaf type:

Family: Fagaceae	Species: *Quercus myrsinifolia*	Author: Blume

Quercus myrsinifolia

Leaves Lanceolate, to 4in (10cm) long and 1¼in (3cm) across, leathery, taper-pointed, with few small teeth, deep bronze-red when young becoming dark green above, blue-green beneath, smooth on both sides. ***Bark*** Dark gray and smooth. ***Flowers*** Males in yellow-green, drooping catkins, females inconspicuous, borne separately on the same plant in early summer. ***Fruit*** An acorn, to ¾in (2cm) long, one-third enclosed in a cup.

NATIVE REGION China, Japan.
HABITAT Forests.

Height: 65ft (20m)	Shape: Broadly spreading	Leaf persistence: Evergreen	Leaf type:

Family: Fagaceae	Species: *Quercus palustris*	Author: Münchh.

Pin Oak

Leaves Elliptic to obovate, to 6in (15cm) long and 4¾in (12cm) across, deeply lobed, glossy green on both sides, paler with tufts of brown hairs in the vein axils beneath. ***Bark*** Gray-brown, smooth. ***Flowers*** Males in yellow-green, drooping catkins, females inconspicuous, borne separately on the same plant in late spring. ***Fruit*** An acorn, to ⅝in (1.5cm) long, one-quarter to one-third enclosed in a broad cup.

NATIVE REGION S.E. Canada, E. US.
HABITAT Swampy woods.

hairy tufts in vein axils on underside of leaves

bristle-tipped teeth at end of leaf lobes

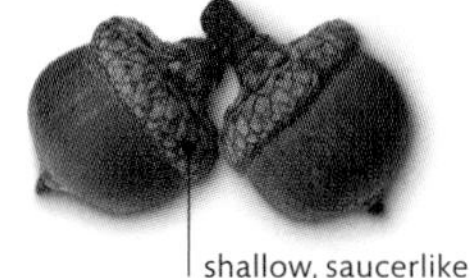

shallow, saucerlike acorn cup

Height: 100ft (30m)	Shape: Broadly conical	Leaf persistence: Deciduous	Leaf type:

Family: Fagaceae	Species: *Quercus petraea*	Author: (Matt.) Liebl.

Sessile Oak

Leaves Elliptic, to 4¾in (12cm) long and 3in (7.5cm) across, with rounded lobes, usually tapered at the base, without auricles, slightly glossy dark green and smooth above, paler and thinly hairy beneath, the stalk to ⅜in (1cm) or more long. ***Bark*** Gray, with vertical ridges. ***Flowers*** Males in yellow-green, drooping catkins, females inconspicuous, borne separately on the same plant in late spring. ***Fruit*** An acorn, to 1¼in (3cm) long, about one-third enclosed in a cup.

NATIVE REGION Europe.
HABITAT Woods.
REMARK Also known as durmast oak.

rounded, untoothed leaf lobes

yellow-green leaf stalk

small scales pressed close to acorn cup

unstalked or very short-stalked acorns

Height: 130ft (40m)	Shape: Broadly spreading	Leaf persistence: Deciduous	Leaf type:

Family: Fagaceae	Species: *Quercus phellos*	Author: L.

Willow Oak

Leaves Narrowly oblong, to 4in (10cm) long and 1in (2.5cm) across, ending in a small, fine point, untoothed, bright green above, paler beneath, smooth on both sides. ***Bark*** Gray and smooth, becoming ridged and cracking into plates with age. ***Flowers*** Males in yellow-green, drooping catkins, females inconspicuous, borne separately on the same plant in late spring. ***Fruit*** An acorn, to ⅝in (1.5cm) long, about one-quarter enclosed in a shallow cup.

NATIVE REGION E. US.
HABITAT Moist and swampy soil.
REMARK Easily distinguished by its leaves, which look very similar to those of certain willows (*Salix*, see pp.271–274).

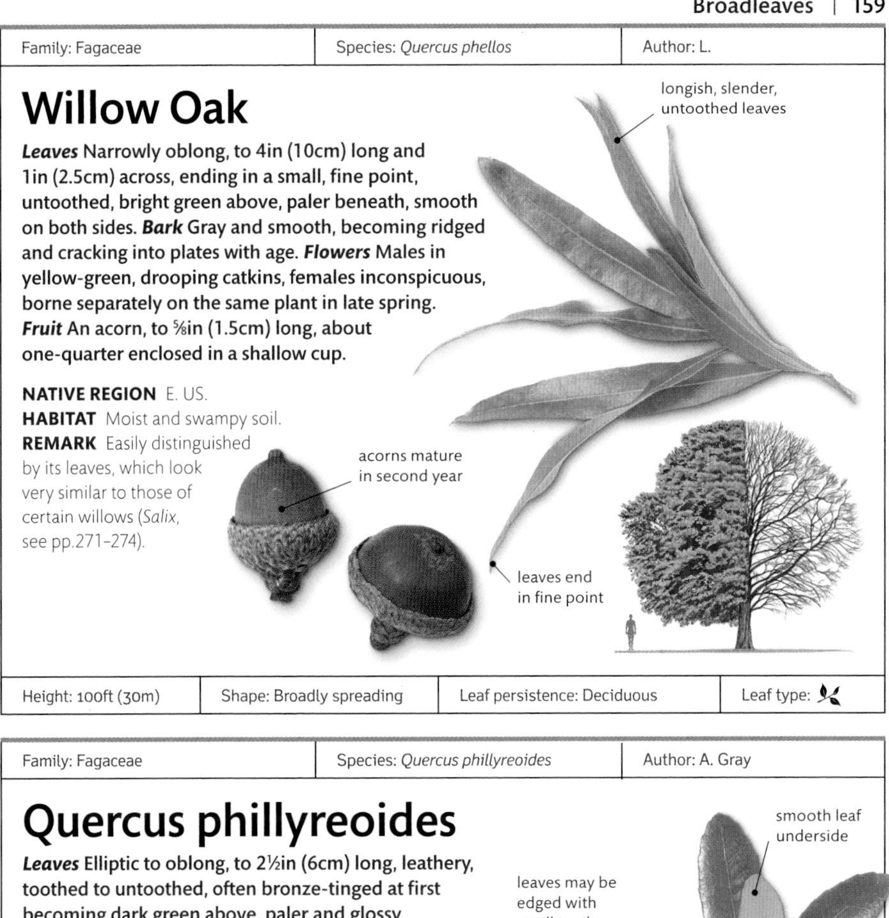

Height: 100ft (30m)	Shape: Broadly spreading	Leaf persistence: Deciduous	Leaf type:

Family: Fagaceae	Species: *Quercus phillyreoides*	Author: A. Gray

Quercus phillyreoides

Leaves Elliptic to oblong, to 2½in (6cm) long, leathery, toothed to untoothed, often bronze-tinged at first becoming dark green above, paler and glossy beneath, smooth on both sides. ***Bark*** Dark gray, with vertical, shallow fissures. ***Flowers*** Males in yellow-green, drooping catkins, females inconspicuous, borne separately on the same plant in late spring. ***Fruit*** An acorn, to ¾in (2cm) long, about one-third enclosed in a cone-shaped cup.

NATIVE REGION China, S. Japan.
HABITAT Cliffs and rocky places.
REMARK A rarely seen and unusual small tree or shrub.

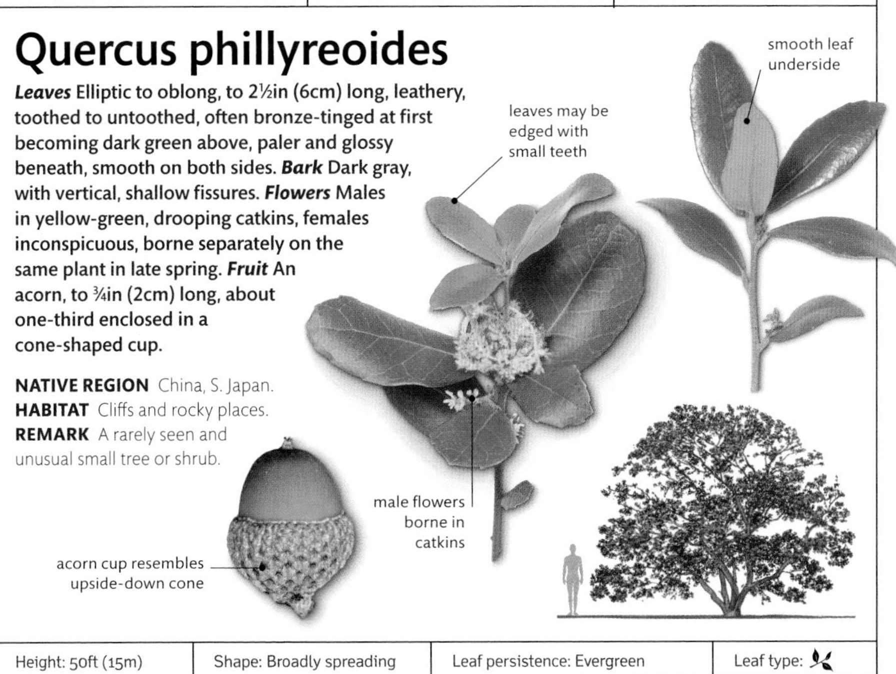

Height: 50ft (15m)	Shape: Broadly spreading	Leaf persistence: Evergreen	Leaf type:

Family: Fagaceae	Species: *Quercus pontica*	Author: K. Koch

Armenian Oak

Leaves Obovate to broadly elliptic, to 6in (15cm) long and 4in (10cm) across, tapered at the base, the numerous parallel veins ending in small, pointed teeth, hairy when young becoming bright green and smooth above, blue-green beneath, turning yellow-brown in fall, carried on stout shoots. ***Bark*** Gray to purple-brown and thinly scaly, becoming rugged with age. ***Flowers*** Males in yellow-green, long, slender, drooping catkins, females inconspicuous, borne separately on the same plant in late spring. ***Fruit*** An acorn, to ¾in (2cm) long, one-half enclosed in a cup.

NATIVE REGION Caucasus, N.E. Turkey.
HABITAT Mountain woods.
REMARK This species can be either a very small tree or a bushy shrub.

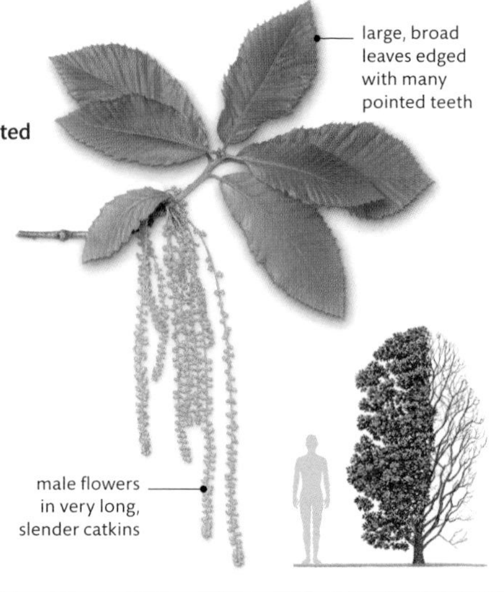

Height: 20ft (6m)	Shape: Broadly columnar	Leaf persistence: Deciduous	Leaf type:

Family: Fagaceae	Species: *Quercus pubescens*	Author: Willd.

Downy Oak

Leaves Elliptic to obovate, to 4in (10cm) long and 2in (5cm) across, with rounded lobes, the lobes ending in a small, sharp point, dark gray-green above, downy beneath, softly gray hairy, at least when young, becoming nearly smooth on both sides. ***Bark*** Dark gray and deeply furrowed. ***Flowers*** Males in yellow-green, drooping catkins, females inconspicuous, borne separately on the same plant in late spring. ***Fruit*** An acorn, to 1½in (4cm) long, about one-third enclosed in a cup, the cup covered in hairy scales.

NATIVE REGION W. Asia, C. and S. Europe.
HABITAT Dry places in hills.

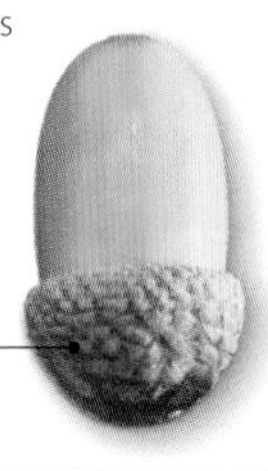

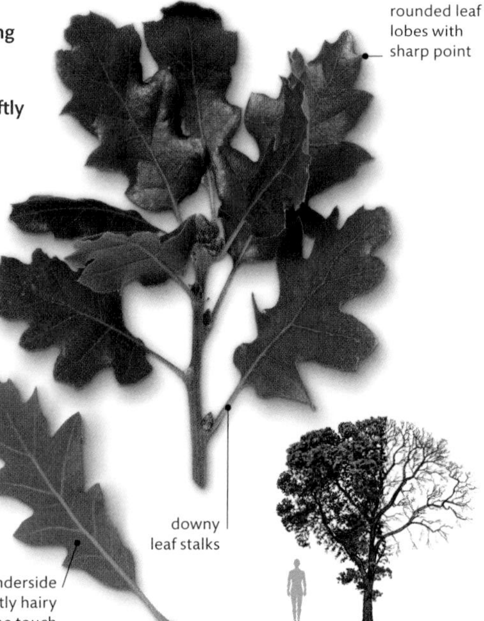

Height: 65ft (20m)	Shape: Broadly spreading	Leaf persistence: Deciduous	Leaf type:

Family: Fagaceae	Species: *Quercus pyrenaica*	Author: Willd.

Pyrenean Oak

Leaves Elliptic to obovate, to 8in (20cm) long and 4in (10cm) across, deeply lobed, often untoothed, hairy on both sides when young becoming deep glossy green and nearly smooth above, hairy beneath. ***Bark*** Pale gray and craggy. ***Flowers*** Males in yellow, drooping catkins, females inconspicuous, borne separately on the same plant in early summer. ***Fruit*** An acorn, to 1½in (4cm) long, one-third to one-half enclosed in a cup.

NATIVE REGION N. Africa, S.W. Europe.
HABITAT Mountain woods.

very hairy young leaves

long, often untoothed leaf lobes

acorn cup covered in dense scales

Height: 65ft (20m)	Shape: Broadly columnar	Leaf persistence: Deciduous	Leaf type:

Family: Fagaceae	Species: *Quercus robur*	Author: L.

English Oak

Leaves Elliptic to obovate, to 4¾in (12cm) long and 3in (7.5cm) across, with three to six lobes on each side, dark green above, blue-green beneath, becoming smooth. ***Bark*** Pale gray and fissured. ***Flowers*** Males in yellow-green, drooping catkins, females inconspicuous, borne separately on the same plant in late spring. ***Fruit*** An acorn, to 1½in (4cm) long, one-third enclosed in a cup.

NATIVE REGION Europe, W. Asia.
HABITAT Woods.

leaves unfold as flowers open

◁▽ ***Quercus robur***

long-stalked acorns

◁ **'Concordia'**
The bright yellow spring leaves of this form turn green after midsummer.

translucent young leaves

red-purple young leaves

'Atropurpurea' ▷
This slower-growing form has ornamental foliage.

Height: 115ft (35m)	Shape: Broadly spreading	Leaf persistence: Deciduous	Leaf type:

Family: Fagaceae	Species: *Quercus rubra*	Author: L.

Red Oak

Leaves Elliptic, ovate, or obovate, to 8in (20cm) long and 6in (15cm) across, with slender-toothed lobes, matte dark green and smooth above, paler and smooth with small tufts of brown hairs in the vein axils beneath, red-brown in fall. ***Bark*** Gray and smooth, becoming deeply furrowed. ***Flowers*** Males in yellowish green, drooping catkins, females inconspicuous, borne separately on the same plant in late spring. ***Fruit*** An acorn, to 1¼in (3cm) long, one-quarter enclosed in a shallow cup.

NATIVE REGION E. North America.
HABITAT Woods, and mountains in the south of its region.

Height: 80ft (25m)	Shape: Broadly spreading	Leaf persistence: Deciduous	Leaf type:

Family: Fagaceae	Species: *Quercus stellata*	Author: Wangenh

Post Oak

Leaves Obovate, to 8in (20cm) long and 4in (10cm) across, with two or three pairs of lobes, the central pair the broadest, narrowing down at the base, dark green and rough above, gray hairy beneath. ***Bark*** Gray-brown, ridged, flaky. ***Flowers*** Males in yellow-green, drooping catkins, females inconspicuous, borne separately on the same plant in late spring. ***Fruit*** An acorn, to 1¼in (3cm) long, about one-third enclosed in a cup.

NATIVE REGION C. and E. US.
HABITAT Dry soil.

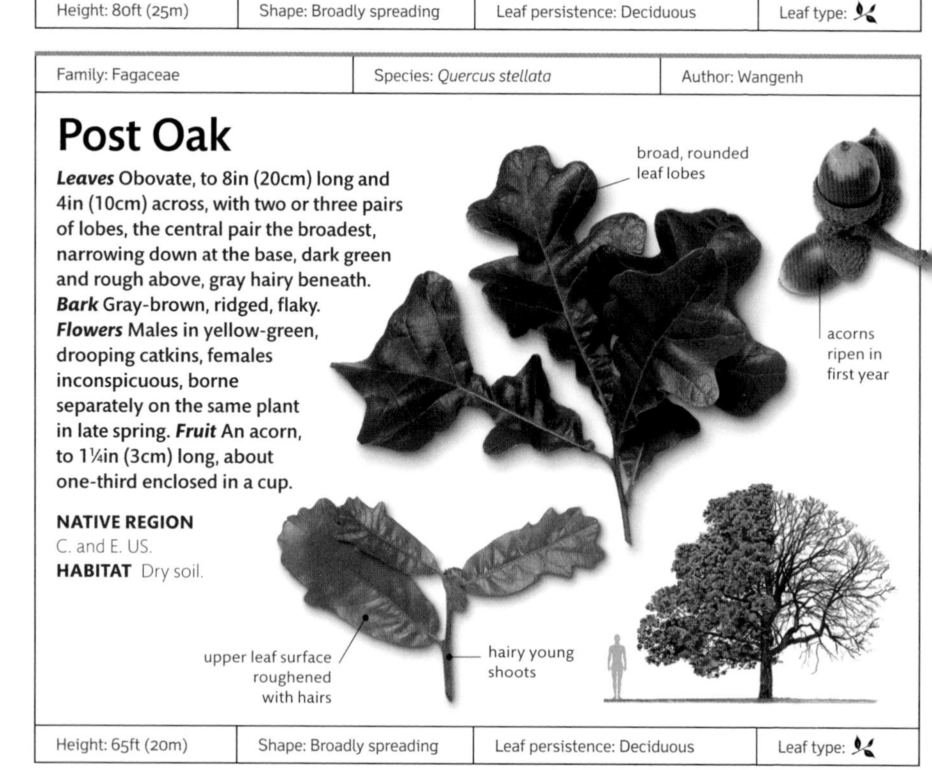

Height: 65ft (20m)	Shape: Broadly spreading	Leaf persistence: Deciduous	Leaf type:

Family: Fagaceae	Species: *Quercus suber*	Author: L.

Cork Oak

Leaves Ovate to oblong, to 2¾in (7cm) long and 1½in (4cm) across, rigid, usually toothed, glossy dark green above, gray hairy beneath. ***Bark*** Pale gray, thick, corky, with prominent ridges; dark red when freshly exposed. ***Flowers*** Males in yellow-green, drooping catkins, females inconspicuous, borne separately on the same plant in late spring. ***Fruit*** An acorn, to 1¼in (3cm) long, about one-half enclosed in a cup.

NATIVE REGION W. Mediterranean.
HABITAT Woods in hills.
REMARK Stripping the bark, from which cork is produced in Portugal and Spain, does not damage the living tissue of the plant.

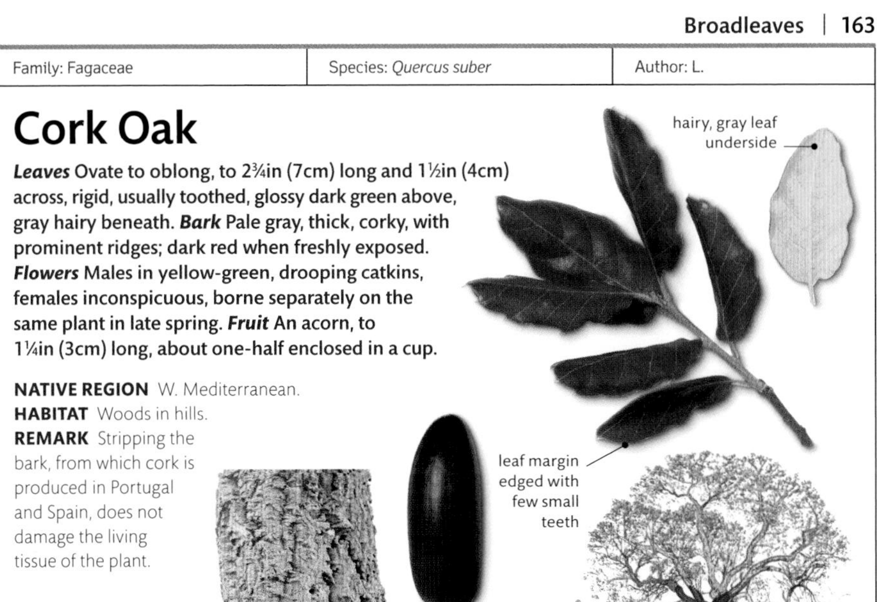

Height: 65ft (20m)	Shape: Broadly spreading	Leaf persistence: Evergreen	Leaf type:

Family: Fagaceae	Species: *Quercus* x *turneri*	Author: Willd.

Turner's Oak

Leaves Oblong to obovate, to 4¾in (12cm) long and 2in (5cm) across, tapered at the base, with three to five triangular teeth on each side, glossy dark green above, paler beneath, some persisting until the following spring. ***Bark*** Dark gray, cracking into plates. ***Flowers*** Males in yellow-green, drooping catkins, females inconspicuous, borne separately on the same plant in late spring. ***Fruit*** An acorn, to ¾in (2cm) long, about one-half enclosed in a cup, usually several together on a long stalk.

NATIVE REGION N. Spain.
REMARK A hybrid between holm oak (*Quercus ilex*, see p.154) and English oak (*Quercus robur*, see p.161). For many years it was only known in yards and gardens.

mature acorns are not always produced

leaves persist far into winter

◁△ **'Pseudoturneri'**

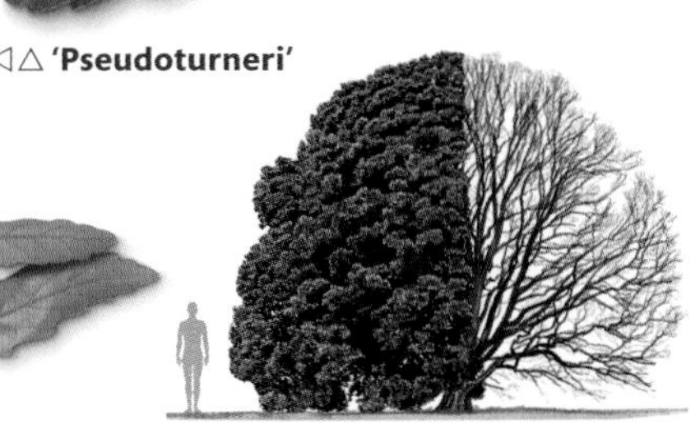

Height: 65ft (20m)	Shape: Broadly spreading	Leaf persistence: Deciduous	Leaf type: 

Family: Fagaceae	Species: *Quercus variabilis*	Author: Blume

Chinese Cork Oak

Leaves Oblong, to 8in (20cm) long and 2in (5cm) across, pointed at the tip, with numerous parallel veins ending in bristle-tipped teeth, glossy dark green and smooth above, gray and thinly hairy beneath. ***Bark*** Pale gray-brown, thick and corky, deeply fissured. ***Flowers*** Males in yellow-green, drooping catkins, females inconspicuous, borne separately on the same plant in late spring. ***Fruit*** An acorn, to ¾in (2cm) long, almost enclosed in a cup, the cup covered in long, curly scales.

NATIVE REGION E. Asia.
HABITAT Mountain woods.

Height: 80ft (25m)	Shape: Broadly spreading	Leaf persistence: Deciduous	Leaf type:

Family: Fagaceae	Species: *Quercus velutina*	Author: Lam.

Black Oak

Leaves Ovate to elliptic, to 10in (25cm) or more long and 6in (15cm) across, with five to seven finely pointed lobes, glossy dark green and smooth above, paler and hairy becoming smooth with tufts of brown hairs in the vein axils beneath. ***Bark*** Dark brown and ridged. ***Flowers*** Males in yellow-green, drooping catkins, females inconspicuous, borne separately on the same plant in late spring. ***Fruit*** An acorn, to 1in (2.5cm) long, one-half enclosed in a cup.

NATIVE REGION E. North America.
HABITAT Dry woods, sand dunes.

Height: 80ft (25m)	Shape: Broadly spreading	Leaf persistence: Deciduous	Leaf type:

HAMAMELIDACEAE

A FAMILY OF ABOUT 25 GENERA and 100 species of deciduous and evergreen trees and shrubs, distributed widely in temperate and subtropical regions, yet unknown in the wild throughout the whole of Europe and most of South America. As well as the two species described here, this family contains genera of ornamental shrubs, such as the witch hazels (*Hamamelis*), which usually flower in winter, *Corylopsis*, and *Fothergilla*.

Family: Hamamelidaceae	Species: *Parrotia persica*	Author: C.A. Mey.

Persian Ironwood

Leaves Elliptic to obovate, to 4¾in (12cm) long and 2½in (6cm) across, wavy at the margin, toothed above the middle, bright glossy green and smooth above, thinly hairy beneath. ***Bark*** Gray-brown, flaking. ***Flowers*** Small, without petals, but with red anthers, in late winter to early spring. ***Fruit*** A nutlike, brown capsule, 3⁄16in (8mm) long.

NATIVE REGION E. Caucasus, N. Iran.
HABITAT Forests.
REMARK Can be either a tree of medium height or a large shrub.

colorful fall foliage

leaves broaden above middle

rounded teeth edge upper half of leaf

Height: 65ft (20m)	Shape: Broadly spreading	Leaf persistence: Deciduous	Leaf type:

Family: Hamamelidaceae	Species: *Parrotiopsis jacquemontiana*	Author: (Decne.) Rehder

Parrotiopsis jacquemontiana

Leaves Rounded, to 3in (7.5cm) long, toothed, glossy green becoming smooth or nearly so above, hairy beneath, on short stalks. ***Bark*** Gray and smooth. ***Flowers*** Small and without petals, with numerous stamens, the stamens with yellow anthers, borne in dense clusters, each cluster surrounded by up to six white bracts, the bracts dotted with numerous tiny brown scales beneath, forming a head to 2in (5cm) across, in mid- to late spring. ***Fruit*** A small, bristly, brown capsule, borne in clusters.

NATIVE REGION W. Himalayas.
HABITAT Forests.
REMARK This shrublike plant is the only species of *Parrotiopsis*. Flowers usually persist till early or midsummer.

tiny clustered flowers have yellow anthers

white bracts surround each flower cluster

rounded leaves

toothed leaf margin

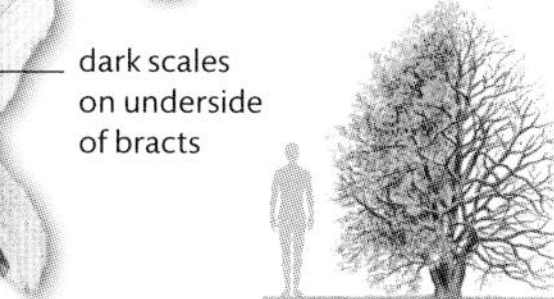

Height: 20ft (6m)	Shape: Broadly conical	Leaf persistence: Deciduous	Leaf type: 

JUGLANDACEAE

MOST MEMBERS OF THIS FAMILY are deciduous plants. Nine genera with some 60 species grow wild in the Americas and from southeast Europe to Japan and Southeast Asia. The leaves are usually alternate and pinnate. The small flowers lack petals, and are clustered in catkins, males and females on the same plant. The fruit is either a large nut, or small and winged.

Family: Juglandaceae	Species: *Carya cordiformis*	Author: (Wangenh.) K. Koch

Bitter Nut

Leaves Pinnate, with usually five to nine sharply toothed leaflets, to 6in (15cm) long, deep green above, turning golden yellow in fall; winter buds with scurfy, yellow scales. ***Bark*** Gray, smooth, becoming thick, furrowed, and ridged. ***Flowers*** Small, without petals, clustered in catkins, male catkins with three hanging branches to 3in (7.5cm) long, females inconspicuous, borne separately on the same plant in late spring to early summer. ***Fruit*** A thin-shelled, bitter, inedible, gray nut, enclosed in a green husk, to 1½in (4cm) long, with four wings.

NATIVE REGION E. North America.
HABITAT Deciduous forests, in swamps, and on riverbanks.

middle leaflets are the largest

yellow-green male catkins

leaflets tapered at both ends

Height: 100ft (30m)	Shape: Broadly columnar	Leaf persistence: Deciduous	Leaf type:

Family: Juglandaceae	Species: *Carya illinoinensis*	Author: (Wangenh.) K. Koch

Pecan

Leaves Pinnate, with 9 to 17 leaflets, to 6in (15cm) long, slender, taper-pointed, the tip curved backward, toothed at the margin, dark green. ***Bark*** Gray, thick, furrowed, and ridged. ***Flowers*** Males and females both small and without petals, clustered in catkins, male catkins yellow-green, with three hanging branches to 3in (7.5cm) long, females inconspicuous, borne separately on the same plant in late spring to early summer. ***Fruit*** A thin-shelled, sweet, edible, red-brown nut, in a green husk, to 2½in (6cm) long, with four wings.

NATIVE REGION S. US.
HABITAT Moist forests and valleys.
REMARK The nuts have an important commercial value.

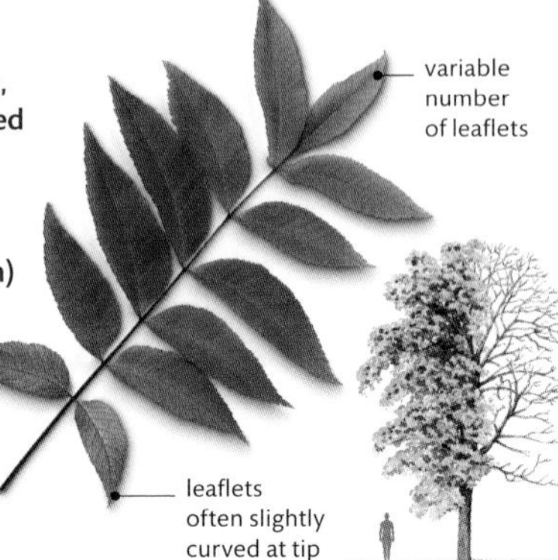

Height: 100ft (30m)	Shape: Broadly columnar	Leaf persistence: Deciduous	Leaf type:

Family: Juglandaceae	Species: *Carya ovata*	Author: (Mill.) K. Koch

Shagbark Hickory

Leaves Pinnate, with usually five taper-pointed leaflets, to 8in (20cm) long, toothed except at the base, deep yellow-green above, turning golden yellow and brown in fall; winter buds with dark scales, the scales spreading at the tips. ***Bark*** Gray to brown, peeling in long, vertical plates with age. ***Flowers*** Males and females both small and without petals, clustered in catkins, male catkins yellow-green, with three hanging branches to 5in (13cm) long, females inconspicuous, borne separately on the same plant in late spring to early summer. ***Fruit*** A thick-shelled, sweet, edible, whitish nut, enclosed in a green husk, to 2½in (6cm) long, with four grooves.

female flowers at end of shoots

strips of bark hang free at either end

terminal leaflet largest

NATIVE REGION E. North America.
HABITAT Rich woods and valleys.
REMARK The distinctively peeling bark gives this species its common name.

Height: 100ft (30m)	Shape: Broadly columnar	Leaf persistence: Deciduous	Leaf type:

Family: Juglandaceae	Species: *Juglans ailantifolia*	Author: Carrière

Japanese Walnut

Leaves Pinnate and very large, with 11 to 17 short-pointed, toothed leaflets, to 6in (15cm) long, dark green above, hairy on both sides, particularly so beneath, borne on stout, sticky, hairy shoots. ***Bark*** Gray-brown, becoming fissured and separating into small plates with age. ***Flowers*** Males and females both small and without petals, clustered in catkins, male catkins greenish, to 12in (30cm) long, hanging, on the old shoots, female catkins to 4in (10cm) long, with red stigmas, at the end of the young shoots, borne separately on the same plant in late spring to early summer. ***Fruit*** A shallowly pitted, brown nut, enclosed in a sticky, green husk, to 2in (5cm) long, in clusters of up to 20.

leaves at end of shoots unfold at flowering time

female flowers have red stigmas

stout, very hairy leaf rachis

NATIVE REGION Japan, Sakhalin.
HABITAT Wet areas and by streams.
REMARK The fruit husk is poisonous. In Japan, it is traditionally used to catch fish. The nuts are also eaten, and the wood is used for making furniture and other purposes.

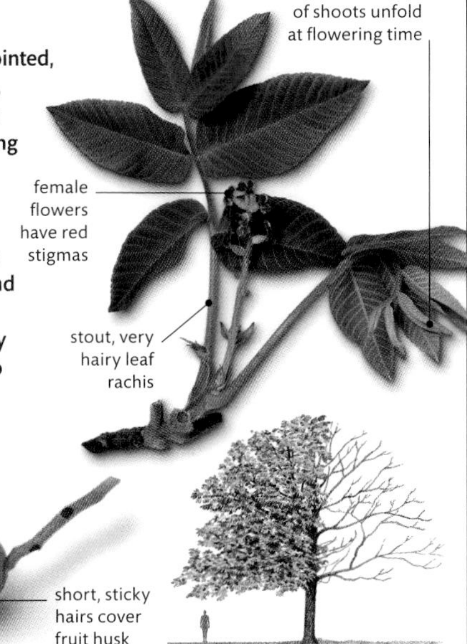

Height: 80ft (25m)	Shape: Broadly spreading	Leaf persistence: Deciduous	Leaf type:

Family: Juglandaceae	Species: *Juglans cinerea*	Author: L.

Butternut

Leaves Pinnate, with 7 to 17 pointed, toothed leaflets, to 5in (13cm) long, all unstalked except for the terminal one, dark green above, hairy on both sides, particularly so beneath. ***Bark*** Gray, furrowed, ridged. ***Flowers*** Males and females both small and without petals, clustered in catkins, male catkins greenish, to 4in (10cm) long, hanging, female catkins short, borne separately on the same plant in late spring to early summer. ***Fruit*** An elongated, rough, sweet, edible, oily nut, enclosed in a pointed, sticky, green husk, to 2½in (6cm) long, in clusters of up to five.

large leaves have numerous leaflets

leaf rachis covered with sticky hairs

NATIVE REGION E. North America.
HABITAT Rich woods or moist soil in valleys and on slopes.
REMARK Also known as white walnut.

Height: 80ft (25m)	Shape: Broadly spreading	Leaf persistence: Deciduous	Leaf type:

Family: Juglandaceae	Species: *Juglans nigra*	Author: L.

Black Walnut

Leaves Pinnate, with 11 to 17 or more slender, taper-pointed, sharply toothed leaflets, to 4¾in (12cm) long, glossy dark green above, hairy, at least beneath, aromatic. ***Bark*** Dark gray-brown to blackish, with narrow, rough ridges. ***Flowers*** Males and females both small and without petals, clustered in catkins, male catkins yellow-green, to 4in (10cm) long, hanging, female catkins short, borne separately on the same plant in late spring to early summer. ***Fruit*** A rounded, edible, brown nut, enclosed in a green husk, to 2in (5cm) long, borne singly or in pairs.

NATIVE REGION C. and E. US.
HABITAT Rich woods.
REMARK Both the wood and the nuts are valuable commodities.

Height: 100ft (30m)	Shape: Broadly spreading	Leaf persistence: Deciduous	Leaf type:

Family: Juglandaceae	Species: *Juglans regia*	Author: L.

Walnut

Leaves Pinnate, with five to nine short-pointed leaflets, to 6in (15cm) long, the terminal leaflet largest, bronze when young becoming dark green, smooth, aromatic when bruised. **_Bark_** Pale gray, smooth, fissured on old plants. **_Flowers_** Males and females both small, without petals, clustered in catkins, male catkins yellow-green, to 4in (10cm) long, hanging, females short, borne separately on the same plant in late spring to early summer. **_Fruit_** An edible nut, creamy white becoming brown, enclosed in a green husk, to 2in (5cm) long.

NATIVE REGION China to S.E. Europe.
HABITAT Valleys and stream banks.

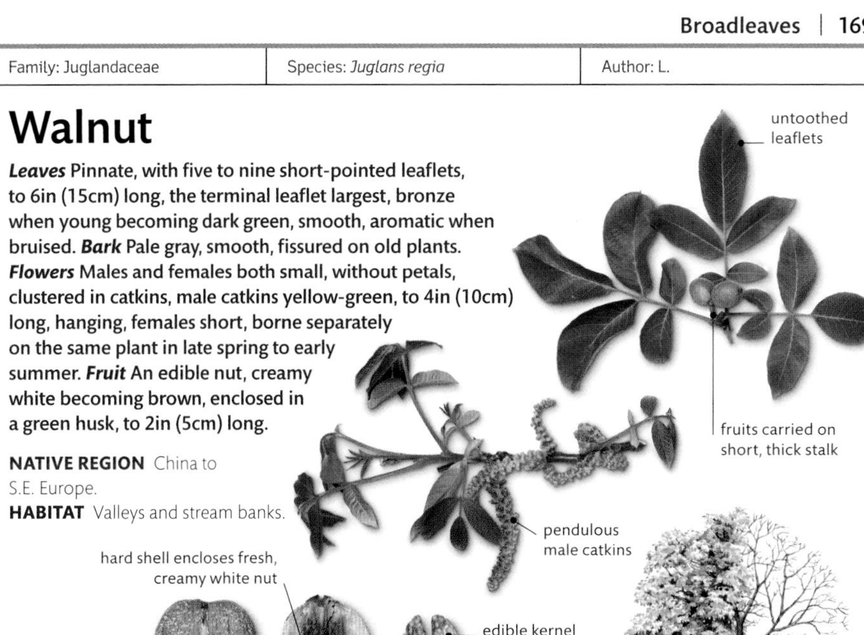

Height: 100ft (30m)	Shape: Broadly spreading	Leaf persistence: Deciduous	Leaf type:

Family: Juglandaceae	Species: *Platycarya strobilacea*	Author: Siebold & Zucc.

Platycarya strobilacea

Leaves Pinnate, with up to 15 taper-pointed, sharply toothed, unstalked leaflets, to 4in (10cm) long and 1¼in (3cm) across, hairy becoming smooth on both sides, dark, slightly glossy green, turning yellow in fall. **_Bark_** Yellow-brown, with vertical fisures. **_Flowers_** Males and females both small, without petals, in upright catkins, male catkins to 4in (10cm) long, clustered together around a single, green female catkin, borne separately on the same plant in summer. **_Fruit_** Conelike, brown, upright, 1½in (4cm) long, persisting for some time.

NATIVE REGION E. Asia.
HABITAT Forests in dry, sunny situations.
REMARK An unusual relative of the wingnuts (*Pterocarya*, see pp.170–171), easily distinguished by its conelike fruit clusters.

leaflets end in slender point

yellowish green male catkins

old fruits remain from previous year

Height: 80ft (25m)	Shape: Broadly spreading	Leaf persistence: Deciduous	Leaf type:

Family: Juglandaceae	Species: *Pterocarya fraxinifolia*	Author: (Poir.) Spach

Caucasian Wingnut

Leaves Pinnate, with 11 to 23 or more toothed, unstalked leaflets, to 6in (15cm) long and 1½in (4cm) across, glossy dark green and smooth above, turning yellow in fall, on an unwinged rachis; leaf buds covered in brown hairs during winter. ***Bark*** Whitish gray, smooth, becoming furrowed with age. ***Flowers*** Small and without petals, with pink stigmas, in green, pendulous catkins, males stout, to 4¾in (12cm) long, females slender, to 6in (15cm) long, borne separately on the same plant in spring; flower stigmas elongate as fruits ripen. ***Fruit*** A small nut, surrounded by two semi-circular, green wings, borne in slender, hanging catkins, to 20in (50cm) long.

NATIVE REGION E. Caucasus, N. Iran.
HABITAT Woods, near rivers, and in bogs.

Height: 100ft (30m)	Shape: Broadly spreading	Leaf persistence: Deciduous	Leaf type:

Family: Juglandaceae	Species: *Pterocarya* x *rehderiana*	Author: C.K. Schneid.

Pterocarya x rehderiana

Leaves Pinnate, with 11 to 21 toothed, unstalked leaflets, to 4¾in (12cm) long, glossy dark green and smooth above, turning yellow in fall, the rachis with small, untoothed, upright wings. ***Bark*** Purple-brown, cracked into diagonal, interlacing ridges; pale orange in the fissures. ***Flowers*** Males and females both small, without petals, in green, pendulous catkins, males to 4¾in (12cm) long, separately on the same plant in spring. ***Fruit*** A small nut, with two elongated, green wings, borne in slender, hanging catkins, to 18in (45cm) long.

NATIVE REGION Of garden and yard origin.
REMARK A hybrid between Caucasian wingnut (*Pterocarya fraxinifolia*, see above) and *Pterocarya stenoptera* (see p.171), raised at the Arnold Arboretum of Harvard University, Boston, MA.

Height: 80ft (25m)	Shape: Broadly spreading	Leaf persistence: Deciduous	Leaf type:

Family: Juglandaceae	Species: *Pterocarya rhoifolia*	Author: Siebold & Zucc.

Japanese Wingnut

Leaves Pinnate, with 11 to 21 taper-pointed, toothed, unstalked leaflets, to 4¾in (12cm) long, glossy green above, turning yellow in fall, on an unwinged rachis; leaf buds covered with scales in winter. ***Bark*** Dark gray, becoming vertically fissured with age. ***Flowers*** Males and females both small and without petals, in green, pendulous catkins, males to 3in (7.5cm) long, at the base of the young shoots, females at the tip, borne separately on the same plant in spring. ***Fruit*** A small nut, with green wings, in clusters on slender, hanging catkins, to 12in (30cm) long.

NATIVE REGION Japan.
HABITAT Near mountain streams.
REMARK In winter, it is easily distinguished by its scaly leaf buds.

leaflets taper to long, fine point
shoots end in distinct buds
unwinged leaf rachis

Height: 80ft (25m)	Shape: Broadly spreading	Leaf persistence: Deciduous	Leaf type:

Family: Juglandaceae	Species: *Pterocarya stenoptera*	Author: C. DC.

Chinese Wingnut

Leaves Pinnate, with 11 to 21 toothed, unstalked leaflets, bright green and smooth above, turning yellow in fall, the rachis with narrow, often toothed, wings. ***Bark*** Gray-brown, with deep fissures. ***Flowers*** Males and females both small and without petals, in separate, green, pendulous catkins, males to 2½in (6cm) long, on the same plant in spring. ***Fruit*** A small nut, with two narrow wings, in clusters on slender, hanging catkins, to 12in (30cm) long.

NATIVE REGION China.
HABITAT Moist woods and stream banks.
REMARK This species is easily distinguished by the characteristically angled wings on the leaf rachis.

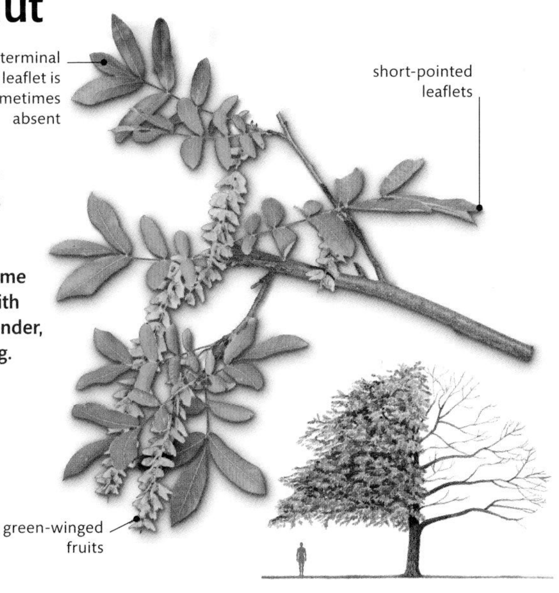

Height: 80ft (25m)	Shape: Broadly spreading	Leaf persistence: Deciduous	Leaf type: 

LAURACEAE

SOME 50 GENERA and more than 2,000 species belong to this widespread family; many grow wild in tropical South America and Southeast Asia. The deciduous and evergreen, usually aromatic, trees and shrubs have untoothed, either opposite or alternate, leaves. Flower petals and sepals, which resemble each other, are arranged in threes. The fruit is usually fleshy.

Family: Lauraceae	Species: *Laurus nobilis*	Author: L.

Bay Laurel

Leaves Elliptic to ovate, to 4in (10cm) long and 1½in (4cm) across, pointed at the tip, with a wavy margin, glossy dark green above, paler beneath, smooth, leathery, aromatic when crushed. ***Bark*** Dark gray, smooth. ***Flowers*** About ⅜in (1cm) across, yellow-green, males with numerous yellow stamens, in clusters in the leaf axils, on separate plants in spring. ***Fruit*** A rounded berry, about ⅜in (1cm) long, green ripening to black.

NATIVE REGION Mediterranean.
HABITAT Evergreen woods, thickets, and rocky places.
REMARK Also known as sweet bay. This species and the related Canary Island laurel (*Laurus azorica*) are the only members of the family native to Europe.

wavy, untoothed leaf margins
berries ripen from green to black
leaves taper gradually toward base
male flowers have many yellow anthers

Height: 50ft (15m)	Shape: Broadly conical	Leaf persistence: Evergreen	Leaf type:

Family: Lauraceae	Species: *Persea americana*	Author: Mill.

Avocado

Leaves Elliptic, to 10in (25cm) long and 4in (10cm) across, pointed at the tip, dark green and smooth above, blue-green beneath, sometimes with a slightly wavy margin. ***Bark*** Smooth and pale gray on young trees, cracking with age. ***Flowers*** ⅜in (1cm) across, with six pale yellow-green tepals, in clusters to 6in (15cm) long in spring to summer. ***Fruit*** Spherical to pear-shaped, to 6in (15cm) long, bright green to nearly black, smooth or warty, the flesh edible.

NATIVE REGION Central Mexico to Central America. Naturalized and cultivated in warm regions.
HABITAT Evergreen forests.
REMARK Warmer summers have enabled this tree to be grown in areas such as southern England.

Height: 131ft (40m)	Shape: Broadly conical	Leaf persistence: Evergreen	Leaf type:

Family: Lauraceae	Species: *Sassafras albidum*	Author: (Nutt.) Nees

Sassafras

Leaves **Elliptic to ovate, to 6in (15cm) or more long and 4in (10cm) across, untoothed but sometimes with a lobe on one or both sides, bright green above, blue-green and smooth beneath, turning yellow to orange or purple in fall, aromatic.** ***Bark*** **Red-brown, thick, furrowed, aromatic.** ***Flowers*** **Males and females both very small, yellow or greenish yellow, without petals, in small clusters or short racemes on separate planes in spring.** ***Fruit*** **An egg-shaped, deep blue berry, ⅜in (1cm) long.**

NATIVE REGION E. North America.
HABITAT Woods and thickets.
REMARK Also known as *Sassafras officinale*. Leaves may appear similar in outline to those of the common fig (*Ficus carica*, see p.195). The root bark is traditionally used to make tea and root beer.

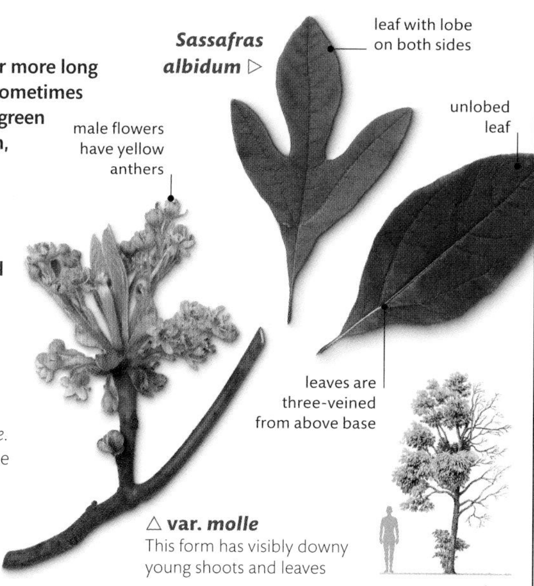

△ **var. *molle***
This form has visibly downy young shoots and leaves

Height: 65ft (20m)	Shape: Broadly columnar	Leaf persistence: Deciduous	Leaf type:

Family: Lauraceae	Species: *Umbellularia californica*	Author: (Hook. & Arn.) Nutt.

California Laurel

Leaves **Elliptic to oblong, to 4in (10cm) long and 1in (2.5cm) across, untoothed, bright green or deep yellow-green.** ***Bark*** **Dark gray, cracking into rectangular plates with age.** ***Flowers*** **⅜in (1cm) across, without petals, with six yellow-green sepals, in clusters of up to 10, in the leaf axils in late winter to spring.** ***Fruit*** **A rounded to egg-shaped berry, about 1in (2.5cm) long, green at first ripening to deep purple.**

NATIVE REGION US: S.W. Oregon, California.
HABITAT Evergreen forests and scrub in canyons and valleys.
REMARK Also known as California bay, California olive, Oregon myrtle. Forms a large tree in moist, sheltered situations, but can be reduced to the size of a small shrub in dry, exposed conditions. When crushed, the leaves emit an acrid odor. This poisonous vapor may induce nausea and headaches.

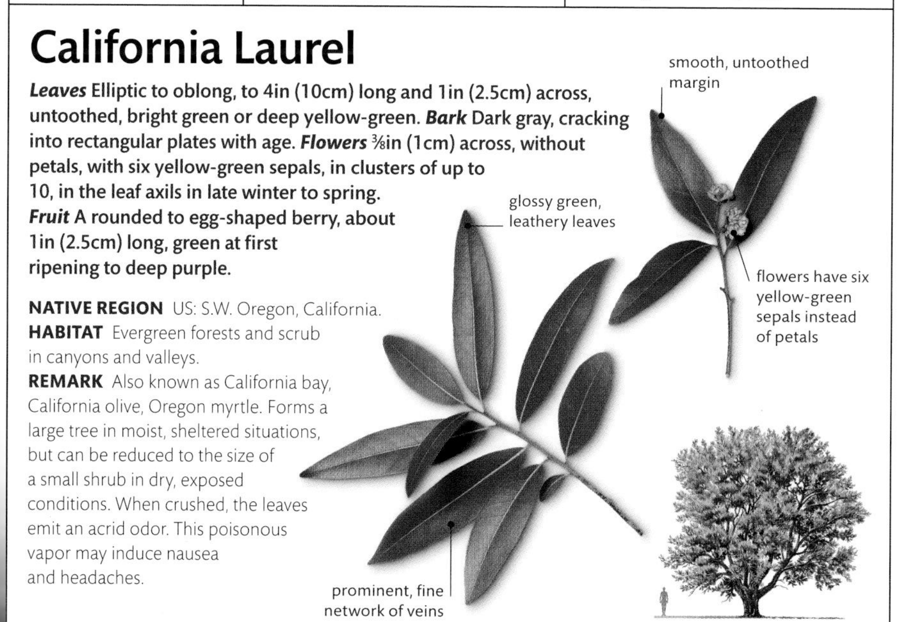

Height: 100ft (30m)	Shape: Broadly spreading	Leaf persistence: Evergreen	Leaf type:

MAGNOLIACEAE

THIS FAMILY OF TWO GENERA and about 340 species is distributed in two main areas. Most species are found in east Asia, from the Himalayas through China to Japan, and in Southeast Asia to New Guinea; others occur from the eastern United States through Mexico to tropical South America, with none in Europe, Africa, or Australia. The deciduous and evergreen trees and shrubs have alternate, untoothed, and (only occasionally) lobed leaves. The showy flowers are borne singly.

Family: Magnoliaceae	Species: *Liriodendron chinense*	Author: (Hemsl.) Sarg.

Chinese Tulip Tree

Leaves To 6in (15cm) or more long, with two lobes at the tip and two at the side, dark green above, bluish white beneath, turning yellow in fall. ***Bark*** Gray, rough, fissured with age. ***Flowers*** To 1½in (4cm) long, with nine tepals, three green, reflexed, six green with yellow veins, upright, borne singly at the ends of the shoots in midsummer. ***Fruit*** A conical, pale brown cluster.

NATIVE REGION China, Vietnam.
HABITAT Mountain woods.

deeply lobed leaves

cut-off, indented leaf tip

large stipules soon fall

Height: 50ft (15m)	Shape: Broadly columnar	Leaf persistence: Deciduous	Leaf type:

Family: Magnoliaceae	Species: *Liriodendron tulipifera*	Author: L.

Tulip Tree

Leaves To 6in (15cm) or more long, with two lobes at the tip and two at the side, dark green above, bluish white beneath, turning yellow to orange in fall. ***Bark*** Gray-brown, furrowed with age. ***Flowers*** To 2½in (6cm) long, with nine tepals, three green, reflexed, six pale green banded orange near the base, borne singly at the ends of the shoots in midsummer. ***Fruit*** A conical, pale brown cluster.

NATIVE REGION E. North America.
HABITAT Deciduous woods.

three outer tepals spread horizontally

△▽ ***Liriodendron tulipifera***

lobes are usually shallow

pale green young fruit

yellow border turns green

◁ **'Aureomarginatum'**
The leaves of this impressive form have a broad, golden yellow margin at first.

Height: 164ft (50m)	Shape: Broadly columnar	Leaf persistence: Deciduous	Leaf type: 

Family: Magnoliaceae	Species: *Magnolia acuminata*	Author: (L.) L.

Cucumber Tree

Leaves **Elliptic to ovate, to 10in (25cm) long and 6in (15cm) across, taper-pointed, untoothed, light to dark green above, blue-green and usually hairy beneath.** ***Bark*** **Brown-gray and furrowed.** ***Flowers*** **Cup-shaped, to 3½in (9cm) long, with nine blue-green to yellow-green, upright tepals, borne singly at the ends of the shoots in early to midsummer.** ***Fruit*** **A cylindrical cluster, to 3in (7.5cm) long, green becoming pink, ripening to red.**

NATIVE REGION E. North America.
HABITAT Rich woods.
REMARK The species gets its common name from the color and shape of the unripe fruit, which resembles a cucumber. The flowers are often hidden by the large leaves.

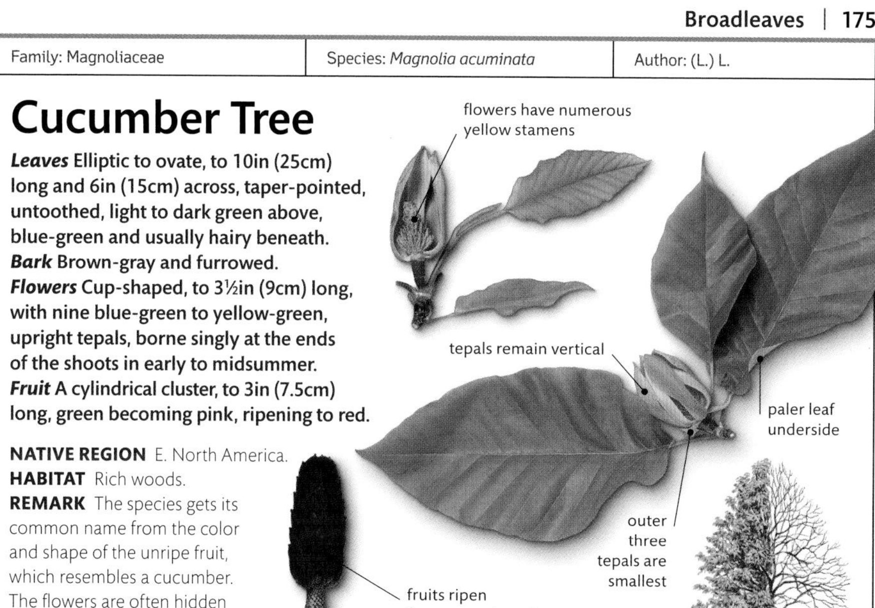

Height: 100ft (30m)	Shape: Broadly conical	Leaf persistence: Deciduous	Leaf type:

Family: Magnoliaceae	Species: *Magnolia ashei*	Author: Weath.

Ashe Magnolia

Leaves **Broadly elliptic to oblong-obovate, to 12in (30cm) or more long and 8in (20cm) or more across, rather thin, usually auricled at the base, green and smooth above, blue-white and finely hairy beneath, carried in large whorls at the ends of the shoots.** ***Bark*** **Pale gray and smooth.** ***Flowers*** **Cup-shaped, 12in (30cm) across, white, fragrant, with nine tepals, the inner tepals usually marked with purple toward the base, borne at the ends of the shoots in early to midsummer with the leaves.** ***Fruit*** **A conical to egg-shaped, pink cluster, about 3in (7.5cm) long.**

NATIVE REGION US: N.W. Florida.
HABITAT Moist woods.
REMARK This species is closely related to *Magnolia macrophylla* (see p.181). It is rare, and of very restricted distribution in the wild, where it can be either a small tree or a large shrub.

young leaves have large stipules
inner tepals blotched purple
whitish green outer tepals

Height: 33ft (10m)	Shape: Broadly columnar	Leaf persistence: Deciduous	Leaf type:

Family: Magnoliaceae	Species: *Magnolia campbellii*	Author: Hook. f. & Thomson

Campbell's Magnolia

Leaves Oblong to ovate or obovate, to 10in (25cm) or more long, usually abruptly pointed, untoothed, bronze when young becoming dark green and smooth above, paler and smooth or hairy beneath, ***Bark*** Gray and smooth. ***Flowers*** Very large, 12in (30cm) across, pale to deep pink to purplish pink or white, slightly fragrant, with up to 16 tepals, the outer tepals spreading, the inner tepals upright, giving the flower its characteristic cup-and-saucer shape, on smooth stalks, opening in late winter to early spring before the leaves. ***Fruit*** A cylindrical, conelike, red cluster, to 6in (15cm) long.

NATIVE REGION S.W. China, Himalayas.
HABITAT Forests in mountainous areas.
REMARK A magnificent, large tree, much sought after in gardens and yards for its huge flowers. On plants raised from seed, flowers are produced only after 20 years.

△▷ ***Magnolia campbellii***

▽ **Mollicomata Group**
The flowers of this form are produced slightly earlier in the year, on younger plants.

Height: 100ft (30m)	Shape: Broadly conical	Leaf persistence: Deciduous	Leaf type:

Family: Magnoliaceae	Species: *Magnolia dawsoniana*	Author: Rehder & E.H. Wilson

Dawson's Magnolia

Leaves Elliptic to obovate, to 6in (15cm) long and 3in (7.5cm) across, rounded at the tip, dark green and smooth above, paler and smooth beneath except for hairs along the veins. ***Bark*** Gray, smooth, with conspicuous raised lenticels, fissured at the base. ***Flowers*** Held horizontally, to 4¾in (12cm) long, pale pink, slightly fragrant, with 9 to 12 drooping tepals, opening in late winter or early spring before the leaves. ***Fruit*** A cylindrical, reddish green cluster, to 4in (10cm) long.

NATIVE REGION China.
HABITAT Mountain woods.
REMARK One of the earliest-flowering magnolias.

color becomes paler as flowers age

leaf buds unfold after flowers open

dark green leaf upperside

paler leaf underside

Height: 40ft (12m)	Shape: Broadly conical	Leaf persistence: Deciduous	Leaf type:

Family: Magnoliaceae	Species: *Magnolia delavayi*	Author: Franch.

Delavay's Magnolia

Leaves Elliptic to oblong, to 12in (30cm) long and 6in (15cm) across, dark green above, downy when young, becoming more or less smooth on both sides. ***Bark*** Dark brown, vertically fissured. ***Flowers*** Saucer-shaped, to 8in (20cm) across, fragrant, with nine fleshy tepals, the outer three greenish white, reflexed, the inner six creamy white, spreading, opening in late summer. ***Fruit*** A cylindrical cluster, to 4in (10cm) long, green ripening to pale brown.

NATIVE REGION S.W. China.
HABITAT Scrubland and open places.

Height: 33ft (10m)	Shape: Broadly spreading	Leaf persistence: Evergreen	Leaf type: 

Family: Magnoliaceae	Species: *Magnolia fraseri*	Author: Walter

Ear-leaved Umbrella Tree

Leaves **Obovate, to 16in (40cm) long and 8in (20cm) across, auricled at the base, pointed at the tip, bronze when young becoming pale green, smooth on both sides.** ***Bark*** **Brown or gray, smooth.** ***Flowers*** **Vase-shaped in bud, to 4¾in (12cm) long, opening saucer-shaped, the nine tepals creamy white flushed green on the outer surface, borne singly at the ends of the shoots in late spring to early summer.** ***Fruit*** **A conelike, red cluster, to 4in (10cm) long.**

NATIVE REGION S.E. US.
HABITAT Rich mountain forests.

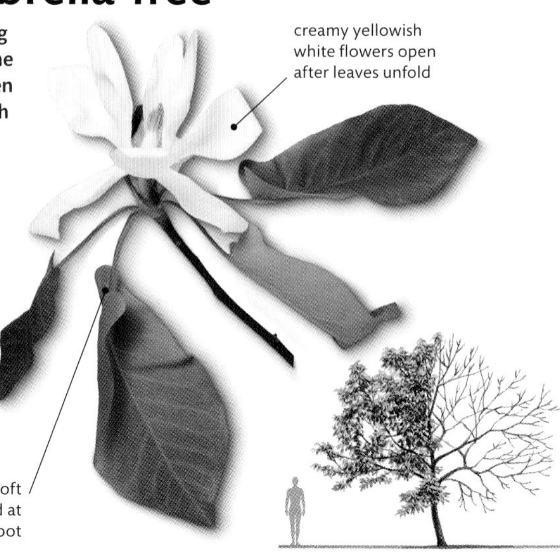

Height: 46ft (14m)	Shape: Broadly spreading	Leaf persistence: Deciduous	Leaf type:

Family: Magnoliaceae	Species: *Magnolia grandiflora*	Author: L.

Bull Bay

Leaves **Elliptic to ovate or lanceolate, to 10in (25cm) long and 4in (10cm) across, rigid and leathery, glossy dark green and smooth above, paler or covered in rusty hairs beneath.** ***Bark*** **Gray, cracking into small plates.** ***Flowers*** **Cup-shaped, to 12in (30cm) across, creamy white, very fragrant, with 9 to 12 or more thick tepals, borne singly at the ends of the shoots in early summer.** ***Fruit*** **An egg-shaped, red cluster, to 4in (10cm) long.**

NATIVE REGION S.E. US.
HABITAT Riverbanks and moist places on coastal plains.
REMARK Plants cultivated in areas that are cooler than the native region flower from late summer to fall.

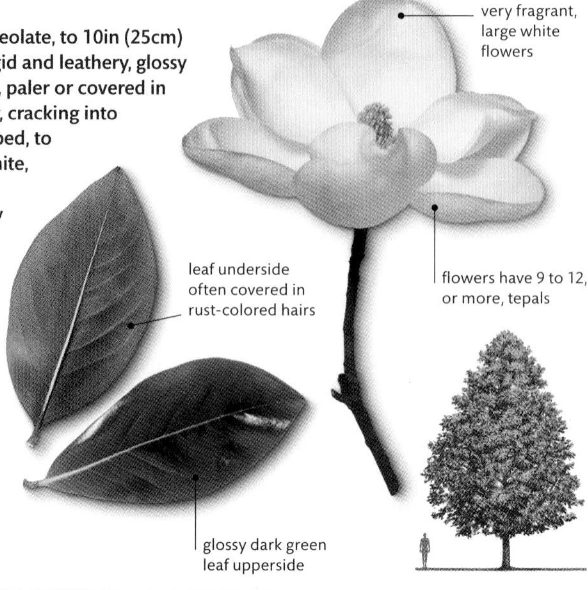

Height: 80ft (25m)	Shape: Broadly conical	Leaf persistence: Evergreen	Leaf type:

Family: Magnoliaceae	Species: *Magnolia* 'Heaven Scent'	Author: None

Magnolia 'Heaven Scent'

Leaves **Broadly elliptic, to 8in (20cm) long, pointed at the tip, glossy green above, paler beneath.** ***Bark*** **Gray and smooth.** ***Flowers*** **Upright and vase-shaped, 5in (13cm) long, narrow at first later opening more widely, strongly fragrant, the nine tepals pale pink but more deeply shaded toward the base, with a distinct, darker pink band on the back, opening in spring to early summer before and with the leaves.** ***Fruit*** **Conelike, the ripe seeds protruding and hanging for some time.**

NATIVE REGION Of garden and yard origin.
REMARK This hybrid between the shrubby *Magnolia liliiflora* 'Nigra' and *Magnolia* x *veitchii* (see p.186) is one of the Gresham Hybrids that resulted from Drury Todd Gresham's program of hybridization in California in the 1950s. By careful selection of both parents and offspring, he produced small trees that combine attributes of some of the best magnolias. 'Peppermint Stick' and 'Sayonara' also belong to this group.

pointed tepals spread slightly as flower ages

◁ **'Heaven Scent'**

◁ **'Peppermint Stick'**
The buds of this hybrid between *M. liliiflora* and *M.* x *veitchii* are 4½in (11cm) long.

tepals eventually spread wider

very faint pink flush at flower base

distinctively narrow buds

△ **'Sayonara'**
This tree is a hybrid between *Magnolia* x *soulangeana* 'Lennei Alba' and *Magnolia* x *veitchii* 'Rubra.' The abundant flowers, which have fleshy tepals, are 4in (10cm) long.

Height: 33ft (10m)	Shape: Broadly spreading	Leaf persistence: Deciduous	Leaf type: 

Family: Magnoliaceae	Species: *Magnolia kobus*	Author: DC.

Northern Japanese Magnolia

Leaves **Elliptic to obovate, to 6in (15cm) long and 3½in (9cm) across, tapered at the base, short-pointed at the tip, dark green and smooth above, paler and hairy along the veins beneath.** ***Bark*** **Gray and smooth.** ***Flowers*** **Usually held horizontally, to 4in (10cm) across, creamy white sometimes flushed pink at the base, slightly fragrant, with six petal-like tepals and three smaller, sepal-like tepals, opening in early spring before the leaves emerge.** ***Fruit*** **A cylindrical, pink to red cluster, to 4in (10cm) long, from which red seeds hang when ripe.**

NATIVE REGION Japan, S. Korea.
HABITAT Mountain forests.
REMARK This is a very hardy species, popular for planting in cold regions, although flowers can be damaged by late frosts.

Height: 65ft (20m)	Shape: Broadly conical	Leaf persistence: Deciduous	Leaf type:

Family: Magnoliaceae	Species: *Magnolia* x *loebneri*	Author: Kache

Magnolia x loebneri

Leaves **Oblanceolate to elliptic, to 6in (15cm) long, glossy green, usually smooth.** ***Bark*** **Gray, smooth.** ***Flowers*** **Upright to horizontal, to 6in (15cm) across, white to pink, with up to 16 or more tepals, opening in early to mid-spring.** ***Fruit*** **A cylindrical, pinkish red cluster, to 4in (10cm) long.**

NATIVE REGION Of garden and backyard origin.
REMARK Hybrids between *Magnolia kobus* (above) and *Magnolia stellata*.

◁▽ 'Leonard Messel'
Each lilac-pink flower of this form has about 12 drooping tepals.

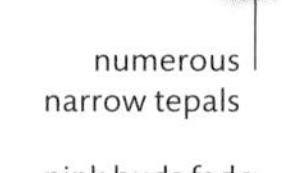

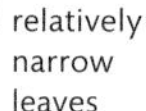
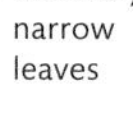

◁'Merrill'

△▷ 'Merrill'
This vigorous plant bears large, white flowers, flushed faint pink at first. Each flower has up to 15 tepals.

Height: 33ft (10m)	Shape: Broadly spreading	Leaf persistence: Deciduous	Leaf type: 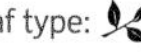

Family: Magnoliaceae	Species: *Magnolia macrophylla*	Author: Michx.

Big-leaf Magnolia

Leaves Very large and rather thin, broadly elliptic to oblong-ovate, to 24in (60cm) or more long and 12in (30cm) across, usually auricled at the base, green and smooth above, blue-green to blue-white and finely hairy beneath, in large whorls at the ends of stout shoots. ***Bark*** Pale gray and smooth. ***Flowers*** Very large and broadly cup-shaped, 12in (30cm) across, creamy white to yellowish, fragrant, with nine tepals, the inner tepals petal-like, usually marked with purple toward the base, the outer tepals sepal-like, held upright, at the ends of the shoots in early to midsummer with the leaves. ***Fruit*** A rounded pink cluster, about 3in (7.5cm) long, from which red seeds hang when ripe.

NATIVE REGION S.E. US.
HABITAT Rich, moist woods.
REMARK The enormous leaves and flowers of this species are among the largest of those of all deciduous trees that are native to temperate regions.

Height: 50ft (15m)	Shape: Broadly columnar	Leaf persistence: Deciduous	Leaf type: 

Family: Magnoliaceae	Species: *Magnolia obovata*	Author: Thunb.

Japanese Big-leaf Magnolia

Leaves Obovate, to 18in (45cm) long and 8in (20cm) across, short-pointed at the tip, deep green and smooth above, pale blue-green and hairy, at least when young, beneath, in large whorls at the ends of the shoots. ***Bark*** Gray and smooth. ***Flowers*** Large, cup-shaped, 8in (20cm) across, very strongly fragrant, with 9 to 12 creamy white tepals, the outer tepals sometimes tinged pink, the filaments and stigmas bright red, opening in summer. ***Fruit*** A cylindrical, large, red cluster, to 8in (20cm) long, from which red seeds hang when ripe.

NATIVE REGION Japan.
HABITAT Woods in mountainous areas.
REMARK Also known as *Magnolia hypoleuca.* The powerful scent of the flowers provides an easy clue to distinguishing this species. In Japan, the large leaves are used to wrap food.

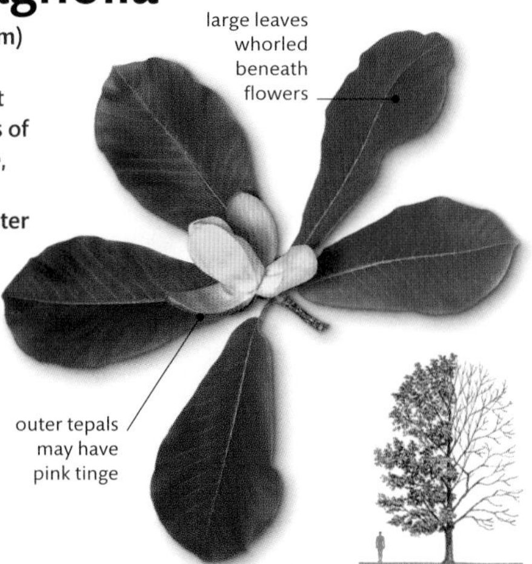

Height: 100ft (30m)	Shape: Broadly columnar	Leaf persistence: Deciduous	Leaf type:

Family: Magnoliaceae	Species: *Magnolia officinalis*	Author: Rehder & E.H. Wilson

Houpu Magnolia

Leaves Obovate, to 18in (45cm) long and 8in (20cm) across, tapered at the base, rounded to short-pointed at the tip, rather pale green and smooth above, whitish and softly hairy when young beneath, carried in whorls at the ends of the shoots. ***Bark*** Pale gray and smooth. ***Flowers*** Cup- to saucer-shaped, 6in (15cm) across, creamy white, fragrant, the stamens with red filaments, borne at the ends of the shoots in late spring to early summer. ***Fruit*** An oblong, pinkish red cluster, to 6in (15cm) long, from which bright red seeds emerge and hang.

NATIVE REGION C. China.
HABITAT Broad-leaved forests.
REMARK This is a rare species with restricted distribution. The bark is used medicinally, which may have caused a decrease in its population. Some bark is now obtained from cultivated plants. The form shown here, var. *biloba*, differs only in the large notch at the tip of the leaves.

△▽ var. ***biloba***

Height: 65ft (20m)	Shape: Broadly columnar	Leaf persistence: Deciduous	Leaf type:

Family: Magnoliaceae	Species: *Magnolia salicifolia*	Authors: (Siebold & Zucc.) Maxim.

Willow-leaved Magnolia

Leaves Ovate to lanceolate or elliptic, to 6in (15cm) long and 2½in (6cm) across, dark green above, blue-green and smooth beneath, aromatic when crushed. ***Bark*** Gray, smooth, lemon-scented when bruised. ***Flowers*** Usually held horizontally, to 5in (13cm) across, white, fragrant, with six narrow tepals, the inner three petal-like, the outer three smaller and sepal-like, opening in early spring before the leaves emerge. ***Fruit*** A cylindrical, pink cluster, to 3in (7.5cm) long.

NATIVE REGION Japan.
HABITAT Oak and beech woods in mountains.

yellow stamens

young leaves may be reddish

leaf buds

dark green mature leaves

Height: 33ft (10m)	Shape: Broadly conical	Leaf persistence: Deciduous	Leaf type:

Family: Magnoliaceae	Species: *Magnolia* x *soulangeana*	Author: Soul.-Bod.

Magnolia x soulangeana

Leaves Elliptic to obovate, to 8in (20cm) long and 4¾in (12cm) across, tapered at the base, usually rounded at the tip, with a short point, dark green and nearly smooth above, paler and finely hairy beneath. ***Bark*** Gray and smooth. ***Flowers*** Variable, from goblet- to cup- or saucer-shaped, to 10in (25cm) across, fragrant, with usually nine white to pink or deep purple-pink tepals, in spring to early summer from before to after the leaves emerge. ***Fruit*** A cylindrical cluster, to 4in (10cm) long, green ripening to pink.

NATIVE REGION C. China.
REMARK A hybrid between *Magnolia denudata* and *Magnolia liliiflora.*

Height: 30ft (9m)	Shape: Broadly spreading	Leaf persistence: Deciduous	Leaf type:

▽ 'Brozzonii'

This conical tree has large, white flowers, faintly flushed pink at the base. They can reach 10in (25cm) across and are produced continuously over a long period from mid-spring to early summer.

△ 'Picture'

The flowers of this form are strongly marked with purplish pink. The plant tends toward a compact and upright, rather than broadly spreading, habit.

'Rustica Rubra' ▷

This form bears large, goblet-shaped flowers. The tepals are shaded deep purplish pink on the outer surface, particularly at the base. The color fades to cream flushed pink at the tip.

Family: Magnoliaceae	Species: *Magnolia tripetala*	Author: (L.) L.

Umbrella Tree

Leaves **Obovate to elliptic, to 20in (50cm) long and 8in (20cm) across, tapered at the base, pointed at the tip, dark green above, gray-green and hairy beneath, in large whorls at the ends of the shoots. *Bark* Pale gray and smooth. *Flowers* To 8in (20cm) across, creamy white, pungently fragrant, with usually 12 narrow, spreading tepals, the three outer tepals opening first from distinctive, slender buds at the ends of the shoots in late spring to early summer with the young leaves. *Fruit* A cylindrical to cone-shaped, pinkish red cluster, to 4in (10cm) long.**

NATIVE REGION E. US.
HABITAT Rich woods.
REMARK The scientific name, meaning "three-petaled," may seem inappropriate, but refers most likely to the three outer, sepal-like tepals. The strong scent of the flowers is an unpleasant odour to some people.

three outer tepals open first

tightly closed inner tepals eventually open wider

Height: 40ft (12m)	Shape: Broadly spreading	Leaf persistence: Deciduous	Leaf type:

Family: Magnoliaceae	Species: *Magnolia* x *veitchii*	Author: Bean

Magnolia x veitchii

Leaves **Obovate to oblong, to 12in (30cm) long and 6in (15cm) across, short-pointed at the tip, bronze-purple at first becoming dark green and smooth above, downy at least on the veins beneath. *Bark* Gray and smooth. *Flowers* Vase-shaped, to 6in (15cm) long, white to pink, fragrant, with around nine tepals, opening in mid-spring usually before the leaves. *Fruit* A cylindrical cluster, to 4in (10cm) long, pinkish green ripening to purple-brown.**

NATIVE REGION Of garden and yard origin.
REMARK Hybrids between the often shrubby yulan (*Magnolia denudata*) and *Magnolia campbellii* (see p.176), these vigorous trees owe their large size to the latter parent, which can also reach 100ft (30m) in the wild. They are attractive plants, usually producing abundant flowers and attractively colored young foliage.

lustrous young leaves tinged bronze

inner and outer tepals are upright

◁▷ **'Isca'**
This cultivar flowers in mid-spring.

flowers flushed slightly pink at base

mature leaves are dark green and smooth on upper surface

◁ **'Peter Veitch'**
The goblet-shaped, soft pink blooms of this hardy magnolia appear in mid-spring before the leaves. Flowers are produced even on young plants.

white flowers flushed deep pink appear pale pink from a distance

Height: 100ft (30m)	Shape: Broadly columnar	Leaf persistence: Deciduous	Leaf type:

Family: Magnoliaceae	Species: *Magnolia* 'Wada's Memory'	Author: None

Magnolia 'Wada's Memory'

Leaves Obovate to narrowly ovate, to 7in (17.5cm) long, tapered at the base, abruptly pointed, red-purple when young becoming glossy dark green above, blue-green beneath, smooth on both sides. ***Bark*** Gray, smooth. ***Flowers*** Held horizontally, 6in (15cm) across, creamy white becoming white, fragrant, the tepals soon drooping, opening from felted buds. ***Fruit*** A cylindrical, pink to red cluster, to 4in (10cm) long, not usually produced.

NATIVE REGION Of garden or yard origin.
REMARK Probably a hybrid between *Magnolia kobus* (see p.180) and *Magnolia salicifolia* (see p.183), which originated in Japan. It is named after the Japanese nurseryman, Koichiro Wada.

much smaller tepals at base of flower

tepals soon flop as flower buds open

young leaves colored reddish purple

silky scales enclose flower bud

new leaves emerge just after first flowers

leaves mature to olive green

Height: 30ft (9m)	Shape: Broadly conical	Leaf persistence: Deciduous	Leaf type:

MALVACEAE

WITH ABOUT 240 GENERA and more than 4,000 species, the mallow family is found worldwide, except in the very coldest parts. The plants are deciduous and evergreen trees and shrubs, as well as herbaceous. The alternate leaves are often palmately lobed. Flowers vary from large and showy to very small.

Family: Malvaceae	Species: *Hoheria glabrata*	Author: Sprague & Summerh.

Mountain Ribbonwood

Leaves Ovate, to 4in (10cm) long and 2in (5cm) across, heart-shaped at the base, toothed, dark green above, smooth or nearly so on both sides, turning yellow in fall. ***Bark*** Gray, smooth. ***Flowers*** To 1½in (4cm) across, white, with five petals and yellow anthers, in clusters in the leaf axils in summer. ***Fruit*** Small and brown.

NATIVE REGION New Zealand.
HABITAT Forests and scrubland.

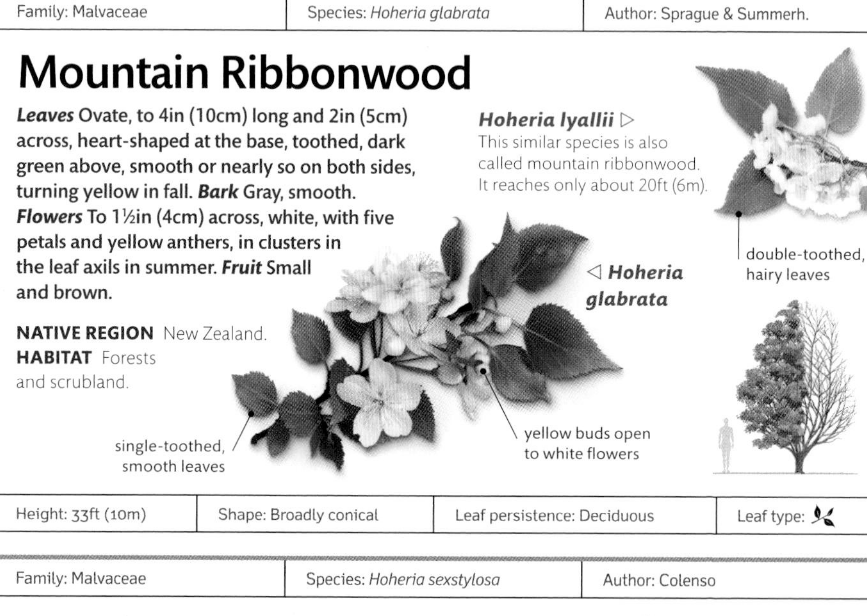

Height: 33ft (10m)	Shape: Broadly conical	Leaf persistence: Deciduous	Leaf type:

Family: Malvaceae	Species: *Hoheria sexstylosa*	Author: Colenso

Lacebark

Leaves Lanceolate, to 6in (15cm) long and 2in (5cm) or less across, narrowed at the base, taper-pointed at the tip, sharply toothed, glossy dark green above, paler beneath, smooth on both sides. ***Bark*** Gray, smooth. ***Flowers*** To ¾in (2cm) across, white, with five petals, in small clusters in the leaf axils in late summer. ***Fruit*** Small and brown.

NATIVE REGION New Zealand.
HABITAT Forests.
REMARK In its juvenile stage, the plant is bushy, and has more deeply toothed, or sometimes even lobed, leaves.

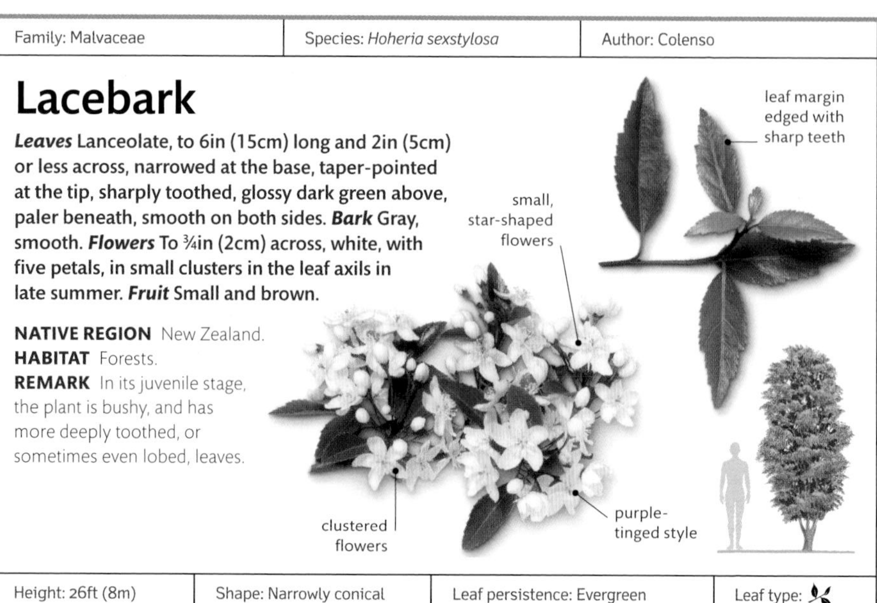

Height: 26ft (8m)	Shape: Narrowly conical	Leaf persistence: Evergreen	Leaf type:

Family: Malvaceae	Species: *Tilia americana*	Author: L.

American Lime

Leaves Broadly ovate to nearly rounded, to 8in (20cm) long and 6in (15cm) across, abruptly tapered to a fine point at the tip, with coarse, pointed teeth, matte deep green above, paler and rather glossy beneath, becoming smooth on both sides except for tufts of brown hairs in the vein axils beneath. ***Bark*** Brown to gray, cracked into long, scaly ridges. ***Flowers*** ⅝in (1.5cm) across, pale yellow, with five petals, fragrant, in pendulous clusters of up to 10, each cluster with an oblong bract to 4in (10cm) long, in midsummer. ***Fruit*** Rounded, woody, pale gray-green, about ⅜in (1cm) across.

NATIVE REGION E. Canada, E. US, Mexico.
HABITAT Moist woods.
REMARK Also known as basswood.

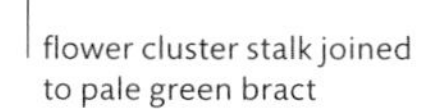

Height: 80ft (25m)	Shape: Broadly columnar	Leaf persistence: Deciduous	Leaf type: 

Family: Malvaceae	Species: *Tilia cordata*	Author: Mill.

Small-leaved Lime

Leaves Rounded, to 3in (7.5cm) long and across, heart-shaped at the base, taper-pointed, toothed, glossy green above, blue-green beneath, smooth except for hairs in the vein axils beneath, turning yellow in fall. ***Bark*** Gray and smooth, becoming gray-brown and furrowed with age. ***Flowers*** ¾in (2cm) across, pale yellow, with five petals, fragrant, in clusters of up to 10, each with a green bract to 4in (10cm) long, in midsummer. ***Fruit*** Rounded, woody, gray-green, about ¼in (6mm) across.

NATIVE REGION
W. Asia, Europe.
HABITAT On limestone.

Height: 100ft (30m)	Shape: Broadly columnar	Leaf persistence: Deciduous	Leaf type:

Family: Malvaceae	Species: *Tilia* x *euchlora*	Author: K. Koch

Caucasian Lime

Leaves Broadly ovate, to 4in (10cm) long and across, pointed, dark green above, paler and smooth beneath, except for hairs in the vein axils. ***Bark*** Gray, smooth, cracked with age. ***Flowers*** ¾in (2cm) across, pale yellow, with five petals, in clusters of up to seven, with a green bract to 3in (7.5cm) long, in midsummer. ***Fruit*** Woody, gray-green, about ½in (1.2cm) long.

NATIVE REGION Crimea, Iran.
REMARK May be a hybrid between *Tilia dasystyla* and *Tilia cordata* (above).

leaf margin edged with fine teeth

very glossy leaf upperside

hairy vein axils on leaf underside

up to seven flowers in each cluster

unequal-sided leaf base

Height: 65ft (20m)	Shape: Broadly columnar	Leaf persistence: Deciduous	Leaf type:

Family: Malvaceae	Species: *Tilia* x *europaea*	Author: L.

Common Lime

Leaves Broadly ovate to rounded, to 4in (10cm) long and across, heart-shaped at the base, abruptly short-pointed at the tip, coarsely toothed, dark green above, paler beneath, smooth except for tufts of hairs in the vein axils beneath. ***Bark*** Gray-brown, with shallow fissures. ***Flowers*** Small, ¾in (2cm) across, pale yellow, fragrant, with five petals, in clusters of up to 10, each cluster with a pale green bract to 4in (10cm) long, in midsummer. ***Fruit*** Egg-shaped, woody, gray-green, about ½in (1.2cm) long.

NATIVE REGION Europe.
HABITAT With the parents.
REMARK Also known as *Tilia* x *vulgaris*. A hybrid between small-leaved lime (*Tilia cordata*, see p.190) and broad-leaved lime (*Tilia platyphyllos*, see p.192).

tufts of hairs in vein axils on leaf underside

each flower cluster has pale green bract

△ ***Tilia* x *europaea***

◁ **'Wratislaviensis'**
The glowing, bright yellow young foliage of this form eventually matures to green.

Height: 130ft (40m)	Shape: Broadly columnar	Leaf persistence: Deciduous	Leaf type:

Family: Malvaceae	Species: *Tilia mongolica*	Author: Maxim.

Mongolian Lime

Leaves Broadly ovate, to 3in (7.5cm) long and across, with three to five lobes, taper-pointed at the tip, sharply toothed, reddish when young becoming glossy dark green above, blue-green beneath, smooth on both sides except for tufts of hairs in the vein axils beneath, turning yellow in fall, carried on red stalks. ***Bark*** Gray and smooth: ***Flowers*** Small, ¾in (2cm) across, pale yellow, fragrant, with five petals, borne in drooping clusters of up to 20, each cluster with a narrow, pale green bract to 4in (10cm) long, in midsummer. ***Fruit*** Rounded, woody, gray-green, about ½in (1.2cm) long.

NATIVE REGION N. China.
HABITAT Mountain slopes.
REMARK This species is easily identified in season by its distinctively lobed, sharply toothed leaves.

lobed leaves edged with sharp teeth

upper leaf surface matures to dark green

tiny tufts of hairs in vein axils

Height: 50ft (15m)	Shape: Broadly spreading	Leaf persistence: Deciduous	Leaf type: 

Family: Malvaceae	Species: *Tilia platyphyllos*	Author: Scop.

Broad-leaved Lime

Leaves Rounded to broadly ovate, to 4¾in (12cm) long and across, heart-shaped at the base, tapering to a short point at the tip, sharply toothed, dark green above, paler beneath, hairy on both sides especially beneath, turning yellow in fall. ***Bark*** Gray, with shallow fissures. ***Flowers*** Small, ¾in (2cm) across, pale yellow, fragrant, with five petals, in drooping clusters of about five, each cluster with a pale green bract to 4¾in (12cm) long, in early to midsummer. ***Fruit*** Rounded, woody, gray-green, about ½in (1.2cm) long, with five ribs.

NATIVE REGION S.W. Asia, Europe.
HABITAT Moist woods.

deeply veined leaves

flower clusters hang from pale green bracts

△ ***Tilia platyphyllos***

leaves edged with large, sharp teeth

◁ **'Laciniata'**
This unusual form has narrowly ovate, twisted leaves.

Height: 100ft (30m)	Shape: Broadly columnar	Leaf persistence: Deciduous	Leaf type:

Family: Malvaceae	Species: *Tilia tomentosa*	Author: Moench

Silver Lime

Leaves Rounded, to 4¾in (12cm) long and 4in (10cm) across, often slightly lobed, usually obliquely heart-shaped at the base, tapering to a short point at the tip, sharply toothed, dark green above, white-hairy beneath. ***Bark*** Gray, with shallow ridges. ***Flowers*** Small, ¾in (2cm) across, pale yellow, highly fragrant, with five petals, in drooping clusters of up to 10, each cluster with a pale green bract to 4in (10cm) long, in mid- to late summer. ***Fruit*** Rounded to egg-shaped, woody, gray-green, to ½in (1.2cm) long.

leaves may be slightly lobed

flowers hang up to 10 together

△▽ ***Tilia tomentosa***

distinctive silvery leaf underside

NATIVE REGION S.W. Asia, S.E. Europe.
HABITAT Mixed deciduous and evergreen woods.
REMARK Also known as *Tilia argentea*.

◁ **'Petiolaris'**
The weeping silver lime is a form selected for its pendulous shoots and longer-stalked leaves.

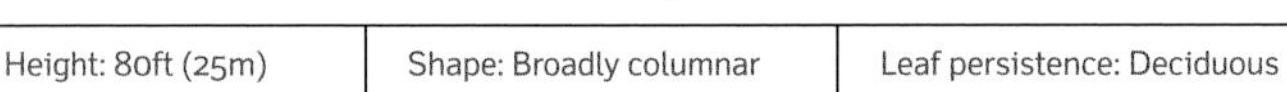

Height: 80ft (25m)	Shape: Broadly columnar	Leaf persistence: Deciduous	Leaf type:

MELIACEAE

OCCURRING IN TEMPERATE regions of east Asia, this largely tropical and subtropical family is composed of some 50 genera and more than 700 species. The plants, which are evergreen and deciduous trees and shrubs, have leaves that are most often pinnate, arranged alternately. The flowers are usually small, frequently borne in large clusters. The fruit is a woody capsule. Many trees that belong to Meliaceae have an important commercial value for their timber: several of the species produce the hardwood, mahogany.

Family: Meliaceae	Species: *Toona sinensis*	Author: (Juss.) M. Roem.

Chinese Cedar

Leaves Pinnate, to 24in (60cm) long, with up to 26 oblong-lanceolate, taper-pointed, remotely toothed leaflets, to 6in (15cm) long, the terminal leaflet often missing, bronze to pinkish and downy when young becoming dark green and smooth or nearly so, tinged yellow in fall, smelling of onions when crushed. ***Bark*** Brown, peeling in long strips. ***Flowers*** Small and white, fragrant, in large, drooping panicles 12in (30cm) or more long, from the ends of the shoots in midsummer. ***Fruit*** A woody, brown capsule, 1¼in (3cm) long.

NATIVE REGION China.
HABITAT Woods.
REMARK Also known as *Cedrela sinensis*.

terminal leaflet is usually absent

leaflets edged with very small teeth

bark peels in long strips on older plants

smallest leaflets at leaf base

Height: 65ft (20m)	Shape: Broadly columnar	Leaf persistence: Deciduous	Leaf type:

MORACEAE

THIS LARGE FAMILY includes the figs (*Ficus*, see p.195) and mulberries (*Morus*, see p.196). Its 50 genera and some 1,200 species of deciduous and evergreen trees, shrubs, and climbing and herbaceous plants are distributed worldwide. The leaves are usually alternate and simple, and, occasionally, lobed. Male and female flowers are borne separately, in small clusters.

Family: Moraceae	Species: *Broussonetia papyrifera*	Author: (L.) L'Hér. ex Vent.

Paper Mulberry

Leaves Ovate to broadly ovate, to 8in (20cm) long and 6in (15cm) across, sometimes lobed, coarsely toothed, purplish at first becoming matte dark green, roughly hairy above, softly hairy beneath. ***Bark*** Gray-brown, shallowly fissured. ***Flowers*** Males and females both small, males white, in stout, drooping catkins, females green, with slender, purple, protruding stigmas, borne in dense, rounded heads on separate plants in late spring to early summer. ***Fruit*** Red, protruding from a rounded cluster, ¾in (2cm) across.

NATIVE REGION China, Japan.
HABITAT Sunny, fertile situations.
REMARK In Japan, the bark is traditionally used to make paper.

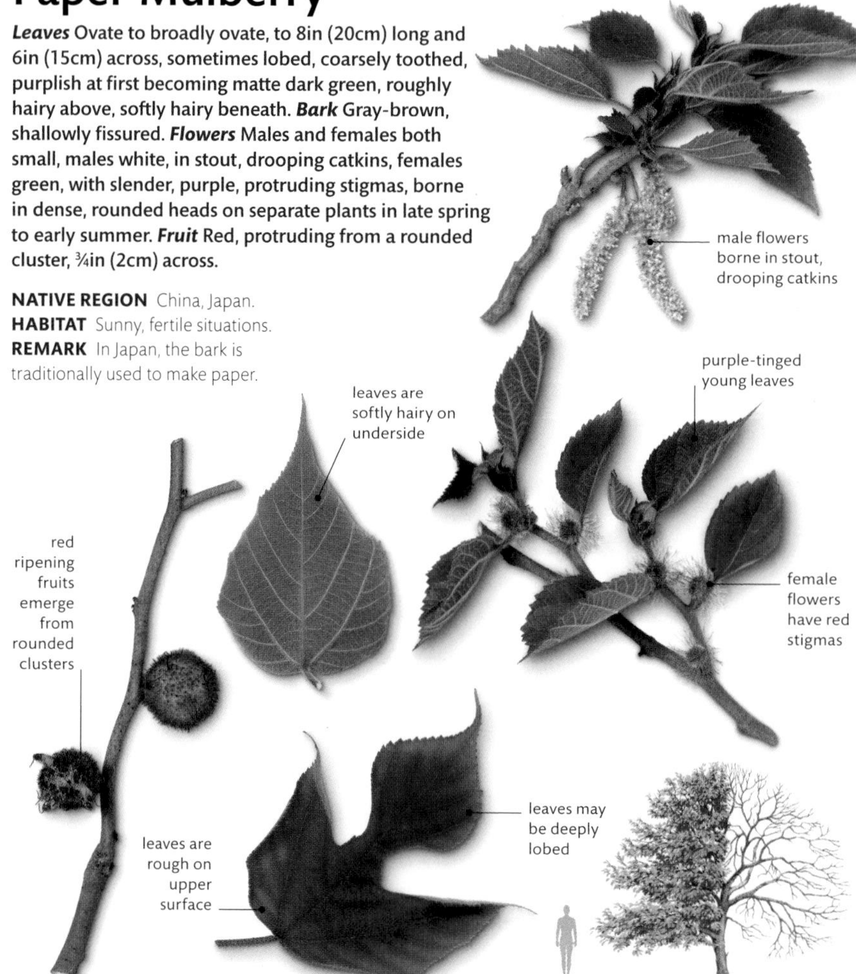

Height: 50ft (15m)	Shape: Broadly spreading	Leaf persistence: Deciduous	Leaf type:

Family: Moraceae	Species: *Ficus carica*	Author: L.

Common Fig

Leaves **Rounded in outline, to 12in (30cm) long and across, deeply cut into three to five lobes, heart-shaped at the base, toothed, glossy green above, rough with hairs on both sides, turning yellow in fall.** ***Bark*** **Gray and smooth.**
Flowers **Males and females both very small, borne inconspicuously inside a fleshy, green receptacle, on separate plants in late spring.**
Fruit **Numerous small seeds borne inside a receptacle, the whole green ripening to brown or purple, forming the edible fig.**

NATIVE REGION S.W. Asia.
HABITAT Broadleaf forests.
REMARK This species is commonly naturalized in the Mediterranean. It favors rocky places, including old walls. Plants are fertilized by female wasps, which take pollen from the tree in which they hatched to one in which they lay their eggs. Most cultivated plants produce fruit without pollination.

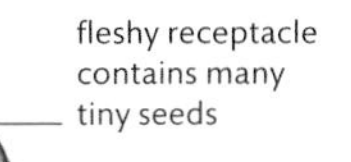

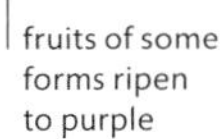

Height: 33ft (10m)	Shape: Broadly spreading	Leaf persistence: Deciduous	Leaf type:

Family: Moraceae	Species: *Maclura pomifera*	Author: (Raf.) C.K. Schneid.

Osage Orange

Leaves Ovate, to 4in (10cm) long and 2in (5cm) across, untoothed, glossy bright green above, smooth, turning yellow in fall. ***Bark*** Orange-brown, fissured. ***Flowers*** Males and females small, yellow-green, in clusters ⅜in (1cm) long, on separate plants in early summer. ***Fruit*** A wrinkled, yellow-green cluster, to 4in (10cm) across.

NATIVE REGION C. and S. US.
HABITAT Rich, moist soil.

small fruits fuse to form heavy fruit mass

leaves taper to long, slender point

Height: 50ft (15m)	Shape: Broadly spreading	Leaf persistence: Deciduous	Leaf type:

Family: Moraceae	Species: *Morus alba*	Author: L.

White Mulberry

Leaves Ovate to rounded, to 8in (20cm) long and 4¾in (12cm) across, toothed, bright green above, turning yellow in fall. ***Bark*** Orange-brown. ***Flowers*** Males and females green, in clusters about ⅜in (1cm) long, on the same or separate plants in early summer. ***Fruit*** A white to pink or red cluster, to 1in (2.5cm) long.

NATIVE REGION N. China.
HABITAT Hill slopes.

heart-shaped leaf base

smooth leaf upperside

stalked, edible fruit clusters

Height: 50ft (15m)	Shape: Broadly spreading	Leaf persistence: Deciduous	Leaf type:

Family: Moraceae	Species: *Morus nigra*	Author: L.

Black Mulberry

Leaves Ovate, to 6in (15cm) long and 4¾in (12cm) across, heart-shaped at the base, toothed, green above, hairy beneath. ***Bark*** Orange-brown, ridged. ***Flowers*** Males and females tiny, green, in small clusters on the same or separate plants in early summer. ***Fruit*** A dark red cluster, 1in (2.5cm) long.

NATIVE REGION Iran.
HABITAT Deciduous forest.
REMARK Widely cultivated and naturalized.

Height: 33ft (10m)	Shape: Broadly spreading	Leaf persistence: Deciduous	Leaf type:

MYRTACEAE

THIS LARGE FAMILY is distributed most widely in the southern hemisphere. Despite the fact that it extends to temperate regions of the northern hemisphere, it does not grow wild in North America, and is represented in Europe only by the shrubby myrtle (*Myrtus communis*). It contains more than 5,000 species of usually evergreen, frequently aromatic, trees and shrubs, in over 100 genera. The leaves are often opposite. The flowers have usually four or five petals and numerous stamens. In *Eucalyptus* species, the petals form a cap over the flower, which falls as the flower opens.

Family: Myrtaceae	Species: *Eucalyptus coccifera*	Author: Hook. f.

Mount Wellington Peppermint

Leaves Juvenile leaves rounded, usually glaucous, unstalked, adult leaves lanceolate, to 2in (5cm) long and ¾in (2cm) across, with a hooked tip, green to blue-green, smooth on both sides, aromatic, carried on often bloomy shoots. ***Bark*** Gray and white, smooth, peeling in long strips; creamy white when freshly exposed. ***Flowers*** White, with numerous stamens, borne in clusters of three to seven in the leaf axils in early summer. ***Fruit*** Resembling an inverted cone, small and woody, ⅜in (1cm) long.

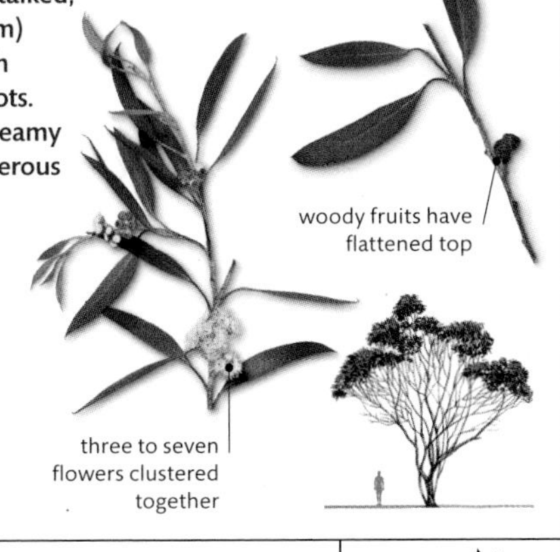

NATIVE REGION Tasmania.
HABITAT Mountains.
REMARK Also known as Tasmanian snow gum. Juvenile leaves are opposite, adult leaves alternate: plants often bear both stages together. On mature plants, juvenile foliage is produced on shoots from the base of the trunk.

Height: 80ft (25m)	Shape: Broadly spreading	Leaf persistence: Evergreen	Leaf type:

Family: Myrtaceae	Species: *Eucalyptus cordata*	Author: Labill.

Silver Gum

Leaves Nearly rounded to ovate, to 4in (10cm) long and 2½in (6cm) across, with rounded, shallow teeth, blue-gray and bloomy on both sides, very aromatic. ***Bark*** Smooth and white, with gray and green patches, peeling in long ribbons. ***Flowers*** Creamy white, with numerous stamens, opening from bloomy buds in winter. ***Fruit*** A hemispherical, bloomy capsule, ⅜in (1cm) long.

leaves overlap each other at base
four-angled shoots
very small, bloomy fruits
flower buds clustered three together

NATIVE REGION Tasmania.
HABITAT Woods in hills and mountains.
REMARK Juvenile and adult leaves are similar.

Height: 50ft (15m)	Shape: Broadly columnar	Leaf persistence: Evergreen	Leaf type:

Family: Myrtaceae	Species: *Eucalyptus dalrympleana*	Author: Maiden

Mountain Gum

Leaves Juvenile leaves rounded, unstalked, adult leaves lanceolate, to 7in (17.5cm) long and 1¼in (3cm) across, tapered to a fine point, bronze when young becoming blue-green and smooth on both sides. ***Bark*** Gray-brown and smooth, peeling in large flakes; creamy white when freshly exposed. ***Flowers*** White, with numerous stamens, in clusters of three in the leaf axils in late summer. ***Fruit*** Hemispherical, small, woody, ⅜in (1cm) long.

NATIVE REGION S.E. Australia, Tasmania.
HABITAT Mountain slopes.
REMARK Juvenile leaves are opposite, adult leaves alternate: plants often bear both stages together.

peeling bark exposes creamy layer beneath

slender, curved adult leaves

Height: 100ft (30m)	Shape: Broadly columnar	Leaf persistence: Evergreen	Leaf type:

Family: Myrtaceae	Species: *Eucalyptus gunnii*	Author: Hook. f.

Cider Gum

Leaves Juvenile leaves rounded, unstalked, to 1½in (4cm) long, gray-blue, adult leaves ovate to lanceolate, to 4in (10cm) long and 1½in (4cm) across, silvery becoming gray-green, smooth on both sides. ***Bark*** Gray, green, or orange, rough at the very base, peeling in large patches; creamy when freshly exposed. ***Flowers*** White, with numerous stamens in clusters of three in the leaf axils in late spring to summer. ***Fruit*** Cup-shaped, green or bloomy, 3/16in (5mm) long.

NATIVE REGION Tasmania.
HABITAT Alpine woods.
REMARK Juvenile leaves are opposite, adult leaves alternate: plants often bear both stages together.

silvery gray-blue young leaves

rounded juvenile leaves

cup-shaped fruits

bark peels in large patches

long, pointed adult leaves

Height: 80ft (25m)	Shape: Broadly columnar	Leaf persistence: Evergreen	Leaf type:

Family: Myrtaceae	Species: *Eucalyptus pauciflora*	Author: Sieber ex Spreng.

Snow Gum

Leaves Juvenile leaves ovate to rounded, to 2½in (6cm) long, leathery, gray, adult leaves lanceolate, to 6in (15cm) long and 1½in (4cm) across, often curved, glossy green and smooth. ***Bark*** Gray and white, peeling in large flakes. ***Flowers*** White, with numerous stamens, in clusters in the leaf axils in summer. ***Fruit*** Rounded, woody, ¼in (6mm) long.

NATIVE REGION S.E. Australia, Tasmania.
HABITAT From sea level to the tree line.

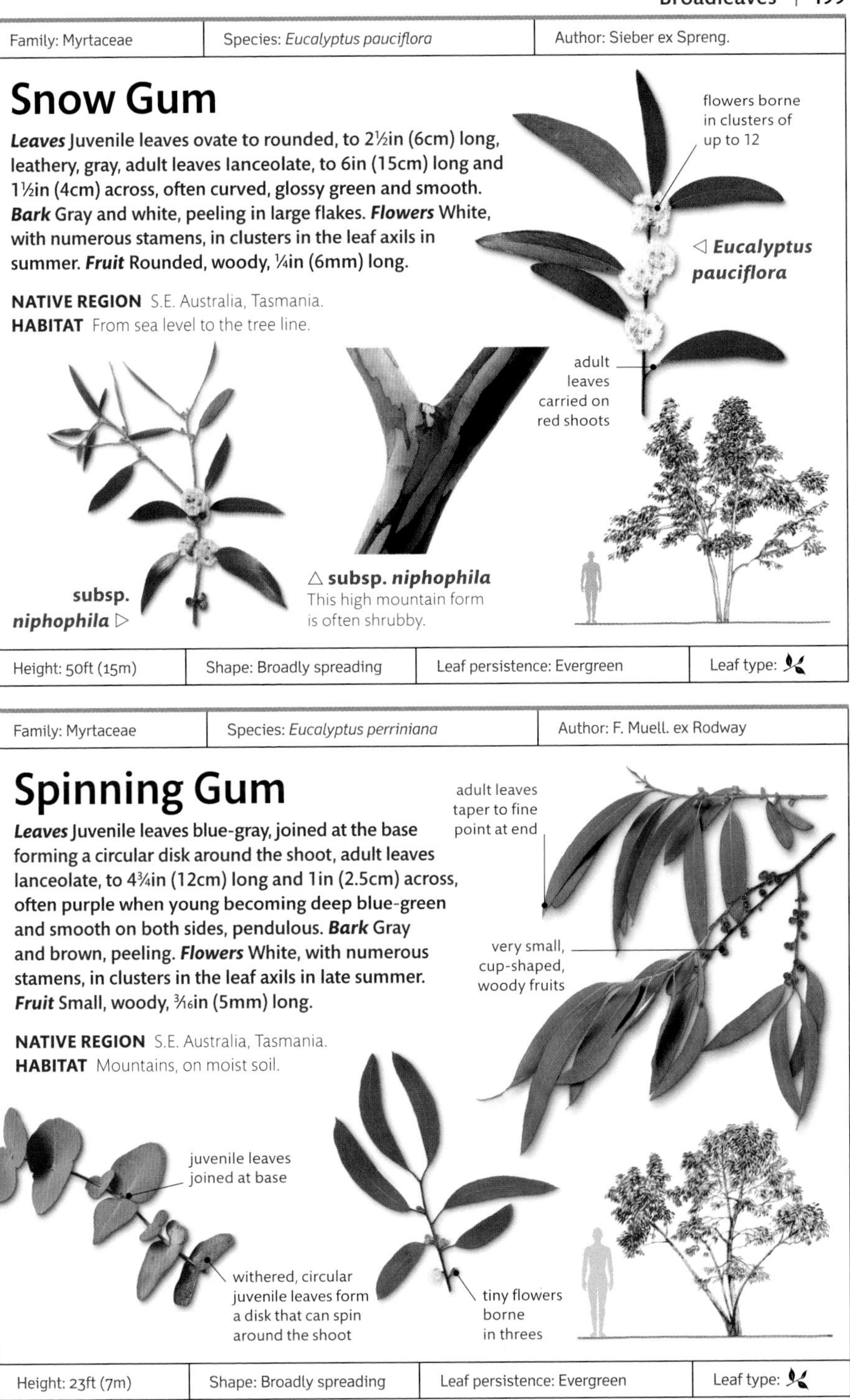

Height: 50ft (15m)	Shape: Broadly spreading	Leaf persistence: Evergreen	Leaf type:

Family: Myrtaceae	Species: *Eucalyptus perriniana*	Author: F. Muell. ex Rodway

Spinning Gum

Leaves Juvenile leaves blue-gray, joined at the base forming a circular disk around the shoot, adult leaves lanceolate, to 4¾in (12cm) long and 1in (2.5cm) across, often purple when young becoming deep blue-green and smooth on both sides, pendulous. ***Bark*** Gray and brown, peeling. ***Flowers*** White, with numerous stamens, in clusters in the leaf axils in late summer. ***Fruit*** Small, woody, 3⁄16in (5mm) long.

NATIVE REGION S.E. Australia, Tasmania.
HABITAT Mountains, on moist soil.

Height: 23ft (7m)	Shape: Broadly spreading	Leaf persistence: Evergreen	Leaf type:

Family: Myrtaceae	Species: *Eucalyptus urnigera*	Author: Hook. f.

Urn Gum

Leaves **Juvenile leaves rounded, to 2in (5cm) long, with a blue-white bloom, adult leaves ovate to lanceolate, to 4¾in (12cm) long and 2in (5cm) across, glossy green to blue-green, smooth on both sides.** ***Bark*** **Pale gray to creamy white or orange-yellow, peeling vertically in long ribbons.** ***Flowers*** **White, with numerous stamens, in clusters of three in the leaf axils in spring.** ***Fruit*** **Urn-shaped, ¼in (6mm) long, distinctly constricted below the rim.**

NATIVE REGION S.E. Tasmania.
HABITAT Rocky slopes in the mountains.
REMARK Juvenile leaves are opposite, adult leaves alternate: plants bear both stages together. Similar to cider gum (*Eucalyptus gunnii*, see p.198), this species is distinguished by its fruits.

rounded juvenile leaves arranged in opposite pairs

urn-shaped fruits

conspicuous white stamens

elongated adult leaves arranged alternately

flowers clustered in threes

Height: 40ft (12m)	Shape: Broadly columnar	Leaf persistence: Evergreen	Leaf type:

Family: Myrtaceae	Species: *Luma apiculata*	Author: (DC.) Burret

Luma apiculata

Leaves **Broadly elliptic, to 1in (2.5cm) long, short-pointed, untoothed, bronze-purple when young becoming glossy dark green and smooth above, paler beneath, aromatic.** ***Bark*** **Bright cinnamon-orange, flaking in patches; nearly white when freshly exposed.** ***Flowers*** **¾in (2cm) across, white, with four petals, numerous stamens, and yellow anthers, borne singly in the leaf axils of young shoots in late summer to fall.** ***Fruit*** **Rounded and fleshy, ⅜in (1cm) long, red ripening to purple-black.**

NATIVE REGION Argentina, Chile.
HABITAT Forests.
REMARK Also known as *Myrtus apiculata*.

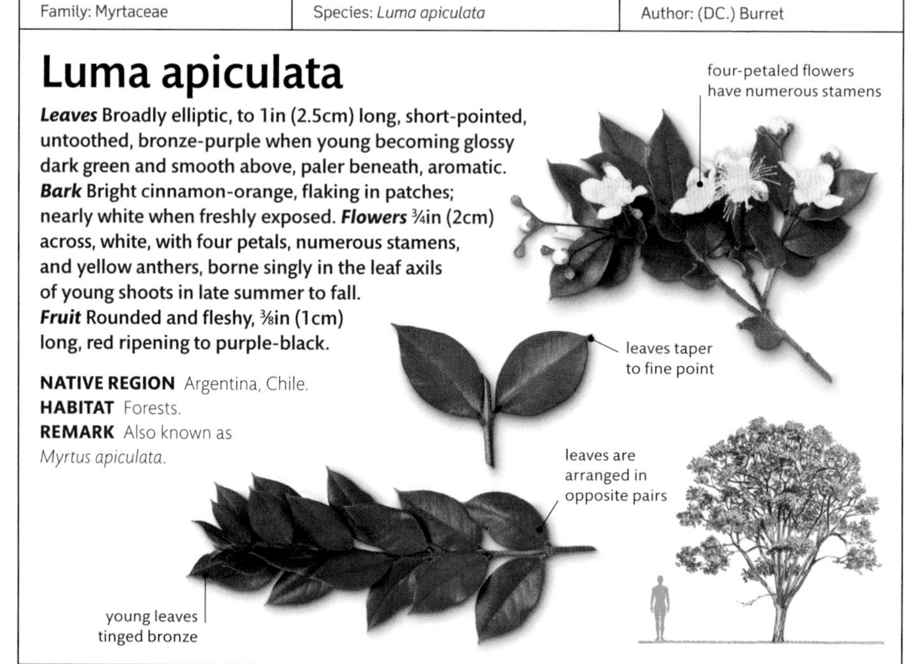

Height: 40ft (12m)	Shape: Broadly spreading	Leaf persistence: Evergreen	Leaf type:

Family: Myrtaceae	Species: *Melaleuca* species	Author: None

Bottlebrushes

The bottlebrushes are all native to Australia, and can be found growing usually in moist habitats. Some make small trees, reaching about 33ft (10m), such as *Melaleuca viminalis*, although most are shrubby. These evergreen plants usually have narrow, pointed leaves, often colored bronze or red when young. The flowers have very small petals, but their numerous long stamens, which range in color from creamy white or yellow to red, pink, or purplish, radiate around the stem, forming dense spikes, and giving the flower clusters their characteristic appearance.

young shoot extends from end of flower cluster

red stamens make flower cluster conspicuous

woody fruits borne in clusters on shoots

△ ***Melaleuca subulata***

This native of S.E. Australia has slender, pointed leaves, covered in silky hairs when young. The large flower clusters, which have numerous crimson stamens, open in summer.

long, greenish stamens tipped with bright yellow anthers

narrow, pointed leaves

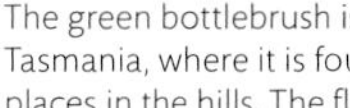

△ ***Melaleuca virens***

The green bottlebrush is a native of Tasmania, where it is found in moist places in the hills. The flowerheads consist of dense clusters of pale yellow-green stamens. They are produced in the summer months.

Height: To 33ft (10m)	Shape: Broadly columnar	Leaf persistence: Evergreen	Leaf type:

NOTHOFAGACEAE

WITH A SINGLE GENUS and about 35 species of deciduous and evergreen trees, this family is restricted to the southern hemisphere, occurring in tropical and temperate regions from New Guinea to East Australia and New Zealand, to southern South America. It was previously included in Fagaceae.

Family: Nothofagaceae	Species: *Nothofagus alpina*	Author: (Poepp. & Endl.) Oerst.

Rauli

Leaves Oblong, to 4in (10cm) long and 1½in (4cm) across, finely toothed, with 15 to 18 pairs of veins, bronze becoming matte deep green above, hairy on both sides, turning yellow in fall. ***Bark*** Dark gray, fissured with age. ***Flowers*** Very small, greenish, males borne singly, females in clusters of three, in the leaf axils in late spring. ***Fruit*** A bristly husk, to ⅜in (1cm) long, enclosing three small nuts.

NATIVE REGION Argentina, Chile.
HABITAT Forests.
REMARK Also known as *Nothofagus nervosa* and *Nothofagus procera.*

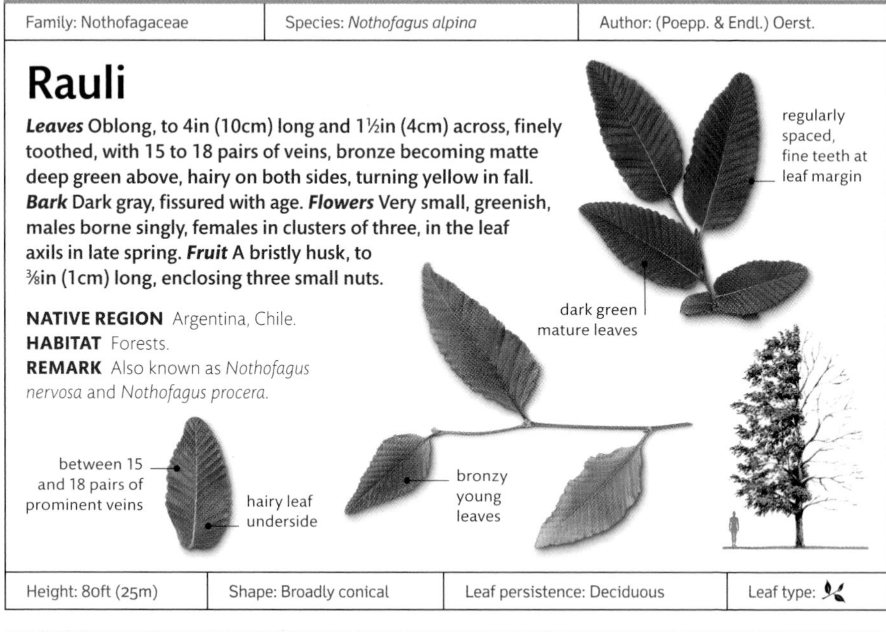

Height: 80ft (25m)	Shape: Broadly conical	Leaf persistence: Deciduous	Leaf type:

Family: Nothofagaceae	Species: *Nothofagus antarctica*	Author: (G. Forst.) Oerst.

Antarctic Beech

Leaves Ovate, to 1¼in (3cm) long and ¾in (2cm) across, finely toothed, with usually four pairs of veins, glossy dark green above, more or less smooth on both sides. ***Bark*** Dark gray, cracking into plates and flaking with age. ***Flowers*** Males and females both very small, males with red anthers, in clusters of one to three, females with red stigmas, in clusters of two to three, in the leaf axils in late spring. ***Fruit*** A smooth husk, to ¼in (6mm) long, enclosing three small nuts.

NATIVE REGION S. Argentina, S. Chile.
HABITAT Deciduous woods and scrub in mountains.
REMARK Also known as nirre. In its native region and habitat, the species is usually a medium-sized tree, but it can also form a large shrub.

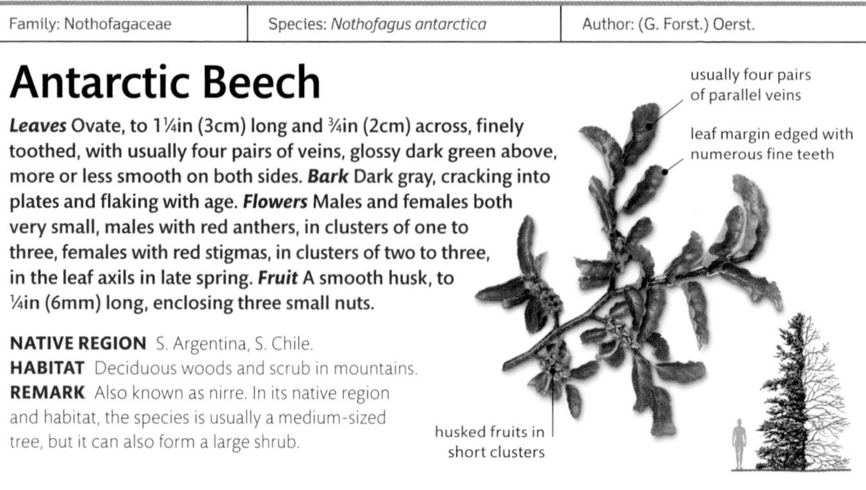

Height: 50ft (15m)	Shape: Broadly columnar	Leaf persistence: Deciduous	Leaf type:

Family: Nothofagaceae	Species: *Nothofagus betuloides*	Author: (Mirb.) Oerst.

Coigüe de Magallanes

Leaves Ovate to elliptic, to 1in (2.5cm) long and ¾in (2cm) across, broadly tapered to the often unequal base, bluntly toothed, glossy dark blackish green above, paler and glossy with a fine network of veins beneath, smooth on both sides; older leaves often with small, dark spots beneath. ***Bark*** Very dark gray, cracking into plates and flaking with age. ***Flowers*** Males and females both very small, males with red anthers, singly, females with red stigmas, in clusters of three, in the leaf axils in late spring. ***Fruit*** A bristly husk, to ¼in (6mm) long, enclosing three small nuts.

NATIVE REGION Argentina, Chile.
HABITAT Evergreen forests.
REMARK Sometimes shrubby.

fine network of veins on paler leaf underside

leaf margin edged with many blunt teeth

young shoots have small red stipules

Height: 80ft (25m)	Shape: Broadly columnar	Leaf persistence: Evergreen	Leaf type:

Family: Nothofagaceae	Species: *Nothofagus dombeyi*	Author: (Mirb.) Oerst.

Coigüe

Leaves Narrowly ovate, to 1½in (4cm) long and ⅝in (1.5cm) across, rounded at the often unequal base, finely and sharply toothed, glossy dark green above, paler and glossy with a fine network of veins beneath, smooth, with small, black spots. ***Bark*** Dark gray, cracking into plates and flaking with age. ***Flowers*** Males and females both very small, males with red anthers, in clusters of three, females with red stigmas, in clusters of three, in the leaf axils in late spring. ***Fruit*** A bristly husk, to ¼in (6mm) long, enclosing three small nuts.

NATIVE REGION Argentina, Chile.
HABITAT Mountain forests.
REMARK This species is similar to *Nothofagus betuloides* (see above), but differs in its larger leaves and taller growing habit.

Height: 130ft (40m)	Shape: Broadly columnar	Leaf persistence: Evergreen	Leaf type:

Family: Nothofagaceae	Species: *Nothofagus obliqua*	Author: (Mirb.) Oerst.

Roble Beech

Leaves Ovate, to 3in (7.5cm) long and 1½in (4cm) across, toothed, dark green above, blue-green beneath, smooth on both sides, turning yellow in fall. ***Bark*** Gray, smooth, cracking into plates with age. ***Flowers*** Tiny, greenish, males singly, females in threes, in late spring. ***Fruit*** A scaly husk, to ⅜in (1cm) long, with three nuts.

NATIVE REGION Argentina, Chile.
HABITAT Forests.

leaves have 8 to 10 pairs of veins

flowers borne in leaf axils

obliquely rounded leaf base

Height: 115ft (35m)	Shape: Broadly columnar	Leaf persistence: Deciduous	Leaf type:

Family: Nothofagaceae	Species: *Nothofagus pumilio*	Author: (Poepp. & Endl.) Krasser

Lenga

Leaves Elliptic to ovate, to 1¼in (3cm) long and ¾in (2cm) across, very dark green above, slightly hairy on both sides, turning yellow in fall. ***Bark*** Purple-brown, with horizontal lenticels and wrinkles, fissured at the base. ***Flowers*** Very small, borne singly in the leaf axils in late spring. ***Fruit*** A scaly husk, to ⅜in (1cm) long, enclosing three small nuts.

NATIVE REGION Argentina, Chile.
HABITAT Forests.

leaves have five to seven pairs of veins

two teeth between ends of adjacent leaf veins

Height: 80ft (25m)	Shape: Broadly columnar	Leaf persistence: Deciduous	Leaf type:

Family: Nothofagaceae	Species: *Nothofagus solandri*	Author: (Hook. f.) Oerst.

Black Beech

Leaves Elliptic, to ⅝in (1.5cm) long and ⅜in (1cm) across, rounded at the tip, untoothed, dark green above, gray-hairy beneath. ***Bark*** Dark gray, rough, furrowed. ***Flowers*** Very small, males with red anthers, singly or in pairs, females in clusters of up to three, in the leaf axils in late spring. ***Fruit*** A scaly husk, enclosing three small nuts.

NATIVE REGION New Zealand.
HABITAT Lowland and mountain forests.

Height: 80ft (25m)	Shape: Broadly conical	Leaf persistence: Evergreen	Leaf type:

NYSSACEAE

THE FIVE GENERA and 35 species of the tupelo family are native to North America and east Asia. The best-known genus is *Nyssa*, whose species display brilliant fall color. The leaves are alternate, and the small flowers petalless, but those of *Davidia involucrata* have conspicuous bracts.

Family: Nyssaceae	Species: *Davidia involucrata*	Author: Baill.

Dove Tree

Leaves Heart-shaped, to 6in (15cm) long and 4¾in (12cm) across, with a slender, pointed tip, sharply toothed, bright green above, densely hairy beneath. ***Bark*** Orange-brown, peeling vertically in small flakes. ***Flowers*** Individually small, in a rounded head ¾in (2cm) across, conspicuous by the purple anthers, surrounded by two white bracts of unequal size, the larger to 8in (20cm) long, in late spring with the leaves. ***Fruit*** Rounded, 1in (2.5cm) across, green ripening to purple-brown.

NATIVE REGION China.
HABITAT Moist mountain woods.

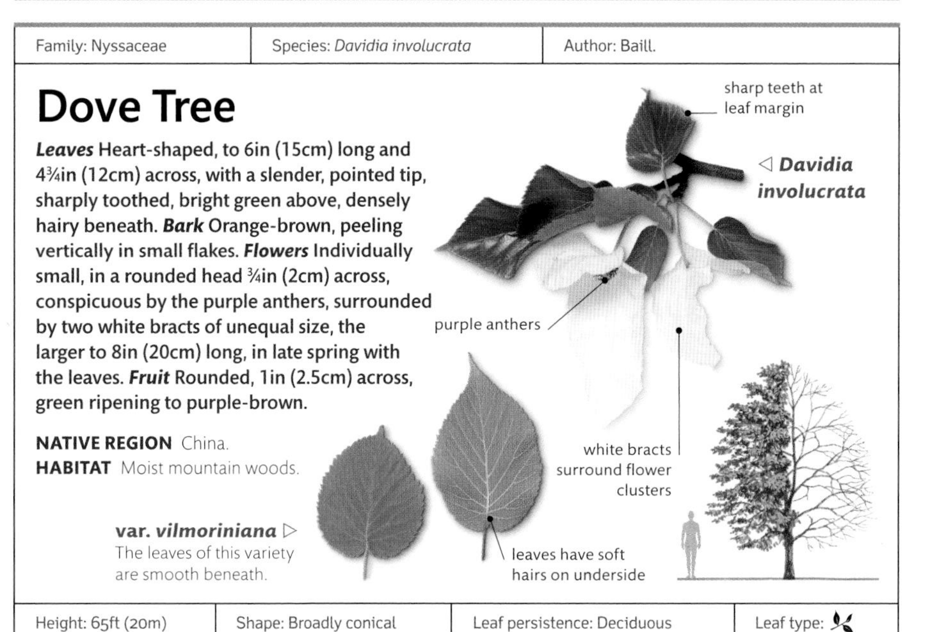

var. *vilmoriniana* ▷
The leaves of this variety are smooth beneath.

Height: 65ft (20m)	Shape: Broadly conical	Leaf persistence: Deciduous	Leaf type:

Family: Nyssaceae	Species: *Nyssa sinensis*	Author: Oliv.

Chinese Tupelo

Leaves Oblong-lanceolate to elliptic, to 8in (20cm) long and 2½in (6cm) across, untoothed, reddish when young becoming deep green above, paler beneath, turning red, orange, and yellow in fall. ***Bark*** Gray-brown, cracked, and flaking with age. ***Flowers*** Males and females both very small and green, with five petals, in usually separate, long-stalked clusters in the leaf axils, on the same plant in summer. ***Fruit*** A bluish berry, about ¾in (1cm) long.

NATIVE REGION S. China, Myanmar, Vietnam.
HABITAT Mountain woods and stream banks.
REMARK A relative of the tupelo (*Nyssa sylvatica*, see p.206).

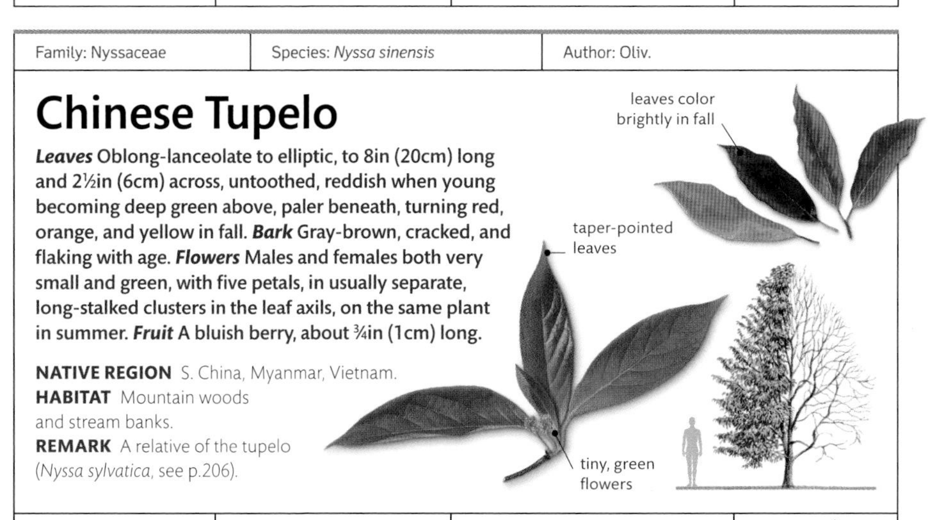

Height: 50ft (15m)	Shape: Broadly conical	Leaf persistence: Deciduous	Leaf type:

Family: Nyssaceae	Species: *Nyssa sylvatica*	Author: Marshall

Tupelo

Leaves Variable, ovate to elliptic or obovate, to 6in (15cm) long and 3in (7.5cm) across, tapering to a short, blunt point at the tip, untoothed, glossy dark green above, blue-green beneath, turning yellow to orange, red, or purple in fall. ***Bark*** Dark gray, vertically ridged and breaking into square plates. ***Flowers*** Males and females both very small and green, with five petals, in usually separate, long-stalked clusters in the leaf axils, on the same plant in summer. ***Fruit*** A bluish berry, about ⅜in (1cm) long.

NATIVE REGION E. North America.
HABITAT Moist woods and swamps.
REMARK Also known as black gum, pepperidge, sour gum.

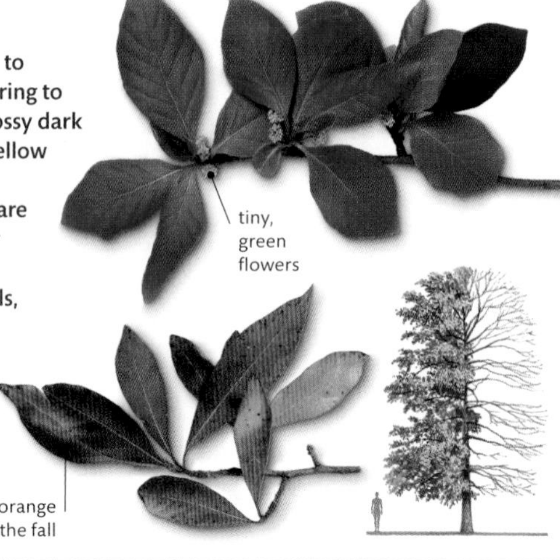

Height: 80ft (25m)	Shape: Broadly columnar	Leaf persistence: Deciduous	Leaf type:

OLEACEAE

A WIDELY DISTRIBUTED family of about 25 genera that contain more than 700 species of deciduous and evergreen trees, shrubs, and climbers. The plants have usually opposite, sometimes compound, leaves. The small flowers are either with four petals, which are frequently joined, or without petals.

Family: Oleaceae	Species: *Chionanthus retusus*	Author: Lindl. & Paxton

Chinese Fringe Tree

Leaves Elliptic to ovate or obovate, to 4in (10cm) long and 2in (5cm) across, bluntly pointed or indented at the tip, finely toothed or untoothed at the margin, glossy green above, paler and downy beneath. ***Bark*** Gray-brown, corky, and deeply furrowed. ***Flowers*** Males and females both about ¾in (2cm) long, white, with four strap-shaped petals, borne in upright panicles at the ends of the young shoots, on separate plants in summer. ***Fruit*** An egg-shaped, deep blue berry, ⅝in (1.5cm) long.

NATIVE REGION China, Japan, Korea.
HABITAT Woods and on cliffs, in sunny, moist places.

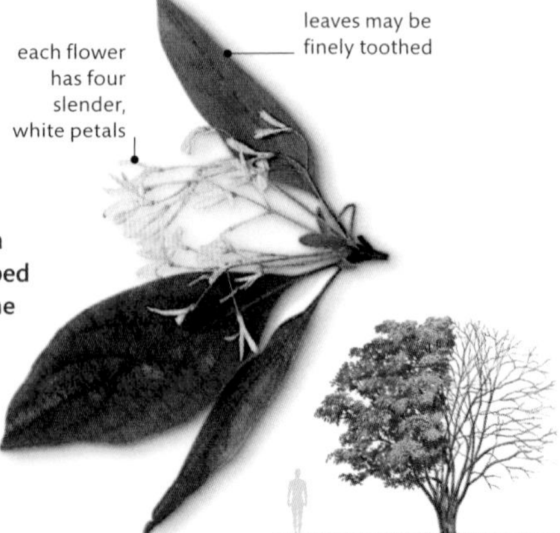

Height: 33ft (10m)	Shape: Broadly spreading	Leaf persistence: Deciduous	Leaf type:

Family: Oleaceae	Species: *Chionanthus virginicus*	Author: L.

Fringe Tree

Leaves Elliptic, to 8in (20cm) long and 4in (10cm) across, tapered to a short point at the tip, untoothed, glossy green above, turning yellow in fall. ***Bark*** Gray and smooth, becoming furrowed with age. ***Flowers*** Males and females both to 1¼in (3cm) long, white, slightly fragrant, with four to six slender, strap-shaped petals, on slender, drooping stalks, borne in conical, upright panicles, male panicles to 8in (20cm) long, females somewhat shorter, usually on separate plants in summer. ***Fruit*** An egg-shaped, bloomy, deep blue berry, ¾in (2cm) long.

NATIVE REGION E. US.
HABITAT Moist woods and riverbanks.
REMARK Also known as old man's beard. This species can be either a shrub or a small tree.

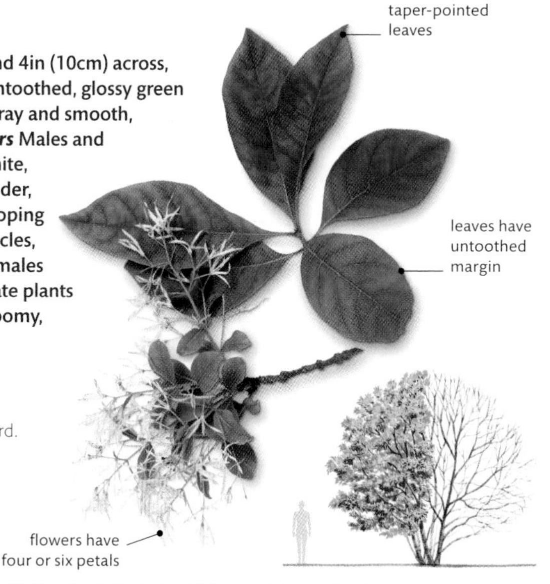

Height: 33ft (10m)	Shape: Broadly spreading	Leaf persistence: Deciduous	Leaf type:

Family: Oleaceae	Species: *Fraxinus americana*	Author: L.

White Ash

Leaves Pinnate, to 14in (35cm) long, with five to nine ovate to lanceolate, taper-pointed, sparsely toothed leaflets, to 4¾in (12cm) long and 3in (7.5cm) across, the lateral leaflets carried on short stalks, dark green and smooth above, blue-green to green and smooth or slightly hairy beneath, usually turning yellow or sometimes purple in fall; winter leaf buds dark brown or nearly black. ***Bark*** Gray-brown, with narrow, interlacing ridges. ***Flowers*** Males and females both very small, green or purple, without petals, borne in clusters on separate plants in spring before the young leaves emerge. ***Fruit*** A key, to 2in (5cm) long, green ripening to pale brown, ending in a flattened wing, hanging in clusters.

NATIVE REGION E. North America.
HABITAT Rich woods.
REMARK The trees produce a close-grained, durable wood, which is traditionally used for making tool handles.

Height: 100ft (30m)	Shape: Broadly columnar	Leaf persistence: Deciduous	Leaf type: 

Family: Oleaceae	Species: *Fraxinus angustifolia*	Author: Vahl

Narrow-Leaved Ash

Leaves Pinnate, to 10in (25cm) long, with 7 to 13 lanceolate leaflets, to 3in (7.5cm) long and ¾in (2cm) across, with a slender, tapered point at the tip, sharply toothed, glossy bright green and smooth above, the lateral leaflets unstalked; winter buds dark brown. ***Bark*** Gray-brown, with prominent ridges. ***Flowers*** Very small, green or purple, without petals, borne in clusters in spring before the leaves. ***Fruit*** With a flattened wing at the end, to 1½in (4cm) long, green ripening to pale brown, in hanging clusters.

NATIVE REGION S. and C. Europe, S.W. Asia, N. Africa.
HABITAT Woods and riversides.

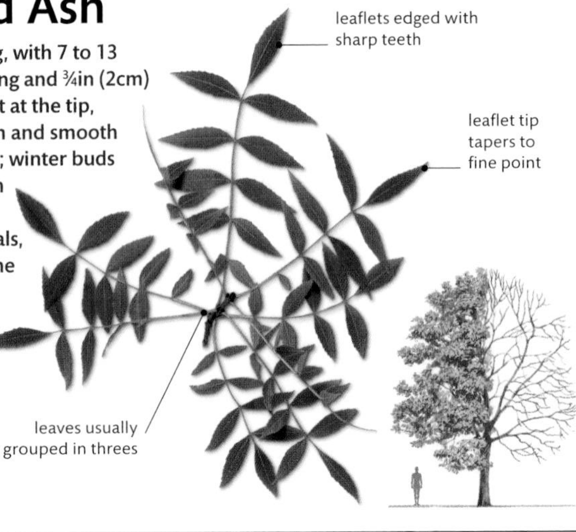

Height: 80ft (25m)	Shape: Broadly columnar	Leaf persistence: Deciduous	Leaf type:

Family: Oleaceae	Species: *Fraxinus excelsior*	Author: L.

Common Ash

Leaves Pinnate, to 12in (30cm) long, with 9 to 13 oblong-ovate to lanceolate leaflets, to 4in (10cm) long and 1¼in (3cm) across, taper-pointed, sharply toothed, dark green above, the lateral leaflets short-stalked. ***Bark*** Pale gray and smooth, fissured with age. ***Flowers*** Tiny, purple, without petals, opening from nearly black buds, on the same or separate plants in spring before the leaves emerge. ***Fruit*** With a flattened wing at the end, to 1½in (4cm) long, green ripening to pale brown, in hanging clusters.

NATIVE REGION Europe.
HABITAT Moist woods, riverbanks.

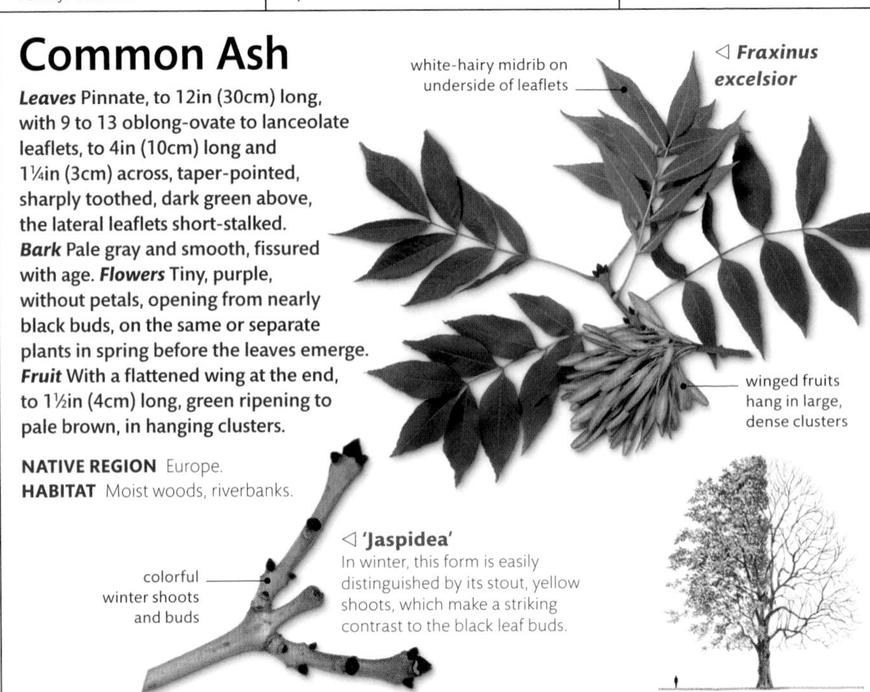

◁ **'Jaspidea'**
In winter, this form is easily distinguished by its stout, yellow shoots, which make a striking contrast to the black leaf buds.

Height: 130ft (40m)	Shape: Broadly columnar	Leaf persistence: Deciduous	Leaf type: 

Family: Oleaceae	Species: *Fraxinus ornus*	Author: L.

Manna Ash

Leaves Pinnate, to 8in (20cm) or more long, with five to nine oblong to ovate, taper-pointed, sharply toothed leaflets, to 4¾in (12cm) long and 2in (5cm) across, the lateral leaflets distinctly stalked, matte green above, paler beneath; winter leaf buds dark gray. ***Bark*** Gray and smooth. ***Flowers*** Small and white, with four slender petals ¼in (6mm) long, fragrant, borne in large, conical, fluffy clusters to 8in (20cm) long, in late spring to early summer. ***Fruit*** A key, to 1½in (4cm) long, green ripening to pale brown, ending in a flattened wing, hanging in clusters.

NATIVE REGION S.W. Asia, S. Europe.
HABITAT Woods on dry, sunny slopes.
REMARK The flowers of most ash (*Fraxinus*) species are inconspicuous. The flower clusters of this species are very showy, and give the tree its alternative common name, flowering ash.

ripening fruits

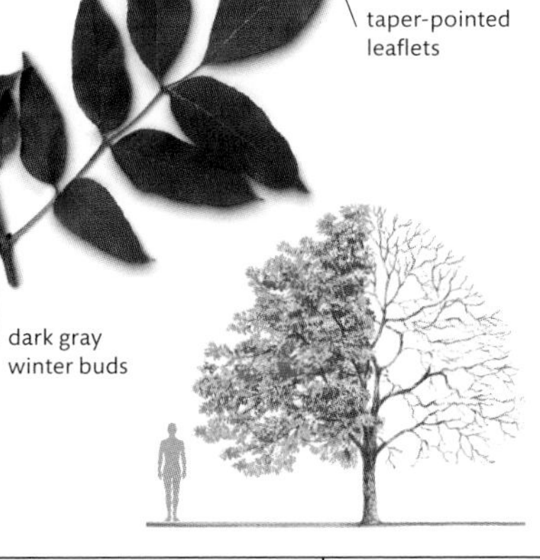

large flower clusters open at same time as young leaves emerge

Height: 65ft (20m)	Shape: Broadly spreading	Leaf persistence: Deciduous	Leaf type: 

Family: Oleaceae	Species: *Fraxinus pennsylvanica*	Author: Marshall

Green Ash

Leaves Pinnate, to 12in (30cm) long, with five to nine ovate to lanceolate, taper-pointed, sharply toothed or sometimes untoothed leaflets, to 4¾in (12cm) long and 2in (5cm) across, the lateral leaflets distinctly stalked, glossy dark green above, turning yellow in fall; winter leaf buds with brown hairs. ***Bark*** Gray-brown, with narrow, interlacing ridges. ***Flowers*** Males and females both very small, green or purple, with no petals, borne in clusters on separate plants in spring before the young leaves emerge. ***Fruit*** A key, to 2in (5cm) long, green ripening to pale brown, ending in a flattened wing, hanging in clusters.

NATIVE REGION North America.
HABITAT Moist woods.

Height: 80ft (25m)	Shape: Broadly columnar	Leaf persistence: Deciduous	Leaf type: 

Family: Oleaceae	Species: *Ligustrum lucidum*	Author: W.T. Aiton

Chinese Privet

Leaves Ovate, to 4in (10cm) long and 2in (5cm) across, tapering to a fine point at the tip, untoothed, bronze when young becoming glossy dark green above, paler and dull beneath, smooth on both sides. ***Bark*** Gray and smooth. ***Flowers*** Small and white, fragrant, with four joined petals, profusely borne in large, conical, upright panicles to 8in (20cm) long, over a long period in late summer and fall. ***Fruit*** A blue-black berry, ⅜in (1cm) long.

NATIVE REGION China, Korea.
HABITAT Hillside woods and river valleys in mountains.
REMARK This species, which can be either a large shrub or a small to medium-sized tree, is one of the evergreen privets. Its flowering season is unusually long.

small, clustered flowers

pale leaf underside

glossy green mature leaves

◁△ ***Ligustrum lucidum***

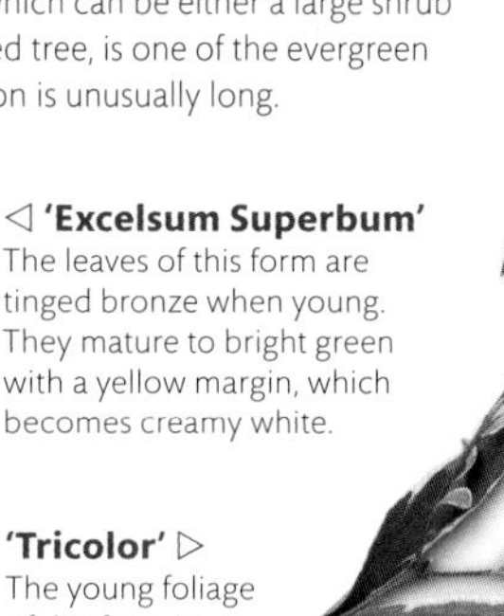

◁ **'Excelsum Superbum'**
The leaves of this form are tinged bronze when young. They mature to bright green with a yellow margin, which becomes creamy white.

'Tricolor' ▷
The young foliage of this form is flushed pink.

Height: 40ft (12m)	Shape: Broadly conical	Leaf persistence: Evergreen	Leaf type:

Family: Oleaceae	Species: *Phillyrea latifolia*	Author: L.

Green Olive

Leaves Ovate to lanceolate, to 2in (5cm) long and 1½in (4cm) across, toothed, glossy very dark green above, paler beneath, smooth on both sides; on juvenile plants, variable in shape and size. ***Bark*** Pale gray and smooth, becoming dark gray and cracking into small, square plates with age. ***Flowers*** Very small and greenish white, the exserted stamens with yellow anthers, borne in clusters in the leaf axils in late spring to early summer. ***Fruit*** A small, rounded, blue-black berry, about ⅜in (1cm) across.

NATIVE REGION Mediterranean.
HABITAT Evergreen woods.

yellow anthers make tiny flowers conspicuous

dark green, leathery leaves

Height: 33ft (10m)	Shape: Broadly spreading	Leaf persistence: Evergreen	Leaf type:

PAULOWNIACEAE

THIS FAMILY CONSISTS OF three genera and 10 species of deciduous and evergreen trees native from the Himalayas to East and Southeast Asia. They have previously been placed in Bignoniaceae or Scrophulariaceae.

Family: Paulowniaceae	Species: *Paulownia tomentosa*	Author: (Thunb.) Steud.

Foxglove Tree

Leaves Ovate, to 12in (30cm) long and 10in (25cm) across, heart-shaped at the base, taper-pointed, sometimes lobed, dark green and hairy above, hairy beneath. ***Bark*** Gray, smooth. ***Flowers*** To 2in (5cm) long, pale purple marked deeper purple and yellow inside, in upright panicles to 16in (40cm) long, in spring. ***Fruit*** A pale brown, woody capsule, to 2in (5cm) long.

NATIVE REGION China, S. Korea.
HABITAT Mountains.

Height: 50ft (15m)	Shape: Broadly columnar	Leaf persistence: Deciduous	Leaf type: 

PITTOSPORACEAE

THE NINE GENERA and nearly 300 species in this family of evergreen trees, shrubs, and climbing plants are native to tropical regions, particularly Australasia. The leaves are alternate, most often untoothed. Small, usually tubular, five-lobed flowers develop into a dry or fleshy fruit.

Family: Pittosporaceae	Species: *Pittosporum tenuifolium*	Author: Gaertn.

Black Matipo

Leaves Oblong to elliptic, to 2½in (6cm) long and ¾in (2cm) across, with a wavy margin, glossy rather light green, smooth, on deep purple-black shoots. ***Bark*** Dark gray, smooth. ***Flowers*** Small and tubular, about ⅜in (1cm) long, whitish at the base, with five reflexed, deep red-purple lobes and yellow anthers, strongly fragrant, borne singly or in clusters in the leaf axils in late spring. ***Fruit*** A rounded capsule, about ½in (1.2cm) across, green ripening to nearly black.

NATIVE REGION New Zealand.
HABITAT Forests from coastline to mountain level.

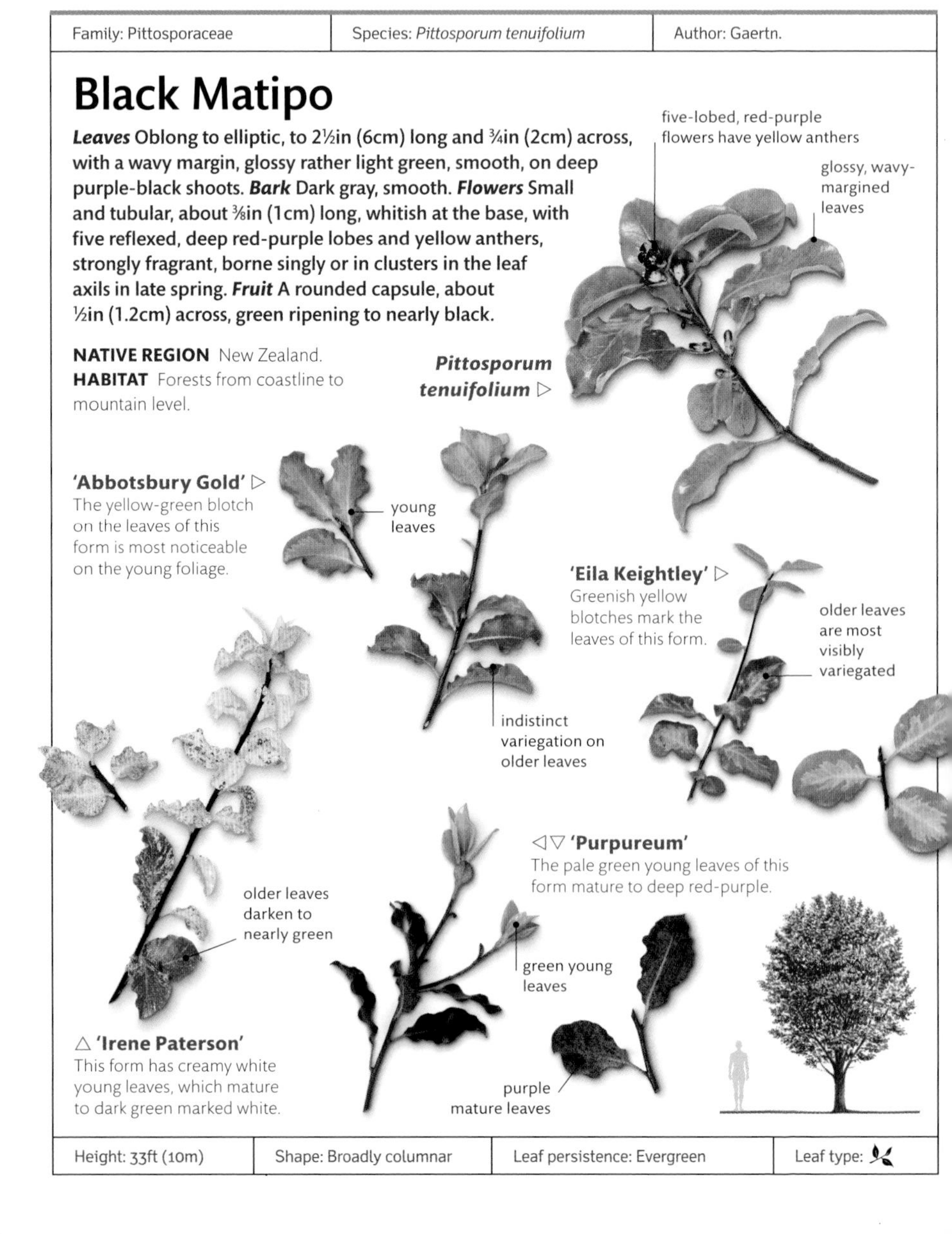

Pittosporum tenuifolium ▷

'Abbotsbury Gold' ▷
The yellow-green blotch on the leaves of this form is most noticeable on the young foliage.

'Eila Keightley' ▷
Greenish yellow blotches mark the leaves of this form.

◁▽ **'Purpureum'**
The pale green young leaves of this form mature to deep red-purple.

△ **'Irene Paterson'**
This form has creamy white young leaves, which mature to dark green marked white.

Height: 33ft (10m)	Shape: Broadly columnar	Leaf persistence: Evergreen	Leaf type:

PLATANACEAE

THE PLANE FAMILY consists of only one genus, *Platanus*, and up to 10 species. The large, deciduous trees grow wild mainly in the US and Mexico. The leaves are alternate and palmately lobed, except for those of the Southeast Asian *Platanus kerrii*, which are unlobed. The dense clusters of tiny flowers hang on slender stalks, either singly or in groups.

Family: Platanaceae	Species: *Platanus* x *hispanica*	Author: Mill. ex Münchh.

London Plane

Leaves Palmately lobed, to 8in (20cm) long and 10in (25cm) across, with three to five large, toothed lobes, glossy bright green above, paler beneath, covered in scurfy brown hairs when young. ***Bark*** Brown, gray, and cream, flaking in patches. ***Flowers*** Males and females both very small, males yellow, females reddish, borne in separate, small, rounded clusters on the same plant in late spring. ***Fruit*** A rounded, dense cluster, 1in (2.5cm) across, green ripening to brown, covered in spiky, brown bristles, hanging two to four together, persisting over winter.

NATIVE REGION Of garden and backyard origin.
REMARK Also known as *Platanus* x *acerifolia*. This species is probably a hybrid between the American sycamore (*Platanus occidentalis*, see p.214) and the oriental plane (*Platanus orientalis*, see p.214).

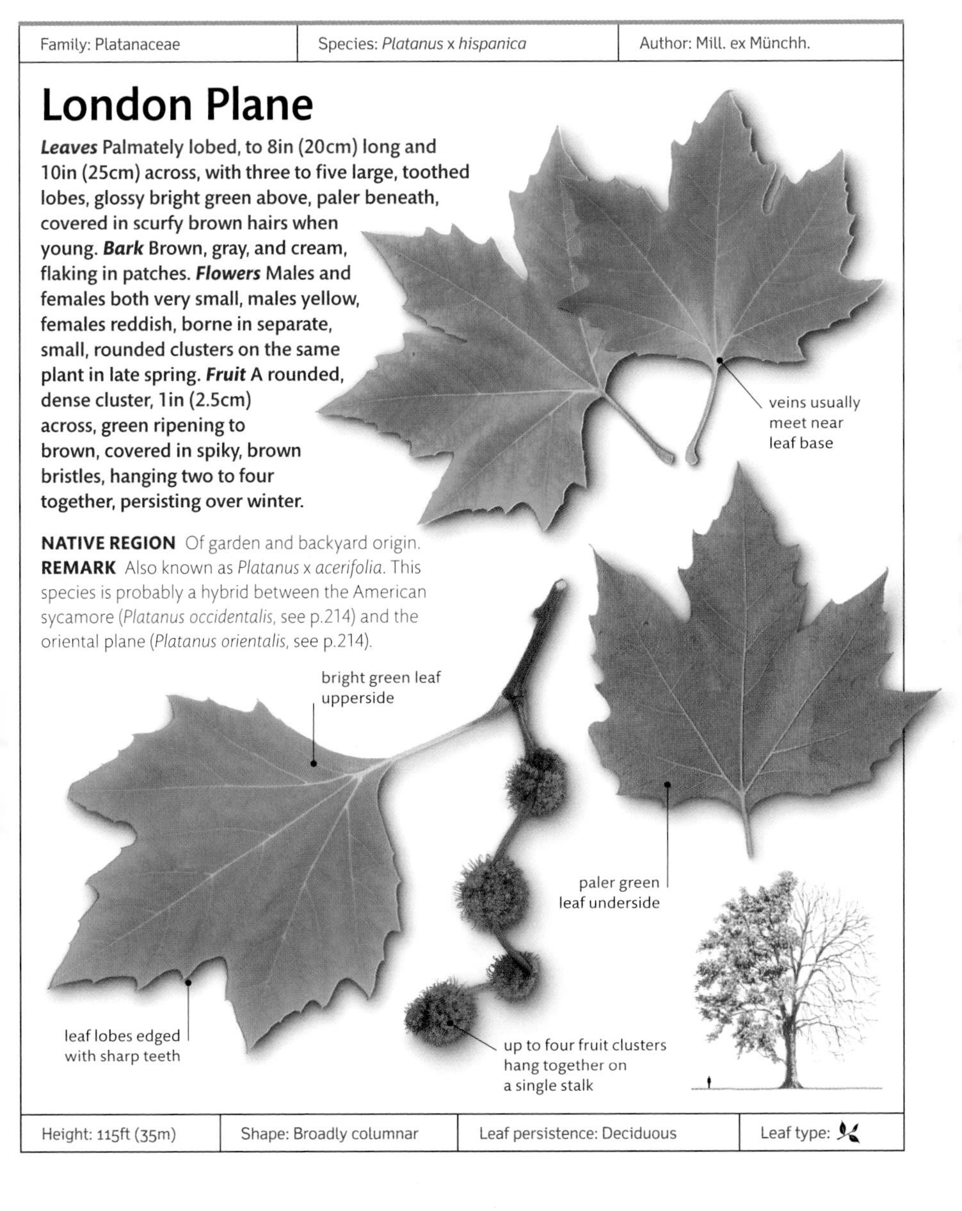

Height: 115ft (35m)	Shape: Broadly columnar	Leaf persistence: Deciduous	Leaf type:

Family: Platanaceae	Species: *Platanus occidentalis*	Author: L.

American Sycamore

Leaves Palmately lobed, to 8in (20cm) long and across, with three lobes, glossy green above, paler beneath. ***Bark*** Gray, brown, cream, flaking. ***Flowers*** Very small, males yellow, females reddish, in separate, rounded clusters on the same plant in late spring. ***Fruit*** A rounded, dense, brown cluster, 1in (2.5cm) across.

NATIVE REGION E. North America.
HABITAT Rich, moist soil.

shallow lobes usually edged with sharp teeth

leaf base may be heart-shaped

Height: 115ft (35m)	Shape: Broadly columnar	Leaf persistence: Deciduous	Leaf type:

Family: Platanaceae	Species: *Platanus orientalis*	Author: L.

Oriental Plane

Leaves Palmately lobed, to 8in (20cm) long and 10in (25cm) across, cut to below the middle into usually five toothed lobes, glossy green above, paler beneath, with scurfy brown hairs when young. ***Bark*** Gray, pinkish brown, and cream, flaking in patches. ***Flowers*** Males and females both very small, males yellow, females reddish, borne in separate, small, rounded clusters on the same plant in late spring. ***Fruit*** A rounded, dense, brown cluster, 1in (2.5cm) across, hanging up to six on each stalk, persisting on the plant over winter.

NATIVE REGION S.E. Europe, S.W. Asia.
HABITAT Mountain woods, riversides, and moist places.

deeply cut, slender leaf lobes

leaves become smooth on underside

bristly fruits break up before falling

up to six fruit clusters hang on a single stalk

Height: 100ft (30m)	Shape: Broadly columnar	Leaf persistence: Deciduous	Leaf type:

PROTEACEAE

SOME 80 GENERA and more than 1,500 species of evergreen trees and shrubs are included in this family. Native to the southern hemisphere, they grow wild throughout this part of the world; some species also extend to warm regions of the northern hemisphere. The leaves are alternate, simple to pinnate; the flowers have a petal-like calyx divided into four lobes, although the petals themselves are very small and inconspicuous.

Proteaceae is best known for its ornamental plants (eg species of *Grevillea*, *Banksia*, *Protea*, and *Telopea*), and for *Macadamia* species, cultivated in Australia and Hawaii for their edible nuts.

Family: Proteaceae	Species: *Embothrium coccineum*	Author: J.R. Forst. & G. Forst.

Chilean Fire Bush

Leaves Elliptic to oblong, variable, to 6in (15cm) long and 1¼in (3cm) across, untoothed, dark green to blue-green above, paler beneath, leathery, smooth on both sides. ***Bark*** Purple-brown, smooth, flaking with age. ***Flowers*** Tubular at first, to 2in (5cm) long, splitting into four lobes, the lobes curling backward leaving the style protruding, bright orange-red, borne in clusters in late spring to early summer. ***Fruit*** A woody capsule, to 1¼in (3cm) long, with a long beak.

NATIVE REGION Argentina, Chile.
HABITAT Open places, at all altitudes from the coast to the mountains.
REMARK This species is one of the most striking representatives of its family.

Height: 30ft (9m)	Shape: Broadly columnar	Leaf persistence: Evergreen	Leaf type:

RHAMNACEAE

THE 60 GENERA AND around 900 species of deciduous and evergreen trees, shrubs, and climbing plants belonging to this family grow wild in all parts of the world. They are sometimes spiny, bearing alternate or opposite leaves, and small male and female flowers, found sometimes on separate plants. Several species of buckthorn (*Frangula* and *Rhamnus*) yield dyes.

Family: Rhamnaceae	Species: *Frangula alnus*	Author: Mill.

Alder Buckthorn

Leaves Obovate, to 2¾in (7cm) long and 1½in (4cm) across, with a short, blunt point, untoothed, glossy dark green above, paler beneath, turning red in fall. ***Bark*** Gray, smooth, with vertical, shallow, pale cracks. ***Flowers*** Very small, with tiny, pink-tinged petals and a green, five-lobed calyx, in clusters in early to late summer. ***Fruit*** Rounded, fleshy, and berrylike, to ⅜in (1cm) across, green becoming red ripening to black.

NATIVE REGION N. Africa, W. Asia, Europe.
HABITAT Woods and scrub, usually on wet soil.
REMARK Also known as *Rhamnus frangula*.

glossy dark leaf surface
fruits ripen from red to black
untoothed leaves
tiny, pink-tinged flowers

Height: 17ft (5m)	Shape: Broadly spreading	Leaf persistence: Deciduous	Leaf type:

Family: Rhamnaceae	Species: *Rhamnus cathartica*	Author: L.

Common Buckthorn

Leaves Broadly ovate to nearly rounded, to 2½in (6cm) long and 1½in (4cm) across, with a short point at the tip, finely toothed, glossy green above, paler beneath, turning yellow in fall, borne on sparsely spiny shoots. ***Bark*** Dark orange-brown and scaly. ***Flowers*** Small, with tiny petals and a green, four-lobed calyx, fragrant, in clusters in early to midsummer. ***Fruit*** Rounded, fleshy, berrylike, to ⅜in (1cm) across, green ripening to black.

NATIVE REGION Asia, Europe.
HABITAT Woods, thickets, and hedgerows, on chalky soil.

Height: 33ft (10m)	Shape: Broadly spreading	Leaf persistence: Deciduous	Leaf type:

ROSACEAE

THIS FAMILY IS a widely distributed and very important collection of deciduous and evergreen trees, shrubs, and herbaceous plants, containing over 100 genera and more than 4,000 species.

The leaves are usually alternate, and vary from simple and untoothed to pinnate. The flowers are usually five-petalled. Several different types of fruit are produced, and the family is divided into groups on the basis of their structure. The trees in this book fall into two of these groups. Both have fleshy, often edible, fruits, but whereas those of *Prunus* species contain only a single seed, those of the other genera listed here contain two or more seeds.

Family: Rosaceae	Species: *Alniaria alnifolia*	Author: (Siebold & Zucc.) Rushforth

Korean Mountain Ash

Leaves Ovate to elliptic, to 4in (10cm) long and 1½in (4cm) across, pointed, toothed, dark green above, downy becoming smooth beneath, turning yellow, orange, or red in fall. ***Bark*** Dark brown, smooth, with shallow fissures. ***Flowers*** ⅜in (1cm) across, white, in clusters in mid-spring. ***Fruit*** A rounded, reddish berry, about ⅜in (1cm) across, marked with lenticels.

NATIVE REGION N.E. Asia.
HABITAT Woods.

fruits ripen from green to red or sometimes pink

five-petalled flowers

Height: 65ft (20m)	Shape: Broadly conical	Leaf persistence: Deciduous	Leaf type:

Family: Rosaceae	Species: *Amelanchier arborea*	Author: (F. Michx.) Fernald

June Berry

Leaves Ovate to obovate, to 3in (7.5cm) long and 1½in (4cm) across, rounded at the base, short-pointed at the tip, finely toothed, white-hairy when young, becoming deep green above, orange to red in fall. ***Bark*** Gray and smooth when young, later ridged and scaly. ***Flowers*** White, with five narrow petals, in upright racemes to 2in (5cm) long, in spring before the leaves are fully open. ***Fruit*** A rounded, sweet, edible, reddish purple berry, to 5⁄16in (8mm) across, ripening in summer.

NATIVE REGION E. Canada, E. and C. US.
HABITAT Woods and thickets, on moist soil.

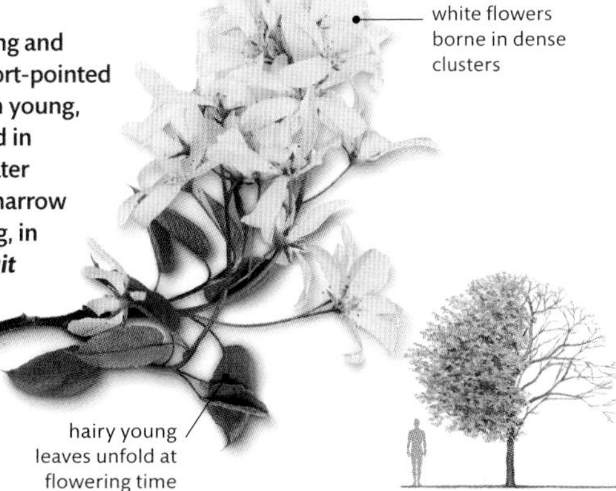

Height: 40ft (12m)	Shape: Broadly spreading	Leaf persistence: Deciduous	Leaf type:

Family: Rosaceae	Species: *Amelanchier asiatica*	Author: (Siebold & Zucc.) Endl. ex Walp.

Asian Serviceberry

Leaves Ovate, to 3in (7.5cm) long and 1½in (4cm) across, rounded at the base, pointed, toothed, dark green above, hairy then smooth beneath, turning orange and red in fall. ***Bark*** Gray-brown, fissured with age. ***Flowers*** White, in upright, later spreading, racemes to 2½in (6cm) long, in spring. ***Fruit*** Black-purple, to ⅜in (1cm) across.

NATIVE REGION China, Japan, Korea.
HABITAT Dry, sunny sites.

five narrow flower petals

finely toothed leaves

pointed leaf tip

Height: 40ft (12m)	Shape: Broadly spreading	Leaf persistence: Deciduous	Leaf type:

Family: Rosaceae	Species: *Amelanchier laevis*	Author: Wiegand

Amelanchier laevis

Leaves Elliptic to ovate or obovate, to 2½in (6cm) long and 1in (2.5cm) across, pointed, finely toothed, bronze-red becoming dark green above, smooth, turning red or orange in fall. ***Bark*** Gray-brown and smooth. ***Flowers*** White, with five narrow petals, in upright to spreading racemes to 3in (7.5cm) long, in spring. ***Fruit*** Rounded, juicy, purple-black, 5/16in (8mm) across.

NATIVE REGION E. North America.
HABITAT Woods, thickets.

flowers borne in open clusters

smooth, bronzy young leaves

Height: 40ft (12m)	Shape: Broadly spreading	Leaf persistence: Deciduous	Leaf type:

Family: Rosaceae	Species: *Amelanchier lamarckii*	Author: F.G. Schroed.

Amelanchier lamarckii

Leaves Ovate to elliptic, to 3in (7.5cm) long and 1½in (4cm) across, usually rounded at the base, pointed, finely toothed, bronzy becoming dark green. ***Bark*** Gray, smooth, developing vertical, narrow cracks. ***Flowers*** White, with five narrow petals, borne in upright or spreading racemes to 3in (7.5cm) long, in spring. ***Fruit*** Rounded, juicy, and purple-black, ⅜in (1cm) across.

NATIVE REGION Europe.
HABITAT Sandy soil.
REMARK Believed by some to be a North American hybrid naturalized in Europe.

Height: 40ft (12m)	Shape: Broadly spreading	Leaf persistence: Deciduous	Leaf type:

Family: Rosaceae	Species: *Aria edulis*	Author: (Willd.) M. Roem.

Whitebeam

Leaves Elliptic to ovate, to 4¾in (12cm) long and 2½in (6cm) across, sharply toothed, pale green with hairs when young becoming glossy dark green above, white with hairs beneath. ***Bark*** Gray and smooth, developing rugged cracks with age. ***Flowers*** About ⅜in (1cm) across, white, with five petals, borne in flattened clusters in late spring. ***Fruit*** A rounded, bright red berry, about ½in (1.2cm) across, speckled with pale lenticels.

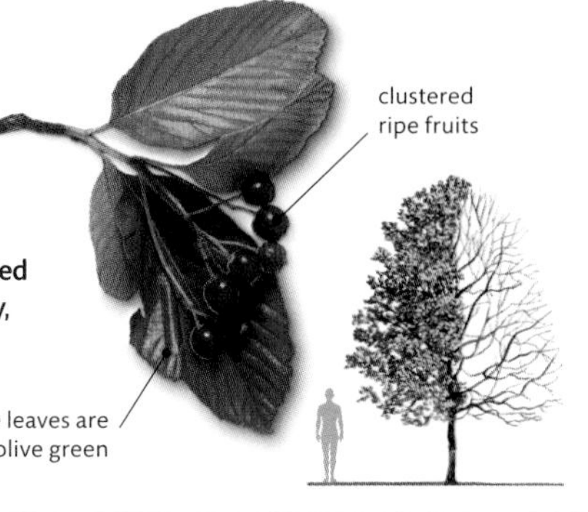

NATIVE REGION Europe, N.W. Africa.
HABITAT From lowland to mountains, on chalk and limestone.

Height: 50ft (15m)	Shape: Broadly columnar	Leaf persistence: Deciduous	Leaf type:

Family: Rosaceae	Species: *Cormus domestica*	Author: (L.) Spach

Service Tree

Leaves Pinnate, to 8¾in (22cm) long, with up to 21 oblong, toothed leaflets, to 2½in (6cm) long and about ⅜in (1cm) across, yellow-green and smooth above, downy beneath when young, turning yellow or red in fall. ***Bark*** Dark brown, scaly, cracking into plates. ***Flowers*** To ⅝in (1.5cm) across, white, with five petals, in rounded clusters about 4in (10cm) across, in late spring. ***Fruit*** Rounded or pear-shaped, yellow-green flushed red, to 1¼in (3cm) long.

NATIVE REGION Europe, N.W. Africa.
HABITAT Mountain slopes, deciduous forests.

flowers borne in rounded heads

parallel-sided leaflets

△ ***Cormus domestica***

Pomifera Group ▷
The fruits of this form resemble tiny apples.

rounded fruits become flushed with red when mature

fruits broaden above center

◁ **Pyrifera Group**
This form has bright red fruits shaped like miniature pears.

teeth at top half of leaflet margin point forwards

Height: 65ft (20m)	Shape: Broadly columnar	Leaf persistence: Deciduous	Leaf type:

Family: Rosaceae	Species: *Cotoneaster frigidus*	Author: Wall ex Lindl.

Cotoneaster frigidus

Leaves Elliptic to ovate, to 4¾in (12cm) long and 2in (5cm) across, rounded at the tip, untoothed, often with a wavy margin, matte dark green and smooth above, gray and hairy beneath, at least when young. ***Bark*** Gray, flaking with age. ***Flowers*** 5⁄16in (8mm) across, white, in dense, flattened heads to 4in (10cm) across, in midsummer. ***Fruit*** Rounded, bright red, 3⁄16in (5mm) across, borne in hanging clusters on thick stems.

NATIVE REGION Himalayas.
HABITAT Thickets and riverbanks.
REMARK Can be either a small tree or a large shrub.

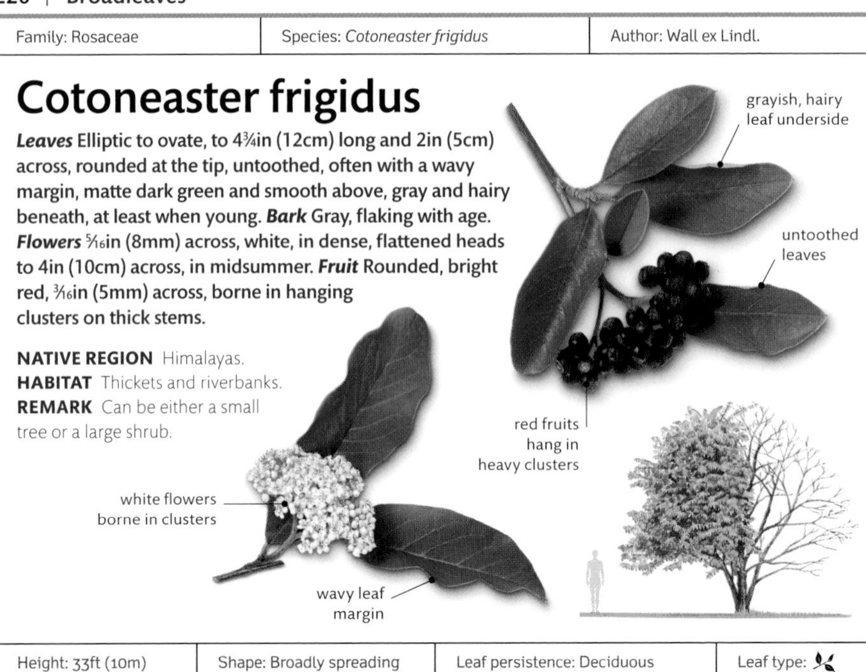

Height: 33ft (10m)	Shape: Broadly spreading	Leaf persistence: Deciduous	Leaf type:

Family: Rosaceae	Species: *Crataegus crus-galli*	Author: L.

Cockspur Thorn

Leaves Obovate, to 4in (10cm) long and 1½in (4cm) across, tapered at the base, rounded at the tip, toothed above the middle, glossy dark green above, paler beneath, smooth, turning orange and red in fall, the shoots with long spines. ***Bark*** Dark brown, scaly. ***Flowers*** ⅝in (1.5cm) across, white, with five petals and pink anthers, in rounded heads in early summer. ***Fruit*** Rounded, fleshy, red, ⅜in (1cm) across.

NATIVE REGION E. North America.
HABITAT Thickets in dry, rocky places.

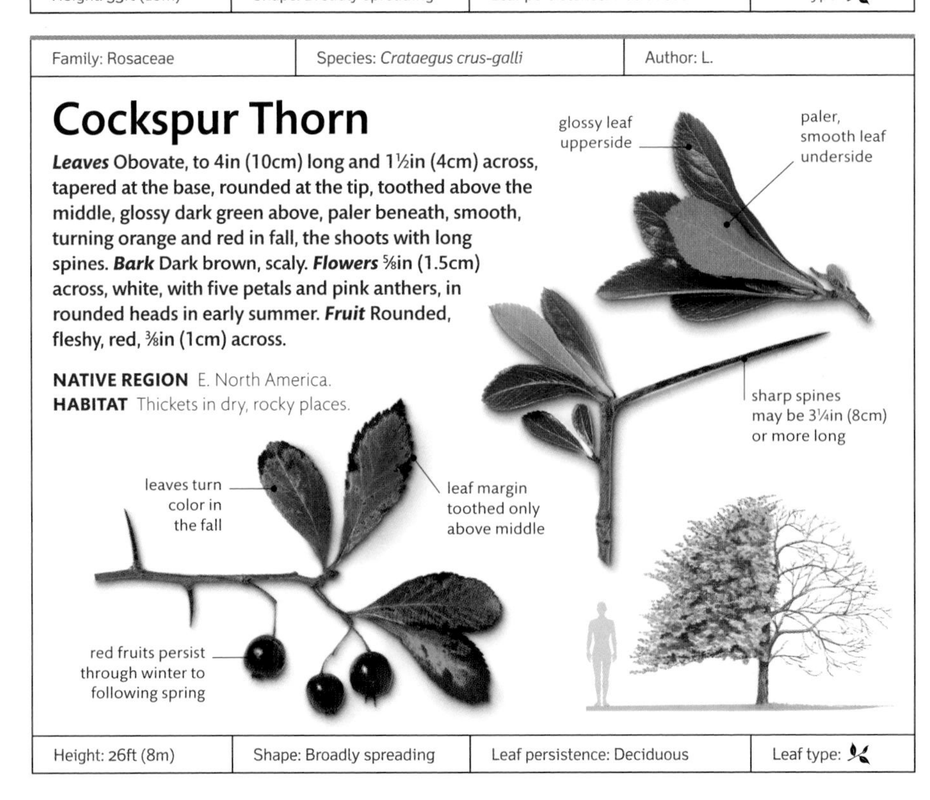

Height: 26ft (8m)	Shape: Broadly spreading	Leaf persistence: Deciduous	Leaf type:

Family: Rosaceae	Species: *Crataegus laevigata*	Author: (Poir.) DC.

Midland Hawthorn

Leaves Ovate to obovate, to 2in (5cm) long and across, shallowly lobed, toothed, glossy dark green above, paler beneath, becoming smooth. ***Bark*** Gray, smooth, cracking with age. ***Flowers*** ¾in (2cm) across, usually white, with five petals, borne in small clusters in late spring. ***Fruit*** Rounded to oval, red, to ¾in (2cm) long.

NATIVE REGION Europe.
HABITAT Woods and hedgerows.

each fruit has two stones

creamy mottled leaves

△ **'Gireoudii'**

'Gireoudii' △
The green young leaves of this form are later followed by variegated foliage.

vibrantly deep pink double flowers

◁ **'Paul's Scarlet'**
This lovely cultivar is selected for its flowers, borne through late spring and early summer.

Height: 33ft (10m)	Shape: Broadly spreading	Leaf persistence: Deciduous	Leaf type:

Family: Rosaceae	Species: *Crataegus* x *lavallei*	Author: Herincq ex Lavallée

Crataegus x lavallei

Leaves Obovate to elliptic, to 4in (10cm) long and 2in (5cm) across, tapered at the base, pointed at the tip, toothed, glossy dark green and smooth above, paler and hairy beneath. ***Bark*** Gray, flaking in plates. ***Flowers*** 1in (2.5cm) across, white, with five petals and pink anthers, in flattened heads on downy stalks in early to midsummer. ***Fruit*** Rounded, red, ¾in (2cm) across.

NATIVE REGION Of garden origin.
REMARK A hybrid between cockspur thorn (*Crataegus crus-galli*, see p.220) and *Crataegus mexicana*, formerly known as *Crataegus carrierei*.

fruits ripen in late fall

dark green leaves turn bronzy red before they fall in late winter

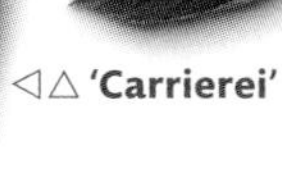

◁△ **'Carrierei'**

hairy flower stalks

Height: 33ft (10m)	Shape: Broadly spreading	Leaf persistence: Deciduous	Leaf type: 

Family: Rosaceae	Species: *Crataegus mollis*	Author: (Torr. & A. Gray) Scheele

Red Haw

Leaves Broadly ovate, to 4in (10cm) long and across, with four or five shallow lobes on each side, sharply toothed, dark green and hairy above, hairy beneath, particularly when young; shoots with glossy spines to 2in (5cm) long. ***Bark*** Red-brown becoming gray-brown, cracking vertically into scaly plates. ***Flowers*** 1in (2.5cm) across, white, with yellow anthers, in broad heads on downy stalks in late spring to early summer. ***Fruit*** Rounded, downy, red, to 1in (2.5cm) across.

NATIVE REGION S.E. Canada, E. US.
HABITAT Near streams in woods, often on limestone.

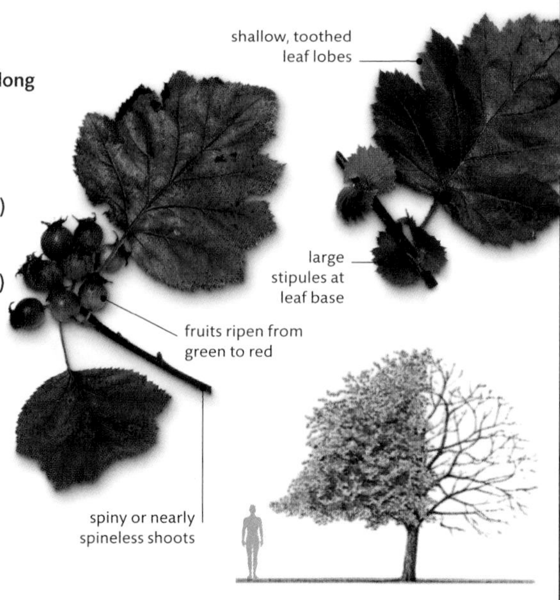

Height: 40ft (12m)	Shape: Broadly spreading	Leaf persistence: Deciduous	Leaf type:

Family: Rosaceae	Species: *Crataegus monogyna*	Author: Jacq.

Common Hawthorn

Leaves Ovate to obovate, to 2in (5cm) or more long and nearly the same across, deeply cut into pointed, toothed lobes, glossy dark green and smooth above, paler and smooth with hairs in the vein axils beneath. ***Bark*** Orange-brown, cracking. ***Flowers*** To ⅝in (1.5cm) across, white, in clusters in late spring. ***Fruit*** Oval, red, to ½in (1.2cm) across.

NATIVE REGION Europe, W. Asia, N. Africa.
HABITAT Woods and thickets.

red berries contain a single seed

flowers have pink anthers

each leaf side has one to three lobes

Height: 33ft (10m)	Shape: Broadly spreading	Leaf persistence: Deciduous	Leaf type:

Family: Rosaceae	Species: *Crataegus orientalis*	Author: Pall. ex M. Bieb.

Eastern Thorn

Leaves Diamond-shaped, to 2in (5cm) long and across, deeply lobed, the lobes often toothed at the tip, glossy dark green above, gray and hairy beneath. ***Bark*** Gray, flaking in thin plates. ***Flowers*** ¾in (2cm) across, white, with five petals and pink anthers, in dense clusters in early summer. ***Fruit*** Rounded or slightly oblong, red or red flushed yellow, ¾in (2cm) long, with a flattened top.

NATIVE REGION S.W. Asia, S.E. Europe.
HABITAT Wood margins and thickets.

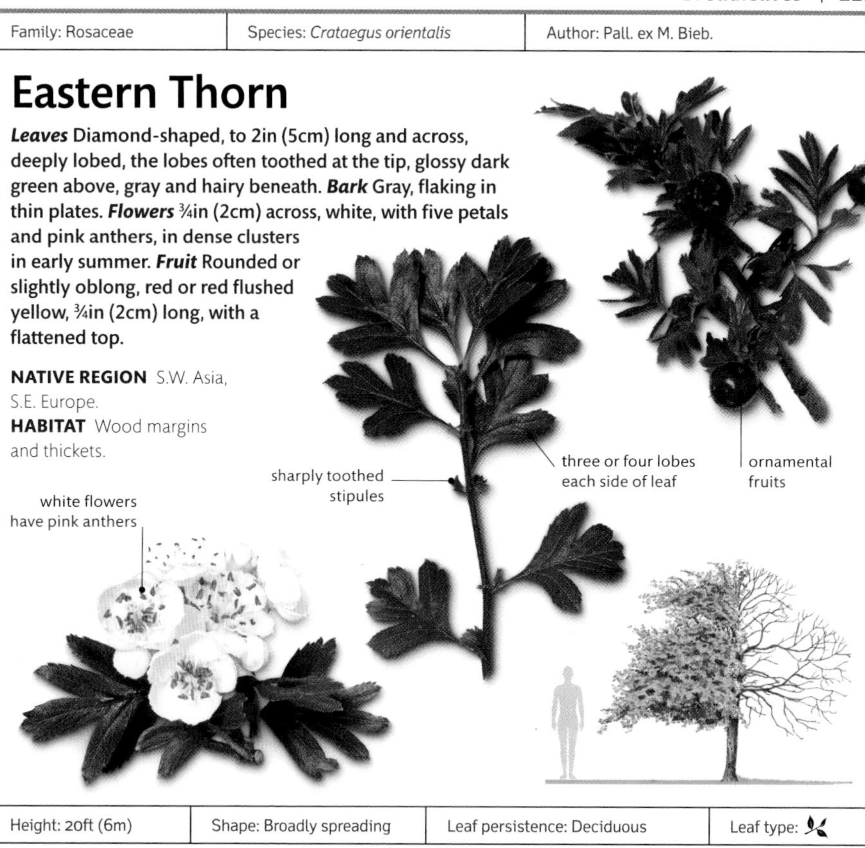

Height: 20ft (6m)	Shape: Broadly spreading	Leaf persistence: Deciduous	Leaf type:

Family: Rosaceae	Species: *Crataegus persimilis*	Author: Sarg.

Crataegus persimilis

Leaves Broadly elliptic to obovate, to 3in (7.5cm) long and 2½in (6cm) across, sharply toothed, glossy dark green and smooth above, hairy on the veins beneath. ***Bark*** Purple-brown and cracking. ***Flowers*** ⅝in (1.5cm) across, white, with five petals, in rounded clusters in early summer. ***Fruit*** Rounded, bright red, ⅝in (1.5cm) across.

NATIVE REGION S.E. Canada, N.E. US.
REMARK It has also been called *Crataegus prunifolia*.

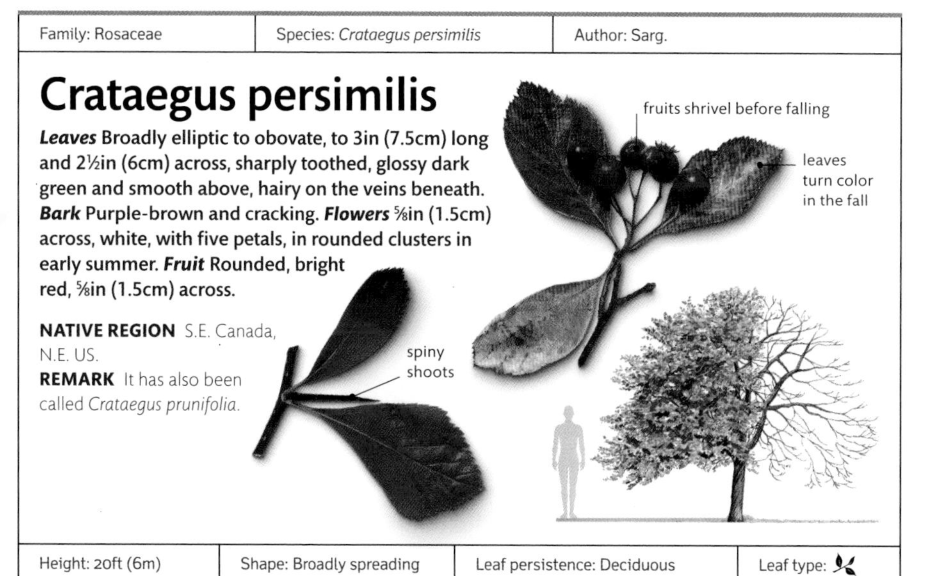

Height: 20ft (6m)	Shape: Broadly spreading	Leaf persistence: Deciduous	Leaf type:

Family: Rosaceae	Species: *Crataegus phaenopyrum*	Author: (L. f.) Medik.

Washington Thorn

Leaves Broadly ovate, with three or five pointed, sharply toothed lobes, glossy dark green and smooth above, paler and smooth or sparsely hairy beneath. ***Bark*** Red-brown to gray-brown, thin, scaly. ***Flowers*** ½in (1.2cm) across, white, with five petals, in clusters in early to midsummer. ***Fruit*** Rounded, small, red, ¼in (6mm) across.

NATIVE REGION S.E. Canada, E. US.
HABITAT Woods and thickets.

shoots carry long spines

fragrant flowers have creamy anthers

Height: 40ft (12m)	Shape: Broadly spreading	Leaf persistence: Deciduous	Leaf type:

Family: Rosaceae	Species: x *Crataemespilus grandiflora*	Author: (Sm.) E.G. Camus

x Crataemespilus grandiflora

Leaves Elliptic to obovate, to 3in (7.5cm) long and 2in (5cm) across, glossy green above, turning bright orange in fall; on vigorous shoots deeply lobed. ***Bark*** Pale orange-brown, flaking in thin plates. ***Flowers*** 1in (2.5cm) across, white, with five petals, borne in clusters of up to three in late spring. ***Fruit*** Rounded, slightly hairy, glossy orange-brown, ¾in (2cm) across.

NATIVE REGION Of garden and backyard origin.
REMARK A possible hybrid between the Midland hawthorn (*Crataegus laevigata*, see p.221) and the medlar (*Mespilus germanica*, see p.236).

△ **x *Crataemespilus grandiflora***

△ **+ *Crataegomespilus dardarii* 'Jules d'Asnieres'**
This graft hybrid has rounded leaf lobes, smaller flowers, and small, brown fruits.

△ **x *Crataemespilus grandiflora***

Height: 26ft (8m)	Shape: Broadly spreading	Leaf persistence: Deciduous	Leaf type:

Family: Rosaceae	Species: *Cydonia oblonga*	Author: Mill.

Quince

Leaves Broadly elliptic to ovate, to 4in (10cm) long and 2½in (6cm) across, untoothed, grayish white and downy when young becoming dark green above, gray and downy beneath, carried on short stalks. ***Bark*** Purple-brown, flaking; orange-brown when freshly exposed. ***Flowers*** 2in (5cm) across, pale pink or white, with five petals, borne singly in late spring. ***Fruit*** Pear- or sometimes apple-shaped, yellow, to 4in (10cm) long, downy at first becoming oily to the touch, very fragrant; on wild plants much smaller.

NATIVE REGION C. and S.W. Asia.
HABITAT Wood margins, forests, and mountain slopes, often on limestone.

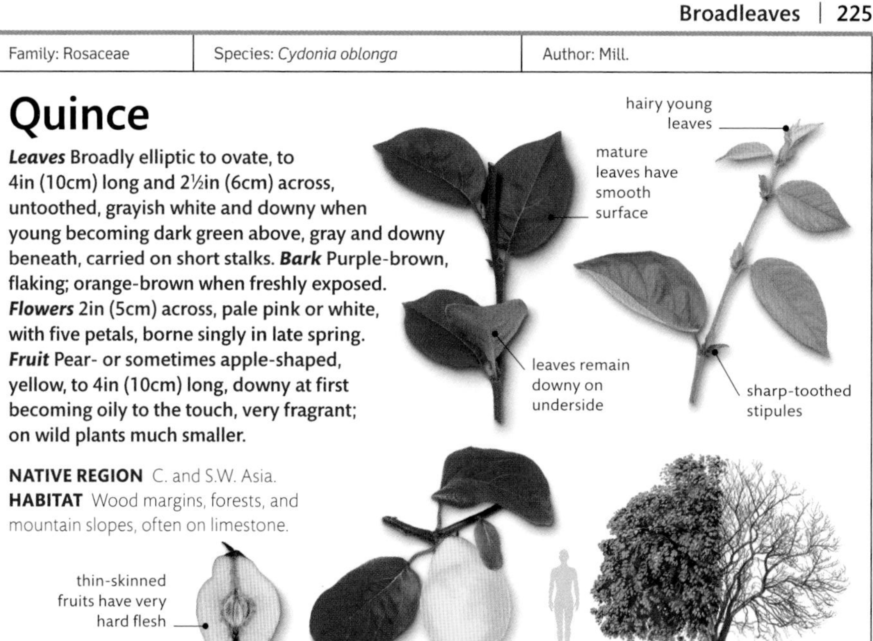

Height: 17ft (5m)	Shape: Broadly spreading	Leaf persistence: Deciduous	Leaf type:

Family: Rosaceae	Species: *Hedlundia thuringiaca*	Author: (Nyman) Sennikov & Kurtto

Hedlundia thuringiaca

Leaves Narrowly ovate to elliptic, to 4in (10cm) long and 2½in (6cm) across, lobed except at the very tip, the lobes deeper toward the base, toothed, glossy dark green above, gray and hairy beneath, often with several free leaflets at the base. ***Bark*** Purple-gray and smooth, cracking and flaking with age. ***Flowers*** ½in (1.2cm) across, white, with five petals, borne in dense clusters in late spring. ***Fruit*** A rounded, bright red berry, ⅜in (1cm) across.

NATIVE REGION Europe, Turkey.
HABITAT Woods, together with the parent plants.
REMARK A naturally occurring hybrid between the whitebeam (*Aria edulis*, see p.219) and the rowan (*Sorbus aucuparia*, see p.256). The form shown here, 'Fastigiata,' is a commonly planted street tree, with upswept branches making a dense, broadly oval crown. Other forms are closer to *Sorbus aucuparia*, and have more numerous free leaflets.

Height: 40ft (12m)	Shape: Broadly conical	Leaf persistence: Deciduous	Leaf type:

Family: Rosaceae	Species: *Karpatiosorbus latifolia*	Author: (Lam.) Sennikov & Kurtto

Service Tree of Fontainebleau

Leaves **Broadly ovate, to 4in (10cm) long and the same across, with shallow, pointed lobes toward the base, sharply toothed, glossy dark green above, gray and downy beneath. *Bark* Dark gray, cracked, flaking. *Flowers* Individually ⅝in (1.5cm) across, white, with five petals, borne in flattened heads in late spring. *Fruit* Rounded, yellow-brown, ½in (1.2cm) across, with conspicuous lenticels.**

NATIVE REGION C. and W. Europe, Algeria.
HABITAT Woods.
REMARK The species probably originated as a hybrid between the whitebeam (*Aria edulis*, see p.219) and the wild service tree (*Torminalis glaberrima*, see p.261).

smooth leaf upperside

leaf underside felted with gray hairs

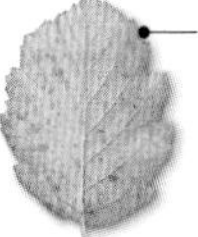

shallow leaf lobes edged with sharp teeth

leaves turn yellow in the fall

Height: 40ft (12m)	Shape: Broadly columnar	Leaf persistence: Deciduous	Leaf type:

Family: Rosaceae	Species: *Malus baccata*	Author: (L.) Borkh.

Siberian Crab Apple

Leaves **Elliptic to ovate, to 3in (7.5cm) long and 1½in (4cm) across, tapered to a pointed tip, finely toothed, dark green above, paler beneath, smooth on both sides. *Bark* Gray-brown, flaking in square plates; red-brown when freshly exposed. *Flowers* Individually to 1½in (4cm) across, white tinged pink, opening white, with five petals and yellow anthers, fragrant, borne in clusters in mid-spring at the same time as the young leaves emerge. *Fruit* Rounded, small, red or yellow, ⅜in (1cm) across.**

NATIVE REGION N.E. Europe, N. Asia, Himalayas.
HABITAT Woods and scrub.

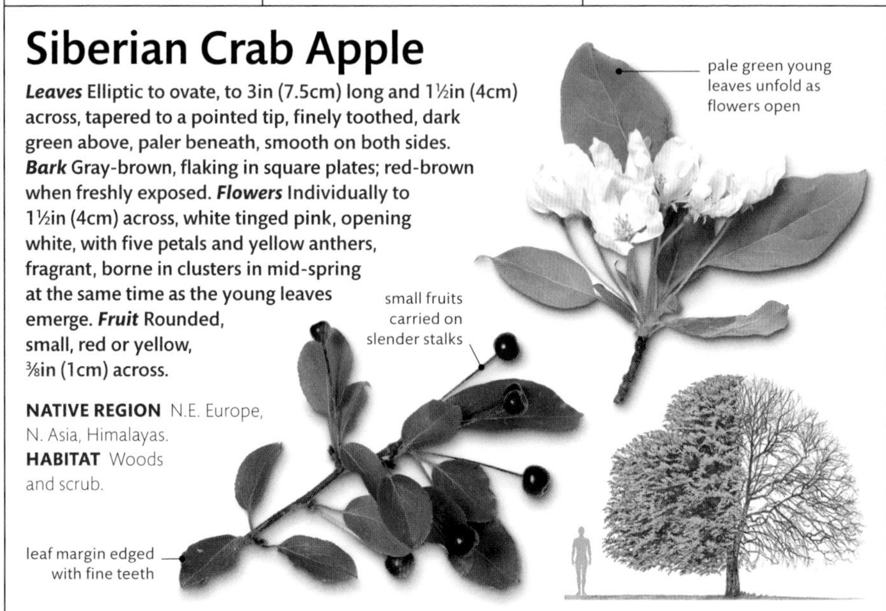

pale green young leaves unfold as flowers open

small fruits carried on slender stalks

leaf margin edged with fine teeth

Height: 50ft (15m)	Shape: Broadly spreading	Leaf persistence: Deciduous	Leaf type:

Family: Rosaceae	Species: *Malus coronaria*	Author: (L.) Mill.

Wild Sweet Crab Apple

Leaves Ovate, to 4in (10cm) long and 2½in (6cm) across, sharply, often double-toothed, reddish and downy becoming deep green above, smooth; on vigorous shoots lobed toward the base. ***Bark*** Red-brown and scaly, with vertical fissures. ***Flowers*** 2in (5cm) across, pink, in clusters in late spring. ***Fruit*** Rounded, green, 1½in (4cm) across, slightly broader than long.

NATIVE REGION E. North America.
HABITAT Woods and thickets.

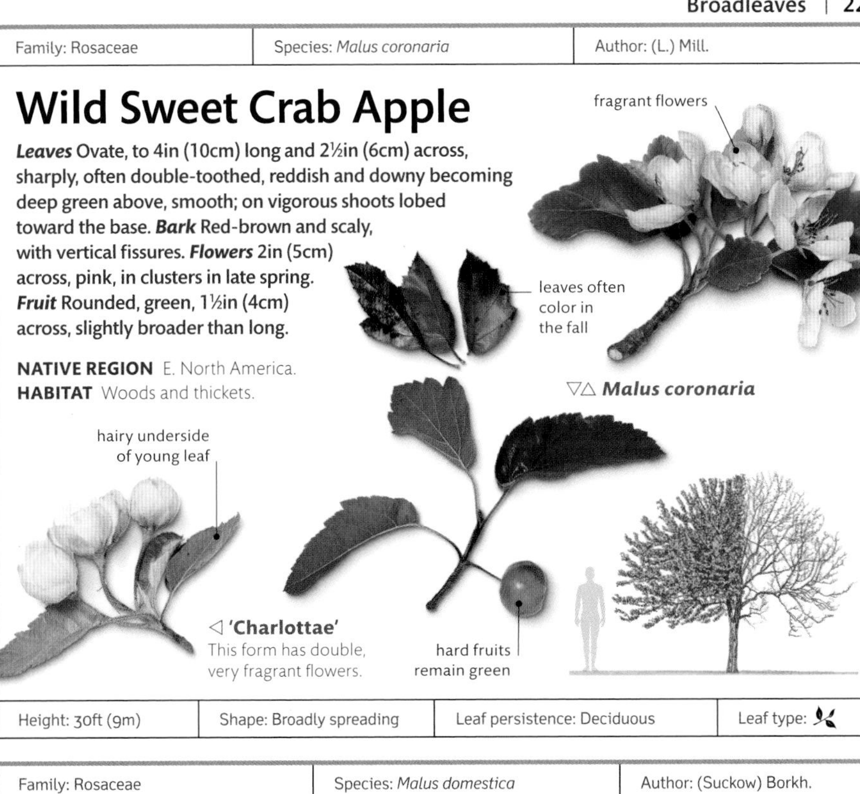

▽△ ***Malus coronaria***

◁ **'Charlottae'**
This form has double, very fragrant flowers.

Height: 30ft (9m)	Shape: Broadly spreading	Leaf persistence: Deciduous	Leaf type:

Family: Rosaceae	Species: *Malus domestica*	Author: (Suckow) Borkh.

Cultivated Apple

Leaves Ovate to broadly elliptic, to 4¾in (12cm) long and 3in (7.5cm) across, toothed, yellowish green becoming dark green above, usually hairy, at least beneath. ***Bark*** Gray-brown to purple-brown, peeling in small, thin flakes. ***Flowers*** To 2in (5cm) across, white flushed pink, with five petals, borne in clusters in late spring. ***Fruit*** Very variable, rounded, sweet to sour, edible, to 4in (10cm) or more across, green to yellow or variously streaked, to entirely, red.

NATIVE REGION Afghanistan to China.
REMARK Grown for its edible fruit for thousands of years; there are now many selections.

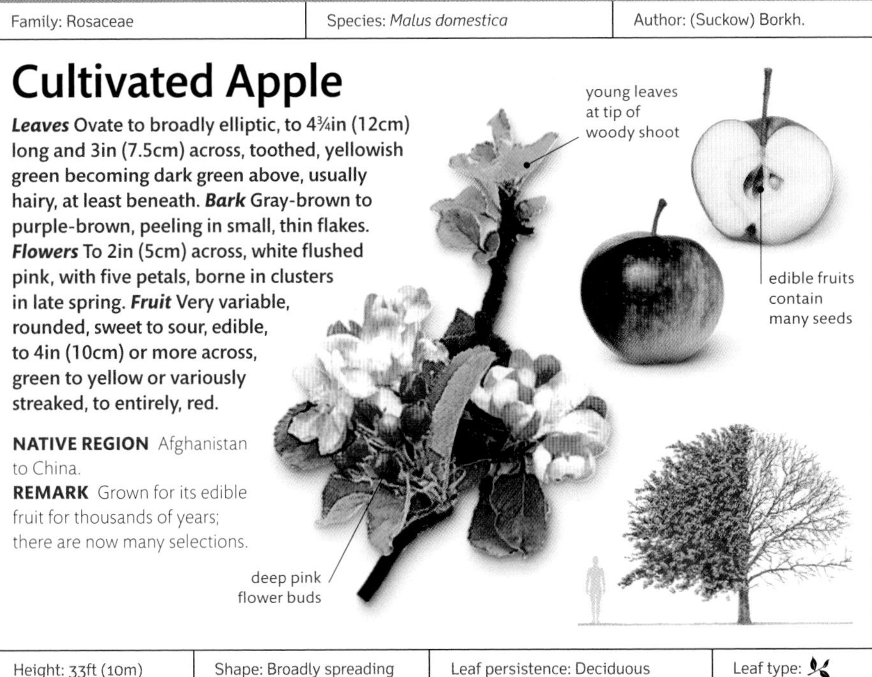

Height: 33ft (10m)	Shape: Broadly spreading	Leaf persistence: Deciduous	Leaf type:

Family: Rosaceae	Species: *Malus florentina*	Author: (Zuccagni) C.K. Schneid.

Florentine Crab

Leaves **Broadly ovate, to 2½in (6cm) long and 2in (5cm) across, lobed, toothed, deep green above, densely hairy beneath, turning purple and red in fall.** ***Bark*** **Red- to purple-brown, flaking freely in small, thin, square plates; orange-brown when freshly exposed.** ***Flowers*** **¾in (2cm) across, white, with five petals and yellow anthers, in clusters in late spring to early summer.** ***Fruit*** **Rounded to pear-shaped, reddish orange, about ⅜in (1cm) across.**

NATIVE REGION Italy to N. Turkey.
HABITAT Scrub and rocky slopes.
REMARK It has been considered to be a hybrid between a crab apple (*Malus*) and the wild service tree (*Torminalis glaberrima*, see p.261), rarely seen in the wild.

Height: 26ft (8m)	Shape: Broadly columnar	Leaf persistence: Deciduous	Leaf type:

Family: Rosaceae	Species: *Malus* x *floribunda*	Author: Siebold ex Van Houtte

Japanese Crab Apple

Leaves **Elliptic, to 4in (10cm) long and 2in (5cm) across, taper-pointed, sharply toothed, dark green and smooth above, hairy beneath when young; on vigorous shoots sometimes lobed.** ***Bark*** **Purple-brown, flaking in thin plates with age.** ***Flowers*** **1in (2.5cm) across, deep red in bud opening pale pink becoming white, with five petals, very profuse, in clusters in mid-spring.** ***Fruit*** **Rounded and yellow, ¾in (2cm) across.**

NATIVE REGION Korea.
REMARK A hybrid between *Malus baccata* (see p.226) and *Malus toringo* (see p.230), introduced to the West from Japan.

sharp teeth at edge of leaf margin

flowers open from deep red buds

one or more fruits clustered together on long, slender stalks

Height: 17ft (5m)	Shape: Broadly spreading	Leaf persistence: Deciduous	Leaf type:

Family: Rosaceae	Species: *Malus hupehensis*	Author: (Pamp.) Rehder

Hupeh Crab

Leaves Elliptic to ovate, to 4in (10cm) long and 2½in (6cm) across, taper-pointed, finely toothed, becoming dark green and smooth above. ***Bark*** Purple-brown, flaking in rectangular plates; orange-brown when freshly exposed. ***Flowers*** 2in (5cm) across, pink in bud opening white, with five broad, overlapping petals, fragrant, usually very profuse, borne in large clusters in mid-spring. ***Fruit*** Rounded and rather flattened, deep red, ⅜in (1cm) across, hanging in clusters on long, slender, red stalks, persisting long after the leaves have fallen.

NATIVE REGION China.
HABITAT Mountain woodlands.

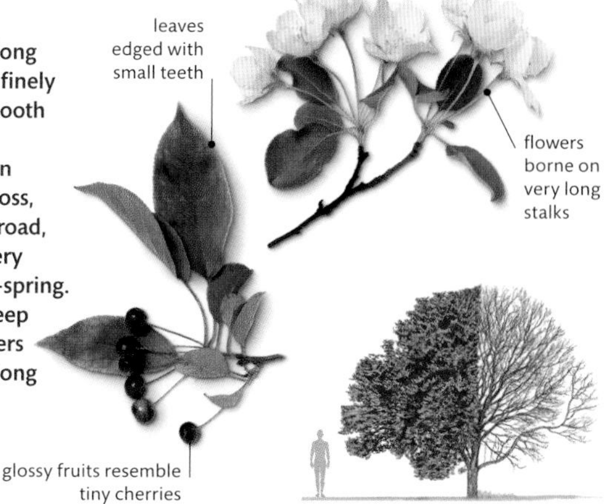

Height: 40ft (12m)	Shape: Broadly spreading	Leaf persistence: Deciduous	Leaf type:

Family: Rosaceae	Species: *Malus ioensis*	Author: (Alph. Wood) Britton

Prairie Crab Apple

Leaves Broadly ovate, to 4in (10cm) long and 2in (5cm) across, shallowly lobed, toothed, glossy green above, downy beneath, turning bright orange-red in fall. ***Bark*** Reddish to purplish brown, and flaking. ***Flowers***. Pink to white, with five petals, borne in clusters of up to six in spring. ***Fruit*** Rounded, smooth, hard, and sour, pale green or green flushed red, 1½in (4cm) across.

NATIVE REGION C. US.
REMARK Moist stream banks and wood margins.

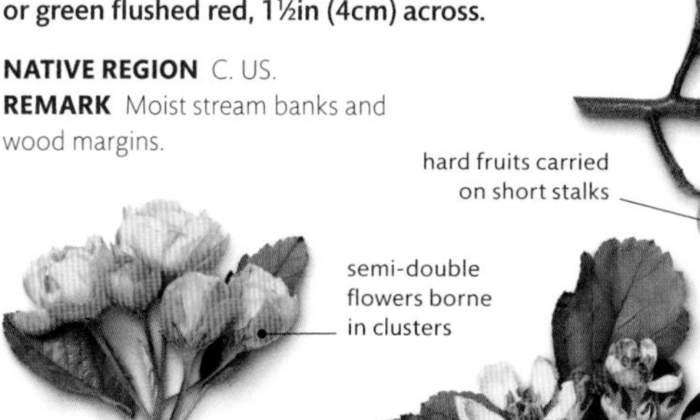

◁△▷ ***Malus ioensis***

△ **'Plena'**
Known as Bechtel's crab, this form has semi-double flowers, which fade from pink to white.

Height: 26ft (8m)	Shape: Broadly spreading	Leaf persistence: Deciduous	Leaf type: 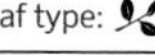

Family: Rosaceae	Species: *Malus prunifolia*	Author: (Willd.) Borkh.

Malus prunifolia

Leaves **Elliptic to ovate, to 4in (10cm) long and 2½in (6cm) across, toothed, dark green.** ***Bark*** **Purple-brown to gray-brown, flaking in rectangular plates; red-brown when freshly exposed.** ***Flowers*** **1½in (4cm) across, pink in bud opening white, with five petals, fragrant, in clusters of up to 10 in mid-spring.** ***Fruit*** **Rounded to egg-shaped, bright red, 1in (2.5cm) across, with persistent, woolly sepals at the top.**

NATIVE REGION N. China.
HABITAT Scrub and rocky slopes.
REMARK This species is thought to be of hybrid origin and is itself the parent of many cultivated hybrids.

flowers borne in compact clusters
leaves vary in shape
persistent sepals at top of fruits

Height: 33ft (10m)	Shape: Broadly spreading	Leaf persistence: Deciduous	Leaf type:

Family: Rosaceae	Species: *Malus* x *purpurea*	Author: (A. Barbier) Rehder

Malus x purpurea

Leaves **Elliptic to narrowly ovate, to 3in (7.5cm) long, pointed, toothed, purplish green.** ***Bark*** **Purple-brown, cracked, flaking.** ***Flowers*** **1½in (4cm) across, opening deep purple-pink, borne in clusters in spring.** ***Fruit*** **Rounded, deep reddish purple, 1in (2.5cm) across.**

NATIVE REGION Of garden and backyard origin.
REMARK A hybrid between *Malus* x *atrosanguinea* and *Malus niedzwetzkyana*.

flowers have five petals

Height: 26ft (8m)	Shape: Broadly spreading	Leaf persistence: Deciduous	Leaf type:

Family: Rosaceae	Species: *Malus toringo*	Author: (Siebold) de Vriese

Toringo Crab

Leaves **Elliptic to ovate, to 2½in (6cm) long and 1¼in (3cm) across, taper-pointed, toothed, matte deep green above, paler beneath, lobed on vigorous shoots.** ***Bark*** **Dark gray, cracking into small plates.** ***Flowers*** **¾in (2cm) across, pink opening white, with five petals, fragrant, in small clusters in mid-spring.** ***Fruit*** **Rounded, red or yellow, ⅜in (1cm) across, with no sepals when ripe.**

NATIVE REGION China, Korea, Japan.
HABITAT Moist, sunny situations.
REMARK Also known as *Malus sieboldii*.

coarsely toothed lobes
green stalks become red as fruits ripen

Height: 33ft (10m)	Shape: Broadly weeping	Leaf persistence: Deciduous	Leaf type: 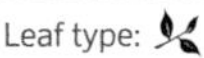

Family: Rosaceae	Species: *Malus transitoria*	Author: (Batalin) C.K. Schneid.

Cut-leaf Crab

Leaves Variable, small, and oblong, to 1in (2.5cm) long on short shoots, larger, to 3in (7.5cm) long and 2½in (6cm) across on vigorous shoots, deeply cut into three lobes, the central lobe with a lobe on each side, sharply toothed, bright green above, paler beneath, thinly hairy. ***Bark*** Purple-brown, cracking into smooth, vertical, rectangular plates. ***Flowers*** ¾in (2cm) across, white, with five petals, in small clusters in late spring. ***Fruit*** Small, yellow, 5⁄16in (8mm) across, slightly flattened, carried on slender, red stalks.

NATIVE REGION N.W. China.
REMARK Woods and thickets.

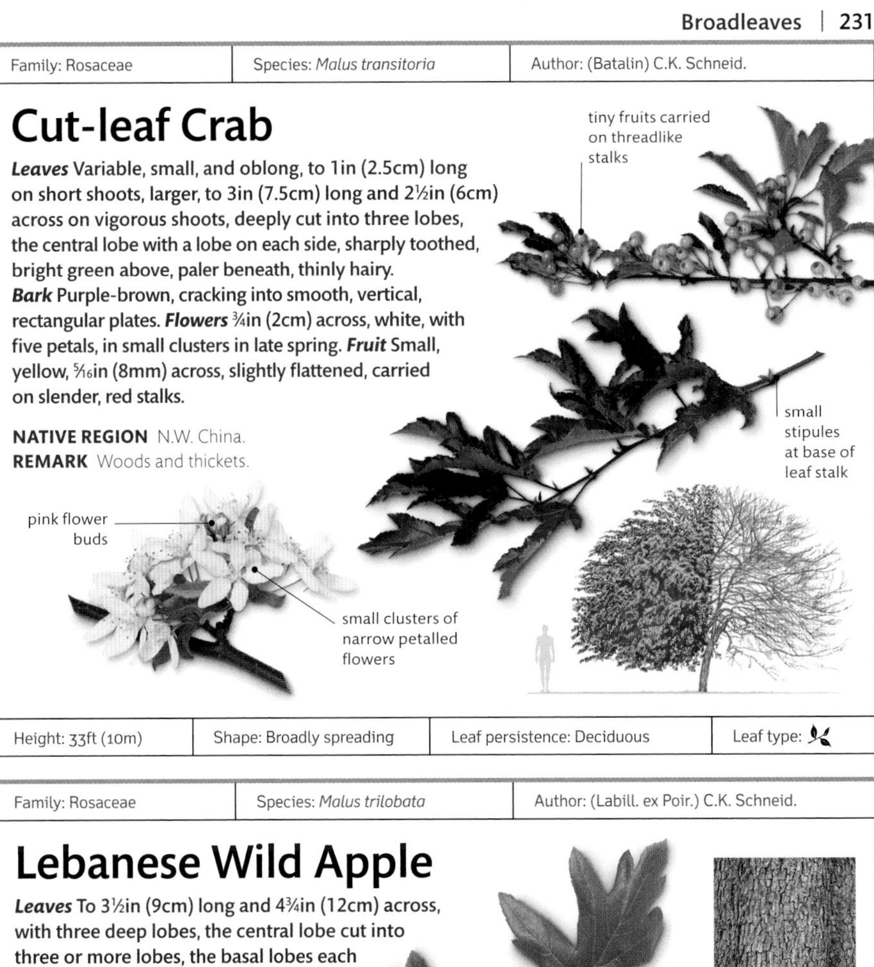

Height: 33ft (10m)	Shape: Broadly spreading	Leaf persistence: Deciduous	Leaf type:

Family: Rosaceae	Species: *Malus trilobata*	Author: (Labill. ex Poir.) C.K. Schneid.

Lebanese Wild Apple

Leaves To 3½in (9cm) long and 4¾in (12cm) across, with three deep lobes, the central lobe cut into three or more lobes, the basal lobes each with one or more lobes, glossy dark green and smooth above, paler and hairy beneath, turning yellow, red, and purple in fall. ***Bark*** Dark gray-brown, cracking into numerous small squares, on a fluted trunk. ***Flowers*** 1½in (4cm) across, white, with five petals and yellow anthers, opening from woolly buds, borne in clusters at the ends of the shoots in summer. ***Fruit*** Small, hard, green or green flushed red, ¾in (2cm) across.

NATIVE REGION S.E. Europe, S.W. Asia
HABITAT Evergreen scrub.
REMARK Also known as *Eriolobus trilobatus*.

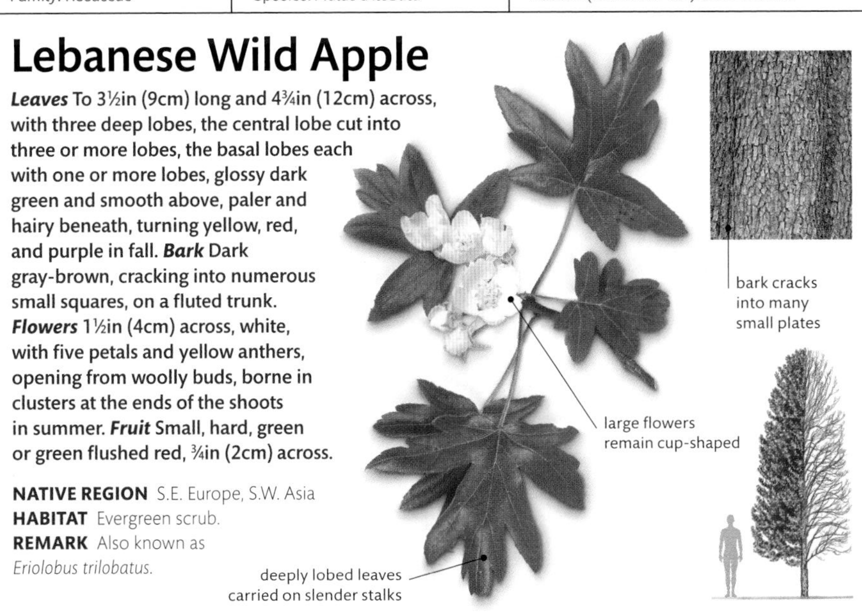

Height: 50ft (15m)	Shape: Narrowly conical	Leaf persistence: Deciduous	Leaf type:

Family: Rosaceae	Species: *Malus tschonoskii*	Author: (Maxim.) C.K. Schneid.

Pillar Crab

Leaves **Broadly ovate, to 4¾in (12cm) long and 3in (7.5cm) across, pointed, sharply toothed, gray and hairy becoming smooth and glossy above, thinly hairy beneath. *Bark* Purple-brown and smooth, becoming fissured and rough with age. *Flowers* 1¼in (3cm) across, white flushed pink, with five petals and yellow anthers, in clusters of up to five in late spring. *Fruit* Rounded, yellow-green flushed red, to 1¼in (3cm) across, speckled with lenticels.**

young leaves have downy upperside

pink flush at tip of petals

NATIVE REGION Japan.
HABITAT Shallow, rocky soil in woods.

red-flushed fruits borne on a short, stout stalk

mature leaves have smooth upperside

Height: 50ft (15m)	Shape: Broadly conical	Leaf persistence: Deciduous	Leaf type:

Family: Rosaceae	Species: *Malus yunnanensis*	Author: (Franch.) C.K. Schneid.

Yunnan Crab

Leaves **Broadly ovate, to 4in (10cm) long and 3½in (9cm) across, heart-shaped at the base, pointed at the tip, shallowly lobed, finely toothed, matte pale green above, softly hairy beneath, turning orange to red and purple in fall. *Bark* Dark gray-brown, peeling in small flakes; orange-brown when freshly exposed. *Flowers* Individually ½in (1.2cm) across, white, with five petals, borne in flattened heads in late spring. *Fruit* Rounded, hard, deep red, ⅝in (1.5cm) across, freely speckled with pale brown lenticels, borne in dense clusters.**

leaves carried on red stalks

var. *veitchii* ▷

NATIVE REGION China, Myanmar.
HABITAT Woods and thickets on mountain slopes.
REMARK The form shown, var. *veitchii*, differs in its brighter fruits, and in its leaves, which are heart-shaped.

◁△ **var. *veitchii***

Height: 33ft (10m)	Shape: Broadly columnar	Leaf persistence: Deciduous	Leaf type: 

Family: Rosaceae	Species: *Malus* hybrids	Author: None

Crab Apple Hybrids

Many of the garden crab apples are hybrids between various species, raised in cultivation and grown for the beauty of their flowers or fruits; the attraction of some of these trees lies in both flowers and the fruits that follow in fall. The plants usually make small, spreading trees, reaching about 20–26ft (6–8m) in height, and flowering in late spring and early summer. Several selections have purplish leaves and flowers. This coloration arises as a result of hybridization with *Malus niedzwetzkyana*, a species found originally in the Central Asian region of Turkestan.

pinkish flower buds

◁ **'Butterball'**
This hybrid was raised in North America. Rounded, yellowish fruits succeed the pink-flushed, white flowers.

▽ **'Butterball'**

fruits persist through fall and winter

fruits mature to orange-yellow

▽ **'Eleyi'**
The fruits of this ornamental form are small, conical, and colored purple.

reddish purple flower petals narrow to white base

bronze-purple young leaves

◁ **'Crittenden'**
This plant bears white flowers flushed slightly pink. They are followed by a profusion of bright scarlet fruits.

▽ **'Dartmouth'**
The small, white flowers of this form open from buds tinged faintly pink. The large fruits are 2in (5cm) across, red-purple and bloomy.

▽▷ **'Crittenden'**

white, tinged pink, flowers borne profusely

clustered flowers open after leaves unfold

fruits ripen from yellow to shades of purple and deep red

Height: To 26ft (8m)	Shape: Broadly spreading	Leaf persistence: Deciduous	Leaf type:

Family: Rosaceae	Species: *Malus* hybrids	Author: None

△ 'Golden Hornet'
The flowers of this form are 1½in (4cm) across, pink in bud opening white flushed pink. The rounded, deep yellow fruits measure 1in (2.5cm) across.

'John Downie' △
The soft pink buds of this form open into small, white flowers with yellow anthers. The egg-shaped fruits are 1¼in (3cm) long and orange-yellow flushed red.

'Lemoinei' ▽▷
This colorful hybrid has deep bronze-purple young leaves, which mature to purplish green. The purplish red flowers are 1½in (4cm) across, and the deep purple fruits ⅝in (1.5cm) long.

'Liset' ▽▷
The bronze-purple young leaves of this form become dark green, contrasting with the deep purple-pink flowers.

Height: To 26ft (8m)	Shape: Broadly spreading	Leaf persistence: Deciduous	Leaf type:

◁▽▷ 'Profusion'
The purplish red flowers of this plant are 1½in (4cm) across, borne profusely in large clusters. The dark green, red-veined leaves are bronze-purple when young. Deep reddish purple, rounded fruits, ½in (1.2cm) across, are produced in fall.

'Red Sentinel' ▷
The pink buds of this hybrid open into white flowers 1¼in (3cm) across, which set rounded, long-persistent, glossy deep red fruits, 1in (2.5cm) across.

'Red Jade' ▷
This mushroom-shaped tree bears clusters of pink buds, which open to white flowers. The bright red fruits are carried on the branches into late fall.

'Royalty' ▽
The glossy red-purple leaves of this compact tree turn red in late fall. Deep red flower buds open deep red-purple.

'Van Eseltine' ▷
This form is distinguished by its upright habit, double flowers, and the small, yellow or yellow flushed red fruits that follow in fall.

Family: Rosaceae	Species: *Mespilus germanica*	Author: L.

Medlar

Leaves Elliptic to oblong, to 6in (15cm) long and 2in (5cm) across, untoothed or finely toothed, dark green above, usually hairy on both sides, turning yellow and brown in fall, on very short stalks; shoots often thorny. ***Bark*** Gray-brown and smooth at first, cracking into thin plates with age; orange-brown when freshly exposed. ***Flowers*** To 2in (5cm) across, white, with five petals, borne singly on short stalks in late spring to early summer; vigorous plants often flower again in late summer. ***Fruit*** Rounded, flat-topped to pear-shaped, fleshy, brown, to 1¼in (3cm) across, with persistent sepals at the top.

NATIVE REGION S.W. Asia, S.E. Europe.
HABITAT Forests, wood margins, and mountain thickets.
REMARK Wild plants tend to be more shrubby than cultivated forms. The fruit becomes edible only after exposure to frost.

Mespilus germanica ▷

untoothed or finely toothed leaf margin

white flowers borne singly

sepals remain attached to fruits

'Nottingham' ▷

'Nottingham' ▷
This cultivated form is selected for its large fruits.

cultivated form has larger leaves

green sepals appear between petals

Height: 20ft (6m)	Shape: Broadly spreading	Leaf persistence: Deciduous	Leaf type:

Family: Rosaceae	Species: *Photinia davidiana*	Author: (Decne.) Cardot

Photinia davidiana

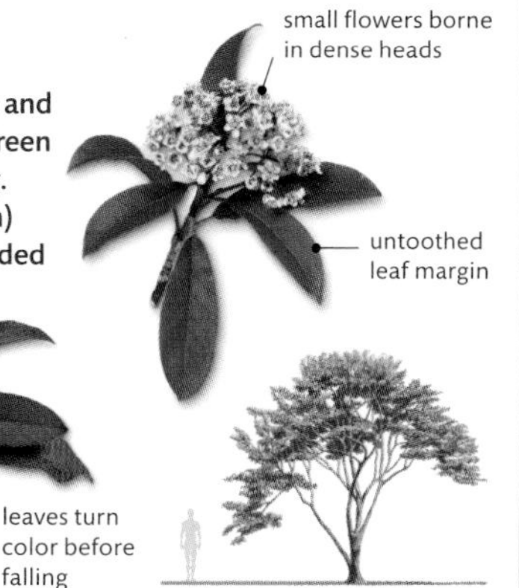

Leaves Elliptic to oblong or oblanceolate, to 4¾in (12cm) long and 1½in (4cm) across, taper-pointed at the tip, untoothed, dark green above, nearly smooth on both sides, turning red before falling. ***Bark*** Gray-brown and smooth. ***Flowers*** Individually ¼in (6mm) across, white, with five petals and pink anthers, in dense, rounded heads about 3in (7.5cm) across, in midsummer. ***Fruit*** Rounded and bright red, about 5/16in (8mm) across, on long stalks, in small clusters.

ripe fruit clusters

leaves turn color before falling

NATIVE REGION China, S.E. Asia.
HABITAT Woods, thickets, and cliffs.

Height: 33ft (10m)	Shape: Broadly spreading	Leaf persistence: Evergreen	Leaf type:

Family: Rosaceae	Species: *Photinia x fraseri*	Author: Dress

Photinia x fraseri

Leaves Oblong to obovate, to 6in (15cm) long and 2½in (6cm) across, toothed, glossy dark green above, smooth. ***Bark*** Gray-brown and smooth, peeling on large trunks. ***Flowers*** White, in flattened heads 4¾in (12cm) across, from late spring to summer. ***Fruit*** Rounded, red, 3/16in (5mm) across.

flowers have five petals and pink anthers

mature leaf

bronzy young foliage

NATIVE REGION Of garden and backyard origin.
REMARK A hybrid between *Photinia glabra* and *Photinia serratifolia* (see below).

Height: 20ft (6m)	Shape: Broadly spreading	Leaf persistence: Evergreen	Leaf type:

Family: Rosaceae	Species: *Photinia serratifolia*	Author: (Desf.) Kalkman

Chinese Photinia

Leaves Oblong to lanceolate, to 8in (20cm) long and 3in (7.5cm) across, toothed, glossy dark green above, smooth, on stout, smooth, red shoots. ***Bark*** Gray-brown, smooth, peeling in irregular flakes. ***Flowers*** ⅜in (1cm) across, white, in large, flattened heads to 6in (15cm) across, at the ends of the shoots in mid- to late spring. ***Fruit*** Rounded, red, ¼in (6mm) across, persisting over winter.

tiny, five-petalled flowers have pink anthers

adult leaf

sharp-toothed juvenile leaf

NATIVE REGION China, Philippines.
HABITAT Thickets.

Height: 33ft (10m)	Shape: Broadly spreading	Leaf persistence: Evergreen	Leaf type: 

Family: Rosaceae	Species: *Pourthiaea arguta*	Author: (Wall. ex Lindl.) Decne.

Christmas Berry

Leaves Elliptic to lanceolate, or obovate, to 4¾in (12cm) long and 2in (5cm) across, narrowed at the base, taper-pointed at the tip, sharply toothed, dark green above, smooth on both sides, turning red in fall. ***Bark*** Gray and smooth, fluted at the base of the trunk. ***Flowers*** Individually ⅜in (1cm) across, white, with five petals, in flattened heads to 2in (5cm) across, in late spring. ***Fruit*** Egg-shaped, 3⁄16in (5mm) across, green ripening to red.

NATIVE REGION W. China.
HABITAT Woods and thickets.
REMARK Shown here is the form previously called *Photinia beauverdiana*, var. *notabilis*, with large leaves and flower clusters.

Height: 20ft (6m)	Shape: Broadly spreading	Leaf persistence: Deciduous	Leaf type:

Family: Rosaceae	Species: *Pourthiaea villosa*	Author: (Thunb.) Decne.

Oriental Photinia

Leaves Elliptic to obovate, to 3in (7.5cm) long and 1½in (4cm) across, taper-pointed, finely toothed, dark green above, turning red and orange in fall. ***Bark*** Gray to gray-brown, shallowly fissured with age. ***Flowers*** Small and white, with five petals and pink anthers, in small, flattened clusters in late spring. ***Fruit*** Egg-shaped, edible, red, about ⅜in (1cm) long.

NATIVE REGION E. Asia.
HABITAT Woods and by streams.

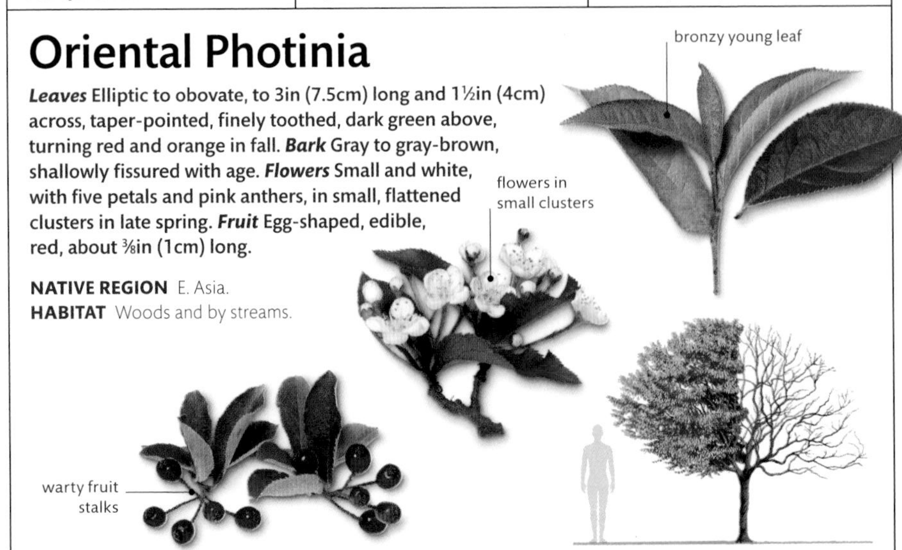

Height: 17ft (5m)	Shape: Broadly spreading	Leaf persistence: Deciduous	Leaf type:

Family: Rosaceae	Species: *Prunus amygdalus*	Author: Batsch

Almond

Leaves Lanceolate to narrowly elliptic, to 4¾in (12cm) long and 1½in (4cm) across, with a long, tapering point, finely toothed, dark green. ***Bark*** Dark gray, cracking into small plates with age. ***Flowers*** To 2in (5cm) across, pink fading to white or completely white, with five petals, borne singly or in pairs in early spring before the young leaves emerge. ***Fruit*** Green and velvety, to 2½in (6cm) long, the flesh dry and leathery, enclosing a single stone with an edible, white seed.

NATIVE REGION Transcaucasus, widely naturalized.
HABITAT Dry slopes, scrub, and woods.

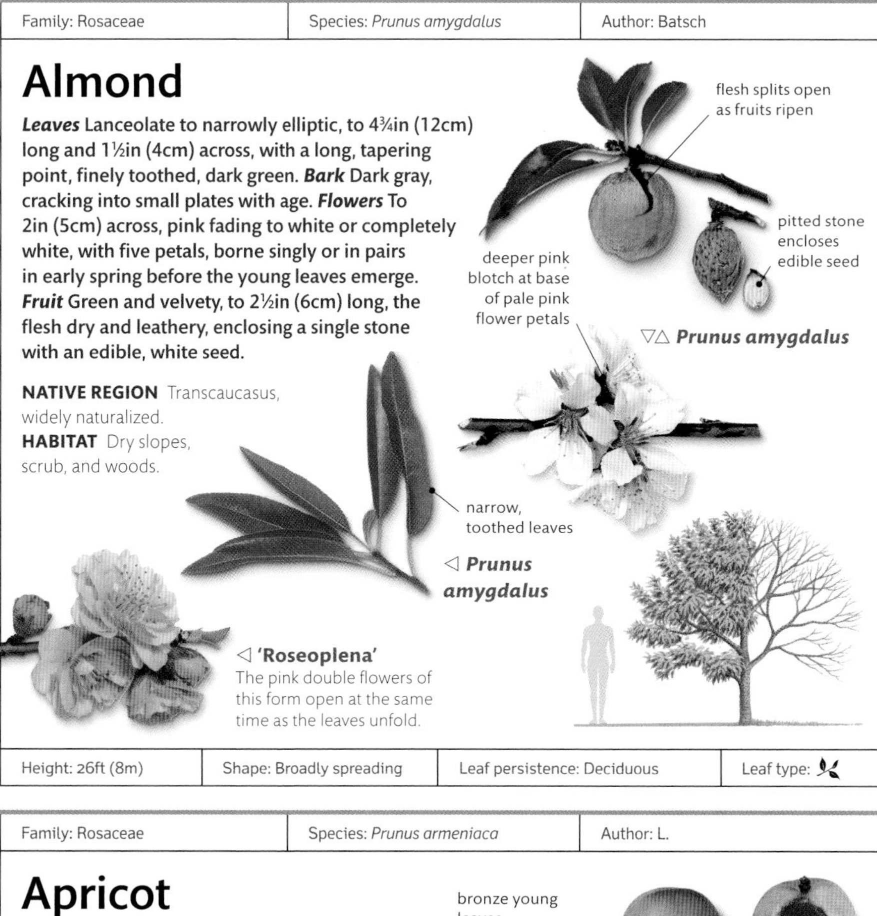

▽△ ***Prunus amygdalus***

◁ ***Prunus amygdalus***

◁ **'Roseoplena'**
The pink double flowers of this form open at the same time as the leaves unfold.

Height: 26ft (8m)	Shape: Broadly spreading	Leaf persistence: Deciduous	Leaf type:

Family: Rosaceae	Species: *Prunus armeniaca*	Author: L.

Apricot

Leaves Broadly ovate to rounded, to 4in (10cm) long and 2½in (6cm) across, with a usually rounded base, abruptly taper-pointed, finely toothed, glossy dark green. ***Bark*** Red-brown, smooth, and glossy. ***Flowers*** 1in (2.5cm) across, pale pink or white, with five petals, nearly stalkless, usually borne singly on old shoots in early spring before the leaves emerge. ***Fruit*** Rounded and fleshy, edible, yellow sometimes flushed red, with a single hard, smooth stone enclosing an edible, white seed.

NATIVE REGION C. Asia, N. China.
HABITAT Hillsides and thickets.
REMARK Naturalized in parts of Europe, and widely cultivated for its edible fruit.

bronze young leaves

sweet, edible flesh

hard stone has smooth surface

small glands along leaf stalk

Height: 33ft (10m)	Shape: Broadly spreading	Leaf persistence: Deciduous	Leaf type:

Family: Rosaceae	Species: *Prunus avium*	Author: (L.) L.

Gean

Leaves **Elliptic to oblong, to 6in (15cm) long and 2½in (6cm) across, taper-pointed, sharply toothed, bronze when young becoming matte deep green above. *Bark* Glossy red-brown, peeling in horizontal bands. *Flowers* 1¼in (3cm) across, white, with five petals, borne in clusters in mid-spring just before, or as, the leaves emerge. *Fruit* A rounded, bitter or sweet, edible, red berry, about ⅜in (1cm) across.**

NATIVE REGION Europe, S.W. Asia, N. Africa.
HABITAT Woods and hedgerows.
REMARK Also known as mazzard, wild cherry. This species is most familiar in flower as a woodland tree. It may reach only 65ft (20m).

sharply toothed leaves

red fruits are edible

Prunus avium △▽

bronzy young leaves emerge with flowers

densely clustered flowers

◁ **'Plena'**
The large, double flowers of this smaller cultivar have numerous petals.

Height: 80ft (25m)	Shape: Broadly columnar	Leaf persistence: Deciduous	Leaf type:

Family: Rosaceae	Species: *Prunus cerasifera*	Author: Ehrh.

Cherry Plum

Leaves **Ovate to obovate, to 2½in (6cm) long and 1¼in (3cm) across, toothed at the margin, glossy dark green and smooth above, downy on the veins beneath. *Bark* Purple-brown, thinly scaly, with horizontal, orange lenticels, fissured with age. *Flowers* 1in (2.5cm) across, white, with five petals and reflexed sepals, borne singly or in small clusters in early spring before the leaves emerge. *Fruit* Rounded, plumlike, edible, and red, 1¼in (3cm) across.**

NATIVE REGION S.E. Europe to Himalayas.
REMARK Also known as myrobalan. A similar species is the yellow-fruiting *Prunus divaricata*, which is native to S.E. Europe, and C. and S.W. Asia.

▽ ***Prunus cerasifera***

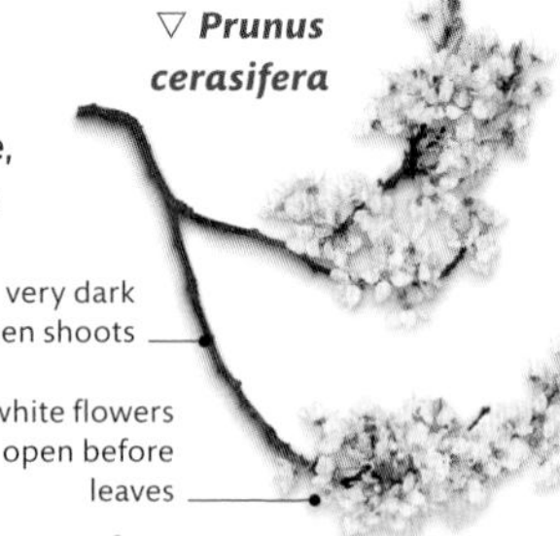

◁ **'Nigra'**
Deep red-purple leaves and pink flowers distinguish this form.

△ **'Pissardii'**
This form has pink buds, opening to white flowers, and purple leaves.

pink flowers have dark center

△ **'Rosea'**
This hybrid has red-purple foliage and small, pink flowers.

Height: 26ft (8m)	Shape: Broadly spreading	Leaf persistence: Deciduous	Leaf type:

Family: Rosaceae	Species: *Prunus cerasus*	Author: L.

Sour Cherry

Leaves Elliptic to ovate, to 3in (7.5cm) long and 2in (5cm) across, taper-pointed, sharply toothed, dark green above, smooth on both sides. ***Bark*** Purple-brown, with horizontal, orange-brown lenticels, peeling horizontally. ***Flowers*** ¾in (2cm) across, white, with five petals, in small clusters in mid-spring. ***Fruit*** An edible, red to black cherry, ¾in (2cm) across.

NATIVE REGION Caucasus.
REMARK The species is related to Gean (*Prunus avium*, see p.240).

Prunus cerasus ▽△

green sepals

ripe fruits remain sour

leaves emerge after flowers open

△ **'Rhexii'**
This form has large, rosettelike flowers.

Height: 26ft (8m)	Shape: Broadly spreading	Leaf persistence: Deciduous	Leaf type:

Family: Rosaceae	Species: *Prunus domestica*	Author: L.

Plum

Leaves Elliptic to obovate, to 3in (7.5cm) long and 2in (5cm) across, short-pointed, bluntly toothed, matte deep green above, downy beneath, on usually spineless shoots. ***Bark*** Gray-brown, fissured with age. ***Flowers*** 1in (2.5cm) across, white, with five petals, singly or in clusters of up to three in spring. ***Fruit*** Rounded to egg-shaped, fleshy, sharp to sweet, edible, yellow, red, or purple, to 3in (7.5cm) long, with a smooth skin, enclosing a single, flattened stone with a white seed.

NATIVE REGION Turkey.
REMARK This was thought to be a hybrid and is widely cultivated and naturalized.

some forms bear red-skinned fruits

flat, loose stone

flowers open before leaves

leaves have two small glands toward the end of the petiole

Height: 33ft (10m)	Shape: Broadly spreading	Leaf persistence: Deciduous	Leaf type:

Family: Rosaceae	Species: *Prunus incisa*	Author: Thunb.

Fuji Cherry

Leaves Ovate to obovate, to 2½in (6cm) long and 1¼in (3cm) across, taper-pointed at the tip, very sharply toothed at the margin, bronze-red when young becoming dark green, hairy on both sides. ***Bark*** Dark gray and vertically fissured. ***Flowers*** ¾in (2cm) across, white or very pale pink, with five notched petals, in small clusters of two or three in mid-spring before the leaves emerge. ***Fruit*** An egg-shaped, purple-black cherry, to 5⁄16in (8mm) long.

NATIVE REGION S.W. Japan.
HABITAT Mountain woods.

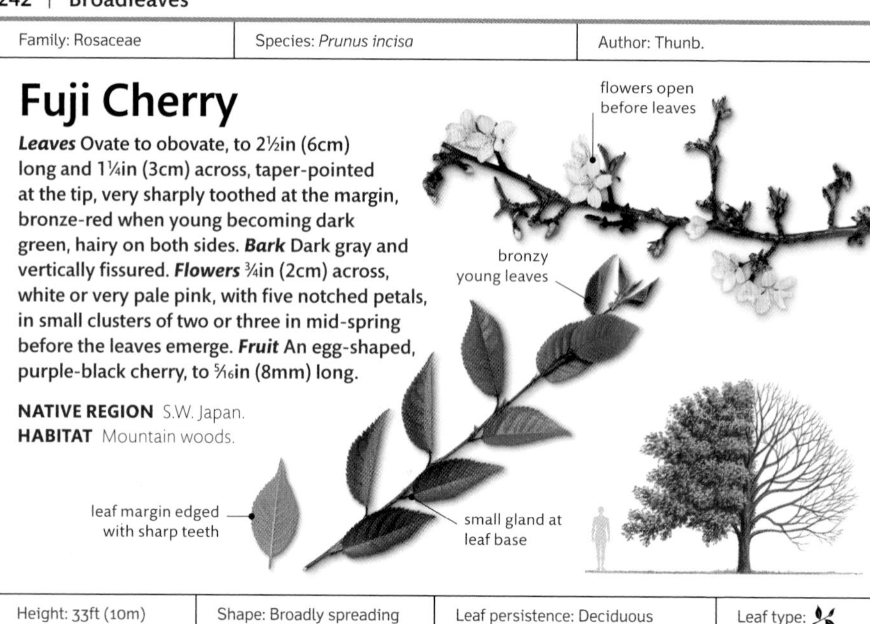

Height: 33ft (10m)	Shape: Broadly spreading	Leaf persistence: Deciduous	Leaf type:

Family: Rosaceae	Species: *Prunus insititia*	Author: L.

Bullace

Leaves Elliptic to obovate, to 3in (7.5cm) long and 2in (5cm) across, abruptly short-pointed at the tip, bluntly toothed, matte deep green above, on often spiny shoots. ***Bark*** Dark gray, smooth, usually fissured with age. ***Flowers*** 1in (2.5cm) across, white, with five petals, borne singly or in small clusters of up to three in spring before the leaves emerge. ***Fruit*** Rounded to egg-shaped, fleshy, edible, purple, to 2in (5cm) long, the nearly rounded stone clinging to the flesh.

NATIVE REGION C. Europe.
REMARK A widely naturalized relative of plum (*Primus domestica*, see p.241). Its varieties include damson and greengage.

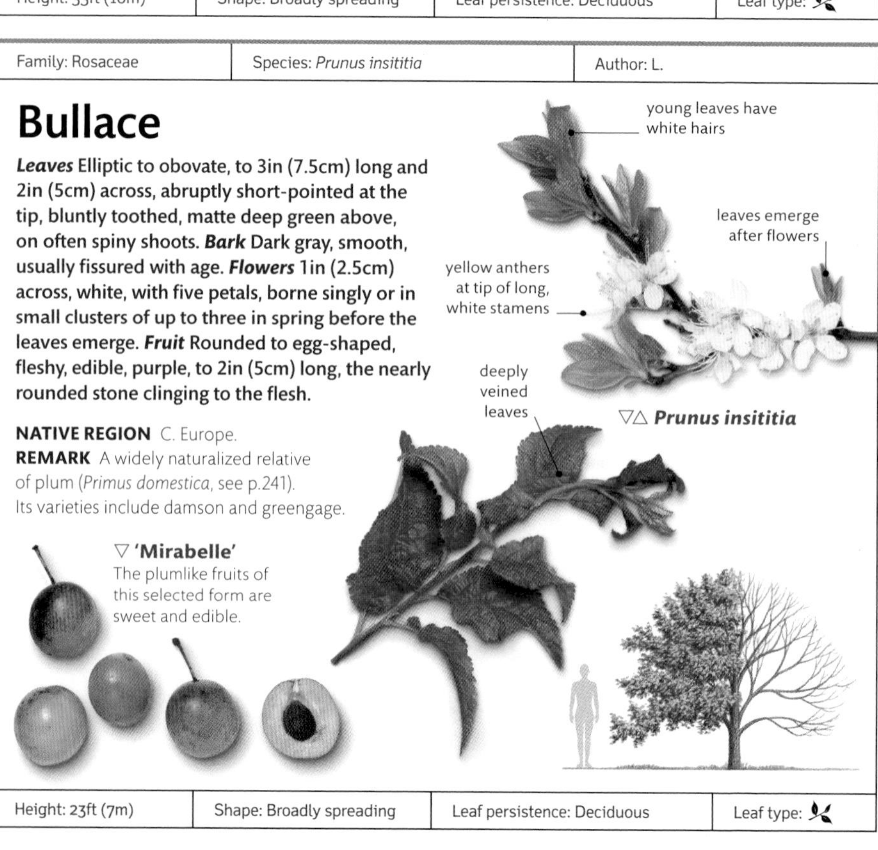

▽△ ***Prunus insititia***

▽ **'Mirabelle'**
The plumlike fruits of this selected form are sweet and edible.

Height: 23ft (7m)	Shape: Broadly spreading	Leaf persistence: Deciduous	Leaf type:

Family: Rosaceae	Species: *Prunus* forms or hybrids	Author: None

Japanese Cherries

The Japanese cherries, or *Sato-zakura*, are ornamental, flowering garden trees raised or selected in Japan. They are thought to be forms or hybrids of two native Japanese species, the hill cherry (*Prunus jamasakura*, see p.247) and the Oshima cherry (*Prunus speciosa*): trees similar to some of them grow wild in the hills and mountains of Japan. They have been cultivated in Japanese gardens for more than 1,500 years, yet are of relatively recent introduction to the West. Most have a spreading habit, but some are weeping or narrowly upright. The showy flowers are single to semi-double or fully double, and range from white to deep pink.

▽ 'Amanogawa'

A distinct tree of narrow, upright habit, to about 26ft (8m) tall. The pale pink double flowers are 1½in (4cm) across, and open in mid-spring before or with the bronze-tinged young leaves.

pale pink flowers have yellow anthers

sharply toothed leaves

deep bronze young leaves

double flowers borne in dense clusters

▽△ 'Kanzan'

By far the most popular and commonly planted Japanese cherry, this tree is vase-shaped at first, the branches eventually spreading and arching, to 33ft (10m) or more tall.

double flowers have numerous petals

bronze-green young leaves

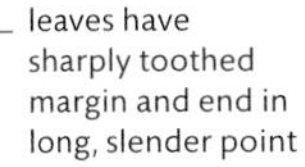

leaves have sharply toothed margin and end in long, slender point

△ 'Kiku-shidare-zakura'

This form usually reaches about 8ft (2.5m). Its long branches arch to the ground, giving the tree a mushroom shape.

Height: To 33ft (10m)	Shape: Variable	Leaf persistence: Deciduous	Leaf type:

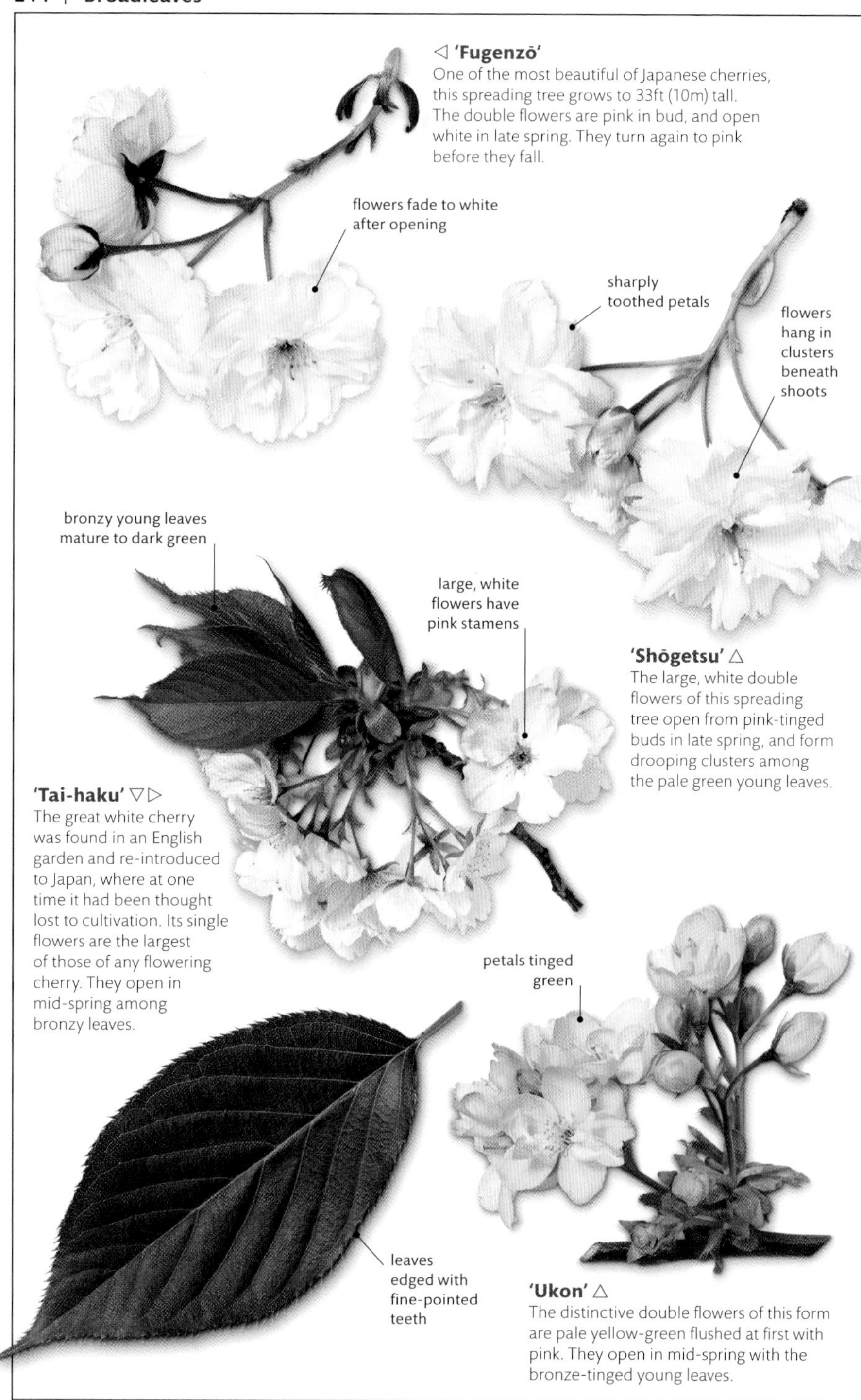

◁ 'Fugenzō'
One of the most beautiful of Japanese cherries, this spreading tree grows to 33ft (10m) tall. The double flowers are pink in bud, and open white in late spring. They turn again to pink before they fall.

'Shōgetsu' △
The large, white double flowers of this spreading tree open from pink-tinged buds in late spring, and form drooping clusters among the pale green young leaves.

'Tai-haku' ▽▷
The great white cherry was found in an English garden and re-introduced to Japan, where at one time it had been thought lost to cultivation. Its single flowers are the largest of those of any flowering cherry. They open in mid-spring among bronzy leaves.

'Ukon' △
The distinctive double flowers of this form are pale yellow-green flushed at first with pink. They open in mid-spring with the bronze-tinged young leaves.

Family: Rosaceae	Species: *Prunus* hybrids	Author: None

Prunus Hybrids

Aside from the Japanese cherries, many other hybrids between various species, either intentionally or accidentally raised and grown for their ornamental flowers and foliage are found in gardens and yards. Their parentage involves several different species and hybrids, including *P. sargentii* (see p.250) and *P.* x *subhirtella* (see p.253), and so these trees are more diverse than the Japanese cherries. They can be upright or spreading, usually reaching no more than 33ft (10m), and are always deciduous; some produce good fall color. The flowers are single to semi-double or fully double, usually opening in early to late spring.

double flowers have yellow anthers

◁△ 'Accolade'
This small tree is thought to be a hybrid between *Prunus sargentii* (see p.250) and *Prunus* x *subhirtella* (see p.253).

leaves edged with sharp-pointed teeth

small glands at base of leaf

△ 'Pandora'
This tree has pale pink single flowers, each with five petals. They open in early spring before the leaves emerge.

single-flower petals have notch at tip

leaves end in short point

leaf margin edged with coarse teeth

pink buds fade to nearly white on opening

◁△ 'Spire'
This vase-shaped tree has matte dark green foliage that turns orange and red in fall.

Height: To 33ft (10m)	Shape: Variable	Leaf persistence: Deciduous	Leaf type:

Family: Rosaceae	Species: *Prunus itosakura*	Author: Siebold

Prunus itosakura

Leaves **Oblong to obovate, to 4¾in (12cm) long and 2½in (4cm) across, with up to 14 pairs of veins, ending in a tapered point, toothed at the margin, dark green and thinly hairy or smooth above, hairy beneath, at least on the veins.** ***Bark*** **Gray-brown, developing vertical fissures with age.** ***Flowers*** **To ¾in (2cm) across, pink, with five petals notched at the tip, borne in clusters of up to five in early spring.** ***Fruit*** **A small, black cherry.**

NATIVE REGION Japan, Korea.
HABITAT Mountain woods.
REMARK This species occurs naturally as an upright tree that has been called *Prunus* x *subhirtella* f. *ascendens*, but is mainly cultivated as weeping forms that make smaller trees and have been called *Prunus pendula* or *Prunus* x *subhirtella* 'Pendula.'

leaves unfold pale green and thin

fine, regularly spaced teeth at leaf margin

◁ 'Pendula Rosea'
The single, pale pink flowers of this form are borne on weeping branches. 'Pendula Rubra' is similar in habit, but has darker flowers. Both of these forms have been listed under *P.* x *subhhirtella* and are of Japanese origin.

petals have notched tip

single flowers borne in dense clusters

flowers borne bunched together along reddish shoots

'Stellata' ▽

cherry fruits ripen in color from deep red to nearly black

leaves mature to dark green

△ 'Stellata'
The name describes the narrow-petalled, starry flowers of this cultivar. This very ornamental and profusely flowering form was raised in the US, where it is also known as 'Pink Star.'

Height: 51ft (15m)	Shape: Broadly columnar	Leaf persistence: Deciduous	Leaf type:

Family: Rosaceae	Species: *Prunus jamasakura*	Author: (Makino) Siebold ex Koidz.

Hill Cherry

Leaves Oblong to obovate, to 4¾in (12cm) long and 2in (5cm) across, abruptly taper-pointed at the tip, sharply toothed, bronze or red becoming deep green above, blue-green beneath, smooth on both sides, turning yellow to red in fall. ***Bark*** Purple-brown, with horizontal lenticels. ***Flowers*** 1¼in (3cm) across, pale pink to nearly white, with five petals notched at the tip, opening in small clusters in mid-spring as the young leaves emerge. ***Center*** A fleshy, deep purple-black berry, 1in (2.5cm) long.

NATIVE REGION Japan.
HABITAT Woods in hills and low mountains.
REMARK Also known as *Prunus serrulata* var. *spontanea*.

notch at tip of petal

sharply toothed leaf margin

folded, soft young leaves

colored fall leaves carried on red stalks

Height: 65ft (20m)	Shape: Broadly spreading	Leaf persistence: Deciduous	Leaf type:

Family: Rosaceae	Species: *Prunus laurocerasus*	Author: L.

Cherry Laurel

Leaves Elliptic to oblong or obovate, to 8in (20cm) long and 2½in (6cm) across, abruptly short-pointed, usually shallowly toothed, at least above the middle, glossy yellowish to very dark green above, pale green beneath, smooth, on short, stout stalks. ***Bark*** Gray-brown and smooth. ***Flowers*** 5/16in (8mm) across, white, with five petals, fragrant, borne in upright racemes to 4¾in (12cm) long, in the leaf axils in mid-spring, sometimes flowering again in fall. ***Fruit*** A rounded berry, ½in (1.2cm) across, green becoming red ripening to black.

NATIVE REGION S.W. Asia, E. Europe.
HABITAT Thickets in forests.

Height: 33ft (10m)	Shape: Broadly spreading	Leaf persistence: Evergreen	Leaf type:

Family: Rosaceae	Species: *Prunus leveilleana*	Author: Koehne

Korean Hill Cherry

Leaves Elliptic to obovate, to 4¾in (12cm) long and 2in (5cm) across, abruptly taper-pointed, sharply toothed, pale green to bronze when young becoming glossy green above, paler beneath, downy on one or both sides, turning red to purple in fall. ***Bark*** Gray-brown, peeling in horizontal bands. ***Flowers*** 1¼in (3cm) across, white or pale pink, with five petals notched at the tip, borne in small clusters in mid-spring before or with the leaves. ***Fruit*** A red to purple cherry, to ⅜in (1cm) across.

NATIVE REGION China, Japan, Korea.
HABITAT Woods in hills and mountains.
REMARK Also known as *Prunus serrulata* var. *pubescens.*

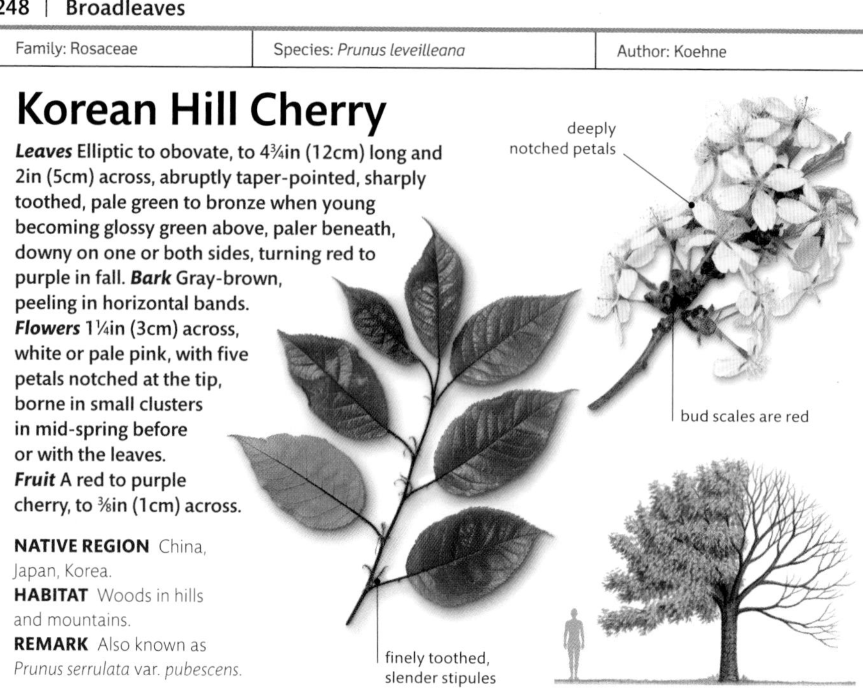

Height: 65ft (20m)	Shape: Broadly spreading	Leaf persistence: Deciduous	Leaf type:

Family: Rosaceae	Species: *Prunus lusitanica*	Author: L.

Portugal Laurel

Leaves Ovate to elliptic, to 4¾in (12cm) long and 2in (5cm) across, taper-pointed at the tip, toothed, glossy dark green above, smooth on both sides, on slender, red stalks. ***Bark*** Dark gray-brown and smooth. ***Flowers*** Individually ⅜in (1cm) across, white, with five petals, fragrant, numerous, borne in spreading racemes to 10in (25cm) long, in midsummer. ***Fruit*** Egg-shaped, ½in (1.2cm) long, green becoming red, ripening to black.

NATIVE REGION S.W. Europe, Morocco.
HABITAT Mountain woods.

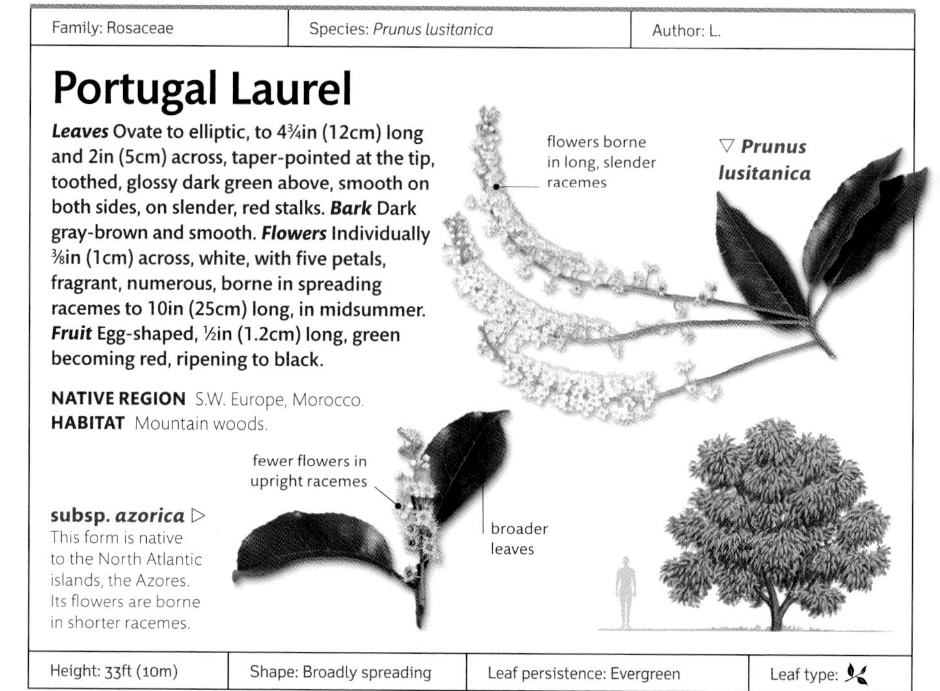

subsp. *azorica* ▷
This form is native to the North Atlantic islands, the Azores. Its flowers are borne in shorter racemes.

Height: 33ft (10m)	Shape: Broadly spreading	Leaf persistence: Evergreen	Leaf type:

Family: Rosaceae	Species: *Prunus maackii*	Author: Rupr.

Manchurian Cherry

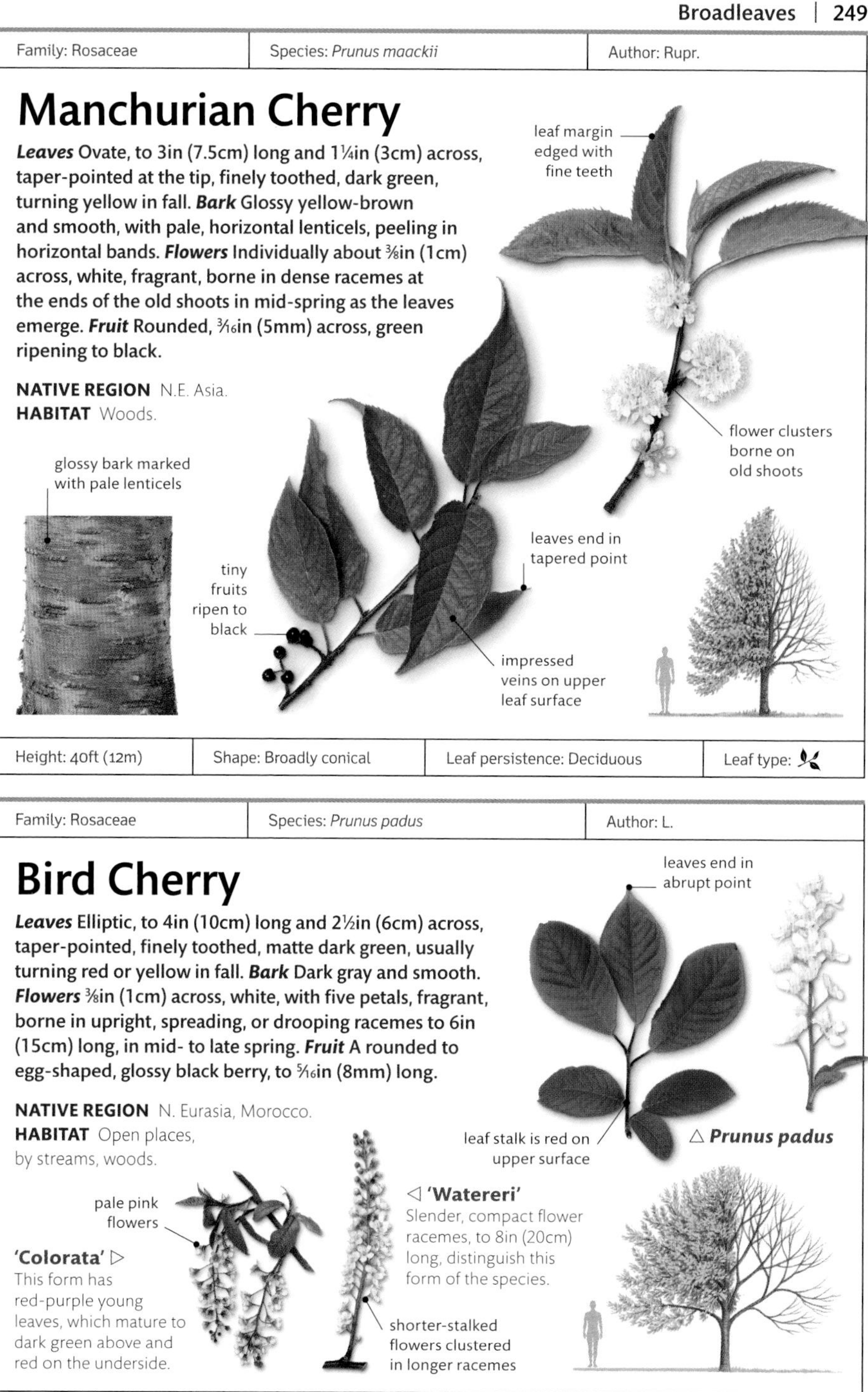

Leaves **Ovate, to 3in (7.5cm) long and 1¼in (3cm) across, taper-pointed at the tip, finely toothed, dark green, turning yellow in fall.** ***Bark*** **Glossy yellow-brown and smooth, with pale, horizontal lenticels, peeling in horizontal bands.** ***Flowers*** **Individually about ⅜in (1cm) across, white, fragrant, borne in dense racemes at the ends of the old shoots in mid-spring as the leaves emerge.** ***Fruit*** **Rounded, 3/16in (5mm) across, green ripening to black.**

NATIVE REGION N.E. Asia.
HABITAT Woods.

Height: 40ft (12m)	Shape: Broadly conical	Leaf persistence: Deciduous	Leaf type:

Family: Rosaceae	Species: *Prunus padus*	Author: L.

Bird Cherry

Leaves **Elliptic, to 4in (10cm) long and 2½in (6cm) across, taper-pointed, finely toothed, matte dark green, usually turning red or yellow in fall.** ***Bark*** **Dark gray and smooth.** ***Flowers*** **⅜in (1cm) across, white, with five petals, fragrant, borne in upright, spreading, or drooping racemes to 6in (15cm) long, in mid- to late spring.** ***Fruit*** **A rounded to egg-shaped, glossy black berry, to 5/16in (8mm) long.**

NATIVE REGION N. Eurasia, Morocco.
HABITAT Open places, by streams, woods.

△ ***Prunus padus***

'Colorata' ▷
This form has red-purple young leaves, which mature to dark green above and red on the underside.

◁ **'Watereri'**
Slender, compact flower racemes, to 8in (20cm) long, distinguish this form of the species.

Height: 50ft (15m)	Shape: Broadly spreading	Leaf persistence: Deciduous	Leaf type:

Family: Rosaceae	Species: *Prunus persica*	Author: (L.) Batsch

Peach

Leaves Narrowly elliptic to lanceolate, to 6in (15cm) long and 1½in (4cm) across, with a long, slender point at the tip, finely toothed, glossy dark green. ***Bark*** Dark gray, becoming fissured with age. ***Flowers*** To 1½in (4cm) across, pale to deep pink or red, sometimes white, short-stalked, borne singly or in pairs, in early spring ***Fruit*** Rounded, fleshy, sweet, edible, usually orange-yellow flushed red, to 3in (7.5cm) across, enclosing a deeply pitted, furrowed stone with a white seed.

NATIVE REGION China.
HABITAT Mountains.

△ ***Prunus persica***

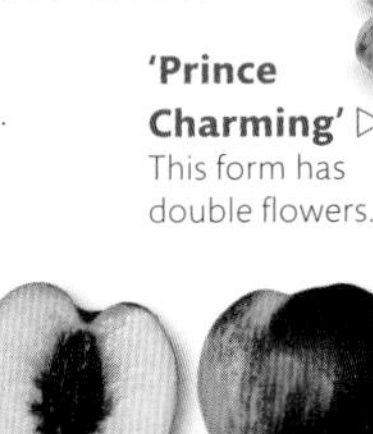

'Prince Charming' ▷
This form has double flowers.

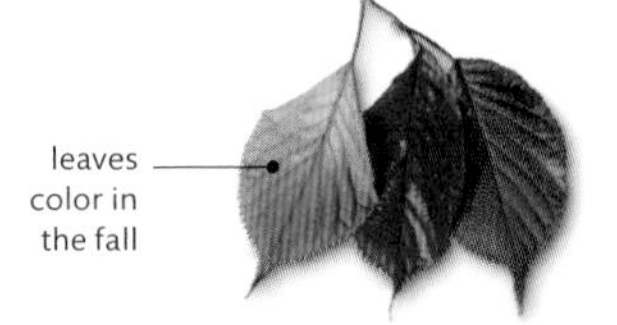

▷ **var. *nectarina***
The fruit of this variety has a smooth and slightly oily skin.

Height: 26ft (8m)	Shape: Broadly spreading	Leaf persistence: Deciduous	Leaf type:

Family: Rosaceae	Species: *Prunus sargentii*	Author: Rehder

Sargent's Cherry

Leaves Elliptic to obovate, to 4¾in (12cm) long and 2½in (6cm) across, abruptly taper-pointed, sharply toothed, reddish when young becoming deep glossy green above, smooth on both sides, turning brilliant orange and red in fall. ***Bark*** Glossy red-brown, with pale, horizontal lenticels. ***Flowers*** 1½in (4cm) across, pink, with five petals notched at the tip, opening in clusters in mid-spring with or just before the leaves. ***Fruit*** A rounded to egg-shaped, glossy, purple-black berry, about ¾in (1cm) long.

NATIVE REGION E. Russia, Korea, Japan.
HABITAT Woods in mountains.

leaves color in the fall

Height: 65ft (20m)	Shape: Broadly spreading	Leaf persistence: Deciduous	Leaf type:

Family: Rosaceae	Species: *Prunus* x *schmittii*	Author: Rehder

Prunus x schmittii

Leaves Elliptic to obovate, to 4½in (11cm) long and 2¼in (5.5cm) across, taper-pointed at the tip, sharply and coarsely toothed at the margin, dark green above, paler beneath, softly downy on both sides. ***Bark*** Purple-red, with horizontal rows of corky, orange-brown lenticels, peeling in narrow, horizontal bands. ***Flowers*** Individually ¾in (2cm) across, deep pink in bud becoming pale pink, with five cupped petals, opening in clusters in mid-spring with the young leaves. ***Fruit*** Not usually produced.

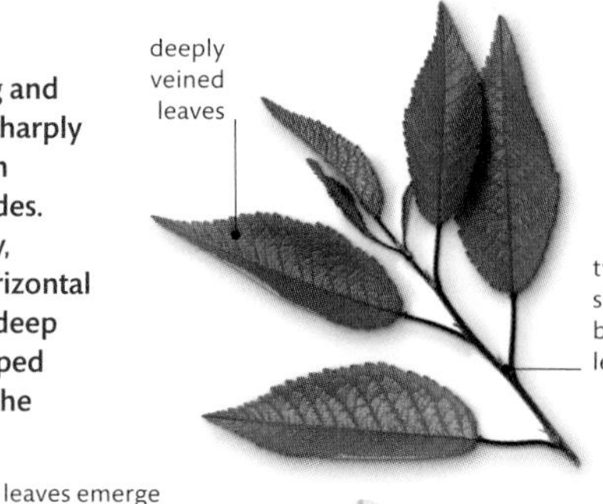

NATIVE REGION Of garden and backyard origin.
REMARK A hybrid between the Gean (*Prunus avium*, see p.240) and *Prunus canescens*.

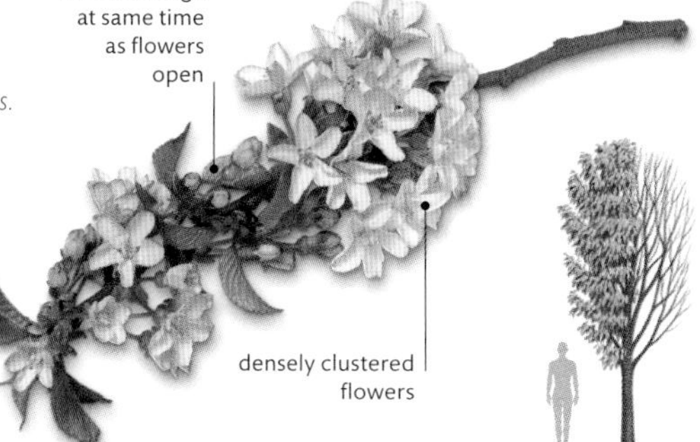

Height: 50ft (15m)	Shape: Narrowly columnar	Leaf persistence: Deciduous	Leaf type:

Family: Rosaceae	Species: *Prunus serotina*	Author: Ehrh.

Rum Cherry

Leaves Elliptic to lanceolate, to 4¾in (12cm) long and 2in (5cm) across, taper-pointed, finely toothed, glossy dark green and smooth above, paler and smooth with hairs along the midrib beneath, turning yellow or red in fall. ***Bark*** Dark gray, smooth. ***Flowers*** ⅜in (1cm) across, white, in spreading to drooping racemes to 6in (15cm) long, at the ends of the shoots in late spring or early summer. ***Fruit*** A rounded, edible cherry, to ⅜in (1cm) across, red ripening to black.

NATIVE REGION Canada to Guatemala.
HABITAT Woods, pastures, and roadsides.

Height: 80ft (25m)	Shape: Broadly columnar	Leaf persistence: Deciduous	Leaf type: 

Family: Rosaceae	Species: *Prunus serrula*	Author: Franch.

Tibetan Cherry

Leaves Lanceolate, to 4in (10cm) long and 1¼in (3cm) across, tapering to a slender point at the tip, finely toothed at the margin, matte dark green. ***Bark*** Glossy red-brown and smooth, conspicuously banded with pale, horizontal lenticels, peeling horizontally in narrow strips. ***Flowers*** White, ¾in (2cm) across, relatively inconspicuous, pendulous, borne singly or in small clusters of up to three in spring just after the young leaves emerge. ***Fruit*** An egg-shaped cherry, about ¾in (1cm) long, yellow ripening to red.

NATIVE REGION W. China.
HABITAT Mountain woods.
REMARK Also known as *Prunus serrula* var. *tibetica*. This species is easily distinguished by its characteristic bark.

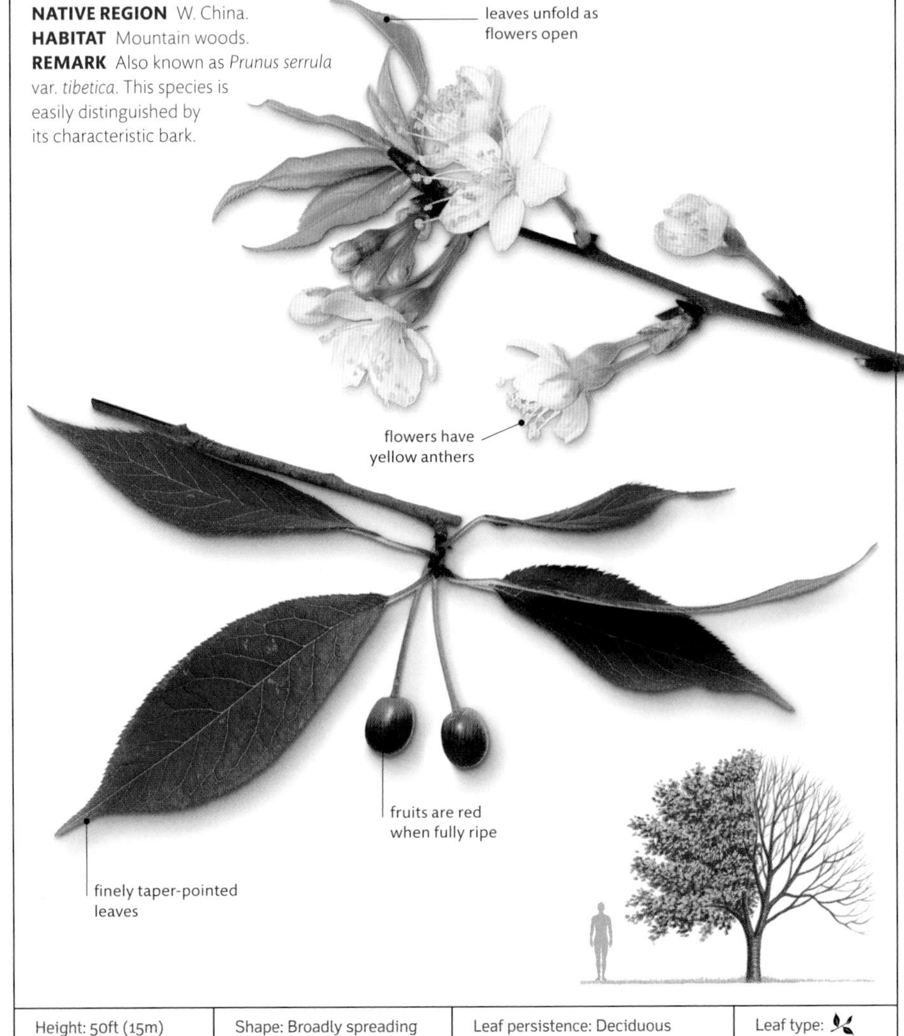

Height: 50ft (15m)	Shape: Broadly spreading	Leaf persistence: Deciduous	Leaf type:

Family: Rosaceae	Species: *Prunus* x *subhirtella*	Author: Miq.

Spring Cherry

Leaves **Elliptic to ovate, to 3in (7.5cm) long and 2in (5cm) across, taper-pointed, sharply toothed, pale bronze when young becoming deep green above, paler beneath, turning yellow in fall. *Bark* Gray-brown and smooth, banded with horizontal lenticels. *Flowers* Individually ¾in (2cm) across, pale pink or white, with five petals notched at the tip, opening from pink buds, in small clusters in early spring either before or as the young leaves emerge. *Fruit* A nearly black cherry, 5⁄16in (8mm) across, sparsely borne.**

NATIVE REGION Japan.
HABITAT In woods with the parents.
REMARK A naturally occurring hybrid between Fuji cherry (*Prunus incisa*, see p.242) and *Prunus itosakura* (see p.246). It is seen only rarely in the wild, but has many garden and backyard forms. 'Autumnalis' is one of the most commonly cultivated varieties.

flowers open from pink buds

semi-double white flowers may open during winter, tinged with pale pink at first

'Autumnalis' △

'Autumnalis' ▷
The semi-double flowers of this form are white, tinged with pale pink. They open in fall, during mild periods in winter, and in spring.

stipules at leaf base

bronze-green young leaves

sharply toothed leaf margin

leaves mature to dark green

△ **'Autumnalis Rosea'**
The semi-double flowers of this cultivar are very similar to those of 'Autumnalis,' but are deeper pink both in bud and when open. Like 'Autumnalis,' it flowers during mild weather in winter, and in spring.

spring flowers open as young leaves emerge

Height: 20ft (6m)	Shape: Broadly spreading	Leaf persistence: Deciduous	Leaf type:

Family: Rosaceae	Species: *Prunus* x *yedoensis*	Author: Matsum.

Yoshino Cherry

Leaves **Elliptic, to 4½in (11cm) long and 2½in (6cm) across, taper-pointed at the tip, sharply toothed at the margin, downy on both sides, but when young, particularly so beneath, becoming smooth and glossy dark green above. *Bark* Purple-gray, with thick bands of corky lenticels. *Flowers* 1½in (4cm) across, pale pink fading to nearly white, with five petals notched at the tip, borne in small clusters in early spring before the young leaves emerge. *Fruit* A nearly rounded cherry, ½in (1.2cm) across, red at first ripening to black in summer.**

NATIVE REGION Japan.
HABITAT Woods in hills together with the parent plants.
REMARK A hybrid between *Prunus itosakura* (see p.246) and *Prunus* x *subhirtella* (see p.253).

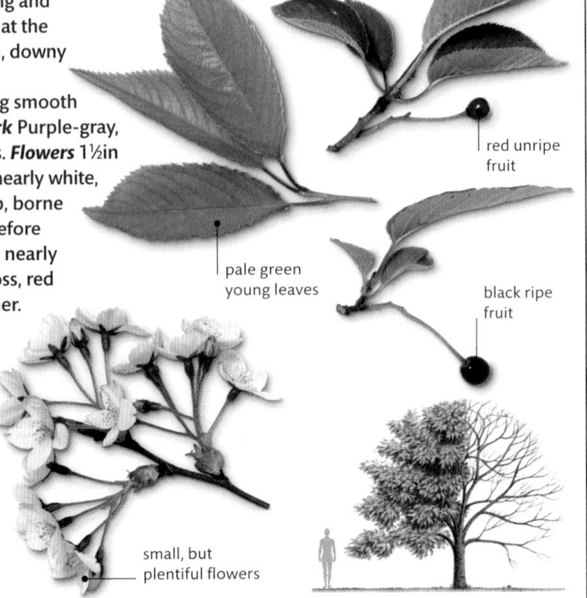

Height: 40ft (12m)	Shape: Broadly spreading	Leaf persistence: Deciduous	Leaf type:

Family: Rosaceae	Species: *Pyrus calleryana*	Author: Decne.

Callery Pear

Leaves **Ovate to elliptic, to 3in (7.5cm) long and 2in (5cm) across, finely toothed, glossy dark green above, smooth, turning red-purple in fall or early winter. *Bark* Dark gray, cracking into scaly ridges; red-brown when freshly exposed. *Flowers* ⅜in (1cm) across, white, with five petals, in spring. *Fruit* Rounded to pear-shaped, fleshy, to ¾in (2cm) across, russet-brown spotted with white.**

NATIVE REGION China, Japan, Vietnam.
HABITAT Thickets and by streams in mountains.

Height: 50ft (15m)	Shape: Broadly conical	Leaf persistence: Deciduous	Leaf type:

Family: Rosaceae	Species: *Pyrus communis*	Author: L.

Common Pear

Leaves Ovate to elliptic, to 4in (10cm) long and 2in (5cm) across, rounded to heart-shaped at the base, taper-pointed, toothed, glossy deep green. ***Bark*** Dark gray, cracking into small plates. ***Flowers*** To 1½in (4cm) across, white, with five petals and deep pink anthers, in clusters in mid-spring. ***Fruit*** Rounded to pear-shaped, fleshy, sweet, edible, greenish to russet or yellow, sometimes flushed red, to 4in (10cm) long.

NATIVE REGION Europe, W. Asia.
REMARK A hybrid involving several species, which probably originated in W. Asia.

fruits vary in size, shape, and color

small, shallow teeth at leaf margin

long-stalked leaves

Height: 50ft (15m)	Shape: Broadly columnar	Leaf persistence: Deciduous	Leaf type:

Family: Rosaceae	Species: *Pyrus salicifolia*	Author: Pall.

Willow-leaved Pear

Leaves Narrowly elliptic to narrowly lanceolate, to 3½in (9cm) long and ¾in (2cm) across, tapering at both ends, usually untoothed, silvery gray and hairy when young, becoming smooth and dark green above. ***Bark*** Pale gray-brown, cracking into smooth plates. ***Flowers*** ¾in (2cm) across, creamy white, with five petals and deep pink anthers, in clusters in spring. ***Fruits*** Pear-shaped, hard, green, to 3cm (1¼in) long.

NATIVE REGION Caucasus, N.E. Turkey.
HABITAT Wood margins, thickets.

young leaves emerge with flowers

fruits have short, stout stalk

downy young leaves

Height: 33ft (10m)	Shape: Broadly weeping	Leaf persistence: Deciduous	Leaf type:

Family: Rosaceae	Species: *Scandosorbus intermedia*	Author: (Ehrh.) Sennikov

Swedish Whitebeam

Leaves Ovate or broadly elliptic, to 4in (10cm) long and 2½in (6cm) across, lobed, the depth of the lobes increasing toward the base of the leaf, toothed, glossy dark green above, gray-green and hairy beneath. ***Bark*** Gray, cracking, and flaking with age. ***Flowers*** Individually ¾in (2cm) across, white, with five petals, in large, dense clusters to 4¾in (12cm) across, in late spring. ***Fruit*** A broadly egg-shaped, bright red berry, to ⅝in (1.5cm) long, with few lenticels.

NATIVE REGION N.W. Europe.
HABITAT Woods.

glossy dark green leaf upperside

egg-shaped, shiny red berries

lobes are deepest below middle of leaf

gray-green, hairy leaf underside

Height: 50ft (15m)	Shape: Broadly columnar	Leaf persistence: Deciduous	Leaf type:

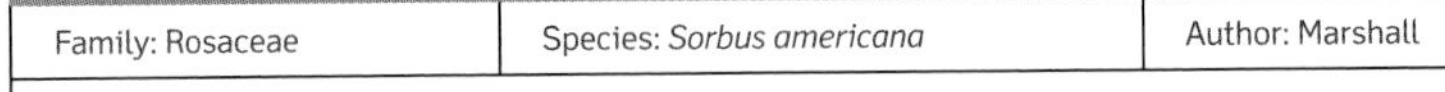

Family: Rosaceae	Species: *Sorbus americana*	Author: Marshall

American Mountain Ash

Leaves Pinnate, to 10in (25cm) long, with about 15 oblong to lanceolate, pointed, toothed leaflets, to 4in (10cm) long and 1in (2.5cm) across, turning yellow or red in late fall. ***Bark*** Gray and smooth. ***Flowers*** 3/16in (5mm) across, white, in dense heads to 8in (20cm) across, in late spring to early summer. ***Fruit*** An orange-red berry, about 3/16in (5mm) across.

NATIVE REGION E. North America.
HABITAT Woods.

Height: 26ft (8m)	Shape: Broadly spreading	Leaf persistence: Deciduous	Leaf type:

Family: Rosaceae	Species: *Sorbus aucuparia*	Author: L.

Rowan

Leaves Pinnate, to 8in (20cm) long, with up to 15 taper-pointed, sharply toothed leaflets, to 2½in (6cm) long, dark green and smooth above, blue-green and usually downy beneath when young, sometimes turning red in fall. ***Bark*** Gray and smooth. ***Flowers*** 5/16in (8mm) across, white, with five petals, borne in large clusters to 6in (15cm) across, in late spring. ***Fruit*** A rounded, orange-red berry, 5/16in (8mm) across, often forming heavy clusters.

NATIVE REGION Asia, Europe.
HABITAT Woods, heathland, moors, and mountains, on moist, acid soil.
REMARK Also known as mountain ash. The berries are used for making jellies and preserves, but can be poisonous if consumed raw.

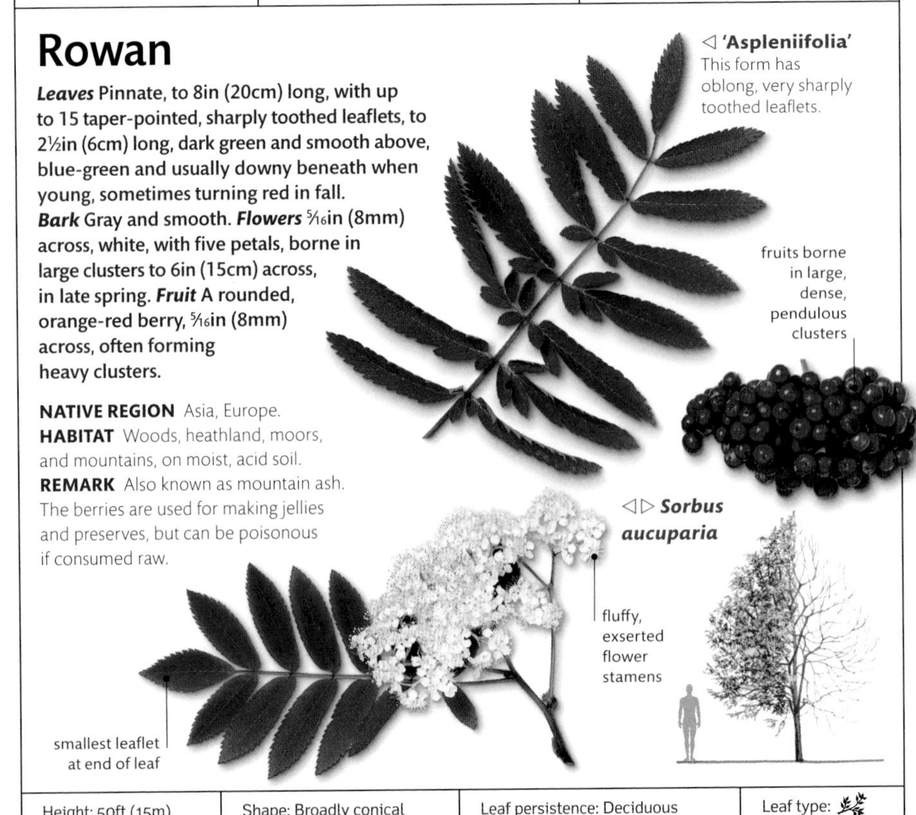

Height: 50ft (15m)	Shape: Broadly conical	Leaf persistence: Deciduous	Leaf type:

Family: Rosaceae	Species: *Sorbus cashmiriana*	Author: Hedl.

Kashmir Rowan

Leaves Pinnate, to 6in (15cm) long, with about 17 sharply toothed leaflets, to 2in (5cm) long and ⅝in (1.5cm) across, deep green above, gray-green beneath, becoming smooth on both sides, turning yellow in fall. ***Bark*** Smooth and gray to reddish gray. ***Flowers*** ⅝in (1.5cm) across, pink, with five petals, in open clusters to 4¾in (12cm) across, in late spring. ***Fruit*** A rounded berry, white tinged pink at first at the top, ½in (1.2cm) across, carried on red stalks.

NATIVE REGION W. Himalayas.
HABITAT Mountain woods.

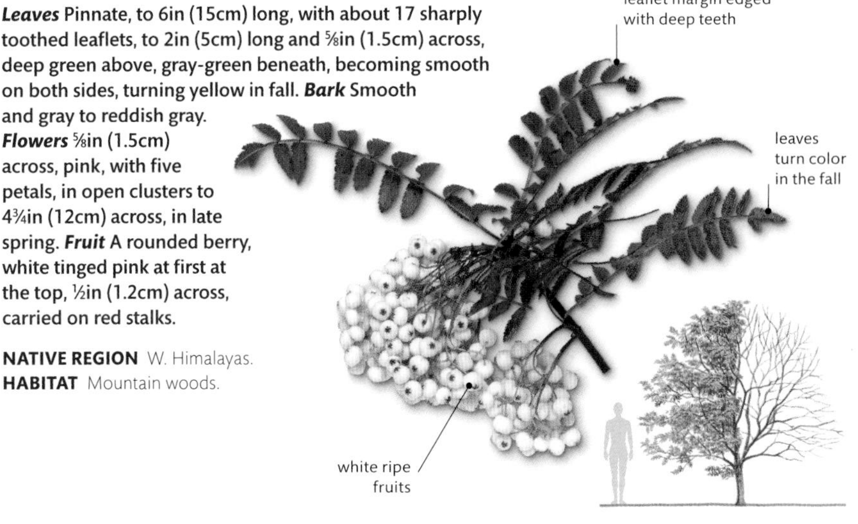

Height: 26ft (8m)	Shape: Broadty spreading	Leaf persistence: Deciduous	Leaf type:

Family: Rosaceae	Species: *Sorbus commixta*	Author: Hedl.

Japanese Rowan

Leaves Pinnate, to 20cm (8in) long, with up to 15 taper-pointed leaflets, to 3in (7.5cm) long and 1in (2.5cm) across, glossy dark green above, blue-green beneath, turning yellow to reddish purple in fall. ***Bark*** Gray and smooth. ***Flowers*** 5/16in (8mm) across, white, with five petals, in clusters to 6in (15cm) across, in late spring. ***Fruit*** Rounded, orange-red, 5/16in (8mm) across.

NATIVE REGION
China, Japan, Korea.
HABITAT Mountain forests.

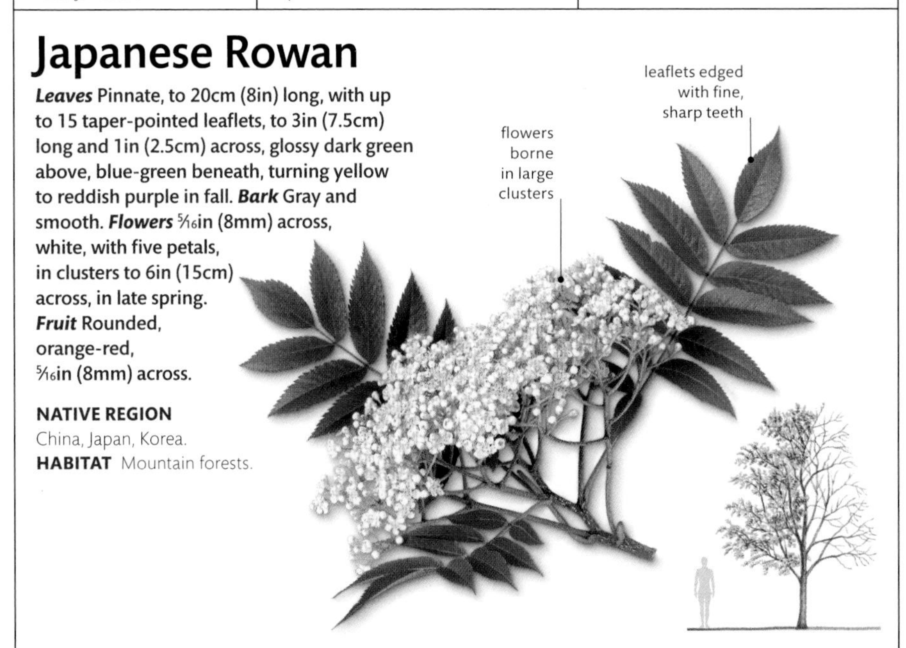

Height: 33ft (10m)	Shape: Broadly conical	Leaf persistence: Deciduous	Leaf type:

Family: Rosaceae	Species: *Sorbus esserteauana*	Author: Koehne

Esserteau's Rowan

Leaves Pinnate, to 10in (25cm) long, with usually up to 15 taper-pointed leaflets, to 4in (10cm) long and 1½in (4cm) across, deep bronze-purple becoming glossy dark green and smooth above, gray-hairy beneath when young, turning red in fall. ***Bark*** Gray-brown, thinly scaly. ***Flowers*** 5⁄16in (8mm) across, white, with five petals, in flattened heads to 4¾in (12cm) across, in late spring. ***Fruit*** Red, 8mm (5⁄16in) across.

NATIVE REGION S.W. China.
HABITAT Mountains, cliffs, woods.
REMARK A cultivated form with yellow fruits is known as *Sorbus esserteauana* 'Flava.'

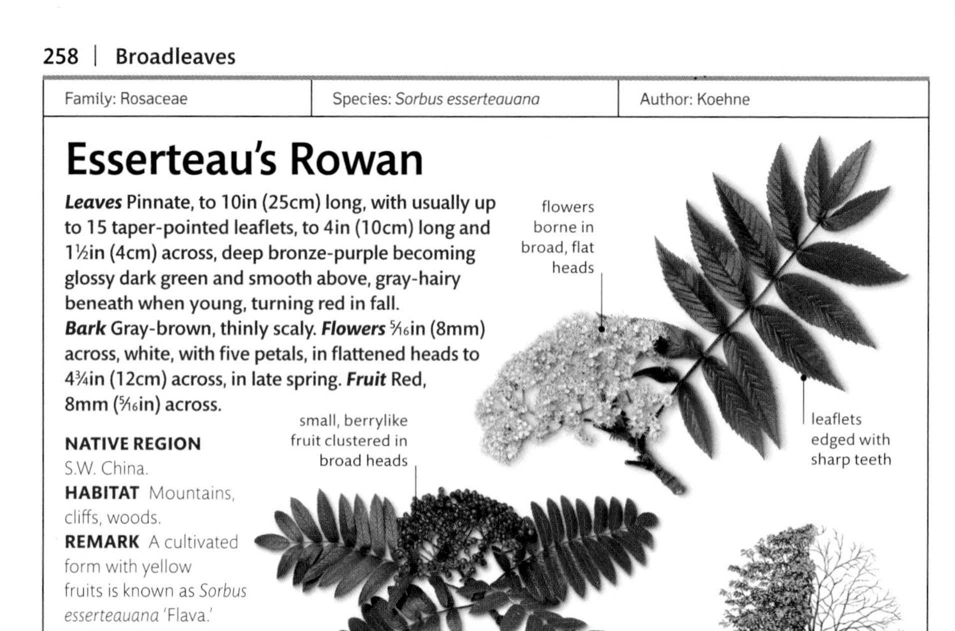

Height: 33ft (10m)	Shape: Broadly spreading	Leaf persistence: Deciduous	Leaf type:

Family: Rosaceae	Species: *Sorbus forrestii*	Author: McAll. & Gillham

Forrest's Rowan

Leaves Pinnate, to 8in (20cm) long, with up to 17 leaflets, to 1½in (4cm) long and ⅝in (1.5cm) across, deep blue-green above, gray-green beneath, becoming smooth. ***Bark*** Purple-gray and smooth, with shallow, vertical fissures. ***Flowers*** ⅜in (1cm) across, white, with five petals, borne in flattened heads in late spring. ***Fruit*** Rounded, ⅜in (1cm) across, green ripening to white.

NATIVE REGION S.W. China.
HABITAT Mountain woods.

upper half of leaflets edged with small teeth

flowers borne in small, loose heads

deep pink tinge around tip of fruit

lower half of leaflets has smooth margin

Height: 20ft (6m)	Shape: Broadly spreading	Leaf persistence: Deciduous	Leaf type:

Family: Rosaceae	Species: *Sorbus glabriuscula*	Author: McAll.

Glabrous Mountain Ash

Leaves **Pinnate, to 6in (15cm) long, with up to 17 leaflets, to 2½in (6cm) long and ¾in (2cm) across, toothed toward the tip, blue-green above, blue-gray and smooth or nearly so beneath, turning red in fall. *Bark* Gray and smooth. *Flowers* Individually ¼in (6mm) across, white, with five petals, in rounded clusters to 6in (15cm) across, in late spring. *Fruit* A rounded berry, about 5⁄16in (8mm) across, white flushed pink at the top.**

NATIVE REGION W. China.
HABITAT Mountain woods.
REMARK This species was called *Sorbus hupehensis* for many years.

Height: 40ft (12m)	Shape: Broadly columnar	Leaf persistence: Deciduous	Leaf type:

Family: Rosaceae	Species: *Sorbus* 'Joseph Rock'	Author: None

Sorbus 'Joseph Rock'

Leaves **Pinnate, to 6in (15cm) long, with up to 17 sharply toothed leaflets, to 1½in (4cm) long and ½in (1.2cm) across, bright green above, gray-green beneath, becoming nearly smooth, turning orange, red, and purple in fall. *Bark* Gray, nearly smooth, with small, orange lenticels. *Flowers* ⅜in (1cm) across, white, with five petals, borne in flattened heads 10cm (4in) across, in late spring to early summer. *Fruit* Rounded, 1cm (⅜in) across, green then yellow-white ripening to orange-yellow.**

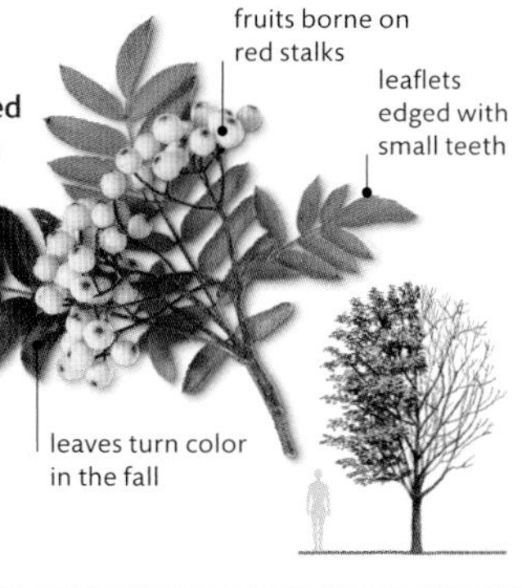

NATIVE REGION Probably China.
HABITAT Not known, it is unknown in the wild.

Height: 33ft (10m)	Shape: Broadly columnar	Leaf persistence: Deciduous	Leaf type:

Family: Rosaceae	Species: *Sorbus sargentiana*	Author: Koehne

Sargent's Rowan

Leaves **Pinnate, to 14in (35cm) long, with about 11 oblong leaflets, to 4¾in (12cm) long and 2in (5cm) across, matte deep green above, gray-green and hairy beneath, orange and red in fall. *Bark* Purple-brown, flaking with age. *Flowers* ¼in (6mm) across, white, in heads to 8in (20cm) across, in early summer. *Fruit* Rounded, bright red, ¼in (6mm) across, borne in large clusters.**

NATIVE REGION S.W. China.
HABITAT Mountain woods.

Height: 33ft (10m)	Shape: Broadly columnar	Leaf persistence: Deciduous	Leaf type:

Family: Rosaceae	Species: *Sorbus scalaris*	Author: Koehne

Ladder-leaf Rowan

Leaves Pinnate, to 8in (20cm) long, with numerous narrowly oblong leaflets, to 1½in (4cm) long and ⅜in (1cm) across, toothed toward the tip, glossy deep green above, gray and hairy beneath, turning red and purple in late fall. ***Bark*** Smooth and gray, with shallow fissures. ***Flowers*** ¼in (6mm) across, white, with five petals, in broad, flattened heads to 6in (15cm) across, in late spring or early summer. ***Fruit*** Rounded, bright red, ¼in (6mm) across, in large clusters.

NATIVE REGION S.W. China.
HABITAT Mountain woods.

Height: 33ft (10m)	Shape: Broadly spreading	Leaf persistence: Deciduous	Leaf type:

Family: Rosaceae	Species: *Sorbus vilmorinii*	Author: C.K. Schneid.

Vilmorin's Rowan

Leaves Pinnate, to 6in (15cm) long, with up to about 25 oblong leaflets, to ¾in (2cm) long, toothed toward the tip, glossy dark green above, gray-green beneath. ***Bark*** Smooth, dark gray. ***Flowers*** ¼in (6mm) across, white, with five petals, in clusters to 4in (10cm) across, in late spring to early summer. ***Fruit*** A roundish berry, ⅜in (1cm) long, deep red at first, ripening to white.

NATIVE REGION S.W. China.
HABITAT Mountain woods.

Height: 26ft (18m)	Shape: Broadly spreading	Leaf persistence: Deciduous	Leaf type:

Family: Rosaceae	Species: *Torminalis glaberrima*	Author: (Gand.) Sennikov & Kurtto

Wild Service Tree

Leaves Broadly ovate, to 4in (10cm) long and nearly the same across, deeply cut into sharply toothed lobes, glossy dark green above, paler beneath, downy when young, turning yellow, red, or purple in fall. ***Bark*** Dark brown, cracking into scaly plates. ***Flowers*** ½in (1.2cm) across, white, in flattened clusters in late spring to early summer. ***Fruit*** A rounded, russet-brown berry, ½in (1.2cm) long.

NATIVE REGION N. Africa, S.W. Asia, Europe.
HABITAT Woods.

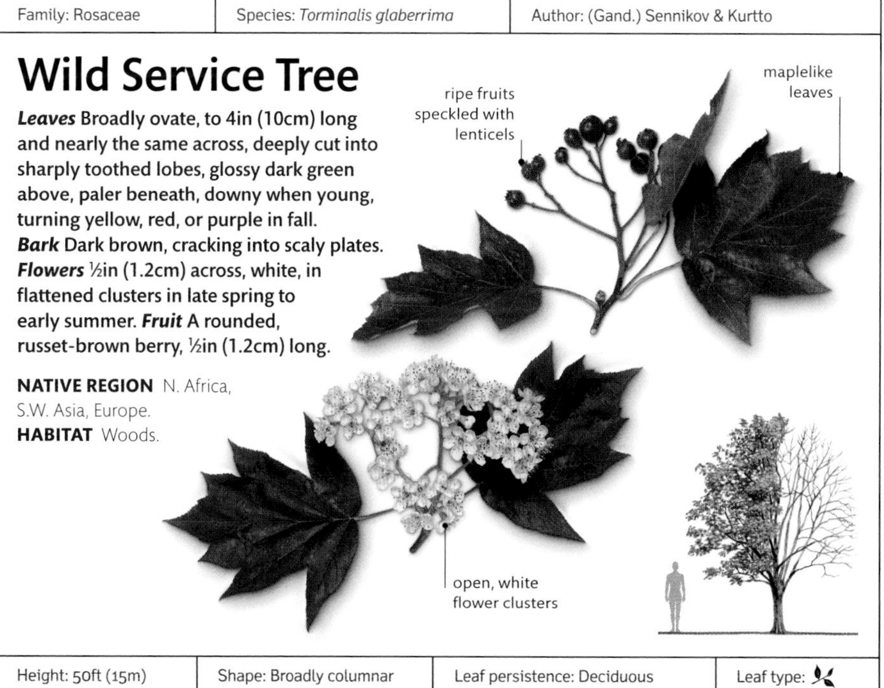

Height: 50ft (15m)	Shape: Broadly columnar	Leaf persistence: Deciduous	Leaf type:

RUTACEAE

ABOUT 2,000 SPECIES of trees, shrubs, and climbing plants belonging to this family are contained in over 150 genera. They are found worldwide, but particularly in tropical and warm temperate regions. The leaves are usually alternate and often compound, and release an aromatic vapor when crushed. Flowers are green to white or yellow, with usually four or five petals.

Family: Rutaceae	Species: *Phellodendron amurense*	Author: Rupr.

Amur Cork Tree

Leaves Pinnate, to 14in (35cm) long, with up to 13 ovate to lanceolate, taper-pointed, untoothed or minutely toothed leaflets, to 4in (10cm) long and 2in (5cm) across, glossy deep green and smooth above, blue-green with hairs at the base of the midrib beneath, turning yellow in fall. ***Bark*** Gray-brown, thick, corky, with prominent ridges. ***Flowers*** Males and females both small and greenish, males with yellow, protruding anthers, borne in conical clusters about 3in (7.5cm) long, on separate plants in midsummer. ***Fruit*** Rounded, ⅜in (1cm) across, green ripening to black.

NATIVE REGION N.E. Asia.
HABITAT Moist places near streams in mountains.

△ var. *lavallei*
Smooth, rather less glossy leaflets, with a gray-green, hairy-veined underside, distinguish this form.

Height: 40ft (12m)	Shape: Broadly spreading	Leaf persistence: Deciduous	Leaf type:

Family: Rutaceae	Species: *Ptelea trifoliata*	Author: L.

Hop Tree

Leaves With three elliptic to ovate, untoothed or sparsely toothed leaflets, to 4in (10cm) long and 1½in (4cm) across, glossy dark green above, usually more or less smooth on both sides, turning yellow in fall, aromatic when crushed. ***Bark*** Dark gray, nearly smooth. ***Flowers*** About ⅜in (1cm) across, yellow-green to green, with four or five petals, in clusters to 3in (7.5cm) across, at the ends of the shoots in early summer. ***Fruit*** With two seeds in the center of a broad, circular wing, to 1in (2.5cm) across, pale green ripening to pale brown.

NATIVE REGION S.E. Canada to Mexico.
HABITAT Moist woods, thickets, and rocky slopes.

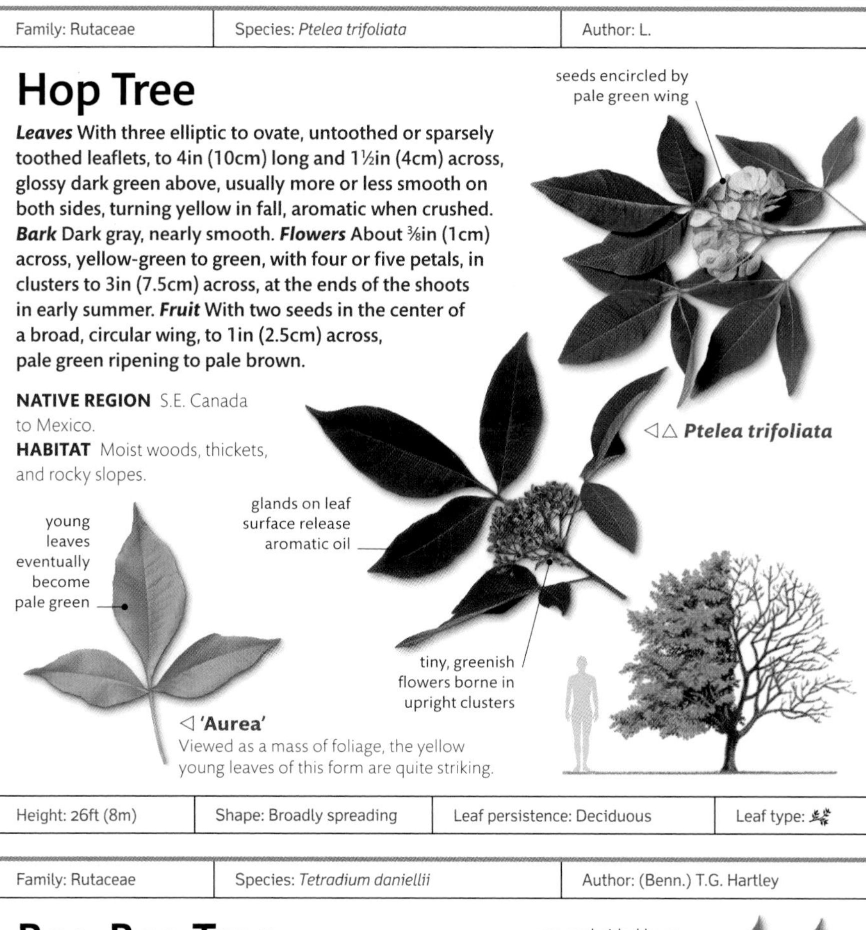
seeds encircled by pale green wing
◁△ *Ptelea trifoliata*
glands on leaf surface release aromatic oil
young leaves eventually become pale green
tiny, greenish flowers borne in upright clusters

◁ **'Aurea'**
Viewed as a mass of foliage, the yellow young leaves of this form are quite striking.

Height: 26ft (8m)	Shape: Broadly spreading	Leaf persistence: Deciduous	Leaf type:

Family: Rutaceae	Species: *Tetradium daniellii*	Author: (Benn.) T.G. Hartley

Bee-Bee Tree

Leaves Pinnate, to 12in (30cm) or more long, with up to 11 ovate or oblong, usually short-pointed, untoothed leaflets, to 4in (10cm) long and 1½in (4cm) across, glossy dark green and smooth above, blue-green and hairy beneath, at least when young. ***Bark*** Gray and smooth. ***Flowers*** Small, white, aromatic, in broadly flattened heads to 6in (15cm) across, at the ends of the shoots in late summer to early fall. ***Fruit*** A small, beaked, red-brown to nearly black capsule, 5/16in (8mm) long, in dense clusters.

NATIVE REGION China.
HABITAT Mountain woods.
REMARK Previously known as *Euodia daniellii.*

unequal-sided base of young leaflets
male flowers have exserted yellow anthers

Height: 50ft (15m)	Shape: Broadly spreading	Leaf persistence: Deciduous	Leaf type:

Family: Rutaceae	Species: *Zanthoxylum ailanthoides*	Author: Siebold & Zucc.

Japanese Prickly Ash

Leaves Pinnate, 12in (30cm) or more long, with up to 15 pairs of oblong, pointed leaflets, to 6in (15cm) long and 2in (5cm) across, light green above, blue-green beneath. ***Bark*** Gray and green, striped, with spiny protuberances. ***Flowers*** Males and females yellow-green, in broad heads at the ends of the shoots, on separate plants in late summer. ***Fruit*** Small, green, with black seeds.

NATIVE REGION E. and S.E. Asia.
HABITAT Wood.

leaflets taper to finely pointed tip

very finely toothed leaflets

Height: 50ft (15m)	Shape: Broadly spreading	Leaf persistence: Deciduous	Leaf type:

Family: Rutaceae	Species: *Zanthoxylum simulans*	Author: Hance

Sichuan Pepper

Leaves Pinnate, to 8in (20cm) long, with up to 11 ovate, sparsely toothed leaflets, glossy green, sometimes prickly above, usually with prickles beneath, the rachis slightly winged, aromatic when crushed, carried on prickly stalks. ***Bark*** Gray, with conical protuberances. ***Flowers*** Small and green, borne in clusters to 2in (5cm) across, in summer. ***Fruit*** Small, round, and warty, very aromatic, 3⁄16in (5mm) across, green ripening to red, drying and splitting open to release glossy black seeds.

NATIVE REGION China, S. Korea.
HABITAT Mountain woods and thickets.
REMARK As the plant grows, spines on the trunk harden, developing into the rough, limpetlike swellings that characterize the bark of this species.

red-stalked, warty fruits

winged leaf rachis

stems carry flattened spines

glands on leaflets release aromatic vapor when crushed

trunk covered in cone-shaped projections

Height: 20ft (6m)	Shape: Broadly spreading	Leaf persistence: Deciduous	Leaf type:

SALICACEAE

THE 50 GENERA and some 1,200 species of deciduous and evergreen trees and shrubs in this family have a worldwide distribution in temperate, tropical, and subtropical regions. Leaves are usually alternate and toothed. The flowers are with or without petals and often have many stamens. Many genera here were previously included in the family Flacourtiaceae.

Family: Salicaceae	Species: *Azara microphylla*	Author: Hook. f.

Azara microphylla

Leaves Obovate to elliptic, to 1in (2.5cm) long, toothed, glossy dark green above, paler beneath, smooth, with a smaller, leaflike stipule at the base. ***Bark*** Gray, with horizontal lenticels, cracking into thin flakes. ***Flowers*** Small, without petals, but with green sepals and conspicuous yellow stamens, in the leaf axils in late winter or early spring. ***Fruit*** A small, orange-red berry.

NATIVE REGION Argentina, Chile.
HABITAT Deciduous forests.

Height: 33ft (10m)	Shape: Narrowly conical	Leaf persistence: Evergreen	Leaf type:

Family: Salicaceae	Species: *Idesia polycarpa*	Author: Maxim.

Idesia polycarpa

Leaves Broadly heart-shaped, to 8in (20cm) long and nearly the same across, heart-shaped at the base, with a short, tapered tip, toothed, bronze-purple becoming dark green above, blue-white beneath, smooth, on long, red stalks. ***Bark*** Gray-white. ***Flowers*** Small and yellow-green, without petals, in large, drooping panicles at the ends of the shoots, on separate plants in early summer. ***Fruit*** A small, red berry, borne in hanging clusters.

NATIVE REGION China, Japan, Korea.
HABITAT Mountain slopes.
REMARK Favors sunny situations.

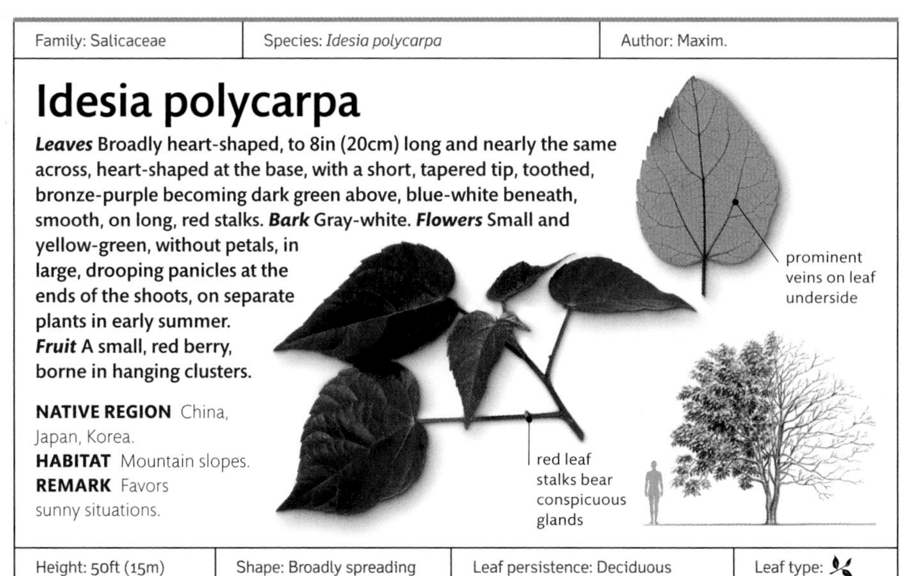

Height: 50ft (15m)	Shape: Broadly spreading	Leaf persistence: Deciduous	Leaf type:

Family: Salicaceae	Species: *Populus alba*	Author: L.

White Poplar

Leaves Variable, on vigorous shoots maplelike, with three to five lobes, to 4in (10cm) long and 3in (7.5cm) across, on short shoots shallowly lobed to wavy-edged, both types white with hairs when young, becoming smooth and dark green above, densely covered in white hairs beneath. ***Bark*** Gray, fissured, dark at the base. ***Flowers*** In drooping catkins, males to 3in (7.5cm) long, gray with red anthers, females to 2in (5cm) long, green, on separate planes in early spring before the young leaves. ***Fruit*** Small, green capsules, borne in catkins to 4in (10cm) long, opening to release tiny seeds held in white, cotton wool-like hairs.

NATIVE REGION N. Africa, C. and W. Asia, Europe.
HABITAT Woods, in moist and dry places.
REMARK Also known as abele.

Height: 100ft (30m)	Shape: Broadly columnar	Leaf persistence: Deciduous	Leaf type: 

Family: Salicaceae	Species: *Populus balsamifera*	Author: L.

Balsam Poplar

Leaves Ovate, to 4¼in (12cm) long and 4in (10cm) across, taper-pointed, finely toothed, glossy green above, whitish and net-veined beneath, smooth on both sides, balsam-scented when young. ***Bark*** Gray, ridged. ***Flowers*** In catkins, males to 2in (5cm) long, females to 3in (7.5cm) long, green, on separate planes in early spring. ***Fruit*** Small green capsules, in catkins to 12in (30cm) long.

NATIVE REGION North America.
HABITAT Moist woods.

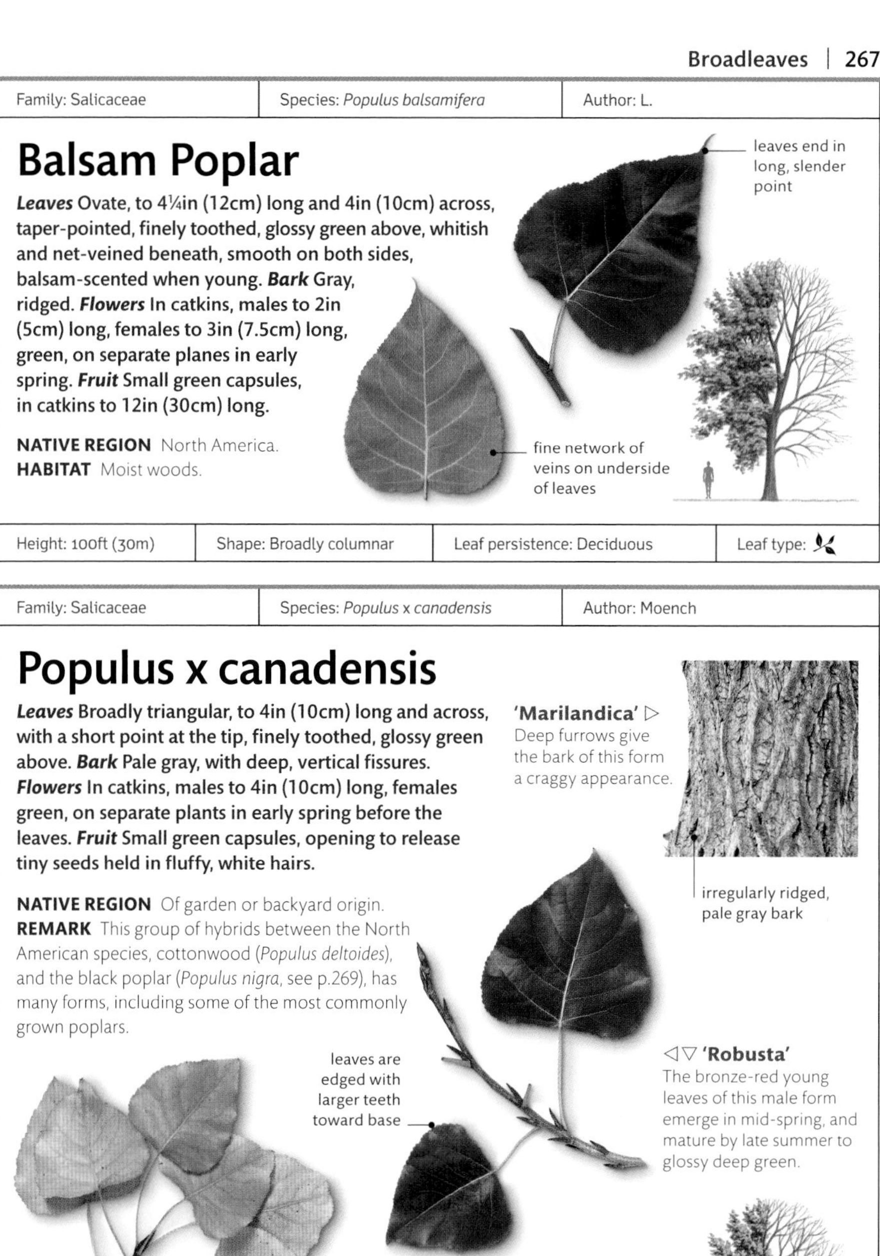

Height: 100ft (30m)	Shape: Broadly columnar	Leaf persistence: Deciduous	Leaf type:

Family: Salicaceae	Species: *Populus* x *canadensis*	Author: Moench

Populus x canadensis

Leaves Broadly triangular, to 4in (10cm) long and across, with a short point at the tip, finely toothed, glossy green above. ***Bark*** Pale gray, with deep, vertical fissures. ***Flowers*** In catkins, males to 4in (10cm) long, females green, on separate plants in early spring before the leaves. ***Fruit*** Small green capsules, opening to release tiny seeds held in fluffy, white hairs.

NATIVE REGION Of garden or backyard origin.
REMARK This group of hybrids between the North American species, cottonwood (*Populus deltoides*), and the black poplar (*Populus nigra*, see p.269), has many forms, including some of the most commonly grown poplars.

'Marilandica' ▷
Deep furrows give the bark of this form a craggy appearance.

irregularly ridged, pale gray bark

leaves are edged with larger teeth toward base

◁▽ **'Robusta'**
The bronze-red young leaves of this male form emerge in mid-spring, and mature by late summer to glossy deep green.

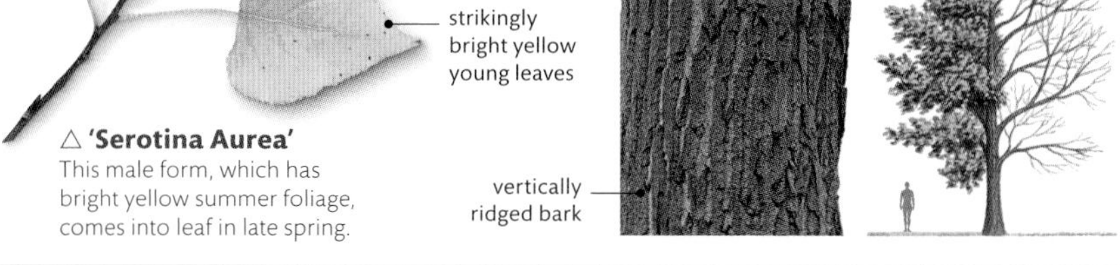

△ **'Serotina Aurea'**
This male form, which has bright yellow summer foliage, comes into leaf in late spring.

Height: 100ft (30m)	Shape: Broadly columnar	Leaf persistence: Deciduous	Leaf type: 

Family: Salicaceae	Species: *Populus* x *canescens*	Author: (Aiton) Sm.

Gray Poplar

Leaves Rounded to ovate, to 3in (7.5cm) long and across, occasionally shallowly lobed, toothed, densely covered in white hairs when young, becoming smooth and glossy deep green above, gray and hairy beneath. ***Bark*** Pale gray, with dark, diamond-shaped fissures when young, becoming dark brown and deeply furrowed with age. ***Flowers*** In drooping catkins, males to 4in (10cm) long, gray with red anthers, females to 4in (10cm) long, green, on separate planes in early spring. ***Fruit*** Small, green capsules, borne in catkins, opening to release tiny seeds held in white, cotton wool-like hairs.

NATIVE REGION Europe to N. China.
HABITAT River valleys.
REMARK A hybrid between the white poplar (*Populus alba*, see p.266) and the aspen (*Populus tremula*, see p.270), widely naturalized from cultivation.

upper leaf surface soon becomes smooth

rounded teeth at leaf margin

slender flattened leaf stalks

gray-hairy leaf underside

young leaves have gray hairs on upper surface

Height: 100ft (30m)	Shape: Broadly columnar	Leaf persistence: Deciduous	Leaf type:

Family: Salicaceae	Species: *Populus* x *jackii*	Author: Sarg.

Balm of Gilead

Leaves Broadly ovate, to 6in (15cm) long and 4in (10cm) across, usually heart-shaped at the base, taper-pointed, toothed, dark green above, whitish and net-veined beneath, slightly downy on both sides. ***Bark*** Gray and smooth, becoming ridged with age. ***Flowers*** Females only, green, in drooping catkins in early spring. ***Fruit*** Small, green capsules, borne in catkins to 6in (15cm) long, opening to release tiny seeds held in white, cotton wool-like hairs.

NATIVE REGION Canada, N.E. US.
REMARK Also known as Ontario poplar. This species is thought to be a hybrid of the balsam poplar (*Populus balsamifera*, see p.267), naturalized from gardens on riverbanks in E. North America. 'Aurora,' a common form, has leaves blotched white, cream, and pink.

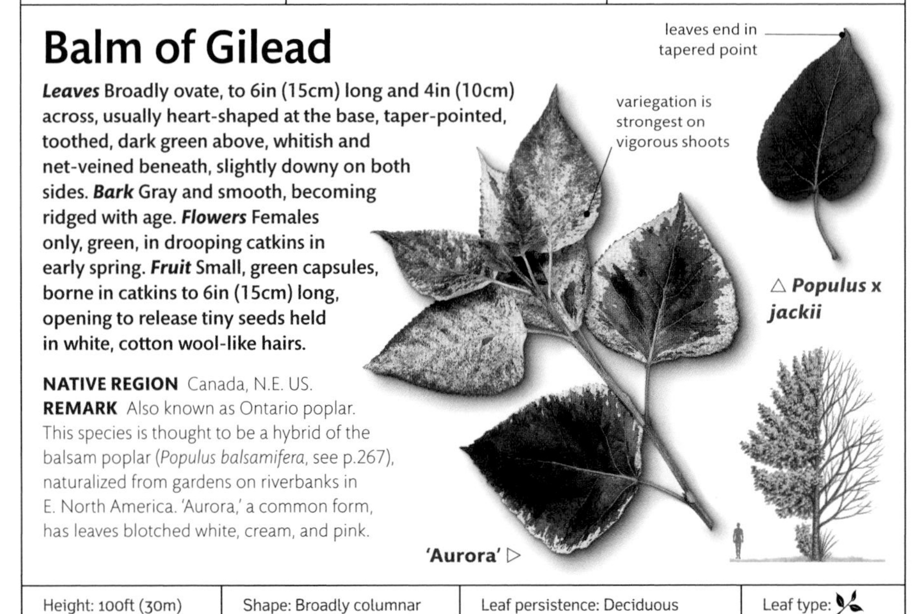

△ ***Populus* x *jackii***

'Aurora' ▷

Height: 100ft (30m)	Shape: Broadly columnar	Leaf persistence: Deciduous	Leaf type:

Family: Salicaceae	Species: *Populus lasiocarpa*	Author: Oliv.

Populus lasiocarpa

Leaves **Broadly ovate and large, to 12in (30cm) long and 8in (20cm) across, deeply heart-shaped at the base, edged with small, rounded teeth at the margin, downy on both sides when young, becoming deep green and smooth above, with red veins and stalk, carried on very stout shoots.** ***Bark*** **Gray-brown and vertically fissured.** ***Flowers*** **Males and females both yellow-green, males with red anthers, borne in stout, drooping catkins to 4m (10cm) long, sometimes on the same spike, usually on separate plants in mid-spring.** ***Fruit*** **Small, green capsules, borne in catkins, opening to release tiny seeds held in white, cotton wool-like hairs.**

NATIVE REGION C. China.
HABITAT Moist woods in mountains.
REMARK The very large, long-stalked leaves easily distinguish this species from others of its genus.

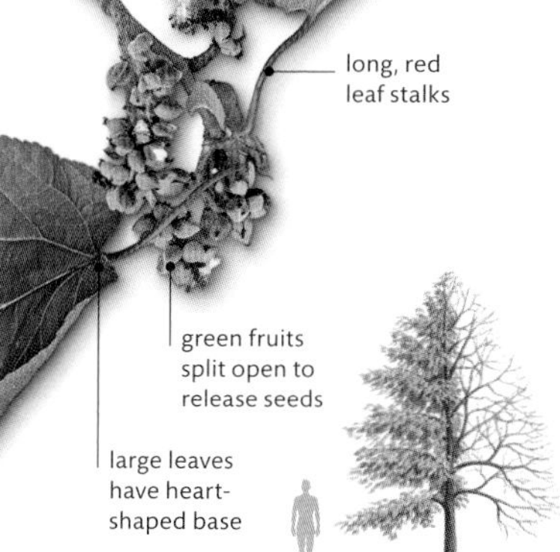

Height: 65ft (20m)	Shape: Broadly conical	Leaf persistence: Deciduous	Leaf type:

Family: Salicaceae	Species: *Populus nigra*	Author: L.

Black Poplar

Leaves **Triangular to ovate, to 4in (10cm) long and nearly the same across, larger on vigorous shoots, taper-pointed at the tip, bluntly toothed, with a narrow, translucent margin, bronze becoming glossy dark green above, paler beneath, smooth on both sides, turning yellow in fall.** ***Bark*** **Dark gray-brown, coarsely fissured, often with large burrs.** ***Flowers*** **Males with red anthers, females green, in drooping catkins to 2in (5cm) long, on separate planes in early spring before the young leaves emerge.** ***Fruit*** **Small, green capsules, borne in catkins, opening to release tiny seeds held in white, cotton wool-like hairs.**

NATIVE REGION N. Africa.
HABITAT River valleys.
REMARK *Populus nigra* 'Italica,' the Lombardy poplar, is an upright form.

leaf tip usually has no teeth

slender, flattened leaf stalks

leaf base has no glands

Height: 100ft (30m)	Shape: Broadly spreading	Leaf persistence: Deciduous	Leaf type: 

Family: Salicaceae	Species: *Populus szechuanica*	Author: C.K. Schneid.

Populus szechuanica

Leaves Ovate, to 12in (30cm) long and 8in (20cm) or more across on vigorous shoots, usually much smaller on short shoots, rounded to heart-shaped at the base, tapered at the tip, blunt-toothed, reddish to bronzy when young, becoming dark green above, paler beneath, smooth on both sides. ***Bark*** Pinkish gray, cracking into large, smooth flakes with age. ***Flowers*** Small and without petals, males with deep red anthers, females green, borne in drooping catkins on separate plants in mid-spring, before the young leaves emerge. ***Fruit*** Small, green capsules, in catkins to 6¼in (16cm) long, opening to release tiny seeds held in white, cotton wool-like hairs.

NATIVE REGION W. China.
HABITAT Moist mountain woods.
REMARK The leaves of the form shown here, var. *tibetica*, are slightly hairy on the underside.

Height: 100ft (30m)	Shape: Broadly columnar	Leaf persistence: Deciduous	Leaf type:

Family: Salicaceae	Species: *Populus tremula*	Author: L.

Aspen

Leaves Rounded to broadly ovate, to 3in (7.5cm) long and across, ovate and larger on sucker shoots, with rounded teeth, bronze when young becoming gray-green above, paler beneath, usually smooth on both sides, turning yellow in fall, carried on flattened stalks. ***Bark*** Gray and smooth, becoming darker and ridged at the base. ***Flowers*** Males with red anthers, females green, borne in drooping catkins to 3in (7.5cm) long, on separate plants in early spring before the young leaves emerge. ***Fruit*** Small, green capsules, in catkins, opening to release tiny seeds held in white, cotton wool-like hairs.

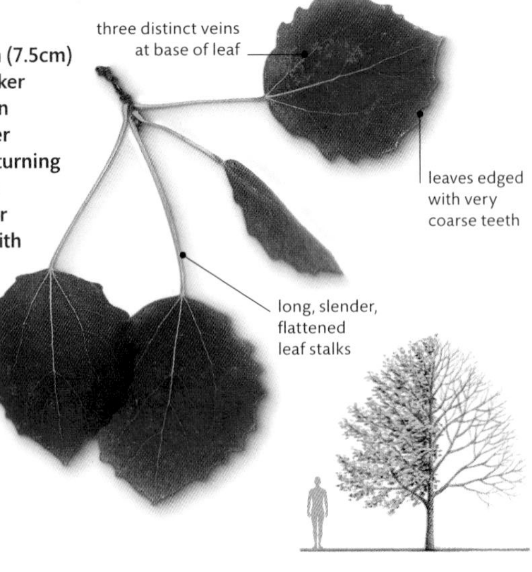

NATIVE REGION Asia, N. Africa, Europe.
HABITAT Woods and scrub on poor soil. In the south of its region, this species occurs in the mountains.

Height: 65ft (20m)	Shape: Broadly spreading	Leaf persistence: Deciduous	Leaf type:

Family: Salicaceae	Species: *Salix alba*	Author: L.

White Willow

Leaves **Lanceolate, to 4in (10cm) long and ⅝in (1.5cm) across, tapered at both ends, more slender at the tip, silvery-hairy when young, becoming green above, gray or blue-green beneath. *Bark* Gray-brown, deeply fissured. *Flowers* Males and females both very small and without petals, clustered in slender, cylindrical, spreading to nearly upright catkins, males to 2in (5cm) long, yellow, females to 1½in (4cm) long, on separate plants in spring as the young leaves emerge. *Fruit* A small, green capsule, 3⁄16in (5mm) long, opening to release fluffy, white seeds.**

NATIVE REGION W. Asia, Europe.
HABITAT Riversides and meadows by water.
REMARK This species is widely cultivated in its native region, where it is planted particularly in moist, coastal areas and by rivers.

male catkins have yellow anthers

green female catkins

△▽ ***Salix alba***

visibly hairy, silvery young foliage

leaves taper to fine point

dark green mature foliage

leaf buds on bare winter shoot

△ **'Britzensis'**
The young shoots of this form, which is commonly known as the scarlet willow, are bright orange-red during the winter months.

var. *caerulea* ▷
Cricket bats are traditionally made from the wood of this variety, hence its common name, cricket-bat willow.

blue-gray, slightly glaucous leaves

Height: 80ft (25m)	Shape: Broadly columnar	Leaf persistence: Deciduous	Leaf type:

Family: Salicaceae	Species: *Salix babylonica*	Author: L.

Chinese Weeping Willow

Leaves Lanceolate, to 4in (10cm) long and ¾in (2cm) across, tapering to a long, slender point at the tip, finely toothed at the margin, green above, bluish green and hairy when young, becoming smooth beneath, carried on hanging, glossy brown shoots. ***Bark*** Gray-brown, fissured into rough, vertical ridges. ***Flowers*** Very small and without petals, borne in slender, cylindrical catkins, males to 2in (5cm) long, yellow, females to 1in (2.5cm) long, green, on separate plants in spring as the young leaves emerge. ***Fruit*** A small, green capsule, 3/16in (5mm) long, opening to release fluffy, white seeds.

NATIVE REGION Korea, N. China.
HABITAT In dry areas, but widely cultivated in warm regions.
REMARK In colder regions the common weeping willow is *Salix* x *sepulcralis* 'Chrysocoma.'

male flowers, with yellow anthers, borne in catkins

◁ ***Salix babylonica***

long slender, drooping shoots

young leaves emerge with flowers

green female flowers, clustered in catkins

▽ **var. *pekinensis***
This form is also known as *Salix matsudana* and Pekin willow. It has a narrowly upright habit.

visibly twisted shoots and leaves

▽ **'Pendula'**
This particularly graceful form of the weeping willow has typically long, drooping shoots and denser foliage.

finely taper-pointed, drooping leaves

'Tortuosa' ▷
Commonly known as dragon's claw willow, this form has curiously contorted shoots and leaves.

Height: 40ft (12m)	Shape: Broadly weeping	Leaf persistence: Deciduous	Leaf type:

Family: Salicaceae	Species: *Salix daphnoides*	Author: Vill.

Violet Willow

Leaves Narrowly elliptic, to 4¾in (12cm) long and 1¼in (3cm) across, taper-pointed, shallowly toothed, glossy dark green above, blue-green beneath, hairy becoming smooth on both sides, the shoots normally bloomy becoming glossy red-brown. ***Bark*** Gray and smooth. ***Flowers*** Males and females both very small and without petals, males with yellow anthers, borne in silky-hairy catkins to 1½in (4cm) long, in late winter to early spring before the leaves emerge. ***Fruit*** A small, green capsule, 3/16in (5mm) long, opening to release fluffy, white seeds.

NATIVE REGION Europe.
HABITAT Moist woods.

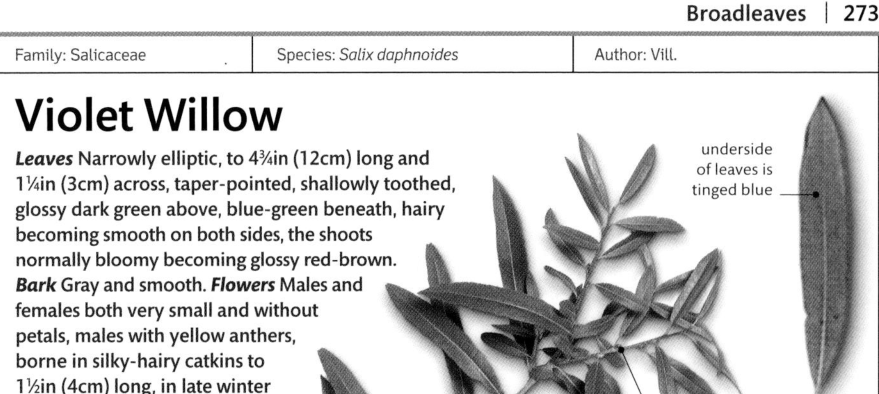

Height: 33ft (10m)	Shape: Broadly conical	Leaf persistence: Deciduous	Leaf type:

Family: Salicaceae	Species: *Salix* x *fragilis*	Author: L.

Crack Willow

Leaves Lanceolate, to 6in (15cm) long and 1¼in (3cm) across, tapered to a fine point at the tip, finely toothed, silky-hairy when young becoming glossy dark green above, blue-green beneath, smooth on both sides. ***Bark*** Dark gray, deeply fissured. ***Flowers*** Males and females both very small and without petals, males yellow, females green, in cylindrical, slender catkins to 2½in (6cm) long, borne on separate plants in spring at the same time as the young leaves emerge. ***Fruit*** A small, green capsule, ⅛in (3mm) long, opening to release fluffy, white seeds.

NATIVE REGION Asia, Europe.
HABITAT Riversides.
REMARK The twigs snap easily from the branches, giving rise to both the scientific and the common name.

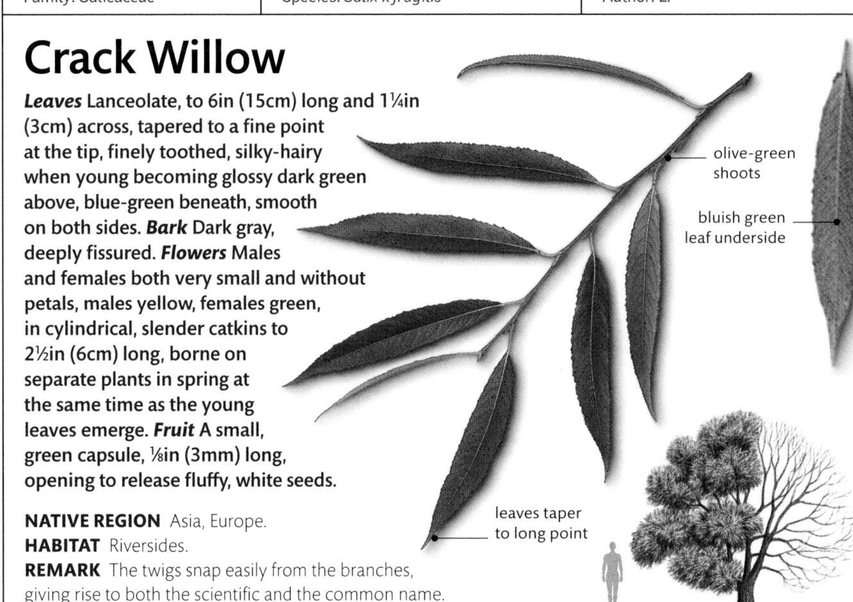

Height: 50ft (15m)	Shape: Broadly spreading	Leaf persistence: Deciduous	Leaf type:

Family: Salicaceae	Species: *Salix pentandra*	Author: L.

Bay Willow

Leaves Elliptic to narrowly ovate, to 4¾in (12cm) long and 2in (5cm) across, tapering to a short point, finely toothed, glossy, very dark green above, paler beneath, smooth on both sides, slightly aromatic. ***Bark*** Gray-brown, with shallow fissures. ***Flowers*** Males and females both very small and without petals, males bright yellow, females green, in cylindrical catkins to 2in (5cm) long, on separate plants in early summer after the young leaves emerge. ***Fruit*** A small, green capsule, ¼in (6mm) long, opening to release fluffy, white seeds.

NATIVE REGION Asia, Europe.
HABITAT Riverbanks and meadows.

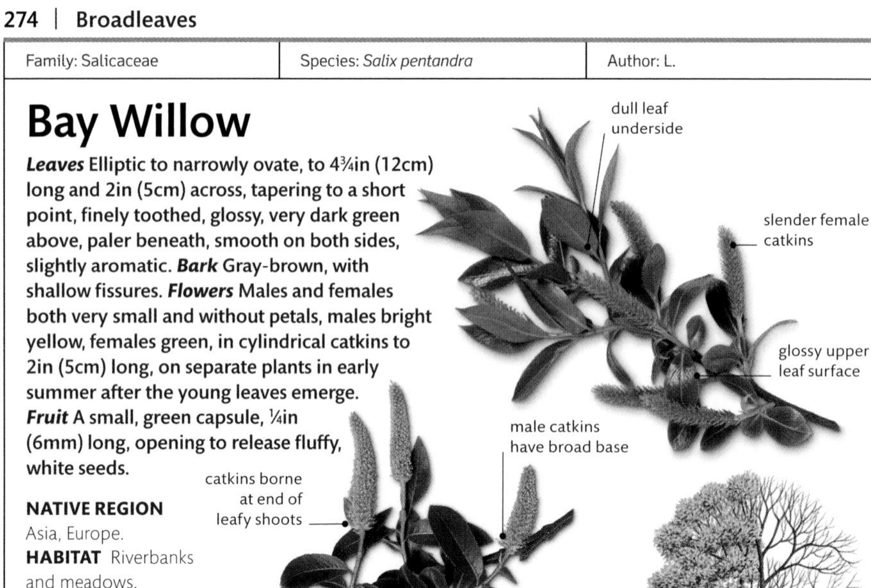

Height: 50ft (15m)	Shape: Broadly spreading	Leaf persistence: Deciduous	Leaf type:

Family: Salicaceae	Species: *Salix* x *sepulcralis*	Author: Simonk.

Salix x sepulcralis

Leaves Narrowly lanceolate, to 4¾in (12cm) long and ¾in (2cm) across, taper-pointed, finely toothed, thinly hairy when young, becoming bright green above, blue-green beneath, smooth, on slender, hanging, yellowish shoots. ***Bark*** Pale gray-brown, with shallow fissures. ***Flowers*** Yellow-green, small and without petals, in catkins to 3in (7.5cm) long, both sexes often on the same spike, in spring. ***Fruit*** A small, green capsule, ⅛in (3mm) long, opening to release fluffy, white seeds.

NATIVE REGION Of garden or backyard origin.
REMARK A hybrid between white willow (*Salix alba*, see p.271) and Chinese weeping willow (*Salix babylonica*, see p.272). Of its many different forms, 'Chrysocoma'—the familiar weeping willow shown here—is the most well known.

▽ **'Chrysocoma'**

long, fine point at tip of slender leaves

upright, curved catkins

blue-green leaf underside

Height: 65ft (20m)	Shape: Broadly weeping	Leaf persistence: Deciduous	Leaf type:

SAPINDACEAE

WIDELY DISTRIBUTED MAINLY in tropical and subtropical regions, this family has nearly 2,000 species of deciduous trees, shrubs, and climbers, collected in about 140 genera.

The leaves are alternate or opposite and can be simple or compound. The often small flowers usually have five petals. The fruit is dry and winged, a capsule, nut, or berry.

Family: Sapindaceae	Species: *Acer buergerianum*	Author: Miq.

Trident Maple

Leaves Palmate, to 4in (10cm) long and across, narrowed at the base, with three forward-pointing lobes, usually untoothed or sparsely toothed at the margin, dark green above, bluish beneath, becoming smooth on both sides, turning red in fall.
Bark Gray-brown, peeling in scaly plates with age.
Flowers Small and yellow-green, in broadly conical, upright clusters in spring with the young leaves.
Fruit With parallel, upright wings, to 1in (2.5cm) long, green or reddish at first, ripening to brown.

NATIVE REGION China, Japan.
HABITAT Mountain woods.

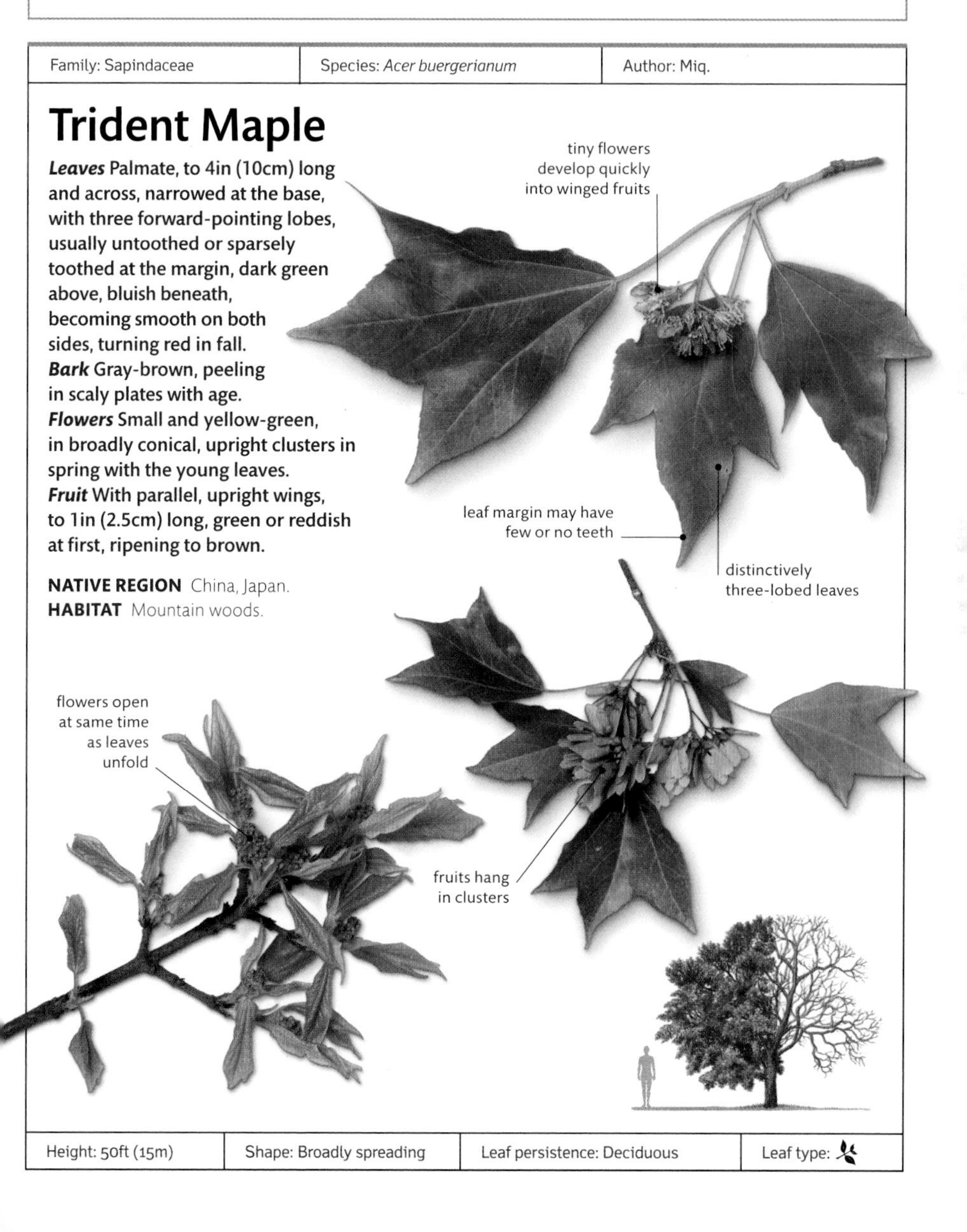

Height: 50ft (15m)	Shape: Broadly spreading	Leaf persistence: Deciduous	Leaf type:

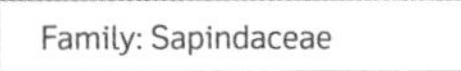

Family: Sapindaceae	Species: *Acer campestre*	Author: L.

Field Maple

Leaves Palmately lobed, to 3in (7.5cm) long and 4in (10cm) across, with five lobes, heart-shaped at the base, dark green above, paler and downy beneath, turning yellow in fall; leaf stalk with milky juice when cut. ***Bark*** Pale brown, corky, fissured with age. ***Flowers*** Small and green, in upright clusters in spring with the leaves. ***Fruit*** To 1in (2.5cm) long, sometimes red at first, in hanging clusters.

NATIVE REGION N. Africa, S.W. Asia, Europe.
HABITAT Woods, scrub, and hedgerows.

larger leaf lobes have smaller lobes toward tip

◁△ ***Acer campestre***

widely spreading fruit wings

young leaves expand at flowering time

▷ **'Pulverulentum'**
The smaller leaves of this form are heavily mottled with white.

variable leaf markings

Height: 50ft (15m)	Shape: Broadly spreading	Leaf persistence: Deciduous	Leaf type:

Family: Sapindaceae	Species: *Acer capillipes*	Author: Maxim.

Red Snake-bark Maple

Leaves To 6in (15cm) long and 4in (10cm) across, with three lobes, the central lobe much the largest, the side lobes short, all tapering to a slender point, toothed, red when young, becoming rich green above, paler and smooth beneath, usually red in fall, on red stalks. ***Bark*** Green and gray, with vertical, white stripes. ***Flowers*** Small and green, borne in drooping racemes in late spring at the same time as the young leaves emerge. ***Fruit*** With spreading wings, to ¾in (2cm) long, green ripening to red.

flowers borne in slender racemes

leaves color in the fall

NATIVE REGION Japan.
HABITAT Woods by mountain streams, on moist soil.
REMARK This species is one of the snake-bark maples, which are easily distinguished by their characteristically striped bark.

tiny pegs in vein axils on leaf underside

gray-green, white-striped bark

Height: 65ft (20m)	Shape: Broadly columnar	Leaf persistence: Deciduous	Leaf type:

Family: Sapindaceae	Species: *Acer cappadocicum*	Author: Gled.

Cappadocian Maple

Leaves Palmately lobed, to 4in (10cm) long and 6in (15cm) across, with five to seven taper-pointed, untoothed lobes, heart-shaped at the base, bright green above, smooth on both sides, except for tufts of hairs in the vein axils beneath, turning clear yellow in fall; leaf stalk with milky juice when cut. ***Bark*** Gray and smooth. ***Flowers*** Small and yellow-green, borne in upright clusters in late spring with the young leaves. ***Fruit*** With spreading pale green wings, to 1½in (4cm) long.

NATIVE REGION W. Asia to China.
HABITAT Forests.
REMARK In Tibet, burrs on the trunk of the tree are made into drinking cups. Subsp. *lobelii*, from S. Italy, also known as *Acer lobelii*, is a narrow tree—at least when young—with bloomy shoots and wavy-edged leaves.

◁△ ***Acer cappadocicum***

◁ **'Aureum'**
The yellow leaves of this form turn green in late summer.

◁△▷▽**subsp. *lobelii***

Height: 65ft (20m)	Shape: Broadly spreading	Leaf persistence: Deciduous	Leaf type:

Family: Sapindaceae	Species: *Acer carpinifolium*	Author: Siebold & Zucc.

Hornbeam Maple

Leaves **Oblong, to 6in (15cm) long and 2in (5cm) across, unlobed, taper-pointed at the tip, sharply toothed, with numerous parallel veins, dark green above, paler and downy on the veins when young beneath, turning yellow and brown in fall.** ***Bark*** **Gray and smooth, with conspicuous lenticels.** ***Flowers*** **Small and yellow-green, on slender stalks, borne in hanging clusters in late spring with the young leaves.** ***Fruit*** **With wings, to ¾in (2cm) long.**

NATIVE REGION Japan.
HABITAT Deciduous woods by mountain streams.
REMARK This unusual species is named for the resemblance of its leaves to those of the hornbeams (*Carpinus*, see pp.126-127), which distinguishes it from other maples.

conspicuously veined leaves
leaves edged with sharp teeth
fruit wings arranged at right angles
tiny, slender-stalked flowers

Height: 33ft (10m)	Shape: Broadly conical	Leaf persistence: Deciduous	Leaf type:

Family: Sapindaceae	Species: *Acer circinatum*	Author: Pursh

Vine Maple

Leaves **To 4¾in (12cm) across, with seven to nine toothed lobes, pale green above, downy when young beneath, turning orange and red in fall.** ***Bark*** **Gray-brown, smooth.** ***Flowers*** **Small, with white petals and reddish sepals, borne in drooping clusters in late spring.** ***Fruit*** **With spreading, reddish wings, to 1¼in (3cm) long.**

NATIVE REGION W. US.
HABITAT Evergreen forests.

lobes have pointed teeth
wings turn red as fruits ripen

Height: 20ft (6m)	Shape: Broadly spreading	Leaf persistence: Deciduous	Leaf type:

Family: Aceraceae	Species: *Acer cissifolium*	Author: (Siebold & Zucc.) K. Koch

Ivy-leaved Maple

Leaves **With three ovate to obovate leaflets, to 4in (10cm) long, dark green above, smooth, turning yellow or red in fall.** ***Bark*** **Yellow-gray, rough, with raised lenticels.** ***Flowers*** **Males and females both tiny, yellow, numerous, in slender racemes to 4in (10cm) long, on separate plants in spring.** ***Fruit*** **With nearly parallel wings.**

NATIVE REGION Japan.
HABITAT By streams.

deeply toothed leaflets
green wings ripen to red
female flowers show tiny, developing fruit wings

Height: 50ft (15m)	Shape: Broadly spreading	Leaf persistence: Deciduous	Leaf type: 

Family: Sapindaceae	Species: *Acer crataegifolium*	Author: Siebold & Zucc.

Hawthorn Maple

Leaves Ovate, to 3in (7.5cm) long and 2in (5cm) across, with three toothed lobes, the central lobe long and taper-pointed, dark green above, paler beneath, smooth. ***Bark*** Green, with vertical stripes. ***Flowers*** Small and yellow-green, in upright or drooping racemes in spring with the leaves. ***Fruit*** With spreading, red-tinged wings, to 1¼in (3cm) long.

NATIVE REGION C. and S. Japan.
HABITAT Forests and sunny places on low mountains.

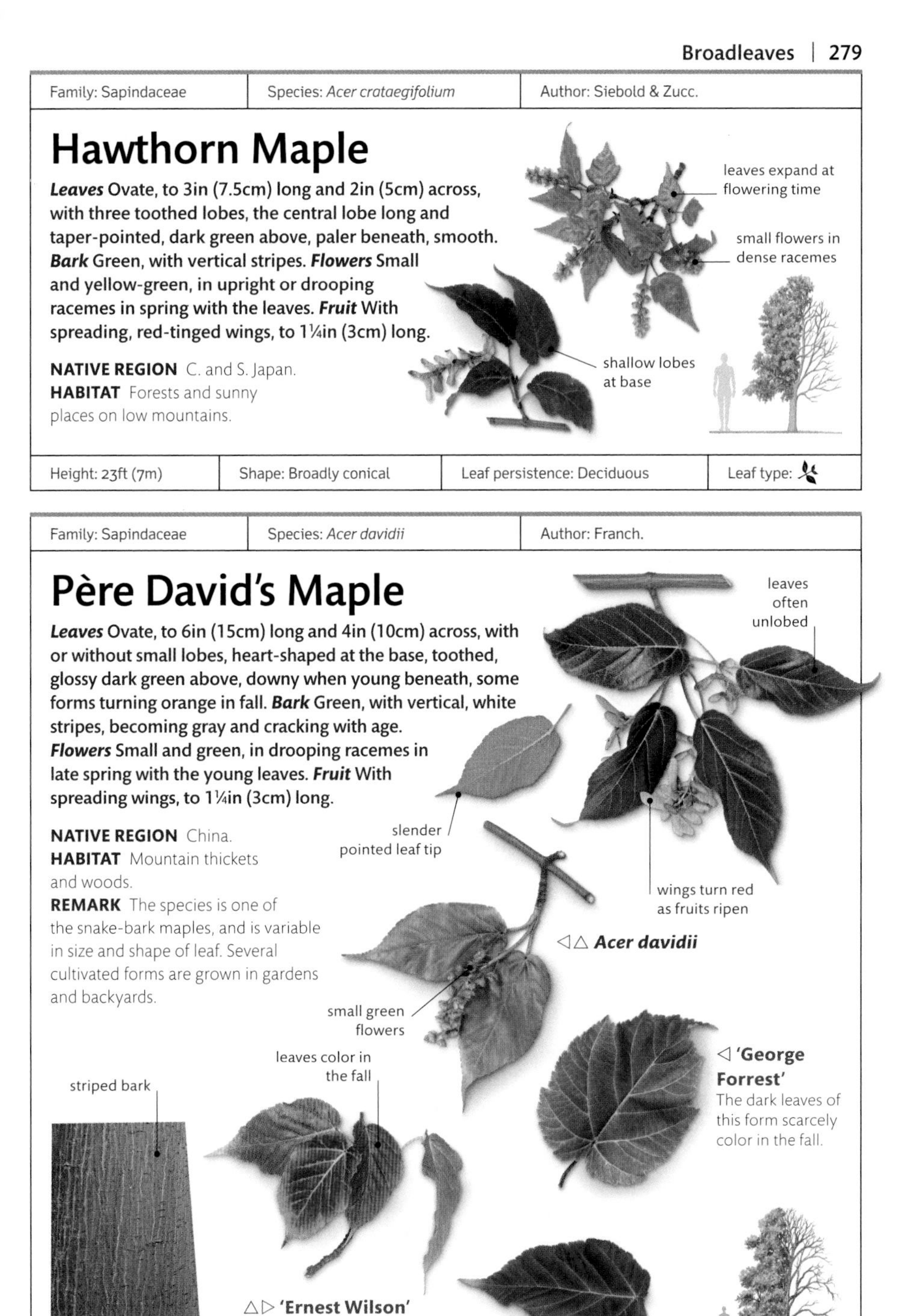

Height: 23ft (7m)	Shape: Broadly conical	Leaf persistence: Deciduous	Leaf type:

Family: Sapindaceae	Species: *Acer davidii*	Author: Franch.

Père David's Maple

Leaves Ovate, to 6in (15cm) long and 4in (10cm) across, with or without small lobes, heart-shaped at the base, toothed, glossy dark green above, downy when young beneath, some forms turning orange in fall. ***Bark*** Green, with vertical, white stripes, becoming gray and cracking with age. ***Flowers*** Small and green, in drooping racemes in late spring with the young leaves. ***Fruit*** With spreading wings, to 1¼in (3cm) long.

NATIVE REGION China.
HABITAT Mountain thickets and woods.
REMARK The species is one of the snake-bark maples, and is variable in size and shape of leaf. Several cultivated forms are grown in gardens and backyards.

◁△ ***Acer davidii***

◁ **'George Forrest'**
The dark leaves of this form scarcely color in the fall.

△▷ **'Ernest Wilson'**
The large leaves of this form turn orange in the fall.

Height: 50ft (15m)	Shape: Broadly conical	Leaf persistence: Deciduous	Leaf type:

Family: Sapindaceae	Species: *Acer griseum*	Author: (Franch.) Pax

Paperbark Maple

Leaves **With three elliptic leaflets, each with several large, blunt teeth on each side, the central leaflet to 4in (10cm) long and 2in (5cm) across, dark green above, blue-white and densely covered with soft hairs beneath, turning red in fall.**
Bark **Reddish to pale cinnamon-brown, peeling in thin,papery flakes.** ***Flowers*** **Small, yellow-green, on hairy stalks, in drooping clusters in late spring with the young leaves.** ***Fruit*** **With broad, pale green wings, to 1¼in (3cm) long.**

NATIVE REGION C. China.
HABITAT Mountain woods.
REMARK Easily distinguished by its peeling bark.

Height: 50ft (15m)	Shape: Broadly columnar	Leaf persistence: Deciduous	Leaf type:

Family: Sapindaceae	Species: *Acer henryi*	Author: Pax

Henry's Maple

Leaves **With three elliptic, untoothed or few-toothed, taper-pointed leaflets, to 4in (10cm) long and 1½in (4cm) across, dark green above, usually hairy beneath, turning brilliant red in fall.** ***Bark*** **Gray, with conspicuous, raised lenticels.** ***Flowers*** **Tiny and yellowish, numerous, borne in slender racemes to 8in (20cm) long, in spring before or with the young leaves.** ***Fruit*** **With nearly parallel wings, to 1in (2.5cm) long, green ripening to red.**

NATIVE REGION
C. China.
HABITAT
Mountain woods.

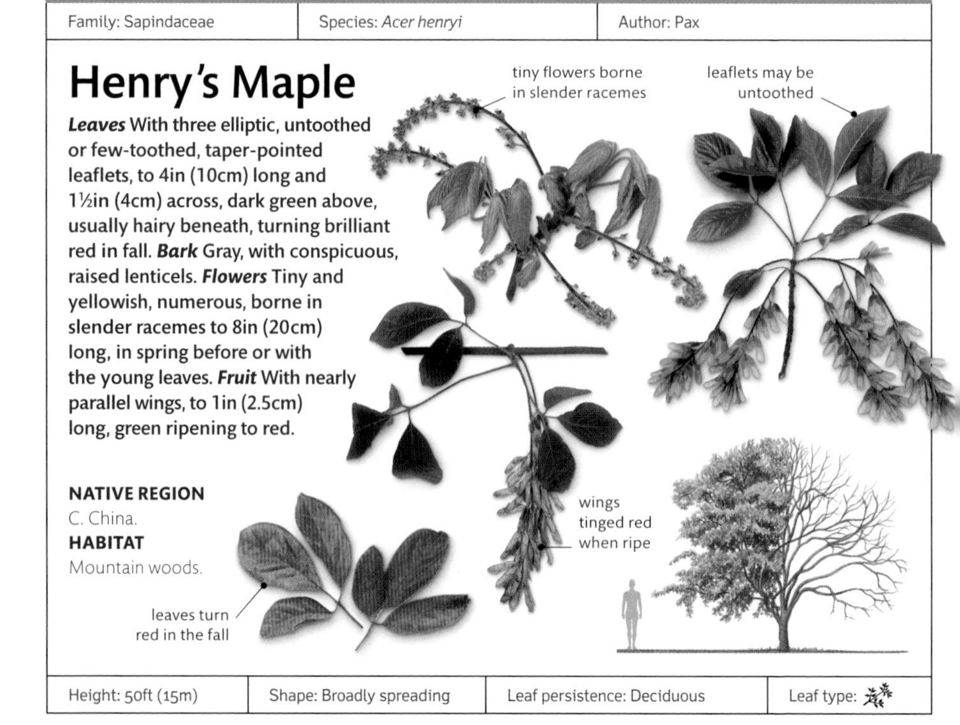

Height: 50ft (15m)	Shape: Broadly spreading	Leaf persistence: Deciduous	Leaf type:

Family: Sapindaceae	Species: *Acer japonicum*	Author: Thunb.

Fullmoon Maple

Leaves Rounded in outline, with 7 to 11 taper-pointed, sharply toothed, ovate to lanceolate lobes, to 5in (13cm) long and across, silky-hairy on both sides when young, becoming dark green above, nearly smooth on both sides, turning red in fall, carried on downy stalks. ***Bark*** Gray-brown and smooth. ***Flowers*** Small and red-purple, with yellow anthers, borne in long-stalked, drooping clusters in spring as the young leaves emerge. ***Fruit*** With spreading wings, green or green tinged red, to 1in (2.5cm) long.

NATIVE REGION Japan.
HABITAT Mountain woods, usually in dry, sunny situations.
REMARK The form shown, 'Vitifolium,' has somewhat larger leaves, with 10 to 12 lobes, and bronzy young foliage.

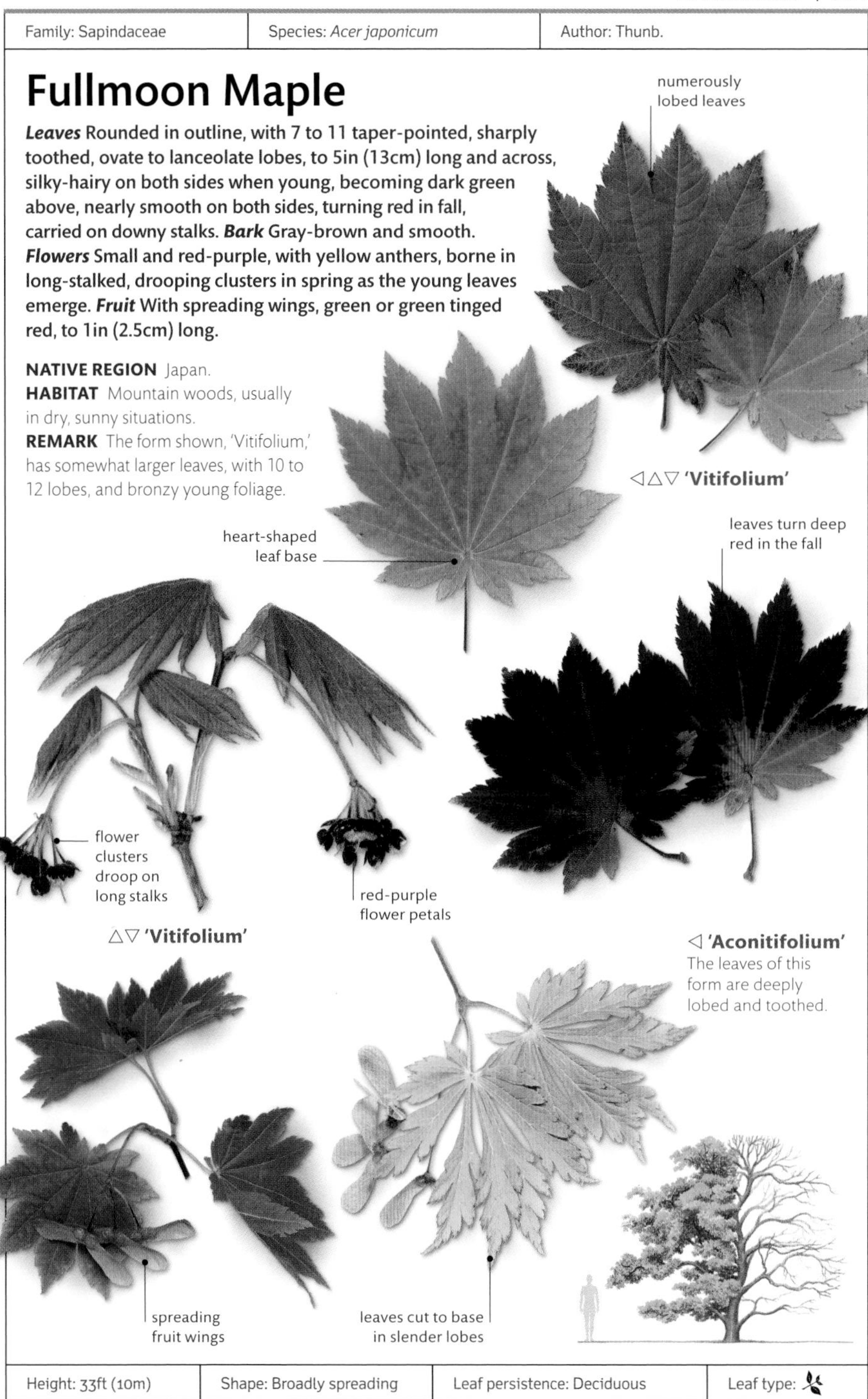

Height: 33ft (10m)	Shape: Broadly spreading	Leaf persistence: Deciduous	Leaf type:

Family: Sapindaceae	Species: *Acer macrophyllum*	Author: Pursh

Oregon Maple

Leaves **Palmately lobed, to 10in (25cm) long and 12in (30cm) across, with three to five lobes, each lobe with few large teeth, dark green above, downy when young beneath, turning deep yellow, orange to brown in fall, on long stalks.** ***Bark*** **Gray-brown, shallowly fissured into vertical ridges.** ***Flowers*** **Yellow, fragrant, in hanging clusters to 10in (25cm) long, in spring as the leaves emerge.** ***Fruit*** **Bristly, with large, smooth wings set at right angles, to 2in (5cm) long, borne in large, hanging clusters.**

NATIVE REGION W. US.
HABITAT Streambanks, moist woods, and canyons.
REMARK Also known as big-leaf maple, canyon maple. Size is a distinguishing feature of this handsome tree, which is bold in leaf, flower, and fruit.

Height: 80ft (25m)	Shape: Broadly columnar	Leaf persistence: Deciduous	Leaf type:

Family: Sapindaceae	Species: *Acer maximowiczianum*	Author: Miq.

Nikko Maple

Leaves With three untoothed or slightly toothed leaflets, the central leaflet to 4in (10cm) long and 2½in (6cm) across, the lateral leaflets smaller and unequal-sided at the base, dark green and smooth above, blue-white and softly hairy beneath, turning red in fall. ***Bark*** Gray-brown and smooth. ***Flowers*** Small and yellow, borne drooping in clusters of three, on downy stalks, in late spring at the same time as the young leaves emerge. ***Fruit*** With broad, spreading, green wings, to 2in (5cm) long.

NATIVE REGION Japan.
HABITAT By streams.
REMARK Also known as *Acer nikoense*. The most notable feature of this species is its fall color. The fruits, though attractive, rarely contain good seed.

Height: 65ft (20m)	Shape: Broadly spreading	Leaf persistence: Deciduous	Leaf type:

Family: Sapindaceae	Species: *Acer miyabei*	Author: Maxim.

Miyabe's Maple

Leaves Palmately lobed, to 5in (13cm) long, with three to five lobes, the larger lobes taper-pointed at the tip, each with a few large, blunt teeth at the margin, heart-shaped at the base, bright green above, paler beneath, downy on both sides, more densely so beneath, turning yellow in fall, carried on slender, red stalks; leaf stalk with milky juice when cut. ***Bark*** Gray-brown, corky, with shallow, orange-brown fissures, peeling in thin scales on old plants. ***Flowers*** Individually either male or male and female, small and yellow-green, borne drooping in slender-stalked clusters at the ends of short, leafy shoots, in spring at the same time as the young leaves emerge. ***Fruit*** With spreading or sometimes slightly curved wings, to 1in (2.5cm) long.

NATIVE REGION Japan.
HABITAT Woods.

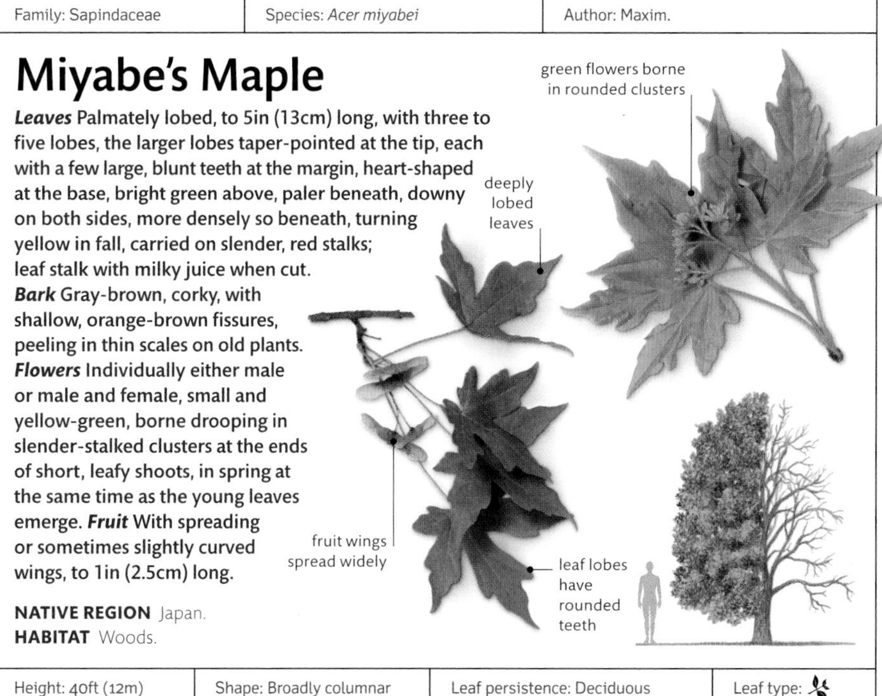

Height: 40ft (12m)	Shape: Broadly columnar	Leaf persistence: Deciduous	Leaf type:

Family: Sapindaceae	Species: *Acer negundo*	Author: L.

Box Elder

Leaves Pinnate, with three to five or seven toothed, sometimes lobed, leaflets, each borne on a slender rachis and ending in a long, tapered point, the terminal leaflet to 4in (10cm) long and 2½in (6cm) across, dark green and smooth above, smooth or downy beneath. ***Bark*** Gray-brown and smooth. ***Flowers*** Males and females both small, yellow-green, or pink in some forms, without petals, the females soon showing small, developing fruit wings, in hanging, tassel-like clusters, on separate plants in spring before or with the leaves. ***Fruit*** With down-pointing, curved wings, to 1½in (4cm) long, persisting on the plant during winter.

NATIVE REGION North and Central America.
HABITAT Riverbanks, on moist soil.
REMARK Also known as ash-leaved maple. The species is variable, and has several cultivated, ornamental forms.

tassel-like male flowers have long filaments

Acer negundo ▷

red anthers

leaflets have broad, yellow margin

'Elegans' ▷
The leaflets of this form have a distinctive yellow variegation.

leaflet margin is tinged pink

'Flamingo' ▷
The pink-tinged leaflets of this form are later margined with white.

deep pink leaf stalk

bronze young leaves

leaflets edged white

◁ **var. *violaceum***
The attractive, bloomy shoots of this form later become purplish. The flowers are pink.

anthers hang on long, pink filaments

△ **'Variegatum'**
This variegated form has white-margined leaflets.

Height: 65ft (20m)	Shape: Broadly columnar	Leaf persistence: Deciduous	Leaf type: 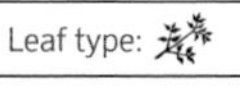

Family: Sapindaceae	Species: *Acer opalus*	Author: Mill.

Italian Maple

Leaves **Palmately lobed, to 4in (10cm) long and across, with three to five bluntly toothed lobes, glossy green and smooth above, downy beneath when young, turning yellow in fall.** ***Bark*** **Gray tinged pink, peeling in large, square places.** ***Flowers*** **Small and bright yellow, opening on the bare shoots in early spring before the young leaves emerge.** ***Fruit*** **With wings, to 1½in (4cm) long.**

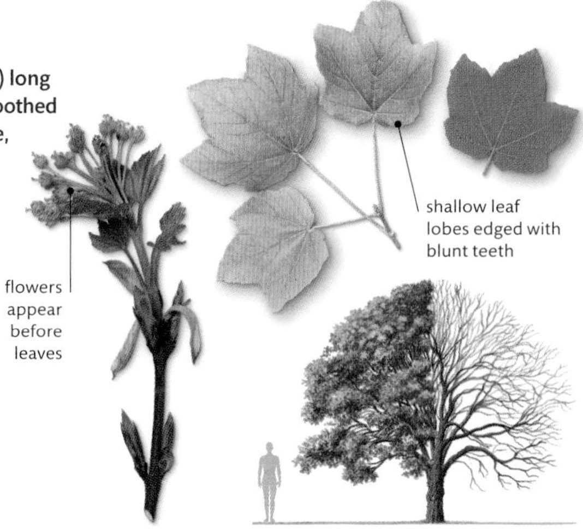

NATIVE REGION W. Europe, S.W. Asia
HABITAT Hills and mountains.
REMARK This species is most beautiful when in flower.

Height: 65ft (20m)	Shape: Broadly spreading	Leaf persistence: Deciduous	Leaf type:

Family: Sapindaceae	Species: *Acer palmatum*	Author: Thunb.

Japanese Maple

Leaves **Rounded in outline, with five to seven deep, taper-pointed, sharply toothed lobes, to 4in (10cm) long and across, bright green, smooth, with tufts of hairs in the vein axils beneath, turning red, orange, or yellow in fall.** ***Bark*** **Gray-brown, smooth.** ***Flowers*** **Small, red-purple, in upright to drooping clusters in spring as the young leaves emerge.** ***Fruit*** **With green or red wings, to ⅜in (1cm) long.**

finely pointed leaf lobes

fruit wings may be tinged red

NATIVE REGION Japan, Korea.
HABITAT Thickets.
REMARK The numerous, mainly shrubby, garden and backyard forms include dwarfs, and those with cut-leaved, colored, or variegated foliage.

variable fall leaf color

slender-stalked flowers

Height: 50ft (15m)	Shape: Broadly spreading	Leaf persistence: Deciduous	Leaf type: 

Family: Sapindaceae	Species: *Acer palmatum*	Author: Thunb.

△ **'Atropurpureum'**
This form is selected for its deep red-purple foliage, which turns brilliant red in the fall. It usually makes a smaller tree.

◁△ **'Sango-kaku'**
Commonly known as coral-bark maple, this form has small leaves, which mature from orange-yellow to pale green, and turn bronzy yellow in the fall.

△ **'Shishi-gashira'**
This smaller form makes a compact plant, reaching about 16ft (5m).

'Linearilobum Atropurpureum' ▷
Spidery, red-purple leaves characterize this form. Its winged fall fruits are tinged red, and hang in small clusters.

Height: 50ft (15m)	Shape: Broadly spreading	Leaf persistence: Deciduous	Leaf type:

Family: Sapindaceae	Species: *Acer pensylvanicum*	Author: L.

Moosewood

Leaves **To 6in (15cm) or more long and nearly the same across, with three triangular, taper-pointed, toothed, forward-pointing lobes toward the end, deep yellow-green and smooth above, with red-brown hairs beneath when young, turning yellow in fall. *Bark* Green, vertically striped red-brown and white, becoming gray with age. *Flowers* Small, yellow-green, borne in drooping racemes in late spring at the same time as the young leaves emerge. *Fruit* With green, down-curved wings, to 1in (2.5cm) long.**

NATIVE REGION E. North America.
HABITAT Moist woods.
REMARK Also known as striped maple. This species is the only North American snake-bark maple. The common name, moosewood, is given because moose eat the bark in winter.

leaves cut into three pointed lobes

yellow-green flower petals

◁△ ***Acer pensylvanicum***

striking winter shoots

short side lobes on leaves

◁ **'Erythrocladum'**
This form is distinguished by its bright pink young shoots and buds.

typically striped bark

◁△ ***Acer pensylvanicum***

larger central lobe

Height: 26ft (8m)	Shape: Broadly columnar	Leaf persistence: Deciduous	Leaf type:

Family: Sapindaceae	Species: *Acer platanoides*	Author: L.

Norway Maple

Leaves **Palmately lobed, to 6in (15cm) long and 7in (17.5cm) across, with five lobes, each lobe ending in several teeth with long, slender points, bright green, smooth when mature on both sides, turning yellow or sometimes red in fall; the long, slender leaf stalk exudes milky juice when cut.** ***Bark*** **Gray and smooth.** ***Flowers*** **Small and bright yellow-green, borne in conspicuous clusters in spring before and with the young leaves.** ***Fruit*** **With large, spreading wings, to 2in (5cm) long.**

NATIVE REGION S.W. Asia, Europe.
HABITAT Mountain woods.
REMARK A fast-growing species, which quickly reaches its maximum height. In cultivation, it has many ornamental forms, selected for both foliage and habit.

leaf lobes end in slender teeth

fruits have large wings

flowers open before leaves

◁△ ***Acer platanoides***

▽ **'Crimson King'**
This form has deep red-purple leaves, and red bud scales and flower stalks.

red bud scales

red flower stalks

△**'Crimson King'**

leaf stalks are deep purple

▽ **'Crimson Sentry'**
The bright red young leaves of this form mature to deep purple-green. The tree has an upright habit.

mature leaves are deep purple-green

young leaves are reddish

◁**'Crimson Sentry'**

Height: 80ft (25m)	Shape: Broadly columnar	Leaf persistence: Deciduous	Leaf type: 

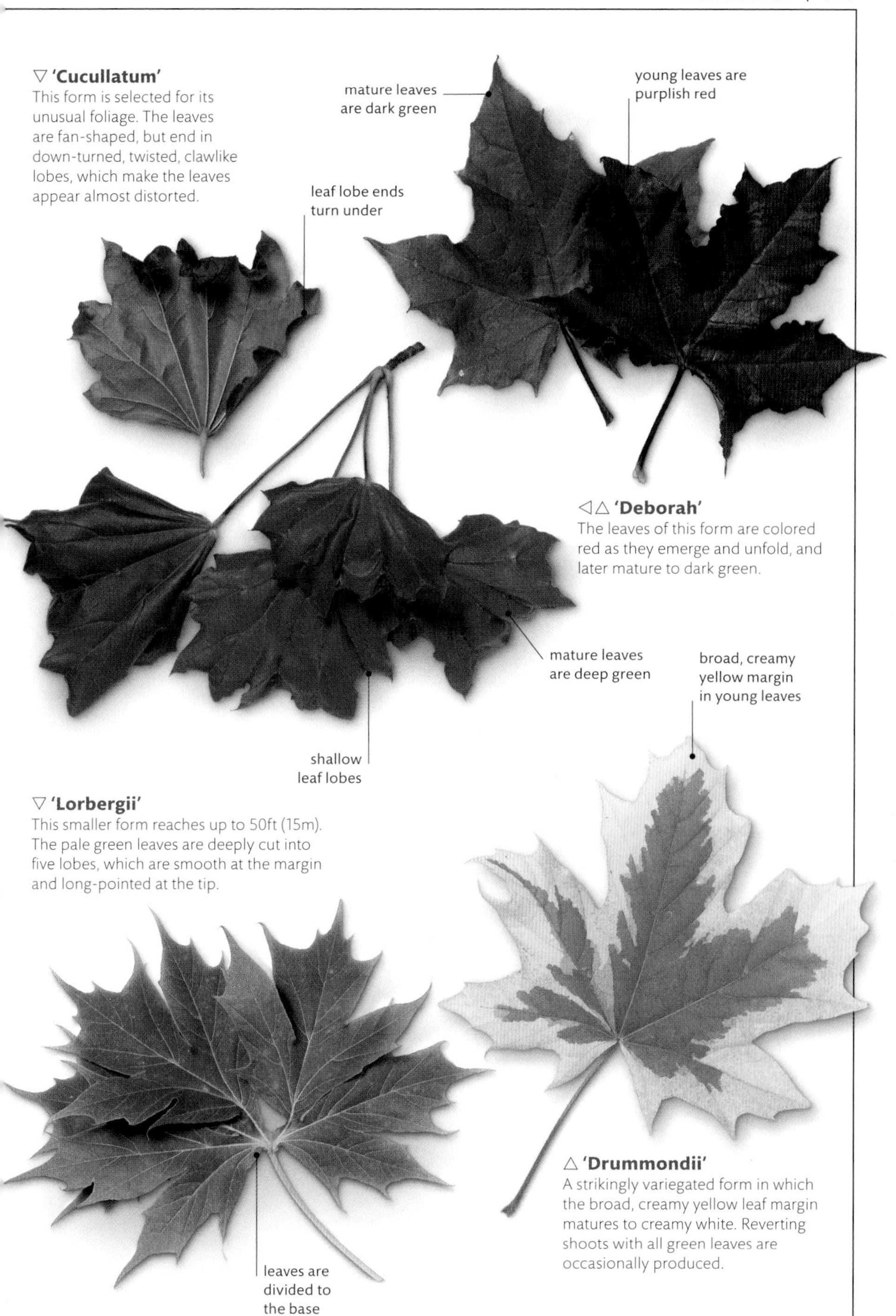

▽ **'Cucullatum'**
This form is selected for its unusual foliage. The leaves are fan-shaped, but end in down-turned, twisted, clawlike lobes, which make the leaves appear almost distorted.

◁△ **'Deborah'**
The leaves of this form are colored red as they emerge and unfold, and later mature to dark green.

▽ **'Lorbergii'**
This smaller form reaches up to 50ft (15m). The pale green leaves are deeply cut into five lobes, which are smooth at the margin and long-pointed at the tip.

△ **'Drummondii'**
A strikingly variegated form in which the broad, creamy yellow leaf margin matures to creamy white. Reverting shoots with all green leaves are occasionally produced.

Family: Sapindaceae	Species: *Acer pseudoplatanus*	Author: L.

Sycamore

Leaves **Palmately lobed, to 4¾in (12cm) long and 6in (15cm) across, with five coarsely toothed lobes, dark green and smooth above, rather blue-gray beneath.** ***Bark*** **Pinkish to yellowish gray, peeling in irregular plates.** ***Flowers*** **Small and yellow-green, without petals, in dense, hanging clusters in spring with the young leaves.** ***Fruit*** **With somewhat down-pointing wings, to 1in (2.5cm) long.**

NATIVE REGION S.W. Asia, Europe.
HABITAT Deciduous mountain woods.
REMARK In Scotland, also known as plane. The species is widely naturalized in North America and Great Britain. In open sites, it may tend toward a spreading shape.

heart-shaped leaf base

pendulous flower clusters

◁ ***Acer pseudoplatanus***

leaves are deep green above

purple underside

△ **'Atropurpureum'**
The special feature of this cultivar is the underside of the leaves, which is colored purple.

fruit wings are bright red

△ **'Erythrocarpum'**
The young fruits of this form have spectacular bright red wings.

attractively colored young foliage

'Brilliantissimum' ▷
The young leaves of this form are bright pink as they unfold, becoming whitish with green veins, maturing to yellow-green.

◁ **'Nizetii'**
The leaves of this selection have bold blotches of pinkish white on the upper surface. The underside is purplish green.

Height: 100ft (30m)	Shape: Broadly columnar	Leaf persistence: Deciduous	Leaf type:

Family: Sapindaceae	Species: *Acer rubrum*	Author: L.

Red Maple

Leaves To 4in (10cm) long and nearly the same across, with three or five toothed lobes, dark green and smooth above, blue-white with hairs on the veins beneath, turning red or yellow in fall. ***Bark*** Dark gray and smooth. ***Flowers*** Small and red, on slender stalks, in dense clusters on the shoots in early spring. ***Fruit*** With red wings, about ¾in (2cm) long.

NATIVE REGION E. North America.
HABITAT Moist ground.

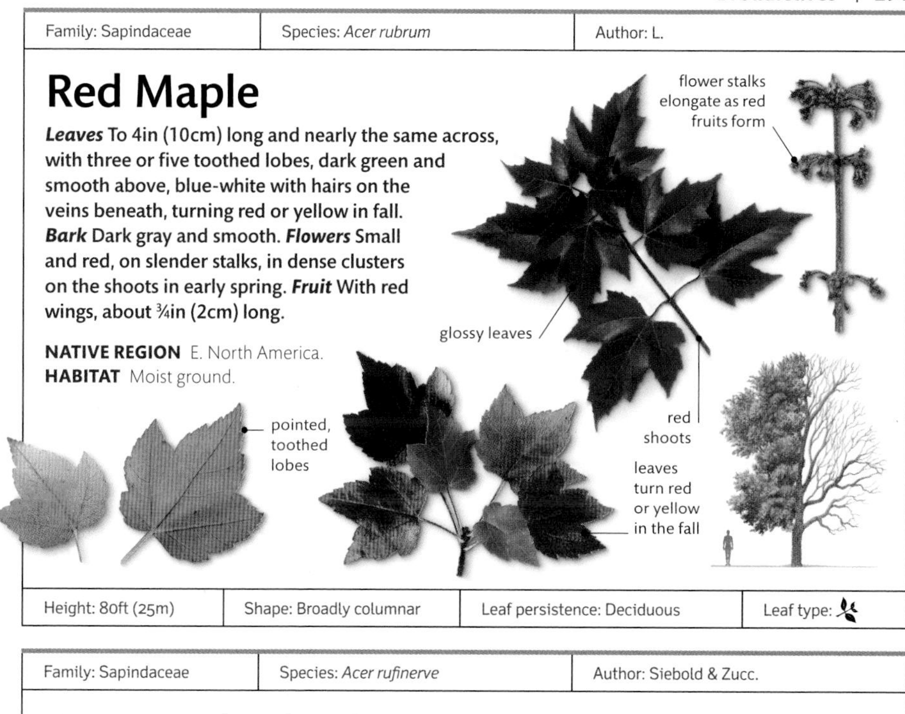

Height: 80ft (25m)	Shape: Broadly columnar	Leaf persistence: Deciduous	Leaf type:

Family: Sapindaceae	Species: *Acer rufinerve*	Author: Siebold & Zucc.

Gray Snake-bark Maple

Leaves To 5in (13cm) long and across, with usually three coarsely toothed lobes, dark green and smooth above, with rust-colored hairs on the veins beneath, turning red in fall. ***Bark*** Dark green striped white and pale green, with diamond-shaped marks, gray and fissured with age. ***Flowers*** Small and yellow-green, in upright racemes in spring. ***Fruit*** With spreading wings, to ¾in (2cm) long.

NATIVE REGION Japan.
HABITAT Mountain woods.

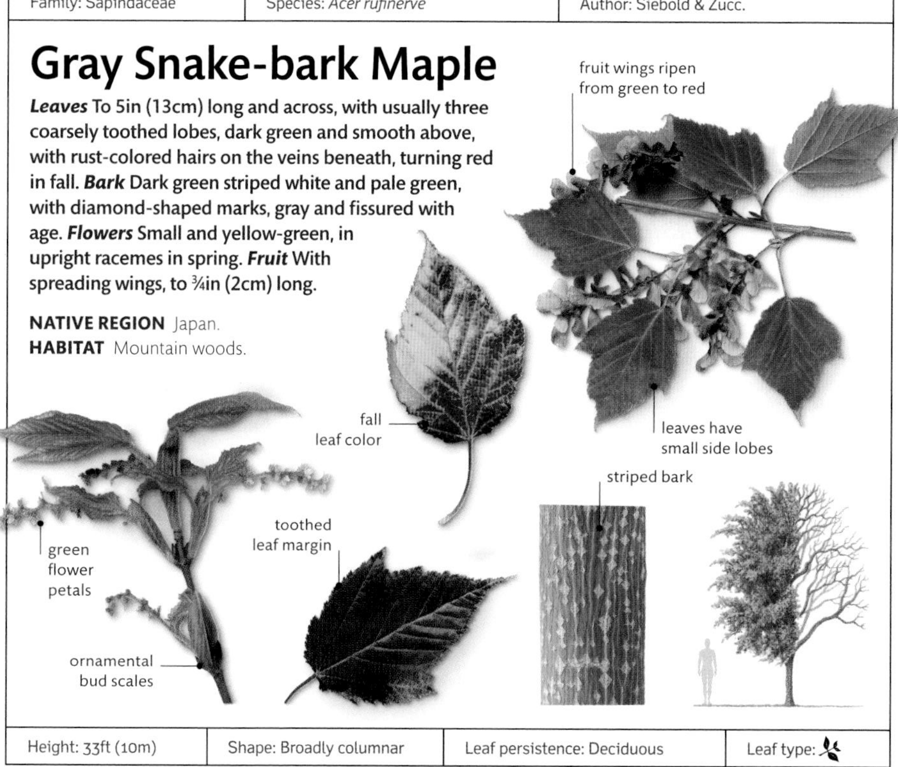

Height: 33ft (10m)	Shape: Broadly columnar	Leaf persistence: Deciduous	Leaf type:

Family: Sapindaceae	Species: *Acer saccharinum*	Author: L.

Silver Maple

Leaves Palmately lobed, to 6in (15cm) long and across, with five lobes, each itself lobed and sharply toothed, light green and smooth above, blue-white and thinly hairy beneath, usually turning yellow in fall. ***Bark*** Gray, smooth, flaking with age. ***Flowers*** Males and females both small and greenish yellow, without petals, in clusters on the shoots in early spring. ***Fruit*** With spreading, green, later pale brown, wings, to ¾in (2cm) long.

NATIVE REGION E. North America.
HABITAT Moist soil and riverbanks.

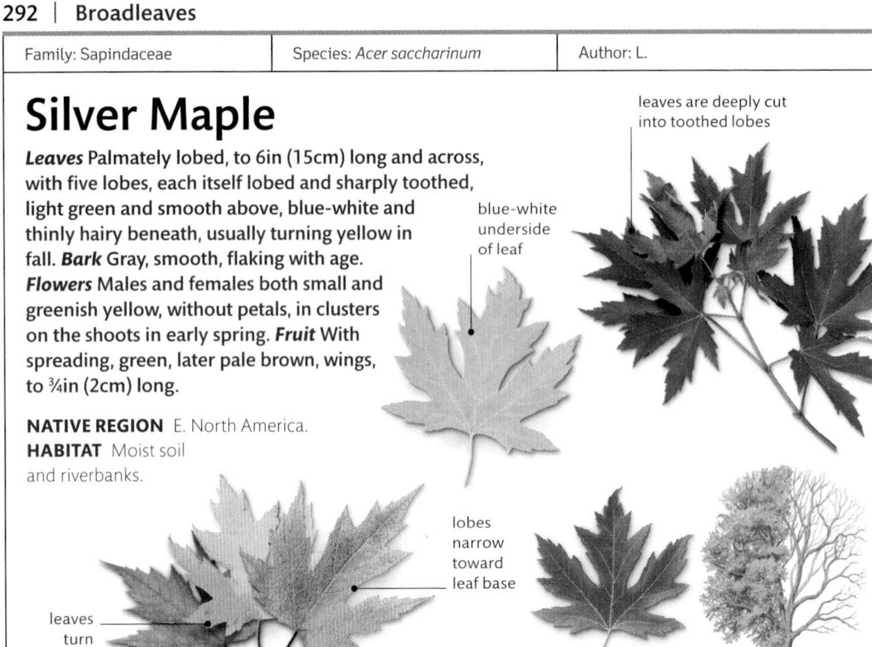

Height: 100ft (30m)	Shape: Broadly columnar	Leaf persistence: Deciduous	Leaf type:

Family: Sapindaceae	Species: *Acer saccharum*	Author: Marshall

Sugar Maple

Leaves Palmately lobed, to 5in (13cm) long and slightly more across, with five lobes, the three largest with few prominent teeth, heart-shaped at the base, mid- to dark green above, with hairs in the vein axils beneath, turning yellow to orange or red in fall. ***Bark*** Gray-brown, smooth, becoming furrowed and scaly with age. ***Flowers*** Small, yellow-green, without petals; drooping on slender stalks, in open clusters in spring with the young leaves. ***Fruit*** With nearly parallel, green, later brown, wings, to 1in (2.5cm) long.

NATIVE REGION E. North America.
HABITAT Rich woods.
REMARK Also known as rock maple. The sap is processed into maple syrup.

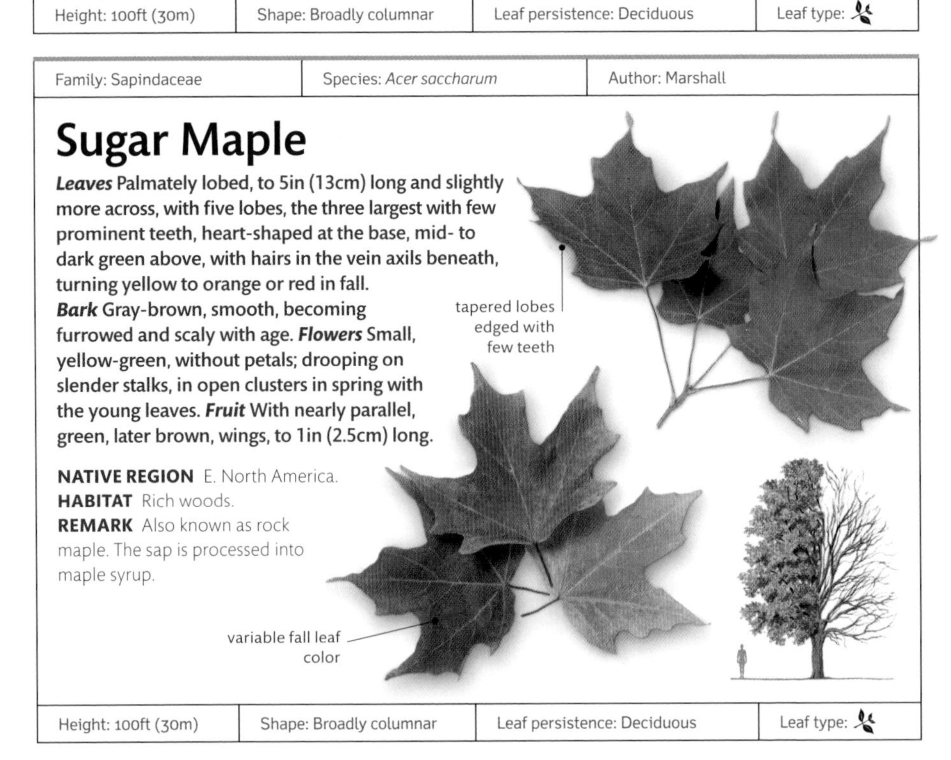

Height: 100ft (30m)	Shape: Broadly columnar	Leaf persistence: Deciduous	Leaf type:

Family: Sapindaceae	Species: *Acer shirasawanum*	Author: Koidz.

Acer shirasawanum

Leaves **Rounded in outline, to 4¾in (12cm) long and across, with about 11 sharply toothed lobes, bright green above, smooth on both sides, turning orange and red in fall.** ***Bark*** **Gray-brown and smooth.** ***Flowers*** **Small, with a pink calyx and cream sepals, spreading to upright clusters in spring with the leaves.** ***Fruit*** **With widely spreading green wings, in upright clusters.**

NATIVE REGION Japan.
HABITAT Mountain slopes and valleys.
REMARK This species is often confused with the full-moon maple (*Acer japonicum*, see p.281), to which it is related.

sharply toothed lobes

▽▷ ***Acer shirasawanum***

upright fruit clusters

flowers in small clusters

◁ **'Aureum'**
This form has golden yellow foliage.

Height: 65ft (20m)	Shape: Broadly spreading	Leaf persistence: Deciduous	Leaf type:

Family: Sapindaceae	Species: *Acer sieboldianum*	Author: Miq.

Siebold's Maple

Leaves **Rounded in outline, to 3in (7.5cm) long and the same across, with seven to nine or sometimes eleven taper-pointed, sharply toothed lobes, cut nearly to the middle, pale green, covered in white hairs when young, becoming dark green above, downy beneath, turning red in fall, on downy stalks.** ***Bark*** **Dark gray-brown and smooth.** ***Flowers*** **Small, with yellow petals and purplish sepals, in long-stalked, drooping, downy clusters in spring at the same time as the young leaves emerge.** ***Fruit*** **With spreading wings, to ¾in (2cm) long, maturing from green to red.**

NATIVE REGION Japan.
HABITAT Sunny ridges, streambanks in the mountains.

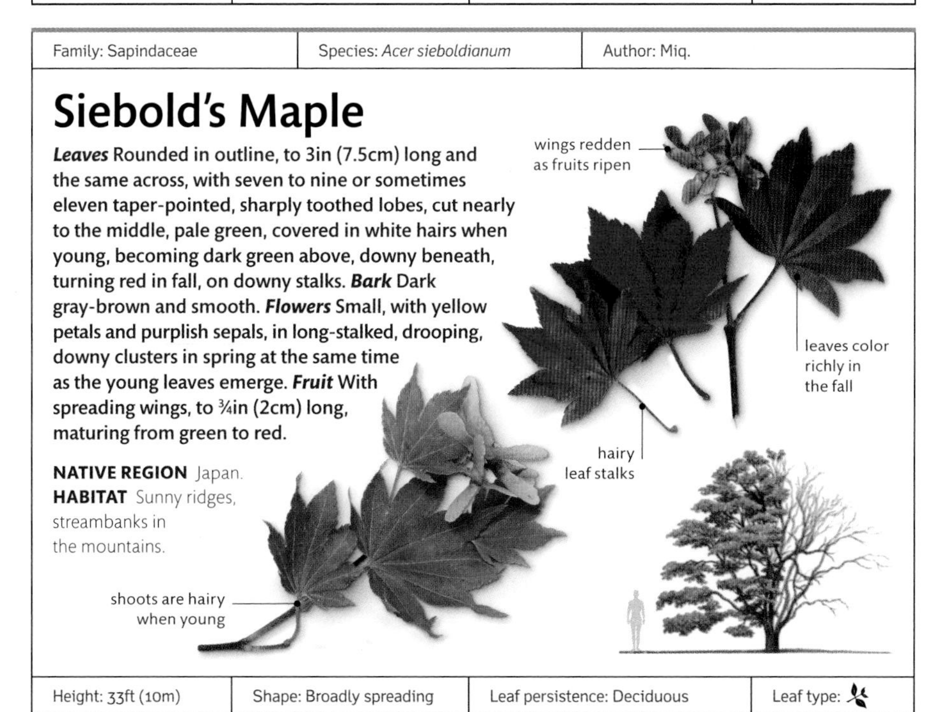

Height: 33ft (10m)	Shape: Broadly spreading	Leaf persistence: Deciduous	Leaf type:

Family: Sapindaceae	Species: *Acer spicatum*	Author: Lam.

Mountain Maple

Leaves Palmately lobed, to 4¾in (12cm) long, with three or five taper-pointed, coarsely toothed lobes, deep yellow-green and smooth with impressed veins above, downy beneath, turning yellow, orange, or red in fall. ***Bark*** Gray-brown and smooth. ***Flowers*** Small and greenish white, numerous, borne in dense, slender, upright panicles to 6in (15cm) long, in early summer. ***Fruit*** With wings spreading at about a right angle, to 1in (2.5cm) long, green often becoming red.

NATIVE REGION E. North America.
HABITAT Cool, moist woods, usually in mountains.
REMARK Can be either a small, bushy tree or a large shrub. It is widely distributed in its habitat. A number of related species are native to E. Asia.

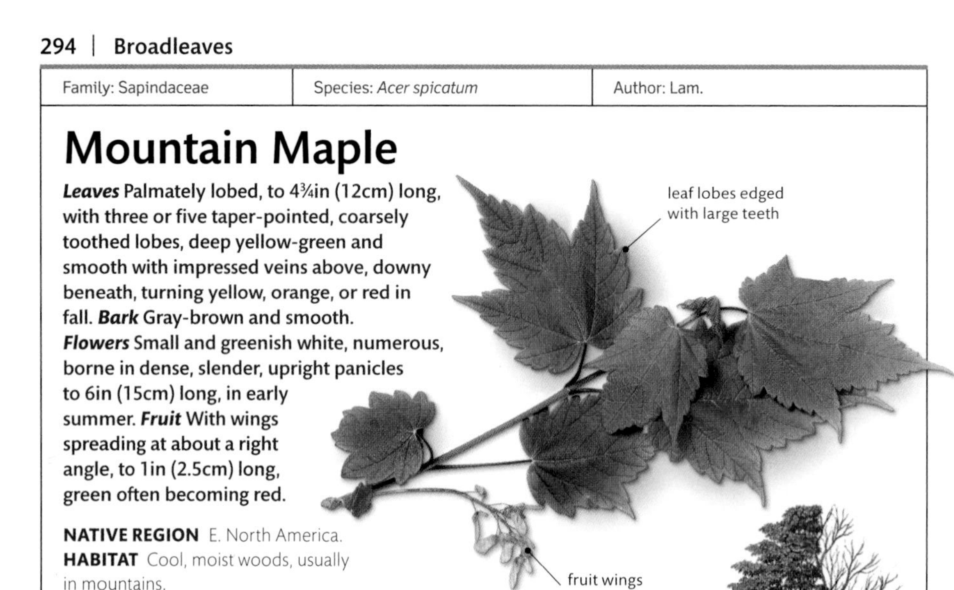

Height: 26ft (8m)	Shape: Broadly spreading	Leaf persistence: Deciduous	Leaf type:

Family: Sapindaceae	Species: *Acer tataricum*	Author: Maxim.

Amur Maple

Leaves Ovate, to 3in (7.5cm) long and 2½in (6cm) across, with three deep lobes, the central lobe largest, toothed, glossy dark green above, smooth, turning bright red in early fall. ***Bark*** Dark gray-brown, smooth. ***Flowers*** Creamy white, fragrant, in upright clusters in late spring after the young leaves. ***Fruit*** With nearly parallel, red-tinged wings, to 1in (2.5cm) long, in drooping clusters.

NATIVE REGION Europe to E. Asia.
HABITAT Thickets by riverbanks and exposed positions in mountain valleys.
REMARK The typical form of this species is from Europe and S.W. Asia. Shown and described here is subsp. *ginnala* from E. Asia.

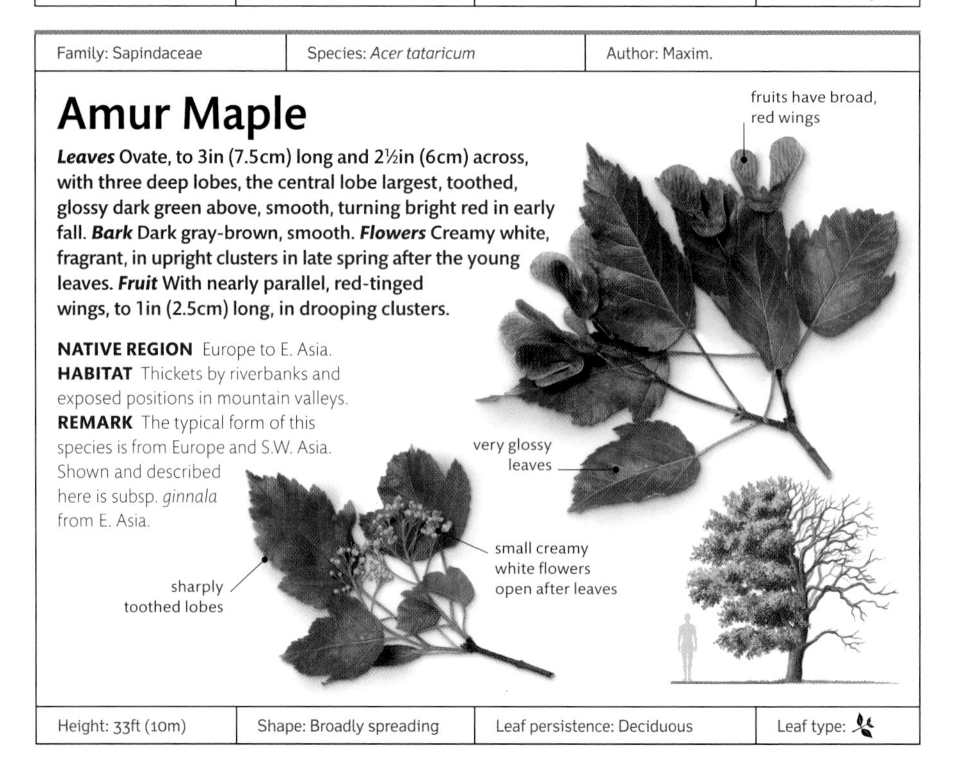

Height: 33ft (10m)	Shape: Broadly spreading	Leaf persistence: Deciduous	Leaf type:

Family: Sapindaceae	Species: *Acer trautvetteri*	Author: Medw.

Red-bud Maple

Leaves Palmately lobed, to 6in (15cm) long and 8in (20cm) across, with five coarsely toothed lobes, cut more than halfway to the base, glossy dark green and smooth above, blue-green with tufts of hairs in the vein axils beneath, turning deep golden yellow in fall, carried on long, red stalks. ***Bark*** Pale gray and smooth. ***Flowers*** Individually small and yellow, borne in upright clusters in spring at the same time as the young leaves emerge among bright red bud scales. ***Fruit*** With broad, bright red, nearly parallel wings, to 2in (5cm) long.

NATIVE REGION S.W. Asia, Caucasus.
HABITAT Mixed deciduous and evergreen forests.
REMARK The fruits are an attractive feature.

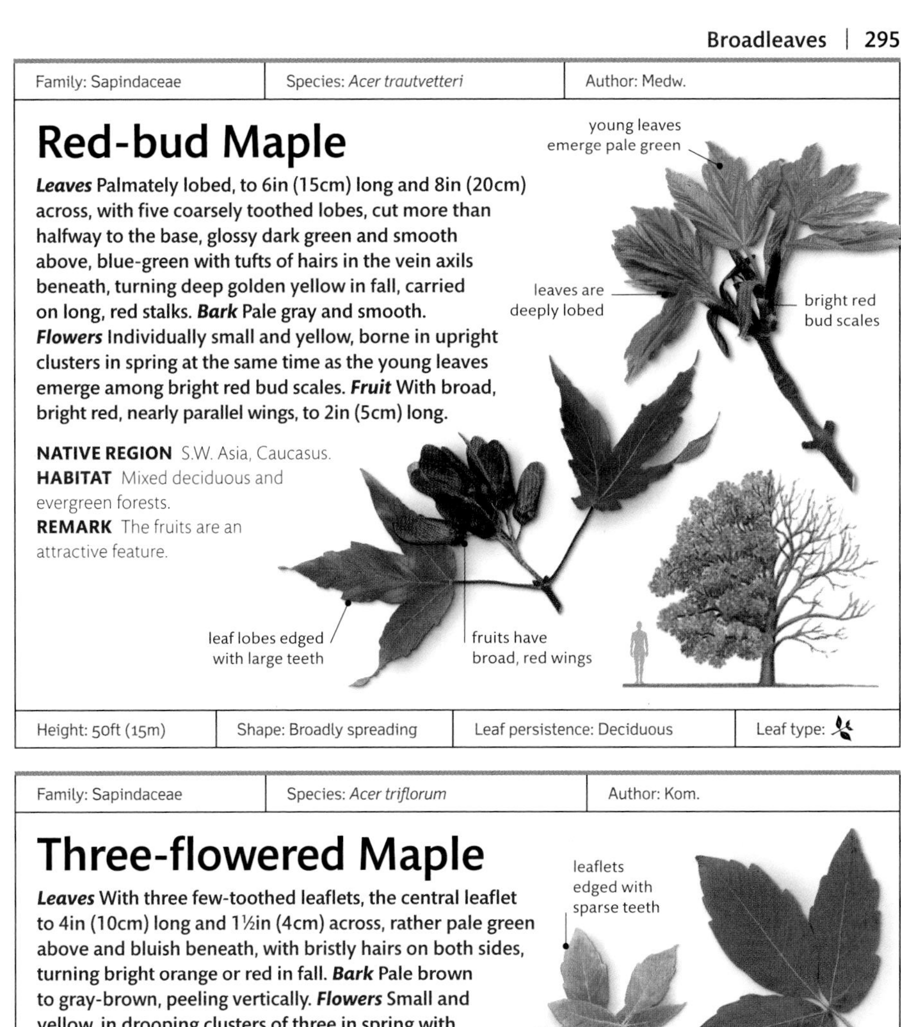

Height: 50ft (15m)	Shape: Broadly spreading	Leaf persistence: Deciduous	Leaf type:

Family: Sapindaceae	Species: *Acer triflorum*	Author: Kom.

Three-flowered Maple

Leaves With three few-toothed leaflets, the central leaflet to 4in (10cm) long and 1½in (4cm) across, rather pale green above and bluish beneath, with bristly hairs on both sides, turning bright orange or red in fall. ***Bark*** Pale brown to gray-brown, peeling vertically. ***Flowers*** Small and yellow, in drooping clusters of three in spring with the young leaves. ***Fruit*** With nearly parallel, pale green wings, to 1¼in (3cm) long.

NATIVE REGION N.E. China, Korea.
HABITAT Mountain woods and ravines.

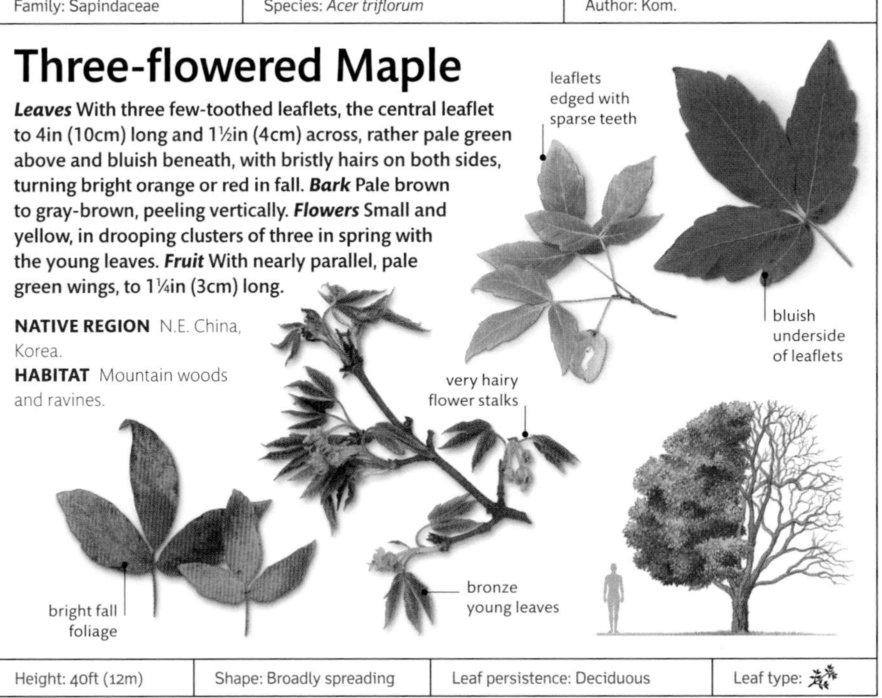

Height: 40ft (12m)	Shape: Broadly spreading	Leaf persistence: Deciduous	Leaf type:

Family: Sapindaceae	Species: *Acer velutinum*	Author: Boiss.

Persian Maple

Leaves Palmately lobed, to 6in (15cm) long and across, with usually five coarsely toothed lobes, yellow-green above, very downy beneath, on long stalks. ***Bark*** Gray-brown and smooth. ***Flowers*** Small and green, in large, upright clusters in late spring just after the young leaves emerge. ***Fruit*** With large, green, later pale brown wings set at right angles, to 1½in (4cm) long.

NATIVE REGION Caucasus, N. Iran.
HABITAT Mountain woods.
REMARK Leaves are similar to, but larger than, those of sycamore (*Acer pseudoplatanus*, see p.290).

Height: 50ft (15m)	Shape: Broadly spreading	Leaf persistence: Deciduous	Leaf type:

Family: Sapindaceae	Species: *Aesculus californica*	Author: (Spach) Nutt.

California Buckeye

Leaves Palmately compound, with five to seven oblong, toothed leaflets, to 6in (15cm) long, deep blue-green above, gray-green beneath. ***Bark*** Pale gray, nearly smooth, thinly scaly. ***Flowers*** White or pale pink, with four petals, in dense, cylindrical, upright panicles to 8in (20cm) long, in summer. ***Fruit*** Gray, smooth, pear-shaped, to 2¾in (7cm) long, with one glossy brown seed, on a long stalk.

NATIVE REGION US: California, Oregon.
HABITAT Dry slopes and canyons in hills.

leaflets have long, tapered point

flowers borne in very dense panicles

long, exserted flower stamens

Height: 33ft (10m)	Shape: Broadly spreading	Leaf persistence: Deciduous	Leaf type:

Family: Sapindaceae	Species: *Aesculus* x *carnea*	Author: Zeyh.

Red Horse Chestnut

Leaves Palmately compound, with five to seven obovate, sharply toothed, stalkless or short-stalked leaflets, to 10in (25cm) long, dark green, on long stalks. ***Bark*** Reddish brown. ***Flowers*** Creamy white blotched yellow becoming pink blotched red, with five petals, in conical, upright, or slightly spreading panicles to 8in (20cm) long, in late spring. ***Fruit*** Green then pale brown, smooth or only slightly spiny, 1½in (4cm) across.

NATIVE REGION Of garden or backyard origin.
REMARK A hybrid between common horse chestnut (*Aesculus hippocastanum*, see p.298) and red buckeye (*Aesculus pavia*, see p.299).

◁▽ ***Aesculus* x *carnea***

◁ **'Briotii'**
Brighter red flowers distinguish this form.

Height: 65ft (20m)	Shape: Broadly columnar	Leaf persistence: Deciduous	Leaf type:

Family: Sapindaceae	Species: *Aesculus flava*	Author: Sol.

Sweet Buckeye

Leaves Palmately compound, with usually five sharply toothed, short-stalked leaflets, to 6in (15cm) long, dark green, turning orange-red in fall. ***Bark*** Gray-brown, peeling in large, smooth scales. ***Flowers*** Yellow with pink blotch, with four petals, in conical, upright panicles to 6in (15cm) long, in late spring to early summer. ***Fruit*** Smooth, rounded, to 2½in (6cm) across, covered in brown scales, usually with two seeds.

NATIVE REGION E. US.
HABITAT Moist, rich woods.
REMARK Also known as *Aesculus octandra*, yellow buckeye. The best buckeye for fall color.

taper-pointed leaflets

Height: 100ft (30m)	Shape: Broadly conical	Leaf persistence: Deciduous	Leaf type:

Family: Sapindaceae	Species: *Aesculus hippocastanum*	Author: L.

Common Horse Chestnut

Leaves Palmately compound, with five to seven obovate, sharply toothed, unstalked leaflets, to 12in (30cm) long, dark green, usually turning yellow in fall, on long stalks. ***Bark*** Red-brown or gray, scaly. ***Flowers*** Creamy yellow blotched yellow, becoming white blotched red, with five petals, in large, conical, upright panicles to 12in (30cm) long, in late spring. ***Fruit*** Rounded, spiny, and green, with up to three glossy brown seeds.

NATIVE REGION Albania, N. Greece.
HABITAT Mountain woods.
REMARK The native region of this species was unknown for many years, because of its introduction to European gardens via cultivation in Turkey.

yellow flower blotch becomes red

large flower panicles borne upright

unstalked leaflets

▷ ***Aesculus hippocastanum***

△ **'Baumannii'**
The double flowers of this form set no fruit.

Height: 100ft (30m)	Shape: Broadly columnar	Leaf persistence: Deciduous	Leaf type: 

Family: Sapindaceae	Species: *Aesculus indica*	Author: (Wall. ex Cambess.) Hook.

Indian Horse Chestnut

Leaves Palmately compound, with usually seven but occasionally five obovate to lanceolate, stalked and finely toothed leaflets, to 1in (25cm) long, bronze when young becoming glossy green above, turning orange or yellow in fall. ***Bark*** Gray and smooth. ***Flowers*** White to pale pink blotched bright yellow, the blotch becoming red, with long, protruding stamens, in conical, upright panicles to 12in (30cm) long, in midsummer. ***Fruit*** Pear-shaped, scaly, and brown, with up to three seeds, on a stout stalk.

NATIVE REGION N.W. Himalayas. S.W. Asia.
HABITAT Forests and shady ravines.
REMARK Flowers much later than the common horse chestnut (*Aesculus hippocastanum*, see above).

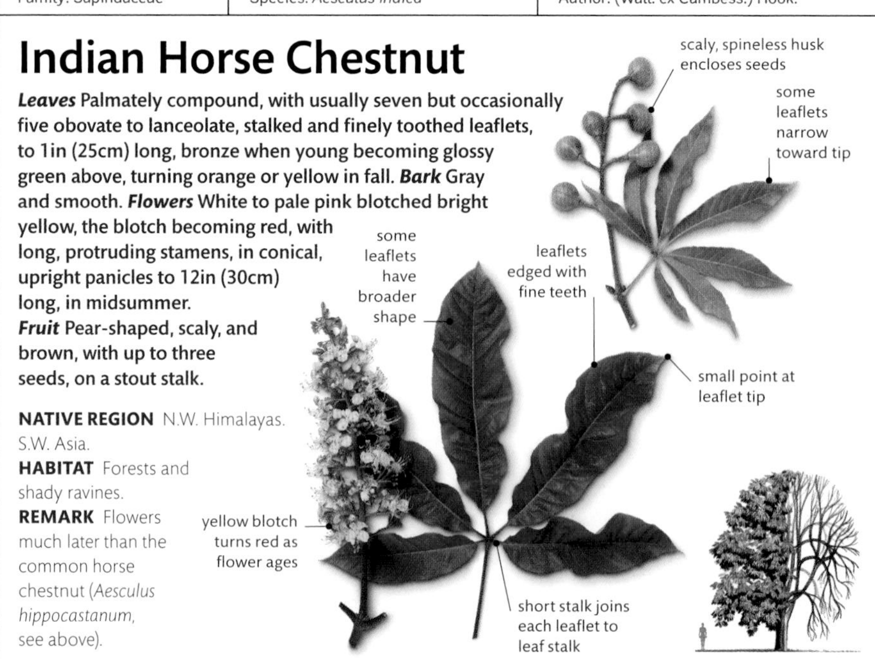

Height: 100ft (30m)	Shape: Broadly columnar	Leaf persistence: Deciduous	Leaf type: 

Family: Sapindaceae	Species: *Aesculus* x *neglecta*	Author: Lindl.

Aesculus x neglecta

Leaves **Palmately compound, with usually five elliptic, taper-pointed, finely toothed, stalked leaflets, to 8in (20cm) long and 3½in (9cm) across, red when young, becoming dark green then red in fall, smooth except for hairs on the veins above, thinly hairy beneath.** ***Bark*** **Gray-brown, with shallow fissures.** ***Flowers*** **1in (2.5cm) long, whitish, borne in conical, upright panicles in late spring to early summer.** ***Fruit*** **Gray-brown, rounded and smooth, about 1½in (4cm) across.**

NATIVE REGION S.E. US.
HABITAT Mainly the coastal plain.
REMARK A hybrid between sweet buckeye (*Aesculus flava*, see p.297) and *Aesculus sylvatica*, most well-known for the cultivar, 'Erythroblastos,' shown here.

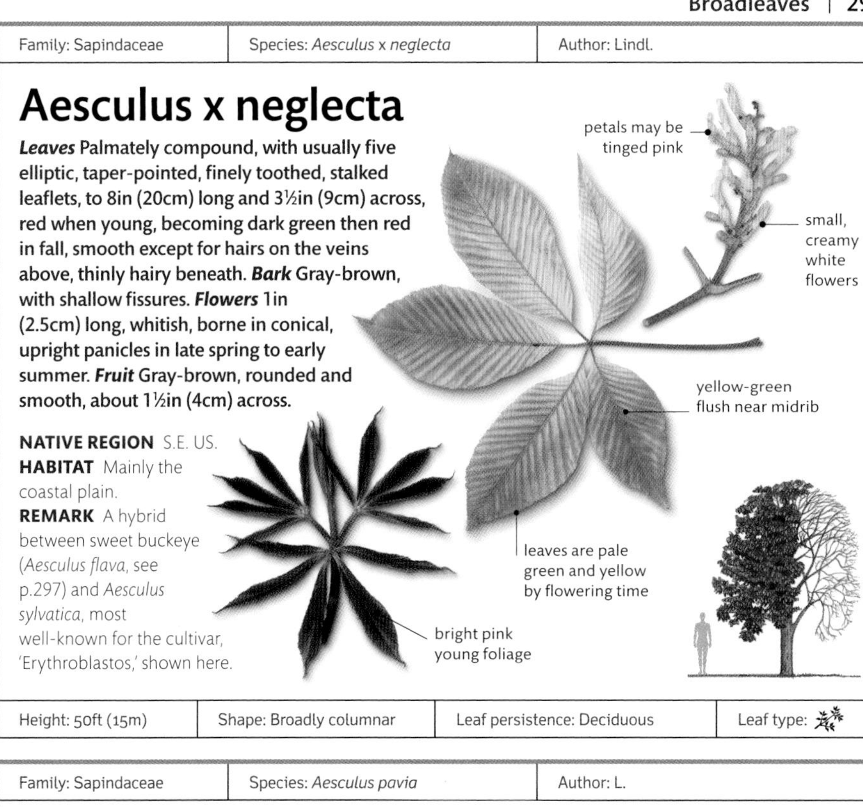

Height: 50ft (15m)	Shape: Broadly columnar	Leaf persistence: Deciduous	Leaf type:

Family: Sapindaceae	Species: *Aesculus pavia*	Author: L.

Red Buckeye

Leaves **Palmately compound, with five elliptic to lanceolate, sharply toothed, stalked leaflets, to 6in (15cm) long, glossy dark green above, turning red in fall.** ***Bark*** **Dark gray and smooth.** ***Flowers*** **Slender and red, 1½in (4cm) long, with four petals, in upright panicles in early summer.** ***Fruit*** **Rounded to slightly elongated, smooth, and brown, enclosing one or two glossy brown seeds.**

NATIVE REGION S.E. US.
HABITAT Moist, rich woods and thickets.
REMARK This species is one parent plant of the hybrid commonly known as red horse chestnut (*Aesculus* x *carnea*, see p.297), to which it gives the color of its flowers.

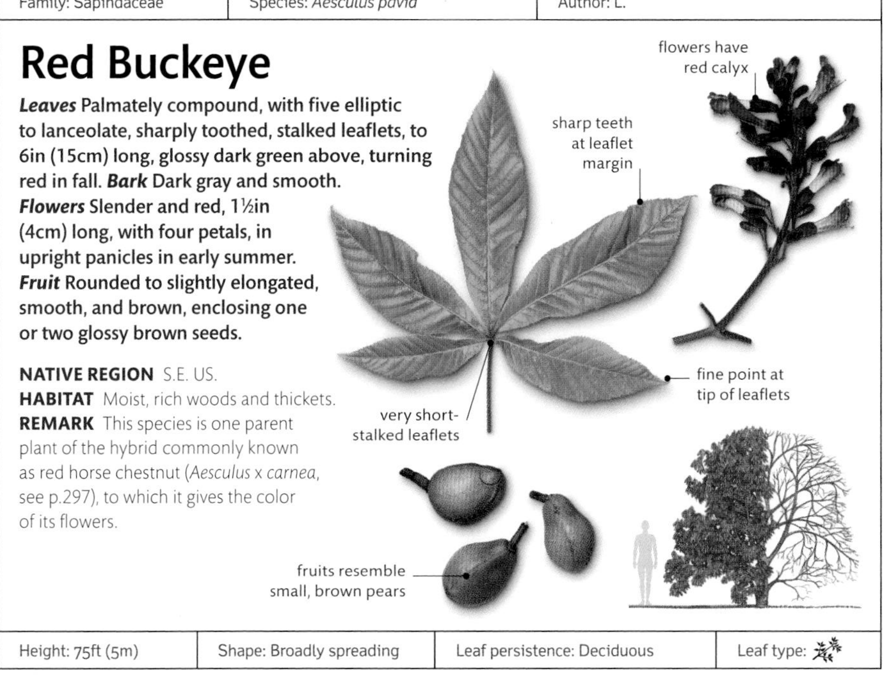

Height: 75ft (5m)	Shape: Broadly spreading	Leaf persistence: Deciduous	Leaf type:

Family: Sapindaceae	Species: *Koelreuteria paniculata*	Author: Laxm.

Golden Rain Tree

Leaves Pinnate or partially bipinnate, to 18in (45cm) long, either lobed or divided into leaflets to 4in (10cm) long, toothed, dark green above, downy, turning yellow in fall. ***Bark*** Pale brown, shallowly fissured. ***Flowers*** About ½in (1.2cm) across, yellow, with four petals, in conical panicles to 18in (45cm) long, at the ends of the shoots in mid- to late summer. ***Fruit*** A bladderlike capsule, to 2in (5cm) long, green or green tinged red ripening to pale brown.

NATIVE REGION China, Korea.
HABITAT Hot, dry, river valleys.

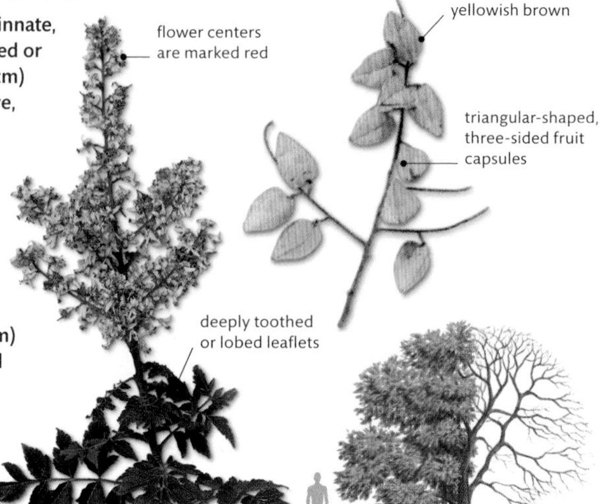

Height: 40ft (12m)	Shape: Broadly spreading	Leaf persistence: Deciduous	Leaf type:

Family: Sapindaceae	Species: *Xanthoceras sorbifolium*	Author: Bunge

Xanthoceras sorbifolium

Leaves Pinnate, to 12in (30cm) long, with up to 17 narrowly elliptic, toothed leaflets, to 2½in (6cm) long, glossy dark green above, smooth. ***Bark*** Gray-brown, fissured into scaly ridges. ***Flowers*** To 1¼in (3cm) across, white, with five petals, the petals blotched yellow-green, becoming red at the base, in upright racemes to 10in (25cm) long, at the ends of the old shoots in late spring as or just after the young leaves emerge. ***Fruit*** A smooth, thick-walled, green capsule, to 2½in (6cm) across, broadest at the top, containing several pea-sized seeds.

NATIVE REGION N. Korea, China.
HABITAT Thickets.

Height: 26ft (8m)	Shape: Broadly columnar	Leaf persistence: Deciduous	Leaf type: 

SIMAROUBACEAE

THIS FAMILY OF SOME 20 genera and about 100 species of trees and shrubs occurs in both tropical and subtropical regions, and temperate regions of Asia. The alternate leaves are often pinnate. The small flowers have five petals; females develop into the fruit, which is dry and winged or a capsule.

Family: Simaroubaceae	Species: *Ailanthus altissima*	Author: (Mill.) Swingle

Tree of Heaven

Leaves Pinnate, to 24in (60cm) long, with 15 or more pairs of leaflets, to 4¾in (12cm) long and 2in (5cm) across, glossy dark green above, paler beneath. ***Bark*** Gray-brown, with pale streaks. ***Flowers*** Males and females greenish yellow, with five or six petals, in large panicles at the ends of the shoots, usually on separate plants in mid- to late summer. ***Fruit*** Winged, to 1½in (4cm) long, ripening from green to yellow then red-brown.

NATIVE REGION China.
HABITAT Mountain woods.

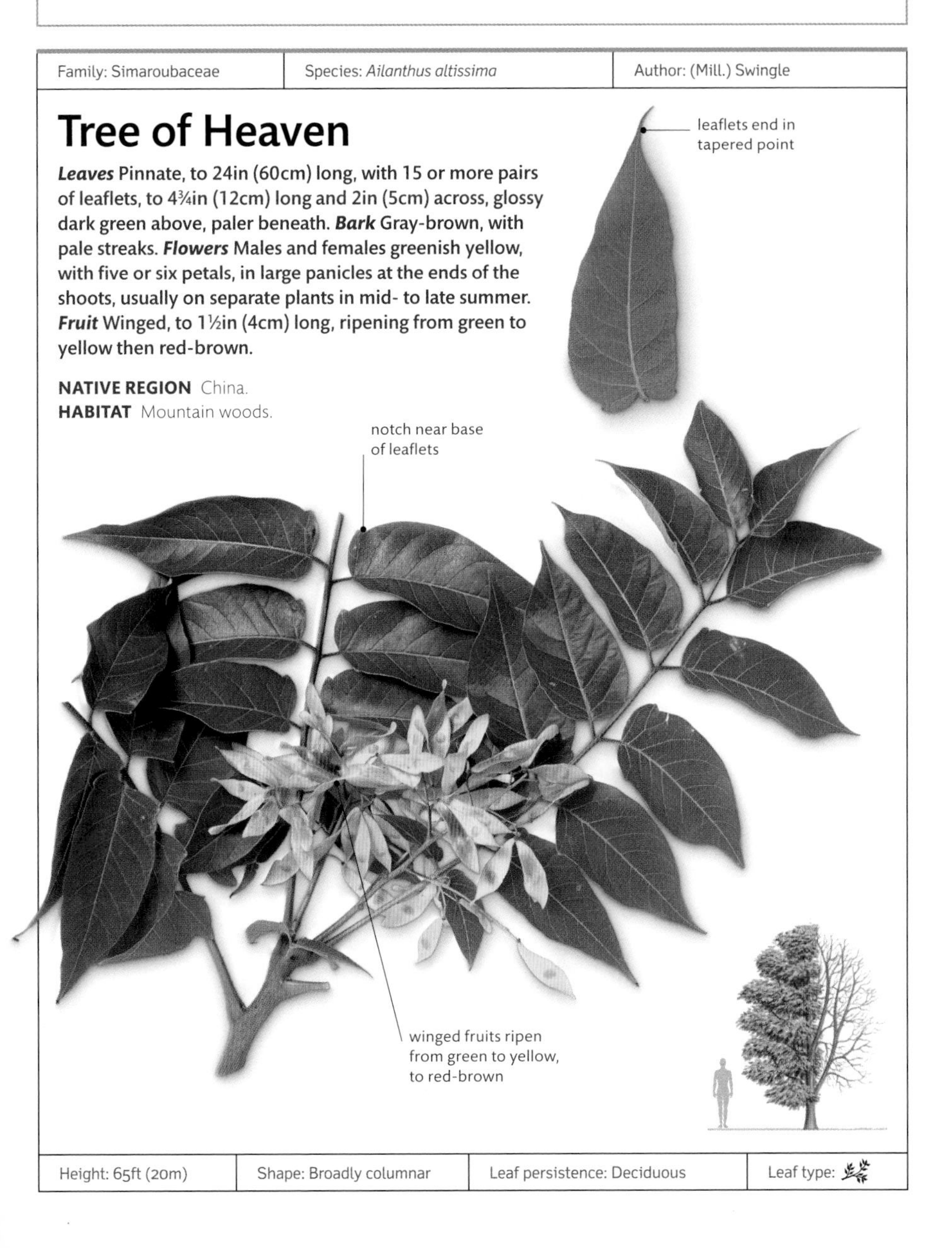

Height: 65ft (20m)	Shape: Broadly columnar	Leaf persistence: Deciduous	Leaf type:

STYRACACEAE

THERE ARE ABOUT 12 GENERA and 150 species of deciduous trees and shrubs in this family, found in East Asia, from the southern United States to Central and South America, and with a single species in the Mediterranean. Leaves are alternate and simple. The flower corolla is tubular at the base, and is divided into five to seven lobes. The fruit is usually a capsule.

Family: Styracaceae	Species: *Halesia carolina*	Author: L.

Snowdrop Tree

Leaves Ovate-oblong, to 8in (20cm) long and 4in (10cm) across, taper-pointed at the tip, finely toothed, bright green above, paler beneath, thinly hairy on both sides, turning yellow in fall. ***Bark*** Pale brown, with scaly, interlacing ridges. ***Flowers*** White or white flushed pink, drooping, the bell-shaped corolla ¾in (2cm) long, with four shallow lobes, in small clusters in mid- to late spring as the young leaves emerge. ***Fruit*** Pear-shaped, to 2in (5cm) long, with four wings, green at first ripening to pale brown.

NATIVE REGION S.E. United States.
HABITAT Rich, moist woods and by streams.
REMARK In unfavorable conditions, this species reaches only about 33ft (10m).

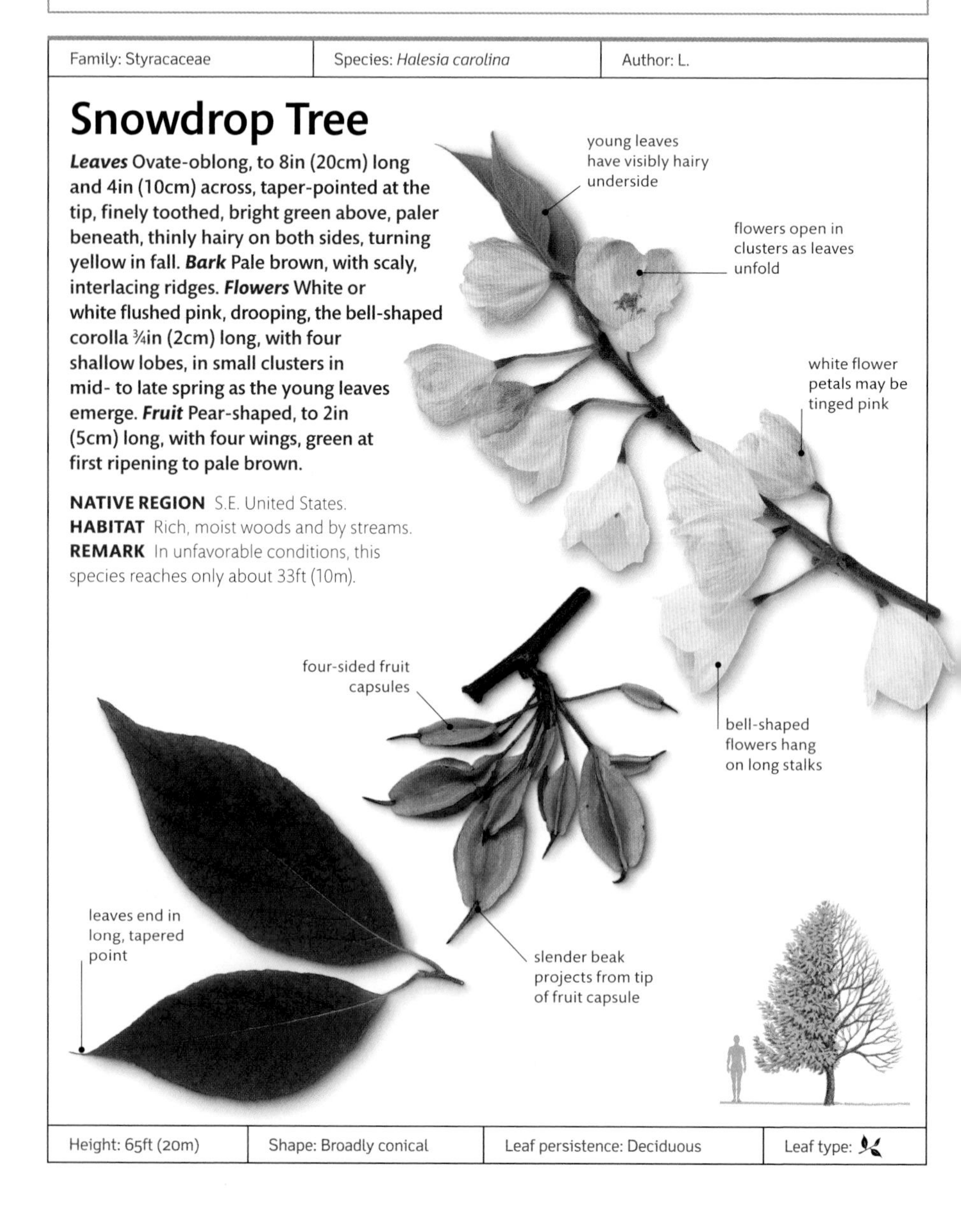

Height: 65ft (20m)	Shape: Broadly conical	Leaf persistence: Deciduous	Leaf type:

Family: Styracaceae	Species: *Pterostyrax hispidus*	Author: Siebold & Zucc.

Epaulette Tree

Leaves Oblong to ovate, to 8in (20cm) long and 4in (10cm) across, tapered at the base, pointed at the tip, bright green and smooth or nearly so above, gray-green and more or less hairy beneath. ***Bark*** Pale gray-brown and corky, with orange fissures. ***Flowers*** Each about ¼in (6mm) long, white, fragrant, with conspicuous, exserted stamens, borne in hanging panicles to 8in (20cm) long, in early to midsummer. ***Fruit*** Small, gray, and dry, about ½in (1.2cm) long, with five ribs, covered with yellow-brown bristles.

NATIVE REGION Japan.
HABITAT Woods, and by streams in mountainous areas.

minutely toothed leaf margin

corolla at first closed over long, projecting stamens

distinctively shaped, drooping, white flower clusters

Height: 40ft (12m)	Shape: Broadly spreading	Leaf persistence: Deciduous	Leaf type:

Family: Styracaceae	Species: *Styrax hemsleyanus*	Author: Diels

Styrax hemsleyanus

Leaves Ovate to obovate, to 5in (13cm) long and 3¼in (8cm) across, oblique at the base, taper-pointed, sparsely toothed, smooth or nearly so. ***Bark*** Pale gray. ***Flowers*** About ⅝in (1.5cm) long, with a five-lobed corolla, white, with golden yellow anthers, the calyx densely covered with dark brown hairs, borne in upright to spreading racemes to 6in (15cm) long, emerging from the ends of short branches in early summer. ***Fruit*** Egg-shaped, gray, and berrylike, ⅝in (1.5cm) long, enclosing a single seed.

NATIVE REGION C. China.
HABITAT Woods and thickets.
REMARK Cultivated plants may grow taller than typical specimens found in the wild. This species is similar to *Styrax obassia* (see p.304), but has exposed, brown leaf buds and less downy leaves.

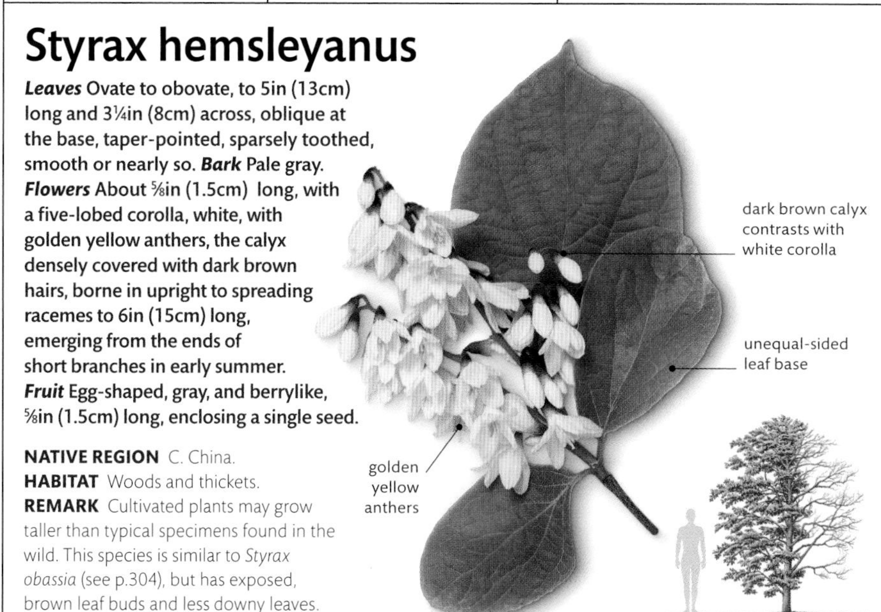

Height: 26ft (8m)	Shape: Broadly columnar	Leaf persistence: Deciduous	Leaf type: 

Family: Styracaceae	Species: *Styrax japonicus*	Author: Siebold & Zucc.

Japanese Snowbell

Leaves Elliptic to ovate, to 4in (10cm) long and 2in (5cm) across, narrowed at the base, abruptly taper-pointed at the tip, with a finely or sparsely toothed margin, rich glossy green above, turning yellow or red in fall. ***Bark*** Dark gray-brown and smooth, developing orange-brown fissures with age. ***Flowers*** Individually about ⅝in (1.5cm) long, with a five-lobed corolla, white or pink-tinged, with yellow anthers, slightly fragrant, on slender stalks, in short racemes or hanging singly beneath the branches in early to midsummer. ***Fruit*** Rounded to egg-shaped, gray, and berrylike, to ⅝in (1.5cm) long, with a single seed.

NATIVE REGION East Asia.
HABITAT Sunny places, usually on wet ground.
REMARK This species makes a beautiful, elegant small tree or large shrub. Some forms with pink flowers are grown in gardens and backyards.

glossy green leaves have duller underside

bell-like flowers hang beneath branches

Height: 33ft (10m)	Shape: Broadly spreading	Leaf persistence: Deciduous	Leaf type:

Family: Styracaceae	Species: *Styrax obassia*	Author: Siebold & Zucc.

Styrax obassia

Leaves Variable, elliptic to rounded, to 8in (20cm) long and nearly the same across, dark green and smooth above, blue-gray and densely hairy beneath, turning yellow in fall. ***Bark*** Gray-brown and smooth, becoming vertically fissured with age. ***Flowers*** Individually about 1in (2.5cm) long, with a five-lobed corolla, white, with yellow anthers, fragrant, borne in horizontally spreading racemes to 6in (15cm) long, in early to midsummer. ***Fruit*** Egg-shaped, gray, and berrylike, about ¾in (2cm) long, with a sngle seed.

NATIVE REGION E. China, Japan, Korea.
HABITAT Moist woods.
REMARK The flower racemes are often almost hidden by the large, broad leaves.

dense hairs cover underside of leaves

Height: 40ft (12m)	Shape: Broadly columnar	Leaf persistence: Deciduous	Leaf type: 

THEACEAE

THE TEA FAMILY has eight genera and over 360 species of deciduous trees and shrubs. They grow mainly in tropical regions, in particular Asia and the Americas, but also in temperate areas of east Asia and the southeast United States. Leaves are simple and usually alternate. Flowers are typically large and showy, with five petals. The fruit is most often a capsule.

Family: Theaceae	Species: *Stewartia malacodendron*	Author: L.

Silky Camellia

Leaves Ovate to elliptic, to 4in (10cm) long and 2in (5cm) across, pointed at the tip, finely toothed, smooth above, paler and hairy beneath. ***Bark*** Pale gray to brown and smooth. ***Flowers*** Cup-shaped at first opening widely, 4in (10cm) across, white, with numerous stamens and bluish anthers, borne singly in summer. ***Fruit*** A woody, red-brown capsule, about ⅝in (1.5cm) across.

NATIVE REGION S.E. United States.
HABITAT Moist woods on coastal plain.

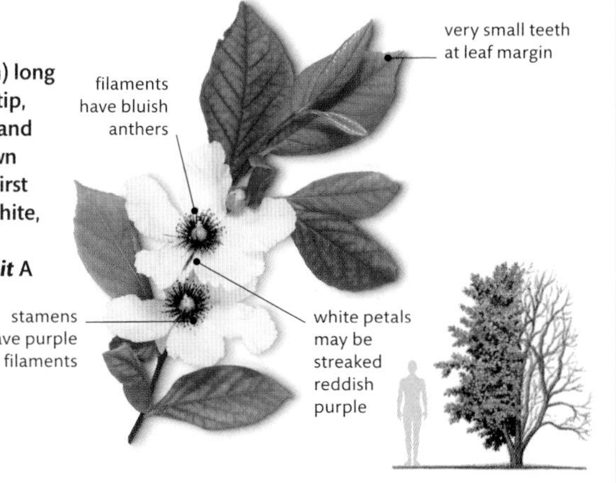

Height: 20ft (6m)	Shape: Broadly columnar	Leaf persistence: Deciduous	Leaf type:

Family: Theaceae	Species: *Stewartia monadelpha*	Author: Siebold & Zucc.

Stewartia monadelpha

Leaves Elliptic to ovate, to 4in (10cm) long and 1¼in (3cm) across, taper-pointed, toothed, glossy dark green above, thinly hairy on both sides, turning deep red-purple in fall. ***Bark*** Smooth, peeling in flakes, leaving gray, pale brown, and red-brown patches. ***Flowers*** 1½in (4cm) across, white, with five petals, the numerous stamens with creamy filaments and dark anthers, with two leafy bracts, borne singly or in pairs in the leaf axils in summer. ***Fruit*** A woody, red-brown capsule, about ⅜in (1cm) long.

NATIVE REGION S. Japan, Korea.
HABITAT Mountain woods.

Height: 80ft (25m)	Shape: Broadly columnar	Leaf persistence: Deciduous	Leaf type:

Family: Theaceae	Species: *Stewartia pseudocamellia*	Author: Maxim.

Stewartia pseudocamellia

Leaves Broadly ovate to elliptic, to 4in (10cm) long and 2½in (6cm) across, tapered to a short point, finely toothed, dark green and smooth above, smooth or hairy beneath, turning yellow to orange or red in fall. ***Bark*** Red-brown, peeling in thin, irregular plates, leaving gray and pink patches. ***Flowers*** 2½in (6cm) across, white, with five petals, the numerous stamens with yellow filaments and darker anthers, with two leafy bracts outside the sepals, borne singly or in pairs in the leaf axils in summer. ***Fruit*** A woody, red-brown capsule, about ¾in (2cm) long.

NATIVE REGION S. Korea, Japan.
HABITAT Mountain woods.
REMARK As in other species of *Stewartia*, the five flower petals are joined together at the base and the flowers fall intact.

flaking bark creates pinkish gray patchwork effect

frilly-petalled flowers

flowers have bright yellow filaments

finely toothed leaf margin

▽ ***Stewartia pseudocamellia***

△ **Koreana Group**
Of South Korean origin, the flowers of this form open more widely than those of the typical form. Its slightly larger leaves color just as well in the fall, however.

paler leaf underside may be smooth or hairy

flower petals covered in silky hairs before opening

dark green leaf upperside

Height: 65ft (20m)	Shape: Broadly columnar	Leaf persistence: Deciduous	Leaf type: 

TROCHODENDRACEAE

THIS FAMILY CONTAINS two genera and two species, native to east Asia from the Himalayas to Japan. Both have small flowers without petals. The apparent lack of vessels in the wood led to the belief that the family was primitive but has more recently been considered close to *Cercidiphyllum* (see p.116).

Family: Trochodendraceae	Species: *Trochodendron aralioides*	Author: Siebold & Zucc.

Trochodendron aralioides

Leaves Narrowly elliptic, to 4¾in (12cm) long and 1½in (4cm) across, toothed except toward the base, dark green above, paler beneath. ***Bark*** Gray to dark brown, with conspicuous lenticels. ***Flowers*** ¾in (2cm) across, bright green, without petals, the stamens radiating from a green disk, in racemes to 4¾in (12cm) long, at the ends of the shoots in late spring and early summer. ***Fruit*** A hemispherical cluster, green ripening to brown, with persistent stigmas.

NATIVE REGION E. Asia.
HABITAT Mountain woods.

leaves end in fine point

slender-stalked leaves

Height: 65ft (20m)	Shape: Broadly columnar	Leaf persistence: Evergreen	Leaf type:

ULMACEAE

THE ELM FAMILY contains seven genera and about 60 species of evergreen and deciduous trees and shrubs, growing wild in tropical and northern temperate regions. Leaves are usually alternate. The small flowers have no petals. The fruit may be winged and dry, fleshy with a single seed, or a nut.

Family: Ulmaceae	Species: *Ulmus davidiana*	Author: Planch.

Japanese Elm

Leaves Elliptic to obovate, to 4in (10cm) long and 2½in (6cm) across, narrowed at the unequal base, taper-pointed at the tip, double-toothed, dark green and rough with hairs above, paler and downy at least on the veins beneath. ***Bark*** Pale gray-brown, fissured. ***Flowers*** Very small, red, in small clusters on the shoots in spring. ***Fruit*** A winged seed, ⅝in (1.5cm), ripening a few weeks after flowering time.

NATIVE REGION N.E. Asia, Japan.
HABITAT Woods, rocky places, and moors.

var. *japonica* ▷
Differs from the typical form in its hairless fruits.

Height: 100ft (30m)	Shape: Broadly spreading	Leaf persistence: Deciduous	Leaf type:

Family: Ulmaceae	Species: *Ulmus* x *hollandica*	Author: Mill.

Ulmus x hollandica

Leaves **Ovate to elliptic, to 4¾in (12cm) long and 2½in (6cm) across, glossy dark green, taper-pointed, toothed, usually hairy beneath. *Bark* Gray-brown, ridged. *Flowers* Tiny, red, in clusters on the shoots in early spring. *Fruit* A winged seed, to 1in (2.5cm) long.**

NATIVE REGION S.W. Asia, Europe.
HABITAT Woods and hedgerows.
REMARK A hybrid between wych elm (*Ulmus glabra*) and smooth-leaved elm (*Ulmus minor*, see below).

unequal-sided leaf base

glossy leaf upperside

'Klemmer'
This form was raised in Belgium. It is a narrowly conical tree.

Height: 100ft (30m)	Shape: Broadly columnar	Leaf persistence: Deciduous	Leaf type:

Family: Ulmaceae	Species: *Ulmus minor*	Author: Mill.

Smooth-leaved Elm

Leaves **Elliptic to obovate, to 4¾in (12cm) long and 2½in (6cm) across, pointed, double-toothed, glossy bright green and smooth above, with hairs in the vein axils beneath. *Bark* Gray-brown, ridged. *Flowers* Tiny, red, in clusters in early spring. *Fruit* A small, winged seed.**

NATIVE REGION N. Africa, S.W. Asia, Europe.
HABITAT Woods and hedgerows.
REMARK This is the once-common English elm, formerly known as *Ulmus procera*.

rounded leaves

leaves edged with sharp, double teeth

Height: 100ft (30m)	Shape: Broadly columnar	Leaf persistence: Deciduous	Leaf type:

Family: Ulmaceae	Species: *Ulmus parvifolia*	Author: Jacq.

Chinese Elm

Leaves **Elliptic to ovate or obovate, to 2½in (6cm) long and 1½in (4cm) across, oblique at the base, pointed, sharply toothed, glossy dark green and sometimes rough above, with hairs in the vein axils beneath, turning yellow, red, or purple in fall. *Bark* Gray-brown, peeling in scales. *Flowers* Tiny, red, in clusters in the leaf axils in early fall. *Fruit* A small seed with a green wing, 5⁄16in (8mm) long.**

NATIVE REGION E. Asia.
HABITAT Rocky places.

Height: 50ft (15m)	Shape: Broadly spreading	Leaf persistence: Deciduous	Leaf type: 

Family: Ulmaceae	Species: *Ulmus pumila*	Author: L.

Siberian Elm

Leaves Elliptic to narrowly ovate, to 2½in (6cm) long and 1in (2.5cm) across, nearly equal-sided at the base, taper-pointed, sharply toothed, dark green above, smooth or nearly so on both sides. ***Bark*** Gray-brown, rough, corrugated. ***Flowers*** Very small, red, in clusters on the shoots in spring before the leaves. ***Fruit*** A small seed surrounded by a rounded, notched, green wing, ½in (1.2cm) long.

NATIVE REGION C. to E. Asia.
HABITAT Sandy or stony soil.

curved point at leaf tip

nearly equal-sided leaf base

Height: 65ft (20m)	Shape: Broadly columnar	Leaf persistence: Deciduous	Leaf type:

Family: Ulmaceae	Species: *Zelkova carpinifolia*	Author: (Pall.) K. Koch

Zelkova carpinifolia

Leaves Elliptic to oblong, to 4in (10cm) long and 2in (5cm) across, with about 10 pairs of veins ending in triangular teeth, dark green and slightly rough above, hairy beneath, turning orange-brown in fall. ***Bark*** Gray and smooth, flaking with age, on a fluted trunk. ***Flowers*** Males and females both small and green, in separate clusters on the same plant in spring. ***Fruit*** Small and rounded.

NATIVE REGION Caucasus, N. Iran.
HABITAT Forests.
REMARK Easily distinguished by its short trunk divided into numerous upright branches.

leaf margin edged with large, broad teeth

short leaf stalk

Height: 80ft (25m)	Shape: Broadly columnar	Leaf persistence: Deciduous	Leaf type:

Family: Ulmaceae	Species: *Zelkova serrata*	Author: (Thunb.) Makino

Keaki

Leaves Ovate to oblong-ovate, to 4¾in (12cm) long and 2in (5cm) across, rounded at the base, taper-pointed, sharply toothed, the teeth ending in a short point, dark green and slightly rough above, paler and nearly smooth beneath, turning yellow, orange, or red in fall. ***Bark*** Pale gray and smooth, flaking with age. ***Flowers*** Males and females both small and green, on the young shoots on the same plant in spring. ***Fruit*** Small and rounded.

NATIVE REGION China, Japan, Korea.
HABITAT Moist soil near streams.

rounded leaf base

▽ ***Zelkova serrata***

leaf margin edged with many sharp teeth

◁ ***Zelkova sinica***
A similar species. Its sparser-toothed leaves taper at the base.

Height: 130ft (40m)	Shape: Broadly spreading	Leaf persistence: Deciduous	Leaf type: 

WINTERACEAE

A PRIMITIVE FAMILY possibly related to the magnolias (*Magnolia*, see pp.175–187). About five genera and about 90 species of evergreen trees and shrubs occur in Madagascar, and from Mexico to South America, and Southeast Asia to Australia and New Zealand. Plants have alternately arranged, untoothed leaves, five- or more petalled flowers, and small, berrylike, clustered fruits.

Family: Winteraceae	Species: *Drimys winteri*	Author: J.R. Forst. & G. Forst.

Winter's Bark

Leaves Oblong to elliptic, to 8in (20cm) long and 2½in (6cm) across, untoothed, glossy dark green above, bluish green to bluish white beneath, leathery, aromatic when crushed. ***Bark*** Gray-brown and smooth, very aromatic. ***Flowers*** 1½in (4cm) across, white, fragrant, with numerous slender petals, borne in large clusters in spring to early summer. ***Fruit*** A small berry, green ripening to purple-black, in clusters at the end of long stalks.

NATIVE REGION S. Argentina, S. Chile.
HABITAT Mountains.
REMARK Named after Captain William Winter, who sailed with Sir Francis Drake in the 16th century. He used the bark (a source of vitamin C) to treat scurvy, a disease caused by a deficiency of the same vitamin.

green unripe fruit

flowers borne in dense, branched clusters

bloomy leaf underside

Height: 50ft (15m)	Shape: Narrowly conical	Leaf persistence: Evergreen	Leaf type:

GLOSSARY

TECHNICAL TERMS HAVE been kept to a minimum, but a limited use of them is unavoidable in a book of this kind. Words in bold in the definitions are explained elsewhere in the glossary.

You may find it useful also to look at Hybrid Plants (p.8), A Family Tree (p.9), What is a Tree? (pp.12–13), The Parts of a Tree (pp.14–15), and Conifer or Broadleaf? (pp.16–17).

■ **ANTHER**
Part of a **stamen** that releases pollen.

■ **ARIL**
Fleshy seed coat.

■ **AURICLE**
Small, earlike **lobe**.

■ **BIPINNATE**
Pinnate, with the divisions themselves pinnate.

■ **BLOOMY**
Covered with a waxy or powdery, blue-white deposit.

■ **BRACT**
Leaflike structure below a flower or flower cluster.

■ **CALYX**
Small part of a flower outside the petals, composed of **sepals**.

■ **CAPSULE**
Dry fruit that splits open to release its seeds.

■ **CATKIN**
Usually pendulous cluster of **bracts** and tiny flowers, most often of one sex.

■ **COMPOUND LEAF**
One that is composed of two or more separate leaflets.

■ **COROLLA**
Often showy and colored part of a flower, composed of petals.

■ **DECIDUOUS**
Without leaves for part of each year.

■ **ENTIRE**
Without teeth or **lobes**.

■ **EVERGREEN**
Retaining leaves for more than one year.

■ **EXSERTED**
Conspicuously protruding.

■ **FILAMENT**
Stalk of an **anther**.

■ **GLAUCOUS**
Bluish white.

■ **HARDY**
Able to withstand winter temperatures.

■ **HERBACEOUS PLANT**
Non-woody plant that dies at the end of the growing season or overwinters by means of underground structures.

■ **LEAFLET**
Single division of a **compound leaf**.

■ **LEAF AXIL**
Angle formed between a leaf and its stem.

■ **LENTICEL**
Usually corky area on a trunk that lets air through the bark.

■ **LOBE**
Rounded segment or part.

■ **MONOTYPIC**
Of a family: containing a single genus that contains only one species; of a genus: containing a single species.

■ **NATIVE**
Growing naturally wild in a specific area.

■ **NATURALIZED**
Introduced by man and growing as if naturally wild in a specific area.

■ **OVARY**
Organ of a flower's female part that, in fruit, contains the seeds.

■ **PALMATE**
Divided into **leaflets** or **lobes** in the manner of a hand.

■ **PANICLE**
Raceme in which the branches are themselves branched.

■ **PEALIKE**
Of a flower: similar in structure to that of a leguminous plant.

■ **PERSISTENT**
Remaining attached.

■ **PINNATE**
Compound leaf, with **leaflets** arranged on opposite sides of a common stalk.

■ **POLLEN**
Spores released from the **anthers**, containing the male reproductive element.

■ **RACEME**
Stalked flowers borne singly along a central axis.

■ **RACHIS**
Stalk of a **pinnate** leaf on which the **leaflets** are borne.

■ **SEPAL**
Individual part of the **calyx**.

■ **SIMPLE LEAF**
One that is not divided into **leaflets**.

■ **SINUS**
Gap between two **lobes**.

■ **SPIKE**
Raceme bearing unstalked flowers.

■ **STAMEN**
Anther, usually on a **filament**. A variable number composes the male part of a flower.

■ **STIGMA**
Organ of a flower's female part, borne at the tip of the **style**, on which the **pollen** is deposited.

■ **STIPULE**
Small, leaflike structure, most often paired, borne where the leaf stalk joins the stem.

■ **STYLE**
Organ of a flower's female part that bears the **stigma**.

■ **TEPAL**
Petal or **sepal**, where there is no distinct difference between the two.

INDEX OF PLANTS

A

B

C

D

E

F

G

H

I

J

K

L

T

Z

ACKNOWLEDGMENTS

The Author and Publisher are greatly indebted to a number of institutions and people, without whom this book could not have been produced. The following supplied and/or collected plant material for photography: Barry Phillips (Curator), Bill George (Head Gardener), and all the staff of the Sir Harold Hillier Gardens, Ampfield, Hampshire; Robert Eburn, P.H.B. Gardner, Bernard and Letty Perrott, and Mrs Eve Taylor; Kate Haywood of The Royal Horticultural Society's Garden Wisley, Woking, Surrey; Hillier Nurseries (Winchester) Limited; Richard Johnston, Mount Annan section of the Royal Botanic Gardens, Sydney, Australia; Longstock Park Gardens; Mike Maunder and Melanie Thomas of the Royal Botanic Gardens, Kew, Surrey; Colin Morgan of the Forestry Commission Research Division, Bedgebury National Pinetum, Cranbrook, Kent; Andrew Pinder (Arboricultural Officer), London Borough of Richmond upon Thames; John White and Margaret Ruskin of the Forestry Commission, Westonbirt Arboretum, Tetbury, Gloucestershire.

The following helped to compile reference material for the illustrators: S. Andrews, T. Kirkham, and Mike Maunder of the Royal Botanic Gardens, Kew, Surrey; the Arnold Arboretum of Harvard University, Jamaica Plain, Massachusetts, USA; Kathie Atkinson; S. Clark and S. Knees of the Royal Botanic Garden Edinburgh, Lothian, Scotland; D. Cooney of the Waite Arboretum, University of Adelaide, S. Australia; B. Davis; Dr T.R. Dudley (Lead Scientist and Research Botanist) of the U.S. National Arboretum, Washington, D.C., USA; M. Flannagan of the Royal Botanic Gardens, Wakehurst Place, Ardingly, West Sussex; the Forestry Commission, Forest Research Station, Alice Holt Lodge, Farnham, Surrey; Anne James of the Parks Department, Dublin County Council, Irish Republic; Roy Lancaster; Scott Leathart; Alan Mitchell; K. Olver; The Royal Horticultural Society's Garden Wisley, Woking, Surrey; V. Schilling of the Tree Register of the British Isles (TROBI), Westmeston, West Sussex; T. Walker of the University of Oxford Botanic Gardens, Oxfordshire; John White and Margaret Ruskin of the Forestry Commission, Westonbirt Arboretum, Tetbury, Gloucestershire; P. Yeo of the University of Cambridge Botanic Garden, Cambridgeshire; Dennis Woodland.

The author would like to express his thanks to: the tremendous team at Dorling Kindersley, especially Vicki James, Gillian Roberts, and Mustafa Sami, for their diligence and commitment to the project; Matthew Ward, for his excellent photography; Roy Lancaster, for reading and commenting on the text.

We acknowledge the invaluable contributions of Mustafa Sami, who shepherded the illustrators with patient good humour, Spencer Holbrook, who gave him vital administrative support, and Donna Rispoli, who researched the references for the illustrators. Special thanks to Mel and Marianne, Witt and Kaye, whose generosity enabled the editor to take a holiday. Thanks also to Michael Allaby, for compiling the index and suggesting words for the glossary; Mike Darton, for reading page proofs, and for commenting on the glossary and introduction; Virginia Fitzgerald, for administrative help with the illustrators' reference material; Angeles Gavira and Ian Hambleton, for cataloguing all the transparencies; Steve Tilling, for commenting on the identification key; Helen Townsend, for caretaking the project while the editor was on holiday; Alastair Wardle, for his computer expertise.

Dorling Kindersley would like to thank the following for their work on this edition: Sulagna Das for design assistance; DTP Coordinators Neeraj Bhatia, Jagtar Singh, and Tarun Sharma; DTP Designers Manish Upreti, Narender Kumar, and Umesh Singh Rawat; Senior Picture Researcher Deepak Negi; Picture Research Administrators Vagisha Pushp and Manpreet Kaur.

PICTURE CREDITS

The publisher would like to thank the following for their kind permission to reproduce their photographs:

(Key: a-above; b-below/bottom; c-center; f-far; l-left; r-right; t-top)

Photographs by Matthew Ward, except:
6 Alamy Stock Photo: David Chapman (bl).
8 Shutterstock.com: dinkaspell (tl). **10 Getty Images/iStock:** FilippoBacci (cla). **12 Dorling Kindersley:** Peter Chadwick (trunk). **15 Dorling Kindersley:** Peter Chadwick (cone section; seed pods).
20 Dreamstime.com: Eddydegroot (cb).
26 Mark Powell: (bl). **28 Dreamstime.com:** Sombra12 (cla). **30 Alamy Stock Photo:** blickwinkel/K. Wagner (cra).
32 Dreamstime.com: Gabriela Beres (cr).
34 Dreamstime.com: Corey A Ford (br); Whiskybottle (crb). **46 Allen Coombes:** crb. **133 Dorling Kindersley:** Kathie Atkinson. **150 Alamy Stock Photo:** shapencolour (crb). **158 Dreamstime.com:** Manfred Ruckszio (bc).
159 Alamy Stock Photo: imageBROKER/Guenter Fischer (bc). **172 123RF.com:** Maksym Bondarchuk (br).
Alamy Stock Photo: TommyK (crb).
246 Dorling Kindersley: Peter Chadwick (tl)

All other images © Dorling Kindersley

Tree illustrations by Laura Andrew 142, 174; Marion Appleton 115 (b), 116–120, 121 (t), 125–129; David Ashby 100–107; Bob Bampton 211, 239–54, 255 (t/c), 266–274, 300–302; Anne Child 108, 109, 296 (b), 297–299; Tim Hayward 95–99, 110–113, 130–131, 148, 175–182, 184, 197–200, 202–210, 212–216, 217 (t), 219, 255 (b), 256–262, 307 (b), 308–310; Janos Marffy 9, 17, 134–137; David More 149–164, 224 (b), 225 (t), 226 (b), 227-233; Sue Oldfield 12–13, 35 (t), 36, 81, -83, 108–113, 188, 189, 196–199, 213–215, 298, 299; Liz Pepperell 182–187, 190, 238–243; Michelle Ross 34, 35 (b), 82 (b), 83 (t), 275–295, 296 (t), 121 (b), 122–124, 143–146, 305, 306, 189, 190, 191, 192, 307 (t), 114, 115 (t); Gill Tomblin 84, 85, 165, 265; Barbara Walker 188, 193–196, 201, 236–238, 263, 264.

Leaf type illustrations by Paul Bailey.

SMITHSONIAN HANDBOOKS

SMITHSONIAN HANDBOOKS
BUTTERFLIES & MOTHS

SMITHSONIAN HANDBOOKS
DINOSAURS
AND OTHER PREHISTORIC LIFE

SMITHSONIAN HANDBOOKS
DOGS

SMITHSONIAN HANDBOOKS
FOSSILS

SMITHSONIAN HANDBOOKS
GEMSTONES

SMITHSONIAN HANDBOOKS
ROCKS & MINERALS

SMITHSONIAN HANDBOOKS
SHELLS

SMITHSONIAN HANDBOOKS
STARS & PLANETS

SMITHSONIAN HANDBOOKS
TREES

For the curious